THE FATHERS
OF THE CHURCH

A NEW TRANSLATION

VOLUME 47

THE FATHERS OF THE CHURCH

A NEW TRANSLATION

EDITORIAL BOARD

Hermigild Dressler, O.F.M.
Quincy College
Editorial Director

Robert P. Russell, O.S.A. Thomas P. Halton
Villanova University *The Catholic University of America*

Robert Sider Sister M. Josephine Brennan, I.H.M.
Dickinson College *Marywood College*

Richard Talaska
Editorial Assistant

FORMER EDITORIAL DIRECTORS

Ludwig Schopp, Roy J. Deferrari, Bernard M. Peebles

SAINT CAESARIUS
OF ARLES

SERMONS
VOLUME II
(81-186)

Translated by
SISTER MARY MAGDELEINE MUELLER, O.S.F.
Cardinal Stritch College
Milwaukee, Wisconsin

THE CATHOLIC UNIVERSITY OF AMERICA PRESS
Washington, D.C.

NIHIL OBSTAT:

   REVEREND HENRY A. ECHLE
     Censor Librorum

IMPRIMATUR:

   ✠ PATRICK A. O'BOYLE, D.D.
    Archbishop of Washington

October 21, 1963

 The *nihil obstat* and *imprimatur* are official declarations that a book or pamphlet is free of doctrinal or moral error. No implication is contained therein that those who have granted the *nihil obstat* and the *imprimatur* agree with the content, opinions, or statements expressed.

Library of Congress Catalog Card No.: 56-8628

Copyright © *1964* by
THE CATHOLIC UNIVERSITY OF AMERICA PRESS, INC.
All rights reserved
Second Printing 1981
ISBN 978-0-8132-2825-9 (pbk.)

CONTENTS

Sermon		Page
81	On the Call of Blessed Abraham	3
82	On the Heifer, the Ram, and the She-goat of Three Years; Also the Turtledove and the Pigeon	6
83	On the Three Men Who Appeared to Blessed Abraham	11
84	On Abraham and His Son Isaac	16
85	On the Servant of Abraham Who Was Sent to Rebecca	20
86	On the Conception of Holy Rebecca	24
87	On Jacob's Ladder	29
88	On Blessed Jacob and Laban	34
89	On Jacob, His Son Joseph, and His Brothers . .	38
*90	On Blessed Joseph	43
91	Likewise on Holy Joseph	49
*92	Again on Holy Joseph	53
*93	On the Blessed Patriarch Joseph	57
*94	On What is Written: Joseph Died and the Children of Israel Increased	61
95	On the Birth of Moses and the Bush	65
96	On the Bush and the Lace of the Shoe	69
*97	On the Three Days' Journey in the Desert . .	74

Sermon		Page
98	On the Spiritual Struggle of the Israelites and Egyptians which can be Inferred when We Read of the Chaff	78
*99	On the Ten Plagues	81
*100	St. Augustine on the Ten Words of the Law and the Ten Plagues	85
*100A	On the Agreement between the Ten Plagues of Egypt and the Ten Commandments of the Law	92
101	On the Words: The Lord Hardened the Heart of Pharao	98
*102	On the Manna and the Bitter Water	103
*103	On Raphidim, Amalec, and the Rock Struck in the Desert	108
104	A Comparison of the Church and the Synagogue when there was a Text in Exodus about the First and Later Tablets	113
*105	On Spiritual Blessings	119
*106	On What the Lord Said to Moses: Send Men to Reconnoiter the Land	125
107	On the Spies and the Cluster of Grapes	131
*108	On the Twelve Scouts	135
109	On the Spies and the Forty Years Spent in the Desert	139
*110	St. Jerome on the Censers of Core and Dathan	144
*111	On the Rod of Aaron	147
112	On the Brazen Serpent and the Rod of Moses	151
*113	St. Jerome in the Middle of Lent on Balaam and Balac	155
114	That the Chanaanites were Driven from the Promised Land through the Just Judgment of God	161
115	Josue Bids the People be Ready to Cross the Jordan; also Something Concerning Rahab the Harlot and the Destruction of Jericho	167

Sermon		Page
116	On Rahab the Harlot and the Two Messengers	171
116A	On the People of Chanaan	175
*117	St. Ambrose, the Bishop, on Holy Gedeon	177
*118	St. Augustine, the Bishop, on Samson	182
119	On Samson	189
120	On the Woman Who Deceived Samson	193
121	St. Augustine on David, Isai His Father, and the Unnatural Goliath	198
122	St. Augustine, Bishop, on the Plague of God	203
*123	St. Augustine the Bishop on the Judgment of Solomon and the Two Harlots	206
124	St. Augustine, the Bishop, on Blessed Elias and the Widow Gathering Two Sticks of Wood	209
125	On Holy Elias and the Two Captains	214
126	On Holy Eliseus and the Spring which was Changed into Sweetness	216
127	On What Is Written Concerning Holy Eliseus: Go Up, Thou Bald Head	220
128	On Blessed Eliseus	223
129	On Blessed Eliseus and His Servant Giezi	228
130	On Eliseus and the Axe Which Fell into the Water; This Ought to be Read as Instruction on the Creed	233
*131	On Holy Job	237
*132	The Bishop St. Augustine on Blessed Job the Prophet and on the Verse of a Psalm: Break into Song, Sing Praise	241
*133	On the Verse of Psalm XLIX Which Says: You Sit Speaking Against Your Brother	244
*134	On a Section of Psalm L, that is, On the Sin of David	250
*135	On a Verse from Psalm LXXV: Make Vows to the Lord Your God and Fulfill Them	257

Sermon		Page
136	Concerning What Is Written: The Sun Knows the Hour of Its Setting	264
*137	On A Verse of Psalm CXVIII: I See That All Fulfillment Has Its Limits	269
*138	An Admonition to the People on the Valiant Woman and the Church	274
*139	That the Church Was Pointed Out Before the Coming of Our Lord As Well As After It . . .	276
*140	St. Augustine on the Words: Happy the Rich Man Who Turns Not Aside After Gain. That If a Man Finds Anything He Should Restore It to the One Who Lost It Without Delay. On the Man Who Found Two Hundred Gold Coins. That a Wolf Came to the Sheepfold and Departed	282
*141	Another Homily on the Words: Happy the Rich Man Who Turns Not Aside After Gain, and So Forth	287
*142	On What Is Written Concerning Our Lord and Savior: He Grew Up Like a Sapling, Like a Shoot from the Parched Earth	291
*143	On the Repentance of the Ninivites	298
*144	On Prayer, Repentance, and the Ninivites . .	300
*145	An Admonition of St. Augustine on What Is Written: 'Come to Terms with Thy Opponent While Thou Art with Him on the Way.' Also on the Mote of Anger Which Is Nourished by False Suspicions and Becomes a Beam	304
146	On the Excerpt of the Gospel Where It Says: 'Do Not Let Thy Left Hand Know What Thy Right Hand Is Doing': Also on Prayer	308
*147	An Explanation of the Lord's Prayer	311

Sermon		Page
148	On Prayer, On What Is Written in the Gospel According to Matthew. 'Do Not Judge, That You May Not Be Judged,' and So Forth	315
149	On the Two Paths, the One to be Desired, and the Other to be Feared	319
150	This Admonition Explains How We Were Cast into the Hell of this World because of the Sin of the First Man, and that We Should Not Deserve to Come to the Lower Darkness on Account of Our Sins, but Should Strive with All Our Strength to Ascend to Our Chief Country by Good Works as by Certain Steps	323
151	On the Earthly Sojourn of Christians, and also on the Easy Way Which Leads to Death and the Rough Road Which Leads to Life; Further on the Fact That Paradise is Our True Country Where All the Saints, Who Have Traveled Out of This World, Await Us with the Extended Arms of Charity	327
152	On What Is Written in the Gospel: 'Where Two or Three Are Gathered Together for My Sake.' .	333
*153	St. Augustine on the Gospel where It Says: 'If Thou Wilt Enter Into Life, Keep the Commandments'	337
154	On What Is Said in the Gospel: 'Woe to Those Who Are with Child, or Have Infants at the Breast'	339
155	On the Ten Virgins	344
156	Likewise a Sermon on the Ten Virgins	348
157	On the Gospel Passage Where It Says: 'Come, Blessed, Receive the Kingdom.' On the Third Rogation Day	354

Sermon		Page
158	On What is Said in the Gospel: 'Come, Blessed'; Also on Almsgiving	359
*158A	A Sermon of Admonition on the Last Judgment	363
*159	On What Is Written: 'If Anyone Wishes to Come After Me, Let Him Take Up His Cross' . . .	365
160	On What Is Written in the Gospel: 'The Good Man from the Good Treasure of His Heart Brings Forth That Which is Good.'	370
160B	On What Is Written: 'The Good Man From the Good Treasure of His Heart Brings Forth That Which Is Good'	374
*161	On What Is Written: 'A Certain Man Was Going Down from Jerusalem to Jericho'	376
*162	A Beautiful Homily of St. Augustine on the Fig Tree Which Did Not Bear Fruit for Three Years; Also That the Tears of a Penitent Are Like a Field in Which Dung Is Spread; and Still Further That If Dung Is Not Put in Its Proper Place It Does Not Make a House Clean, But When It Is Put in Its Right Place It Is Proven to Produce Much Fruit	379
*163	On the Prodigal Son and the One Who Always Remained with His Father	384
*164	On the Rich Man and Lazarus	389
*165	Likewise on the Rich Man and Lazarus . . .	393
166	Another Sermon, This Time on What Is Written in the Gospel: 'The Kingdom of God is Within You'; Also That We Should Decide with a Just Judgment Between the Body and the Soul; Further That We Can Never Possess Peace with God If We Murmur Against Him, and How We Possess Justice and Peace and Even Joy	397

Sermon		Page
*167	From the Gospel According to John Where It Says That on the Third Day a Marriage Took Place at Cana of Galilee	402
*168	On the Words of the Gospel According to John: 'On the Third Day a Marriage Took Place,' and So Forth	409
169	On the Fact That Our Lord Changed Water Into Wine	413
*170	On the Samaritan Woman, and On Not Postponing Baptism	419
171	On the Pool of Siloe	422
172	On the Man Born Blind	424
*173	The Bishop, Augustine, on What Is Written: 'He Who Loves His Life, Loses It.'	427
*174	On the Blessing of Peace, From the Gospel of John	432
*175	On the Gospel Lesson Where the Lord Appeared to His Disciples When the Doors were Closed; Also Against Heretics Who Baptize a Second Time	433
176	A Homily Taken From a Work of the Bishop, St. Augustine, on the Vision of Blessed Peter, the Apostle, and Cornelius, the Centurion	437
*177	St. Augustine on Original Sin	442
*178	A Homily on a Thought of Peter. Also on Judgment Day, and on What the Apostle Says: 'Laying Aside the Works of Darkness, Put on the Armor of Light.'	447
179	An Admonition on the Gospel Text Where it Says: 'If a Man's Work Abides He Will Receive Reward; If His Work Burns He Will Lose His Reward'	449
*180	On What Is Written: 'Put Away Lying.' . . .	456

Sermon		Page
*181	On the Lesson of the Apostle Where It Says: 'Making the Most of Your Time, Because the Days are Evil'; and Also: 'You Give Coins to Buy Bread for Yourself; Forgive a Wicked Man Something, in Order That You May Buy Rest for Yourself.'	461
182	An Admonition of St. Augustine on the Love of Charity and Hatred of Carnal Desires; That the Kingdom of Heaven Can Be Bought, Not Only With Two Mites, But Even with Good Will; Also on the Tribulation of Grapes and Olives . . .	467
*183	A Homily of St. Augustine on the Peril of a Priest; Also on That Rich Man Whose Land Brought Forth Abundant Fruit, and on That Other One Who Was Clothed In Purple and Fine Linen . .	473
184	On the Martyrs, on Phylacteries, and on a Passage From the Eleventh Chapter of the Apostle's Letter to the Hebrews	479
*185	On Harmony Between Brothers	484
186	An Exhortation to the People on the Words of Blessed John the Evangelist: 'Everyone Who Believes That Jesus Is the Christ Is Born of God.' .	489

INTRODUCTION

THIS VOLUME OF THE WORKS of St. Caesarius comprises his sermons on Scripture: Sermons 81-143 are based upon the Old Testament, while 144-186 have texts from the New Testament. Again, the pastoral character of the bishop is everywhere evident, especially in his deep concern for the wayward members of his flock. Present-day congregations might find his applications of Sacred Scripture severe and his examples pointed, but they simply manifest the saint's anxiety over their spiritual welfare. He is ever mindful of the additional account which will be required, on judgment day at the end of the world, from the clergy and especially from bishops, to whom the care of the faithful has been entrusted.

Following the method employed in Volume I of the Sermons of St. Caesarius (Volume 31 of the series), sermons which appear in small type in Morin's edition and those prefixed by a dagger have been distinguished by an asterisk (*).[1] Nos. 93, 100A, 105, 106, 110, 111, 113, 118, 131, 135, 138, 140, 141, 142, 143, 144, 145, 147, 153, 158A, 160A, 162, 164, 165, 167, 170, and 174 belong to the former category, while Nos. 90, 92, 94, 97, 99, 100, 102, 103, 108, 117, 123, 132, 133, 134, 137, 139, 159, 161, 163, 168, 173, 175, 177, 178, 180, 181, 183, and 185 are of the latter variety.

Translation of the biblical text follows the general policy—where possible, the version issued by the Confraternity of Christian Doctrine has been used; in other cases Challoner's revision of the Douay version has been followed.

---

1 For an explanation of these distinctions; also for the *Select Bibliography* and a brief account of St. Caesarius' life and activity, cf. Volume I, xxv, i.e., Volume 31 of the series.

SAINT CAESARIUS OF ARLES

SERMONS

(Volume II)

Sermon 81

On the Call of Blessed Abraham

WHEN THE SACRED LESSON WAS READ just now, we heard the Lord say to blessed Abraham: 'Leave your country, your kinsfolk and your father's house.'[1] Now everything which was written in the Old Testament, dearly beloved, provided a type and image of the New Testament. As the Apostle says: 'Now all these things happened to them as a type, and they were written for our correction, upon whom the final age of the world has come.'[2] Therefore, if what happened corporally in Abraham was written for us, we will see it fulfilled spiritually in us if we live piously and justly. 'Leave your country,' the Lord said, 'your kinsfolk and your father's house.' We believe and perceive all these things fulfilled in us, brethren, through the sacrament of Baptism. Our land is our body; we go forth properly from our land if we abandon our carnal habits to follow the footsteps of Christ. Does not a man seem to you happily to leave his land, that is, himself, if from being proud he becomes humble, from irascible patient, from dissolute chaste, from avaricious generous, from envious kind, from cruel gentle? Truly, brethren, one who is changed thus out of love for God happily leaves his own land. Finally, even in private conversation, if a wicked man suddenly begins to perform good works we are wont to speak thus of him: He has gone out of himself. Indeed, he is properly said to have gone out of himself if he rejects

---
[1] Gen. 12.1.
[2] Cf. 1 Cor. 10.11.

his vices and delights in virtue. 'Leave your country,' says the Lord. Our country, that is, our body, was the land of the dying before Baptism, but through Baptism it has become the land of the living. It is the very land of which the psalmist relates: 'I believe that I shall see the bounty of the Lord in the land of the living.'[3] Through Baptism, as I said, we have become the land of the living and not of the dying, that is, of the virtues and not of the vices. However, this is true only if after receiving Baptism we do not return to the slough of vices, if when we have become the land of the living we do not perform the blameworthy, wicked deeds of death. 'And come,' says the Lord, 'into the land which I will show you.'[4] It is certain that then we will come with joy to the land which God shows us, if with His help we first repel sins and vices from our land, that is, from our body.

(2) 'Leave your kinsfolk.'[5] Our kinsfolk is understood as those vices and sins which are in part born with us in some way, and are increased and nourished after infancy by our bad acts. Therefore, we leave our kinsfolk when through the grace of Baptism we are emptied of all sins and vices. However, this is true only if later we strive as much as we can with God's help to expel vice and to be filled with virtues. If after being freed from all evil through Baptism we are willing to be slothful and idle, I fear that what is written in the Gospel may be fulfilled in us: 'When the unclean spirit has gone out of a man, he roams through dry places in search of rest and finds none. If after he returns he finds his house unoccupied, he takes with him seven other spirits more evil than himself; and the last state of that man becomes worse than the first.'[6] Therefore, let us so go forth from our kinsfolk, that is, from our sins and vices, that we may never again wish to return to them as a dog to its vomit.

---

3 Ps. 26.13.
4 Gen. 12.1.
5 *Ibid.*
6 Cf. Matt. 12.43-45.

(3) 'Leave your father's house.'[7] This we ought to accept in a spiritual manner, dearly beloved. The devil was our father before the grace of Christ; of him the Lord spoke in the Gospel when He rebuked the Jews: 'The father from whom you are is the devil, and the desires of your father it is your will to do.'[8] He said the devil was the father of men, not because of birth from him, but because of imitation of his wickedness. Indeed, they could not have been born of him, but they did want to imitate him. This fact that the devil was our first father the psalmist relates in the person of God speaking to the Church: 'Hear, O daughter, and see; turn your ear, forget your people and your father's house.'[9] Consider what he said, brethren. 'Hear, O daughter,' he says. One who says 'Hear, O daughter,' surely is the father; and when he says: 'forget your people and your father's house,' he clearly advises that the father should be left. Therefore, we are invited by God the Father through a happy, blessed exchange, to abandon our father the devil. We truly leave our father the devil, provided that, with God's help, we always endeavor to avoid and to flee from his cunning wickedness.

(4) Therefore, it is through the gift of Christ's grace, not by our own strength, brethren, that we have merited all these things, so that we can go forth from our country, that is, carnal living, leave our kinsfolk, that is, vices and sins, and flee from the home of the devil our father. For this reason let us labor as much as we can, with His help, that we may never again return to the company or friendship of the devil through vices or carnal desires. As it is written: 'Now thou art cured. Sin no more, lest something worse befall thee.'[10] Instead, by imitating the faith of Abraham and continually doing good works, we may attain not only pardon but even the company and friendship of God. However, we also ought to consider with great fear and dread what the Lord said on this same

---
7 Gen. 12.1.
8 John 8.44.
9 Ps. 44.11.
10 Cf. John 5.14.

subject to Moses. When the Lord handed over to you the land of the Chanaanites, He said: 'Take care, therefore, not to make a covenant with these inhabitants of the land that you are to enter; else they will immediately become a snare among you.'[11] Now we believe that by the grace of Baptism all sins and offenses have been banished from us. If we afterwards make a covenant with those same sins and vices, doubtless this covenant will become a snare for us because of our consent to avarice or dissipation. Therefore, let us with God's help labor for the salvation of our soul as much as we can, and let us take care to introduce virtues in the field of our heart which sins and vices had occupied. Then will be fulfilled in us what blessed Isaac as a type of Christ said in blessing his son: 'The fragrance of my son is like the fragrance of a plentiful field which the Lord has blessed!'[12] May He deign to grant this, to whom is honor and might together with the Father and the Holy Ghost forever and ever. Amen.

Sermon 82

On the Heifer, the Ram, and the She-goat of Three Years; Also the Turtledove and the Pigeon

(1) Dearly beloved, we have heard the Scriptures saying: 'The Lord spoke to Abraham and said: "Bring me a heifer three years old, a she-goat three years old, a ram three years old, a turtledove and a young pigeon." He brought him all these and cut them in two, and laid each half opposite the other; but the birds he did not cut in two. Birds of prey swooped down on the carcasses, but Abraham drove them off. As the sun was setting, Abraham fell into a deep sleep; and terror came upon him, a great darkness. Now when the sun

---
11 Cf. Exod. 34.12.
12 Gen. 27.27.

had set and it was dark, a smoking oven and a fiery torch passed between the pieces.'[1] Therefore, brethren, as far as the Lord grants us we wish to suggest to the ears of your charity what these facts mean. Blessed Abraham was called by the Lord 'the father of a multitude of nations,'[2] for all the nations which now believe in Christ and will believe are sons of Abraham by imitating his faith, not by birth in the flesh. Now just as after being children of Abraham the degenerate Jews by their infidelity became children of the devil and are called in the Gospel a 'brood of vipers,'[3] so on the contrary all the nations who faithfully believe in Christ have merited to become the children of Abraham. Therefore, the heifer, the she-goat, and the ram of three years, as also the turtledove and the pigeon, presented a type of all nations. They were described as of three years, because all the nations were to believe in the mystery of the Trinity. Now the entire Catholic Church has not only spiritual members but carnal ones also, for although some say they believe in the Trinity, they are nevertheless carnal because they neglect to avoid sins and vices. Since there are spiritual souls with the carnal ones, for this reason the turtledove and pigeon were added; in the latter spiritual men can be meant, but in those other three animals carnal men are understood.

(2) Now notice carefully that Abraham is said to have divided the three animals into two parts and to have placed them one against the other. 'The birds,' says Scripture, 'he did not cut in two.' Why is this, brethren? Because in the Catholic Church carnal men are divided, but spiritual men are not at all. And, as Scripture says, they are separated one against the other. Why are carnal men divided and set against each other? Because all wicked lovers of the world do not cease to have divisions and scandals among each other. For this reason they are divided, since they are opposed to one

---
[1] Cf. Gen. 15.9-12; 17. The text has *Abraham*.
[2] Gen. 17.5.
[3] Matt. 3.7.

another. However, the birds, that is, spiritual souls, are not divided. Why not? Because they have 'one heart and one soul in the Lord';⁴ to will and not to will is all one thing to them. Surely the turtledoves and pigeons which we mentioned above are like these souls. In the turtledove chastity is represented, simplicity in the pigeon. All God-fearing people in the Catholic Church clearly are chaste and simple, and with the psalmist they can say: 'Had I but wings like a dove, I would fly away and be at rest.'⁵ And again: 'The swallow finds a nest in which she puts her young.'⁶ And since carnal men, who can be divided, are pressed down by the heavy fetters of vice, spiritual men are raised on high by the wings of various virtues and as if by two wings, that is the two precepts of love of God and charity toward the neighbor, they are lifted up to heaven. With the Apostle they can say: 'But our citizenship is in heaven.'⁷ As often as the priest says: 'Lift up your hearts,'⁸ they can say with assurance and devotion that they have lifted them up to the Lord. However, very few and rare are the people in the Church who can say this with confidence and truth. Therefore, Abraham did not divide the birds, because spiritual souls who have one heart and soul, as I said, cannot be divided or separated from love of God and of neighbor. They exclaim with the Apostle: 'Who shall separate us from the love of Christ? Shall tribulation, or distress, or persecution?'⁹ Other words follow until it is said: 'Nor any other creature will be able to separate us from the love of God, which is in Christ Jesus our Lord.'¹⁰ Therefore, spiritual souls are not separated from Christ by torments, while carnal souls are sometimes separated by idle gossip; the cruel sword cannot separate the former, but carnal affec-

---

4 Cf. Acts 4.32.
5 Ps. 54.7.
6 Cf. Ps. 83.4.
7 Phil. 3.20.
8 These are words addressed to the people by the priest before the Preface of the Mass.
9 Rom. 8.35.
10 Rom. 8.39.

tions remove the latter. Nothing hard breaks down spiritual men, but even flattering words corrupt the carnal. For this reason Abraham divided those animals into two parts, but the birds he did not divide.

(3) 'When the sun had set, Abraham fell into a deep sleep; and terror came upon him, a great darkness. And there appeared a smoking oven and a fiery torch passed between the pieces.'[11] Notice, brethren, that what is called a fiery torch passing between those pieces is also not said to have touched the turtledove and pigeon. That evening signified the end of the world. Those animals, as we already said, showed a type of all the nations who believe in Christ. Because those nations have in them not only spiritual men, as was already said, that is, not only good men but even the wicked, for this reason the animals were divided and the fiery torch passed through them. According to what the Apostle says: 'The day of the Lord will declare it, since it will be revealed in fire,'[12] and so forth. That burning, smoking oven and fiery torch prefigured the day of judgment, and for this reason fear and a darksome horror settled upon blessed Abraham. Therefore, we have realized that: 'If the just man scarcely will be saved,' on the day of judgment, 'where will the impious and the sinner appear?'[13] That burning, smoking oven signified judgment day: the day of judgment, I repeat, on which 'there will be the weeping, and the gnashing of teeth.'[14] On that day there will be wailing and lamenting and repentance that is too late, when the foundations of the mountains will be moved and the earth will burn down to hell. When, as the blessed Apostle Peter says: 'The heavens, being on fire, will be dissolved and the elements will melt away by reason of the heat of the fire!'[15] When, as the Lord Himself asserts in the Gospel: 'The powers of heaven will be shaken,' when 'the sun will be

---

11 Cf. Gen. 15.17, 12, 17.
12 1 Cor. 3.13.
13 1 Peter 4.18.
14 Matt. 8.12.
15 2 Peter 3.12.

darkened, and the moon will not give her light, and the stars will fall from heaven.'[16] Where will the wicked see themselves then? Where will adulterers, drunkards, and railers recognize themselves? Where will lovers of dissipation, robbers, the proud, and the envious appear? What will these unhappy souls say in their own defense, when that day finds they have been admonished so often and still are unprepared? When the whole world begins to groan in answer to the archangel's trumpet which is louder than any other; when, as the prophet says, the Lord shall come 'To lay the world desolate, and to destroy the sinners thereof';[17] when, as Scripture says, wicked sinners will be thrown into the pool of fire, 'And the smoke of their torments goes up forever and ever';[18] then what trembling, what a mist, what darkness will seize those hateful, negligent, tepid souls? Therefore, in order that we may not come to this torture of soul, let us awake while there is time for correction and like good, profitable servants seek the will of our Lord. Then when that dreadful day of judgment comes, which is dreaded exceedingly even by the good and was signified by that burning, smoking oven, we will not be tormented in hell by avenging flames in company with carnal men. These souls were signified by the animals, because they can be divided by various contentious desires. Let us rather show the simplicity of the pigeon and the chastity of the turtledove, so that we may be raised to heaven on the spiritual wings of virtue. According to the Apostle's words: 'We shall be caught up together with them in clouds to meet the Lord in the air, and so we shall ever be with the Lord':[19] with the help of our Lord Jesus Christ, to whom is honor and glory together with the Father and the Holy Ghost world without end. Amen.

---

16 Matt. 24.29.
17 Isa. 13.9. This is an adaptation of the Scriptural text.
18 Apoc. 14.11.
19 1 Thess. 4.17.

Sermon 83

On the Three Men Who Appeared to Blessed Abraham

(1) I have frequently admonished your charity, dearly beloved, that in the lessons which are read in church these days you should not only pay attention to what we know is meant by the letter, but removing the veil of the letter should devoutly seek the life-giving spirit. Thus, indeed, the Apostle says: 'The letter kills, but the spirit gives life.'[1] The unfortunate Jews and still more unfortunate heretics, while they only look to the sound of the letter, thus remain dead without its vivifying spirit. Let us listen to the Apostle when he says that: 'All these things happened to them as a type, and they were written for us.'[2] Therefore, let us see what it is that we heard yesterday when the sacred lesson was read.

(2) 'God appeared to Abraham,' it said, 'as he sat at the entrance of his tent near the holm-oak of Mamre. Behold three men stood at a distance from him, and he went to meet them,'[3] and so forth. Notice, brethren, and see how God appeared to Abraham, and how He appeared to Lot. The three men came to Abraham and stood over him; two came to Lot and stayed in the street. Consider, brethren, whether these things did not happen through the dispensation of the Holy Ghost according to their merits. Indeed, Lot was far inferior to Abraham; if he had not been, he would not have merited to be separated from Abraham, nor would the dwelling of Sodom have pleased him. Now the three men came to Abraham at noon, while the other two came to Lot in the evening for this reason: Lot was unable to endure the power of the noonday sun, but Abraham could stand its full brightness.

---

1 2 Cor. 3.6.
2 Cf. 1 Cor. 10.11.
3 Cf. Gen. 18.1, 2.

(3) Now let us see how Abraham and Lot received the men who came to them. 'Abraham anticipated them and ran to meet them.'[4] When he had come to them, 'He hastened to the tent and said to his wife, "Hasten, moisten three measures of flour, and make three loaves," '[5]—in Greek they are called loaves when baked under ashes, indicating that they are hidden or concealed. 'And Abraham ran to the herd and picked out a bullock.'[6] What kind of a bullock? Perhaps the first one he could find? Not at all, but a 'good, tender'[7] bullock. Therefore, he took the bullock, 'and gave it to the servant who hastened to prepare it.'[8] See, brethren, and notice how you should receive strangers with a warm spirit. Behold Abraham himself runs, his wife hastens, and the servant hurries; no one is lazy in the home of the wise man. Understand what are the duties of Abraham and Sarah's hospitality. Lot, too, received men, but only two, not the whole trinity; moreover in the evening, not at noon. What did he serve them? 'He baked unleavened bread, and they ate.'[9] Because he was much inferior to Abraham in merits he did not have a fatted calf nor did he recognize the mystery of the Trinity in the three measures of flour. However, since he offered what he could in a kindly spirit, he merited to be freed from the destruction of Sodom. Notice, brethren, that even Lot deserved to receive the angels, because he did not reject strangers. Behold angels enter a hospitable home, but houses that are closed to strangers are burned with flames of sulphur.

(4) 'Three men came to Abraham, and stood over him.'[10] Observe how it is that they come upon him, but not against him. He had subjected himself to God's will, and for this reason God is said to stand over him. 'They stood over him'; not against him to repulse him, but over him for protection.

---
4 Cf. Gen. 18.2.
5 Cf. Gen. 18.6.
6 Cf. Gen. 18.7
7 *Ibid.*
8 *Ibid.*
9 Gen. 19.3
10 This is a free version of Caesarius, based only vaguely on Gen. 18.2.

He received the three men and served them loaves out of three measures. Why is this, brethren, unless it means the mystery of the Trinity? He also served a bullock; not a tough one, but a 'good, tender one.'[11] Now what is so good and tender as He who humbled Himself for us even unto death? He Himself is that fatted calf which the father killed upon receiving his repentant son. 'For God so loved the world that he gave his only-begotten Son.'[12] For this reason Abraham went to meet the three men and adored them as one. In the fact that he saw three, as was already said, he understood the mystery of the Trinity; but since he adored them as one, he recognized that there is one God in the three persons. He speaks to one, saying: 'Turn aside to thy servant.'[13] Moreover he adds, as though speaking to the men: 'I will bring water, that you may wash your feet.'[14] Learn from blessed Abraham, brethren, to receive strangers gladly, and to wash their feet with humility and piety. Wash, I repeat, the feet of pious strangers, lest there remain in them some dust which they will be able to shake off of their feet to your judgment. In the Gospel we read: 'Whoever does not receive you—go forth and shake off the dust from your feet. Amen I say to you, it will be more tolerable for the land of Sodom and Gomorrah in the day of judgment than for that town.'[15] Abraham foresaw this in spirit, and for this reason wanted to anticipate it by washing their feet, lest perchance any dust remain which might be kept and shaken off on judgment day as an evidence of unbelief. Therefore, the wise Abraham says: 'I will bring water, that you may wash your feet.'[16] Carefully listen to this, brethren, if you are unwilling to exercise hospitality and to receive even your enemy as a guest. Behold while blessed Abraham welcomed those men warmly, he merited to receive

---

11 Gen. 18.7.
12 John 3.16.
13 This quotation is not found in the reference to Gen. 18.3.
14 Cf. Gen. 18.4.
15 Cf. Matt. 10.14, 15.
16 Cf. Gen. 18.4.

God Himself in consideration of his hospitality. Christ further confirmed this in the Gospel when He said: 'I was a stranger and you took me in.'[17] Therefore, do not despise strangers, lest perhaps He Himself be the one you have rejected.

(5) Now where did this happen? 'Near the holm-oak of Mamre,'[18] which in Latin is interpreted as 'vision' or 'discernment.' Do you see what kind of a place it is in which the Lord can have a feast? The vision and discernment of Abraham delighted Him; he was clean of heart, so that he could see God. Therefore, in such a place and in such a heart the Lord can have His feast. Of this vision our Lord spoke to the Jews in the Gospel when He said: 'Abraham rejoiced that he was to see my day. He saw it and was glad.'[19] He saw my day, He says, because he recognized the mystery of the Trinity. He saw the Father as day, the Son as day, the Holy Ghost as day, and in these three one day. Thus, the Father is God, the Son is God, the Holy Ghost is God, and these three are one God. For individually each person is complete God, and all three together are one God. Moreover, because of the unity of substance, in those three measures of flour the Father, Son, and Holy Ghost is not unfittingly understood. However, this can also be taken in another way by understanding Sarah as the Church; the three measures of flour then are faith, hope, and charity. In these three virtues all the fruits of the Church are contained, so that if a man merits to possess the three within himself, he can with security receive the entire Trinity at the banquet of his heart.

(6) After this the Lord said to Abraham: 'The outcry against Sodom and Gomorrah ascended to me, therefore, I descended to see whether they have done all that the outcry which has come to me indicates; if not, I will know.'[20] These are the words of Scripture; let us see what is fittingly meant in them. 'I descended to see.' When replies are given to Abra-

---

17 Cf. Matt. 25.35.
18 Cf. Gen. 18.1.
19 John 8.56.
20 Cf. Gen. 18.20, 21.

ham, God is not said to descend but to stand over him. However, since it is now a question of sinners, God is said to descend. See to it that do you not feel this ascent and descent of position. It is unbecoming to perceive this in a substance that is immaterial and everywhere entire. God is said to go down when he condescends to care for human frailty. This we should feel in particular concerning our Lord and Savior who 'emptied himself, taking the nature of a slave.'[21]

(7) Now let us see what He means by saying: 'I descended to see whether they have done all that the outcry which has come to me indicates; if not, I will know.' Because of this, pagans, and especially the exceedingly foul Manichaeans, are wont to assail us by saying: Behold, the God of the law did not know what was being done in Sodom. Now we reply with sound understanding and say that God knows the just in one way and sinners in another. What is said concerning the just? 'The Lord knows who are his.'[22] What is said about sinners? 'Depart from me, all you workers of iniquity! I do not know you.'[23] Moreover, the Apostle Paul says: 'If anyone is the Lord's, he knows what I am saying; if anyone ignores this, he shall be ignored.'[24] What does it mean, then, I do not know you? I do not recognize you in my pattern; I do not recognize my image in you. My justice knows something to punish in you, but my mercy does not find anything to crown. For this reason if a man's actions are unworthy of God, he is said to be unworthy of His knowledge also. 'I descended to see'; not in order to know what they are doing, but to make them worthy of my knowledge if I find any of them just, repentant, or such as I should know. Finally, since no one but Lot was found to repent and be converted, he alone was known and saved from the fire. For our part, brethren, let us work hard and, with God's help, strive to be such as are considered worthy of God's notice, so that He may deign to both recognize and

---
21 Phil. 2.7.
22 2 Tim. 2.19.
23 Cf. Matt. 7.23.
24 Cf. 1 Cor. 14.37, 38.

know us: with the help of our Lord Jesus Christ, to whom is honor and glory together with the Father and the Holy Ghost world without end. Amen.

Sermon 84

On Abraham and His Son Isaac

(1) That lesson in which we read that blessed Abraham offered his son Isaac as a holocaust is not read in the right order during the days of Lent, dearly beloved, because as you know it is reserved for the vigil of Easter due to the mystery of the Lord's Passion. Since at that time there is no opportunity to say anything about it, we will now, if you wish, briefly suggest an explanation of it to your heart. Under the Lord's inspiration we shall do so to the best of our ability as the fathers have discussed it.

(2) 'Therefore, the Lord said to Abraham: "Take your son Isaac whom you love and offer him as a holocaust upon one of the mountains, which I shall point out to you." And he, rising up harnessed his ass, and took with him two servants and his son Isaac; and on the third day he came to the place which the Lord had indicated to him.'[1] When Abraham offered his son Isaac he was a type of God the Father, while Isaac prefigured our Lord and Savior. The fact that he arrived at the place of sacrifice on the third day is shown to represent the mystery of the Trinity. That the third day should be accepted in the sense of a promise or mystery of the Trinity is found frequently in the Sacred Books. In Exodus we read: 'We will go a three days' journey into the wilderness.'[2] Again, upon arriving at Mount Sinai it is said to the people: 'Be

---

1 Cf. Gen. 22.2-4.
2 Cf. Exod. 8.27.

sanctified, and be ready for the third day.'³ When Josue was about to cross the Jordan, he admonished the people to be ready on the third day. Moreover, our Lord arose on the third day. We have mentioned all this because blessed Abraham on the third day came to the place which the Lord had showed him.

(3) The two servants whom he ordered to stay with the ass typified the Jewish people who could not ascend or reach the place of sacrifice because they would not believe in Christ. That ass signified the synagogue. The ram which was stuck among the briars with its horns also seems to represent the Lord, for Christ as it were stuck among thorns with horns when He hung on the beam of the cross, fastened with nails. When Isaac himself carried the wood for the sacrifice of himself, in this, too, he prefigured Christ our Lord who carried His own cross to the place of His Passion. Of this mystery much had already been foretold by the prophets: 'And his government shall be upon his shoulders.'⁴ Christ, then, had the government upon His shoulders, when He carried His cross with wonderful humility. Not unfittingly does Christ's cross signify government: by it the devil is conquered and the whole world recalled to the knowledge and grace of Christ. Finally, the Apostle also said this when he spoke of the Lord's Passion: 'He became obedient to death, even to death on a cross. Therefore God also has exalted him and has bestowed upon him the name that is above every name.'⁵ We have said this, brethren, so that your charity may know that the government of Christ of which we read: 'And the government shall be upon his shoulders,' is none other than His cross. For this reason this lesson is read at Easter when the true Isaac, whose type the son of Abraham showed, is fastened to the gibbet of the cross for the human race.

(4) We read in this lesson that when blessed Abraham

---
3 Cf. Exod. 19.15.
4 Cf. Isa. 9.5, 6.
5 Phil. 2.8, 9.

came with his son and saw the place afar off, he said to his servants: 'Sit here with the ass while the boy and I go on; and when we have worshiped we shall come back to you.'[6] Why is it said to the servants who prefigured the Jews: 'Sit here with the ass'? Could that ass sit down, dearly beloved? It is said: 'Sit with the ass,' because the Jewish people who would not believe in Christ could not stand, but like the weak and languid sinner who had despised the staff of the cross were about to fall to the ground. For this reason blessed Abraham said: 'Sit here with the ass while the boy and I go on; and when we have worshiped, we shall come back to you.' What is it that you are saying, blessed Abraham? You are going to sacrifice your son and you say you will return with him? If you offer him as a holocaust, surely he will not be able to return with you. Blessed Abraham could reply: I speak the truth: I am offering my son and I will return to you with him. So great is my faith that I believe that He who deigned to give him to me of a sterile mother could raise him from the dead. For this reason I say with truth: 'When we have worshiped, we shall come back to you.'

(5) But when the ram was killed, and Isaac was not killed, it happened thus because Isaac was a figure and not the reality; for in him was designated what was later fulfilled in Christ. Behold, God contending with men in great devotion. Abraham offered God his mortal son who was not to die, while God surrendered in death His immortal Son for the sake of men. Concerning blessed Isaac and that ram it can be further understood that in Isaac was signified the divinity of Christ, in the ram His humanity. Just as in His Passion not the divinity but the humanity is believed to have been crucified, so the ram but not Isaac was immolated: the only-begotten Son of God is offered, the first-born of the Virgin is sacrificed. Listen to another mystery. Blessed Jerome, a priest, wrote that he knew most certainly from the ancient Jews and elders that Christ our Lord was afterwards crucified in the place where Isaac

---

6 Cf. Gen. 22.5.

was offered. Lastly, from the place whence blessed Abraham was commanded to depart, he arrived on the third day at the place where Christ our Lord was crucified. This, too, is mentioned in the account of the ancients, that in the very place where the cross was fastened the first Adam once was buried. Moreover, it was called the place of Calvary for the very reason that the first head of the human race is said to have been buried there. Truly, brethren, not unfittingly is it believed that the physician was raised up where the sick man lay. It was right that divine mercy should bend down in the place where human pride had fallen. The precious Blood may be believed to have corporally redeemed the ashes of the sinner of old by deigning to touch it with its drops. We have gathered these facts as well as we could, dearly beloved, from the different books of Scripture for the progress of your soul, and we suggest them to the consideration of your charity. If, with the Lord's help, you will read over the Sacred Scriptures rather frequently and heed them carefully, I believe that you can find an even better explanation.

(6) I beseech you, brethren, that anyone who wants his son or slave baptized should not postpone bringing him to church. It is not right for a matter which is considered so important and distinguished to be sought with indifference and later than necessary. I am afraid that some women bring their little babies so reluctantly because they neglect to come to the vigils with them. We believe most certainly that if at the beginning of Lent they will bring those who are to be baptized and devoutly come with them to the vigils, their children will receive the sacrament of Baptism in the proper manner, and they themselves will obtain pardon for their sins: with the help of our Lord Jesus Christ, to whom is honor and might together with the Father and the Holy Ghost world without end. Amen.

Sermon 85

On the Servant of Abraham Who Was Sent to Rebecca

(1) When the sacred lesson was read a little while ago, we heard that blessed Abraham called his servant and said to him: 'Put your hand under my thigh that I may adjure you by the God of heaven and of earth, not to obtain a wife for my son from the daughters of this region,'[1] and that he obediently placed his hand under his thigh and swore to him. Indeed, brethren, all these things which are read in the Old Testament, if we are willing to accept them only according to the letter, will bring us little or no profit of soul. For of what benefit is it to us who assemble in church with devotion to hear the word of God, if it is mentioned that Abraham sent his servant to bring his son a wife from a distant country, when we see this happen frequently also in this land? However, brethren, following the blessed Apostle Paul, we should believe that all things which were written for the Jews 'happened to them as a type,'[2] but in reality were fulfilled for us. Therefore, Abraham said to his servant: 'Put your hand under my thigh and swear by the God of heaven and of earth.' Thus blessed Abraham said: 'Put your hand under my thigh,' as if he were saying, put your hand upon the altar, or put your hand upon the ark of the testament, or stretch forth your hand to God's temple, and swear to me. He touched his thigh and swore by the God of heaven and earth. For blessed Abraham did not err when he commanded that this be done, but because he was filled with the spirit of prophecy and knew that from his own seed Christ the Lord of heaven and earth would be born, therefore, when his servant touched his thigh, he did not utter an oath by any carnal member but by the living and true God: because 'Abraham begot Isaac,

---
1 Cf. Gen. 24.2, 3.
2 1 Cor. 10.11.

Isaac begot Jacob, and Jacob begot Judas,'[3] of whose seed Christ the Lord was born.

(2) 'The servant then journeyed to Syrian Mesopotamia, and standing near a well said in his heart: "Lord, God of my master, if thou hast shown kindness to my master, behold I stand here at the well. Now if a young woman comes to draw water and I say to her, 'Give me to drink,' and she answers, 'Do you drink, and I will also water your camels,' she it is whom you have chosen for my master Isaac." He had not yet finished speaking within his heart when Rebecca came out with a jar on her shoulder. Now the servant said to her: "Give me to drink." Quickly she lowered the jar and said: "Drink, sir, and I will draw water also for your camels." When he had asked whose daughter she was, the young woman answered that she was the daughter of Bathuel and the sister of Laban. So the man bowed and worshiped God, because he knew that they were kinsfolk of his master Abraham. And he brought forth ear-rings for adorning her face and placed bracelets on her wrists. The maiden going informed her parents, who went out and blessed God, with joy and honor receiving Abraham's servant. The latter, however, spoke to them of Rebecca, that he might take her to his master Isaac. But they said: "Let us call the girl and ask her wish." They called Rebecca and asked her: "Will you go with this man?" and she answered: "I will." '[4]

(3) Now, dearly beloved, let us briefly see, as far as we can, what these facts mean. When blessed Abraham directed his servant to take a wife for his son, he portrayed an image of God the Father. Just as when he offered the boy as a holocaust, he then presented an image of God the Father, so also his servant signified the words of prophecy. For this reason Abraham sent his servant into a distant land to take a wife for his son, because God the Father intended to send His prophetic word throughout the world to search for the

---
3 Matt. 1.2.
4 Cf. Gen. 24.10-58. This is an adaptation of the Scriptural passage.

Catholic Church as a spouse for His only-begotten Son. Just as through Abraham's servant a bride is brought for blessed Isaac, so by His prophetic word the Church of the Gentiles is invited to Christ the true bridegroom from distant lands. But where is found that spouse who was to be joined to Christ? Where, unless near the water? It is true, dearly beloved: If the Church had not come to the waters of Baptism, she would not have been joined to Christ. For this reason Rebecca found Abraham's servant at the well, and the Church finds Christ at the sacrament of Baptism. What happened, then, after this? The servant brought gold ear-rings and gold bracelets and gave them to Rebecca. In those gold ear-rings are signified the divine words; in those gold bracelets good works, because works are designated by the hands. Let us see, brethren, how Christ also gave these gifts to the Church. For this reason the servant brought gold ear-rings for adorning Rebecca's face, while Christ put into the Church's ears divine words that are of greater value than all pearls. The servant put bracelets on Rebecca's wrists, while Christ put good works into the Church's hands. Consider, dearly beloved, and rejoice, giving thanks to God because what was prefigured in them has been fulfilled in us by Christ's gift. Moreover, just as Rebecca could not have had the ear-rings or bracelets if Isaac had not sent them through his servant, so also the Church could not have had divine words in her ears or good works in her hands if Christ by His grace and through His apostles had not conferred them. Furthermore, the fact that the girl, when asked by her parents whether she wished to go with the servant, replied, I am going—this we see clearly fulfilled in the Church. There Rebecca's will is asked; here the Church's will is sought. To Rebecca it is said: Are you willing to go with this man? And she replied: I am going. To the Church it is said: Do you believe in Christ? And she replies: I do believe. Rebecca would not be led to Isaac if she did not say: I am going; neither would the Church be joined to Christ if she did not say: I believe.

(4) Therefore, the servant took Rebecca and showed her to Isaac. However, let us see where she found him. 'She found him at the well of the oath.'⁵ Look, brethren: Isaac's servant found Rebecca at the well, and Rebecca in turn found Isaac himself at the well. It is true: Christ does not find the Church, nor the Church Christ, except at the sacrament of Baptism. Therefore, as the Scriptures say: 'Toward evening blessed Isaac went out in the field to meditate.'⁶ That field contained a figure of the world. Isaac went out into the field, because Christ was to come into the world; Isaac toward the evening of the day, Christ at the end of the world. 'He went out,' it says, 'to meditate.' For this reason Isaac went to meditate in the field, because Christ came into the world to fight against the devil, that He might justly conquer him while being unjustly killed by him, so that by dying He might destroy death, and by rising again bring life to all who believe. Moreover, just as Rebecca was corporally joined to Isaac, so the Church was spiritually joined to Christ, receiving at present the Blood of her Spouse as a precious dowry, and later to receive the dowry of His kingdom. The blessed Apostle Peter clearly proclaims this when he says: 'You were redeemed, not with gold or silver, but with the precious blood of Christ, as of a lamb without blemish.'⁷

(5) Therefore, Isaac took Rebecca 'and led her into the tent of his mother.'⁸ Christ also took the Church and established it in place of the synagogue. As by infidelity the synagogue became separated from God and died, so by faith the Church was joined to Christ and received life. As the Apostle says, by pride 'the branches' of the olive tree 'have been broken off,'⁹ in order that the lowly wild olive may be ingrafted. For this reason Isaac took Rebecca, 'and because he loved

---
5 Cf. Gen. 21.32; 24.62.
6 Cf. Gen. 24.63.
7 Cf. 1 Peter 1.18, 19.
8 Cf. Gen. 24.67.
9 Rom. 11.17.

her he was consoled for the loss of his mother.'[10] Christ took the Church and loved her so much that by this very love He tempered the grief which was occasioned by the death of His mother, the synagogue. Indeed, just as the synagogue's infidelity caused Christ sorrow, so the Church's faith produced joy in Him. Likewise, as He lost the one nation of the Jews by the synagogue's wickedness, and still not all of it, so Christ the Lord acquired the whole world by the Church's faith. Moreover, dearly beloved, because from us Christ the Lord prepared for Himself a spiritual spouse which, as I said, He even redeemed with His precious Blood, therefore, with His help, each one of us should not only guard the benefits conferred upon him by divine gift, but should strive to increase them. Thus, there will appear to Him nothing sordid because of luxury, nothing puffed up with pride or consumed with anger, nothing blind with avarice or struck with the snakelike poison of envy. Truly, it is right that our spouse, 'fairer in beauty than the sons of men,'[11] should find in us none of the above-mentioned sins to offend the eyes of His majesty. To Him, together with the Father and the Holy Ghost, is honor and might forever. Amen.

Sermon 86

On the Conception of Holy Rebecca

(1) If we wanted to make known to the ears of your charity an explanation of Sacred Scripture in the same order and language in which the holy fathers expressed it, the food of doctrine could reach only a few scholarly souls, while the remaining crowd of people would remain hungry. For this reason I humbly beg you that learned ears be content to hear

---
10 Cf. Gen. 24.67.
11 Ps. 44.3.

with patience these simple words, provided that all of the Lord's flock can receive spiritual nourishment, as I said, from this homely, prosaic sermon. Since inexperienced, simple souls cannot rise to the height of scholars, the learned should deign to bend down to their ignorance. What is said to simple souls can, indeed, be understood by the educated, but what is preached to the learned cannot be grasped at all by the simple.

(2) On Tuesday there was read to us the lesson concerning blessed Isaac and holy Rebecca, and the children who struggled in her womb. Almost everyone accepts the fact that blessed Isaac represented a type of the Lord our Savior. Therefore, Isaac prefigured Christ and blessed Rebecca the Church, because although like the Church she remained sterile for a long time, she conceived through the prayer of blessed Isaac and the Lord's gift. Now the children struggled in her womb, and not tolerating this annoyance, she said: 'If this be so, why am I pregnant?'[1] Then the Lord replied to her: 'Two nations are in your womb; two peoples shall stem from your body. One people shall be stronger than the other, and the elder shall serve the younger.'[2] Indeed, as the Apostle says, dearly beloved: 'All these things happened to them as a type, and they were written for us.'[3] Therefore, Rebecca corporally conceived of blessed Isaac, because the Church was going to conceive spiritually of Christ. Moreover, just as the two children struggled in Rebecca's womb, so two people continually oppose each other in the Church's womb. If there were only wicked or only good men, there would be just one people. In the Church, so much the worse, both good and bad people are found, two people struggling as in the womb of the spiritual Rebecca—the humble, indeed, and the proud, chaste and adulterous, meek and irascible, kind and envious, merciful and avaricious. For good souls want to win over the evil, but the wicked long to destroy the just. It is the

---
1 Gen. 25.22.
2 Gen. 25.23.
3 Cf. 1 Cor. 10.11.

desire of the good that those who are bad be corrected, while the destruction of the good is the pursuit of the wicked. There is one class of the pious, another of the impious; the class of the good are raised up to heaven through humility, while the class of the wicked are plunged into hell through pride. For all those members of the Catholic Church belong to Esau who are inclined toward earthly possessions, love the earth, desire the earth, and place all their hopes in the earth. Whoever wishes to serve God in order to increase in honors or receive material profits is known to belong to Esau, that is, to earthly happiness. For in Esau carnal souls are understood, spiritual ones truly in Jacob. These are the two people whom the Apostle clearly mentions when he points out the carnal and indicates the spiritual. As he says: 'Now the works of the flesh are manifest, which are immorality, uncleanness, licentiousness, idolatry, witchcrafts, enmities, contentions, jealousies, anger, quarrels, factions, parties, envies, drunkenness, carousings, and suchlike.'[4] Behold the fruits of the people who belong to Esau. In the following passage the same Apostle adds the fruits of those who belong to Jacob, saying: 'But the fruit of the Spirit is: charity, joy, peace, patience, goodness, kindness, faith, modesty, continency.'[5] Behold the spiritual works belonging to blessed Jacob, that is, to people who are pious.

(3) The fact that we read: 'One people shall be stronger than the other, and the elder shall serve the younger,'[6] we do not see fulfilled according to the letter in Esau and Jacob. For Scripture does not mention that Esau served blessed Jacob bodily. Therefore, we ought to inquire how this is to be understood spiritually, or how the elder shall serve the younger, for if this were not to happen Holy Scripture would not mention it. Therefore, if a man pays careful attention, he will know how the elder people shall serve the younger in the case of

---

4 Gal. 5.19-21.
5 Gal. 5.22, 23.
6 Gen. 25.23.

Christians and Jews. The greater and older people of the Jews are proved to serve the younger, that is, the Christian people, for like servants of the Christians they are known to carry the books of the divine law throughout the world for the instruction of all nations. Therefore, the Jews were scattered in every land, so that when we want to invite some pagan to faith in Christ by testifying that Christ Himself was announced by all the prophets, and he resists and says that the holy books of the divine law were written by us rather than the Holy Ghost, we may thus have a means of refuting him with positive arguments. To such a man we may say: If a doubt arises in you concerning my books, behold the books of the Jews, apparently our enemies, which I certainly could neither have written nor changed. Read them over, and when you have found in them the same thing as in my books, 'Be not unbelieving, but believing.'[7] In this way the elder people is known to serve the younger, for through their books the people of the Gentiles are invited to belief in Christ.

(4) In another way, too, the elder people shall serve the younger. In what way, you ask? Surely in the way the wicked serve the good; not by yielding to them, of course, but by persecuting them. How, then, do the wicked serve the good? As persecutors serve the martyrs; as a file or hammer, gold; as a mill, wheat; as ovens, the baking of bread: those are consumed, so that these may be baked. How, I say, do the wicked serve the good? As chaff in the furnace of the goldsmith serves gold; doubtless the gold is proved when the chaff is destroyed. Therefore, the wicked should not glory or extol themselves when they send some tribulations to the good. Although they persecute the latter in body, they are known to kill themselves in heart. If the misfortune of an evil person affects a good man, the iniquity has already caused his own soul to decay. Therefore, if in an evil spirit someone who is inflamed with the fury of wrath tries to stir up a good man, it is still doubtful whether the latter can be consumed with rage; but there

---

[7] John 20.27.

is no doubt that the first one is glowing with anger. Perhaps that good man who is full of spiritual vigor and the refreshment of the Holy Ghost will not get excited, even if the fire of persecution is inflicted; but without any doubt the one who tried to arouse him cannot fail to burn with passion. Both Esau and Jacob were born of the one seed of Isaac, just as Christian people are begotten of our Lord and Savior's one Baptism and one womb of the Church. However, just like Esau and Jacob, these people are divided into two parts because of the difference of morals, for from the fruits of their works one part is known to be carnal, the other spiritual. For this reason, then, Scripture said: 'The elder shall serve the younger,'[8] because the number of the wicked is always greater than that of the good. So just like those two children in the womb of Rebecca, so these people will struggle in the womb of the Church until judgment day, as we said above, while the proud resist the humble, while adulterers persecute the chaste, while drunkards whose number is infinite rail at the sober, while the envious rival the good, while robbers desire to destroy those who give alms like the irascible do the peaceable, and while the dissolute attempt to drag down to earth those who have a taste for heavenly things.

(5) Therefore, I beseech you, brethren, that whoever feels himself guilty in these evils, while there is still time, should, with God's help, strive to be transferred from the left hand to the right. Abandoning the baseness of vice, he should hasten to return to the adornments of the virtues. Then at the day of judgment he will merit to be freed from the evil hearing and to hear that desirable word: 'Well done, good and faithful servant; enter into the joy of thy master.'[9] Yet I exhort and admonish you, brethren, to be more careful to rise earlier for the vigils; come faithfully to Tierce, Sext, and None. Above all observe chastity even with your own wives throughout Lent and to the end of Easter. Give to the poor

---
8 Gen. 25.23.
9 Matt. 25.21.

what you intended to eat for breakfast. Preserve peace yourselves, and recall to harmony those whom you know are at variance. Welcome strangers and do not be ashamed to wash their feet; do not blush to do as a Christian what Christ deigned to perform. With good will give alms to the poor according to your means: 'For God loves a cheerful giver.'[10] If you cannot cut off the impediments of the world entirely, at least moderate them in part, so that you will be able to engage in reading and prayer. By thus storing up more abundant spiritual wine, that is, the word of God, in the holy receptacle of your heart, you will be able to serve God with a clear and upright conscience after rejecting all sins and vices. Then when the holy feast of Easter comes, you can with joy and exultation approach the Lord's altar with a pure heart and chaste body, if you have faithfully and happily observed charity both with the good and the wicked. Then, too, each one of you may merit to receive the Body and Blood of Christ as the remedy of your soul and not unto judgment: with the help of our same Lord Jesus Christ, to whom is honor and might together with the Father and the Holy Ghost world without end. Amen.

Sermon 87

On Jacob's Ladder

(1) When the lesson was read just now, dearly beloved, we heard that in reply to holy Rebecca's plea Isaac called his son Jacob and told him to proceed to Mesopotamia of Syria and take a wife from there. Jacob departed in humble obedience to his father and on the way came to a certain place where he put a stone under his head and went to sleep. In his slumber

---
10 2 Cor. 9.7.

he saw a ladder extending to heaven with angels of God ascending and descending by it, while the Lord leaned on the ladder and said to him: Jacob, Jacob, do not be afraid, I am with you, and I will be the companion of your journey. Now when blessed Isaac directed his son to Mesopotamia, dearly beloved, he represented a type of God the Father, while Jacob signified Christ the Lord. Disregarding the women of the region in which he lived, blessed Jacob sent his son into a distant country to take a wife, because God the Father would reject the synagogue of Jews and send His only-begotten Son to form a Church out of the Gentiles. This was fulfilled in truth when the apostles said to the Jews: 'It was necessary that the word of God should be spoken to you first, but since you judge yourselves unworthy of eternal life, behold, we now turn to the Gentiles.'[1]

(2) We do not read of blessed Jacob that he departed with horses or asses or camels, but we read only that he carried a staff in his hand. Thus, indeed, when entreating the Lord he said: 'Lord, I am not worthy of all thy kindnesses. With only my staff I crossed this Jordan; behold, now I have grown into two camps.'[2] Jacob displayed his staff to take a wife, but Christ bore the wood of the cross to redeem the Church. In his sleep Jacob put a stone under his head and saw a ladder extending to heaven, while the Lord leaned upon the ladder. Consider, brethren, how many mysteries there are in this place. Jacob represented a type of the Lord our Savior; the stone which he put under his head no less prefigured Christ the Lord. Listen to the Apostle telling why the stone at the head signifies Christ: 'The head of man is Christ.'[3] Finally, notice that blessed Jacob anointed the stone. Pay attention to the anointing, and you will recognize Christ: Christ is explained from an anointing, that is, from the grace of anointing.

(3) Now if Jacob sleeping on the ground prefigured the

---
1 Acts 13.46.
2 Cf. Gen. 32.10.
3 1 Cor. 11.3.

Lord, why is it that the Lord in heaven rested and leaned upon the ladder? How was Christ the Lord seen both on top of the ladder in heaven and in blessed Jacob on the ground? Listen to Christ Himself say that He is both in heaven and on earth: 'No one has ascended into heaven except him who has descended from heaven: the Son of Man who is in heaven.'[4] Notice that the Lord Himself said He is both in heaven and on earth. We confess, dearly beloved, that Christ the Lord is head of the Church; if this is true, He is in heaven with regard to the head, but on earth as far as the body is concerned. Moreover, when the blessed Apostle Paul was persecuting the Church, Christ exclaimed from heaven: 'Saul, Saul, why dost thou persecute me?'[5] He did not say: Why do you persecute my servants? Nor did He say: Why do you persecute my members? But He said: 'Why dost thou persecute me?' Now the tongue cries out if the foot is stepped on: You stepped on me, even though the tongue cannot be stepped on at all; through the harmony of charity the head cries out for all the members. Therefore, Jacob was sleeping and saw the Lord leaning on the top of the ladder. What does it mean to lean on the ladder, except to hang on the cross? Consider, brethren, that while hanging upon the wood of the cross He prayed for the Jews, and you will realize who shouted from heaven while leaning on the ladder of Jacob. But, why did this happen on the road, before Jacob obtained a wife? Because our Lord, the true Jacob, first leaned on the ladder, that is, the cross, and afterwards formed a Church for Himself. At the time He gave it the wages of His Blood, intending to give it later the dowry of His kingdom.

(4) Listen and see the sublimity of the fact that both Jacob asleep and the Lord leaning on the ladder prefigured Christ. Indeed, when our Savior in speaking of Nathanael had named blessed Jacob, He said: 'Behold an Israelite in whom there

---

4 John 3.13.
5 Acts 9.4.

is no guile.'⁶ Continuing, He said: 'Presently you shall see heaven opened, and the angels of God ascending and descending upon the Son of man.'⁷ In the Gospels our Lord preached concerning himself what Jacob had seen prefigured in his sleep: 'You shall see heaven opened, and the angels of God ascending and descending upon the Son of man.' If the angels of God were descending to the Son because He was on earth, how is it that those same angels were ascending to the Son of man except because He is in heaven? Therefore, He Himself was sleeping in Jacob, and from heaven He likewise called to Jacob.

(5) 'All these things," as the Apostle proclaims, brethren, 'happened to them as a type, and they were written for us, upon whom the final age of the world has come.'⁸ Carefully notice, brethren, how the angels of God ascend to the Son of man in heaven, and descend to the same Son on earth. When God's preachers announce deep and profound truths from Sacred Scripture which are understood only by devout men, they ascend to the Son of man; when they preach matters pertaining to the correction of morals which all the people can understand, they descend to the son of man. Thus the Apostle says: 'Wisdom we speak among those who are mature, yet not a wisdom of this world nor of the rulers of this world, but a secret, hidden wisdom which God foreordained before the world unto our glory.'⁹ When the Apostle said these words, doubtless he was ascending to the Son of man. However, when he said: 'Flee immorality';¹⁰ when he said: 'do not be drunk with wine, for in that is debauchery';¹¹ when he declared 'covetousness is the root of all evils';¹² in these words he descended like the angel of God to the son of man. When he

---

6 John 1.47.
7 Cf. John 1.51.
8 Cf. 1 Cor. 10.11.
9 Cf. 1 Cor. 2.6, 7. ·
10 1 Cor. 6.18.
11 Eph. 5.18.
12 1 Tim. 6.10.

further said: 'Mind the things that are above, not the things that are on earth,'[13] he was ascending. However, when he taught, 'Be sober, and do not sin,'[14] and preached the other truths which pertain to the correction of morals, he was descending; ministering the milk of doctrine like a nurse to children, he spoke words which even the ignorant could grasp. In this manner, then, there is ascending and descending to the son of man, since solid food is offered to the perfect while the milk of doctrine is not denied even to the young. Blessed John also was ascending when he said: 'In the beginning was the Word, and the Word was with God; and the Word was God';[15] by these words he ascended on high sufficiently. However, since God's angels not only ascend but also descend, bending down he says to the little ones: 'The Word was made flesh, and dwelt among us.'[16]

(6) In order that what we have mentioned above may adhere more firmly to your pious hearts, we will briefly repeat what was said. Blessed Isaac, as we said, sending his son away was a type of God the Father; Jacob who was sent signified Christ our Lord. The stone which he had at his head and anointed with oil also represented the Lord our Savior. The ladder touching heaven prefigured the cross; the Lord leaning on the ladder is shown to be Christ fastened to the cross. The angels ascending and descending on it are understood to be the apostles, apostolic men, and all doctors of the Church; they ascend by preaching perfect truths to the just, they descend by telling the young and ignorant what they can understand. For our part, brethren, we who see fulfilled in the New Testament all the truths which were prefigured in the Old, should thank God as well as we can because He has deigned to give us such great gifts without any preceding merits on our part. With His help let us labor with all our strength so that these great benefits may not bring us judgment

---

13 Col. 3.2.
14 Cf. 1 Cor. 15.34.
15 John 1.1.
16 John 1.14.

but progress. Rather let us be zealous to live spiritually and always to engage in good works in such a way that when the day of judgment finds us chaste, sober, merciful, and pious, we may not be punished with wicked sinners, but with the just and all who fear God we will merit to arrive at eternal bliss: with the help of our Lord who together with the Father and the Holy Ghost lives and reigns world without end. Amen.

Sermon 88

On Blessed Jacob and Laban

(1) We have frequently mentioned to your charity, dearly beloved, that blessed Jacob was a type and figure of our Lord and Savior. Moreover, how Christ was to come into the world to be joined to the Church was prefigured also in blessed Jacob when he traveled into a distant country to choose a wife. Therefore, blessed Jacob, as you have heard, went into Mesopotamia to take a wife. When he had come to a certain well, he saw Rachel coming with her father's sheep; after he recognized her as his cousin he kissed her as soon as the flock was supplied with water. If you notice carefully, brethren, you can recognize that it was not without reason that the holy patriarchs found their wives at wells or fountains. If this had happened only once someone might say it was accidental and not for some definite reason. Blessed Rebecca who was to be united to blessed Isaac was found at the well; Rachel whom blessed Jacob was to marry was recognized at the well; and Sephora who was joined to Moses was found at the well. Doubtless, then, we ought to understand some mysteries in these facts. Since all three of those patriarchs typified our Lord and Savior, for this reason they found their wives at fountains or wells, because Christ was to find His

Church at the waters of Baptism. Moreover, when Jacob came to the well Rachel first watered the flock and then he kissed her. It is true, dearly beloved; unless the Christian people are first washed from all evil by the waters of Baptism, they do not deserve to possess the peace of Christ. Could not blessed Jacob have kissed his cousin upon seeing her, before the flock was watered? Doubtless he could have, but a mystery was involved: for it was necessary for the Church to be freed from all iniquity and dissension by the grace of Baptism, and thus to merit peace with God.

(2) In that journey Jacob took two wives, and those two wives prefigured the two people of the Jews and the Gentiles. For at Christ's coming not a small number even of the Jewish people are read to have believed in Him, and again in the Acts of the Apostles there is recorded the fact that on one day three thousand people believed, on another day five thousand, and afterwards many thousands more. The Lord Himself in the Gospel confirms the fact that the two people believed in Christ when He said: 'And other sheep I have that are not of this fold. Them also I must bring, so that there may be one fold and one shepherd.'[1] Therefore, those two women who were married to blessed Jacob, that is, Lia and Rachel, prefigured those two people: Lia the Jews and Rachel the Gentiles. Like a cornerstone Christ is joined to those two people, like two walls coming from different directions. In Him they have kissed and in Him they have merited to find eternal peace, as the Apostle says: 'For he himself is our peace, he it is who has made both one.'[2] How did He make both one? By uniting the two flocks, and connecting the two walls to Himself.

(3) Now see what happened afterwards, for Scripture says that after this blessed Jacob became rich. Just as holy Jacob increased and grew rich so that he returned to his own country with immense wealth, so the true Jacob, our Lord Jesus

---
1 Cf. John 10.16.
2 Eph. 2.14.

Christ, came into this world and by uniting to Himself those two people, the Jews and Gentiles, bore countless spiritual sons of them, increased, and became exceedingly rich. Finally, listen to Him say: 'All power in heaven and on earth has been given to me.'[3] After despoiling the devil He carried great riches with Him back to the Father, in fulfillment of what the psalmist had predicted much earlier: 'Ascending on high, thou hast led captivity captive.'[4]

(4) As Jacob was returning to his own country, Laban and his companions pursued them. Upon examination of Jacob's substance Laban found nothing of his, and, therefore, he could not hold him. Laban here is not unfittingly said to represent a type of the devil, because he both served idols and was opposed to blessed Jacob who prefigured the Lord. For this reason he pursued Jacob but was unable to find anything of his own with him. Listen to the true Jacob declaring this fact in the Gospel: 'Behold the prince of the world is coming, and in me he will find nothing.'[5] May the divine mercy grant that our adversary may find nothing of his works in us, for if he finds nothing of his own he will not be able to keep us or recall us from eternal life. Therefore, dearly beloved, let us look at the treasury of our conscience, let us examine the secret places of our heart, and if we find nothing there which belongs to the devil let us rejoice and thank God. With His help let us strive as well as we can that the doors of our heart may always be open for Christ but closed forever to the devil. However, if we recognize something of the devil's works or cunning in our souls, let us hasten to cast it out and get rid of it as deadly poison. Then when the devil wants to ensnare us and can find nothing which belongs to him, he will depart in confusion while we can thank God with the prophet and shout to the Lord: 'You freed us from our foes, and those who hated us you put to shame.'[6] Therefore, Lia,

---

3 Matt. 28.18.
4 Cf. Ps. 67.19.
5 Cf. John 14.30.
6 Cf. Ps. 43.8.

as we said above, signified the people of the Jews who were joined to Christ; Rachel typified the Church, that is, the nation of the Gentiles. For this reason Rachel, not Lia, stole the idols of her father, because after Christ's advent the synagogue of the Jews is not known to have served idols everywhere, as is clearly proved concerning the Church of the Gentiles. Besides, not with Lia, that is, the synagogue, do we read that Laban's idols were hidden, but with Rachel who typified the Gentiles.

(5) Now as to the fact that Jacob came to the Jordan and after sending over all his possessions remained alone and wrestled with a man until the break of day. In that struggle Jacob prefigured the people of the Jews; the angel with whom he wrestled typified our Lord and Savior. Jacob wrestled with the angel because the Jewish people were to wrestle with Christ even to death. However, not all the Jews were unfaithful to Christ, as we said above, but a considerable number of them are read to have believed in His name, and for this reason the angel touched Jacob's thigh which began to be lame. That foot with which he limped typified the Jews who did not believe in Christ; the one which remained uninjured signified those who received Christ the Lord. Finally, notice carefully that in the struggle Jacob was victorious and sought a blessing. When the angel had said to him: 'Let me go,' Jacob replied, 'I will not let you go till you bless me.'[7] In the fact that he was victorious Jacob signified the Jews who persecuted Christ; inasmuch as he asked a blessing he prefigured the people who were to believe in Christ the Lord. What, then, did the angel say to him? 'You have contended with God and men, and have triumphed.'[8] This was fulfilled at the time when the Jewish people crucified Christ the Lord. 'Let me go,' said the angel, 'it is dawn.'[9] This prefigured the Lord's Resurrection, for the Lord, as you know very well, is read to have risen before dawn.

---
7 Gen. 32.27.
8 Gen. 32.29.
9 Gen. 32.27.

(6) The fact that Jacob typified the Lord we know again from the fact that he prayed God to deliver him from the hand of Esau his brother. 'O Lord, I am not worthy of all your kindnesses. With only my staff I crossed this Jordan; now I have grown into two camps.'[10] It is true, dearly beloved; with the staff of His cross Christ took possession of the world and returned in triumph to His Father with two companies, that is, two people. Therefore, think over these truths, beloved brethren, and like clean animals spiritually chew them over, providing useful energy and necessary food for your souls. Surely this is the food of which the Lord said in the Gospel: 'Do not labor for the food that perishes, but for that which endures unto life everlasting.'[11] May the Lord in His goodness lead you to this: to whom is honor and might together with the Father and the Holy Ghost world without end. Amen.

Sermon 89

On Jacob, His Son Joseph, and His Brothers

(1) As often as lessons from the Old Testament are read to you, dearly beloved, you should not only heed what is said in word, but also what is understood and perceived in spirit, as I have frequently advised. The Apostle also calls our attention to this when he says: 'The letter kills, but the spirit gives life.'[1] Now all these things which are read in the Old Testament, as the Apostle says: 'happened to them as a type, and they were written for us.'[2] When the Christian people devoutly come to church, of what benefit is it that they hear how the

---

10 Gen. 32.10.
11 John 6.27.

---

1 2 Cor. 3.6.
2 Cf. 1 Cor. 10.11.

holy patriarchs took their wives or begot their children, unless they perceive in a spiritual sense why these things happened or what the facts prefigured? Behold, we have heard that blessed Jacob begot a son and called his name Joseph, and that he loved him more than the rest of his sons. In this place blessed Jacob prefigured God the Father; holy Joseph typified our Lord and Savior. Therefore, Jacob loved his son because God the Father loved His only-begotten Son, as He Himself said: 'This is my beloved Son.'³ Jacob sent his son to manifest solicitude for his brothers, and God the Father sent His only-begotten Son to visit the human race which was weak from sin and like lost sheep. When Joseph was looking for his brothers he wandered in the desert. Christ also sought the human race which was wandering in the world; He, too, as it were, wandered in the world because He was seeking the erring. Joseph searched for his brothers in Sichem. Sichem is interpreted as a shoulder, for sinners always turn their backs in the face of the just, and shoulders are behind. Just as Joseph's brothers, struck with envy, offered their back rather than their face to fraternal love, so also the unhappy Jews preferred to envy rather than to love the author of salvation who came to them. Of such men it is said in the psalms: 'Let their eyes grow dim so that they cannot see, and keep their backs always feeble.'⁴

(2) So Joseph found his brothers in Dothain. Dothain is interpreted as rebellion. Truly, those men who thought about killing their brother were in a state of great rebellion. Upon seeing Joseph, his brothers discussed his death; just as when the Jews saw the true Joseph, Christ the Lord, they all resolved with one plan to crucify Him. His brothers robbed Joseph of his outside coat that was of divers colors; the Jews stripped Christ of His bodily tunic at His death on the cross. When Joseph was deprived of his tunic he was thrown into a cistern, that is, into a pit; after Christ was despoiled of human flesh,

---
3 Matt. 3.17.
4 Ps. 68.24.

He descended into hell. Afterwards, Joseph is lifted up out of the cistern and is sold to the Ismaelites, that is, to the Gentiles; when Christ returns from hell, He is bought by all nations at the price of faith. Upon the advice of Juda, Joseph is sold for thirty pieces of silver; Christ is sold for the same amount upon the counsel of Judas Iscariot. Now in different translations Joseph is not written as sold at the same price, for some say it was twenty pieces of silver and others thirty. This spiritually signifies that Christ was not to be believed and loved equally by all men. In fact, even in the Church some love Him more, others less, for Christ means more to the soul which loves Him with greater charity. Joseph went down to Egypt, Christ went into the world. Joseph saves Egypt from want of grain, Christ frees the world from a famine of the word of God. If Joseph had not been sold by his brothers, Egypt would have failed. It is true, brethren, that if the Jews had not crucified Christ, the world would have been lost.

(3) Let us see, dearly beloved, why his brothers raged so cruelly against blessed Joseph. Why, unless because of the poison of envy through which 'Death entered the world'?[5] Moreover, listen to the Scriptures saying: 'His brothers hated him and could not even greet him.'[6] Blessed Joseph had a dream as though he was standing in the field with his brothers binding sheaves, and the sheaves of his brothers adored his sheaf. This was fulfilled in Joseph in Egypt, when his brothers worshiped him. Not unfittingly were the sterile sheaves forced to adore the fruitful one through which they were to be freed from the danger of famine.

(4) Moreover, Joseph had another dream in which the sun, the moon, and eleven stars worshiped him. His father replied to him: 'Can it be that I and your mother and your brothers will come to bow to the ground before you?'[7] This could not be fulfilled in that Joseph; but in our true Joseph, that is, our Lord Jesus Christ, the mysteries of that dream were ful-

---

5 Wisd. 2.24.
6 Cf. Gen. 37.4.
7 Gen. 37.10.

filled. The sun, the moon, and eleven stars worshiped Him when after the Resurrection holy Mary as the moon, blessed Joseph as the sun, and eleven stars, that is, the blessed apostles, bent down and prostrated before Him. Then was fulfilled the prophecy which said: 'Praise him, sun and moon; praise him, all you shining stars.'[8] The interpretation of this dream was not accomplished in that Joseph for the important reason that we read his mother had died many years before he saw the aforementioned dreams. Truly, how could it happen to his brothers that they should adore him like the stars, since the night of envy had made them obscure and gloomy? They had lost the brightness of the stars, because they had extinguished in themselves the light of charity. We truly believe that this was deservedly fulfilled in our Lord and Savior, for, as I already said, we read that blessed Joseph, blessed Mary, and the eleven apostles worshiped Him quite frequently. That the apostles possessed the light of the stars our Lord Himself tells us in the Gospel: 'You are the light of the world.'[9] Again, He says concerning the same men and those who are similar: 'Then the just will shine forth like the sun in the kingdom of their Father.'[10]

(5) Joseph is interpreted as an increase or growth. In that Joseph nothing but Egypt alone had a growth, while in our true Joseph the whole world merited to have an increase. That Joseph distributed wheat, but ours deigned to dispense the word of God. 'For through all the earth their voice resounds, and to the ends of the world, their message.'[11]ABearly beloved, we have received so many good things through the mercy of the true Joseph, our Lord Jesus Christ, and without any preceding merits on our part. To us has come, not the shadow of the Old Testament, but its reality. Let us, then, with God's grace labor as hard as we can so that when He comes to judge us, our Judge may find what He has conferred

---

8 Ps. 148.3.
9 Matt. 5.14.
10 Matt. 13.43.
11 Ps. 18.5.

upon us whole and entire. He knows how much to demand in return, since He bestowed so much upon you. Truly, when He comes He will pay what He has promised, but He will also ask for what He redeemed; what He gave at His first coming, He will exact at the second. Therefore, let no one return evil for good to Christ our Lord. Who is there who could act so wickedly, except the man who receives sweetness and returns bitterness, who has been given life but restores death? If a man kills himself by an evil life, surely he gives back death. Who is it that repays good with evil, except the man who seizes what belongs to another although he should give his own goods, or returns hatred for love, envy for kindness, pride for humility, dissipation for chastity? Who is it that returns evil for good to Christ, except one who chooses to play at draughts and to frequent furious, bloody, or shameful spectacles when he should be engaged in reading or hurrying to church? While he ought to be destroying his sins by prayer, reading, and almsgiving, he strives rather to increase and augment them. Who is it that repays good with evil? Anyone who gives darkness instead of light, malice for kindness, drunkenness for sobriety, greediness for almsgiving, iniquity for justice. Therefore, if, with the Lord's help, a man does not commit these evils, he should protect the divine gifts within him to the best of his ability. However, if a man feels himself subject to these vices and overwhelmed by them, he should have recourse to the remedies of repentance at once. Before his gloomy soul departs from the body of its death, he should by almsgiving, fasts, and prayers obtain for himself a remedy against the day of wrath. For this reason let us so live, brethren, that before the tribunal of Christ those who are good may receive a crown and those who are careless may obtain pardon, in order that an innocent life may adorn the former and an amended one be able to excuse the latter. May He deign to grant this, to whom together with the Father and the Holy Ghost is honor and glory forever and ever. Amen.

* *Sermon 90*

On Blessed Joseph

(1) It is written concerning blessed Joseph, dearly beloved, that his brothers envied him and, therefore, 'could not even greet him.'¹ It is true, beloved brethren, that so dangerous is the disease of envy that it cannot even spare brothers, not to mention strangers. Indeed, at the very beginning of the world Cain, a wicked brother, killed the just Abel through envy. Hc¹y and faithful Joseph, then, was shown to be a more just servant of the Lord because of his tribulations. Through envy he was first sold by his brothers to the Ismaelites as a slave, and after having been sold by the very people by whom he had seen himself worshiped, was later handed over to an Egyptian master. However, he always kept the dignity of a noble soul, by his example teaching both slaves and freemen that in sin, not a man's condition, but his mind is a hindrance.

(2) The young man is desired by his mistress, but is not provoked to lust. He is asked and runs away. She who commanded in other matters, in this one thing coaxes and pleads. She loved him, or was it rather herself? I think that it was neither him nor herself. If she loved him, why did she want to ruin him? If she loved herself, why did she want to perish? Behold I have proved that she did not love: she burned with the poison of lust, but did not shine with the flame of charity. He, however, knew how to see what she did not know. Joseph was more beautiful within than without, fairer in the light of his heart than in the beauty of his body. Where the eye of that woman could not penetrate, there he enjoyed his own beauty. Therefore, as he beheld the interior beauty of chastity in the mirror of his conscience, when would he allow it to be stained or violated by the temptation of that

---

1 Gen. 37.4.

woman? For this reason what he saw you, too, can see if you will—namely, the interior and spiritual beauty of chastity—provided that you have eyes for it. I will tell you something by way of an example. You love it in your wife; therefore, do not hate in the wife of another what you love in your own. What do you love in your own wife? Chastity, of course. You hate it in another's wife, when you are willing to destroy chastity by intimacy with her. What you love in your own wife you want to kill in the wife of another. How can you have a prayer of devotion, O murderer of chastity? Therefore, preserve in the wife of another what you want to protect in your own, for in your wife you love her chastity rather than her body.

(3) Perhaps you think you love the flesh of your wife, and not her chastity. Indeed, this is a base thought and miserable, pleasurable lust. Moreover, I will not dismiss you without an example; I will give you a very definite reason. You think you love your wife's body; I tell you that you love chastity still more in her. To show you very clearly that you love her chastity more than her flesh, you love it more in your daughter. What man is there who does not want his daughters to be chaste? What man does not rejoice in the chastity of his daughters? Do you love the flesh there? Do you desire a beautiful body, when you dread an unchaste one? Behold I have convinced you that you love chastity more than the flesh. Finally, if you have a beautiful wife but perhaps an unchaste or wicked one, do you love her beautiful body and not rather detest it? External physical beauty is indeed considered, but the interior loveliness of chastity is sought. If this does not exist, all love of the body immediately grows cold; because although beauty is to be considered, an interchange of love within is sought still more. If, then, I have proved that you love chastity, why have you offended yourself by not loving it within you? What you love in your daughter love also in the wife of another, because your daughter will become another's wife. Therefore, love chastity in

yourself also. If you love the wife of another, presently you will not have it, but if you love chastity, with the Lord's help you will presently possess it. You ought to love a beautiful servant or the elegant wife of another in such a way that you seek it everywhere outside of you. If you love chastity, what you love is yours. Holy chastity coaxes you within the chamber of your heart; sweet is its embrace, 'For association with her involves no bitterness.'[2] Chastity does not quarrel with you, subvert you, or in any way contradict you in the home of your conscience. Therefore, love it both in yourself and in others, in order that you may possess eternal bliss. If, then, you love this very beautiful virtue which is called chastity, you will imitate blessed Joseph who refused to consent to illicit intimacy with an unchaste woman, spurned the lust of another, and esteemed his own virtue. That woman, however, did what she threatened, lied to her husband and was believed; and still God was patient. Holy Joseph was thrown into prison. He was held captive like a guilty man, although God was not offended by him. Nor did God fail him there, since he was not guilty in His sight. The Lord was with holy Joseph; because he loved what was holy, he was not overcome by the love of a woman. Her age did not arouse the chaste mind of the youth, nor did the authority of the one who loved him move him to associate with his despised mistress. With her own lips she plotted against the young man. Secretly and without witnesses the shameless woman seized him with her own hand, urging him by her insolent words to sin. Indeed, he is not overcome there, but as words followed words, so one thing followed another; although he had refused when asked repeatedly, still he was seized at the time he fled.

(4) You have admired the chastity of Joseph; now behold his generosity. He repays hatred with charity. When he saw his brothers, or rather enemies in his brothers, he gave evidence of the affection of his love by his pious grief when he wanted to be recognized by them. He tenderly kissed each

---
2 Wisd. 8.16.

one of them, and wept over them individually. As he moistened the necks of his frightened brothers with his refreshing tears, he washed away their hatred with the tears of his charity. He loved them always as with the love of their living father and dead brother. He did not recall that pit into which he had been thrown to be murdered; he did not think of himself, a brother, sold for a price. Instead, by returning good for evil, even then he fulfilled the precepts of the apostles which were not yet given. Therefore, by considering the sweetness of true charity, blessed Joseph, with God's help, was eager to repel from his heart the poison of envy with which he knew his brothers had been struck.

(5) Truly, brethren, what does envy offer the unhappy person whom spite gnaws at with the secret claws of conscience, when it makes the happiness of another a source of torment to him? What reward will he receive from his hatred, except terrible darkness of soul and the horror of a mind in confusion? May he who always grieves in countenance and in spirit torture himself with the wish whereby he wants to injure another; when disquieted by these cruel goads, he is deprived of all advice and moderation of mind. Therefore, brethren, let us watch the assault of this vice, lest perchance we become sharers in the works of the devil and together with him be condemned by an equal sentence. As it is written: 'By the envy of the devil, death entered the world, and they who are in his possession experience it.'[3] This vice does not injure very much those at whom it is aimed, but it first afflicts more gravely and dangerously those from whom it proceeds. As rust destroys and consumes iron, so does envy in the case of the soul. Just as they say vipers are born after tearing to pieces and shattering their mother's womb in which they were conceived, so, too, envy consumes and destroys the very soul in which it is conceived. What kind of worm of the soul is this, what corruption of thoughts, what great rust of the heart? It is jealous of God's gift in a man, turns the goods

---
3 Wisd. 2.24, 25.

of another to its own evil, makes the glory of others its own punishment, admits, as it were, tormentors to its own heart, by its thoughts and feelings inviting torturers who tear it to pieces with internal torments. No food can be agreeable to such men, no drink pleasant. There are sighs and groans and grief, day and night the besieged soul is torn apart without respite; for jealousy has no limit, the vice continually and endlessly remains. The more the object of envy proceeds with greater success, the more the jealous soul is inflamed by the fire of malice to greater passion. Because of this there is pallor on the countenance, a trembling of the lips, the gnashing of teeth, savage words, and unrestrained insults. Whoever is persecuted by the jealousy of the envious man probably cannot shun or avoid it. Moreover, the envious man cannot flee from himself. Wherever he is, his adversary is within him, the enemy is always shut up in his heart. Now when the disciples asked Him who was the greatest among them, our Lord in the Gospel replied: 'He who is the least among you, he is the greatest.'[4] By these words He utterly destroyed and took away every reason and cause for biting envy.

(6) Therefore, it is not right for Christian people to be jealous or envious; as the result of humility, they rise to the heights. Listen to blessed John the Apostle say in his epistle: 'Everyone who hates his brother is a murderer';[5] and again: 'He who says that he is in the light, and hates his brother, is in the darkness and walks in the darkness, and he does not know whither he goes; because the darkness has blinded his eyes.'[6] If a man hates his brother, he says, he walks in darkness and does not know where he is going. In his ignorance he goes down to hell, and in his blindness is thrown headlong into punishment because he withdraws from the light of Christ who says in warning: 'I am the light of the world. He who believes in me does not walk in the darkness, but will have

---

4 Cf. Luke 9.48.
5 1 John 3.15.
6 1 John 2.9, 11.

the light of life.'[7] Moreover, how can a man preserve either the peace or charity of the Lord, if he cannot be peaceable or untroubled because of the vice of envy? For our part, brethren, let us, with God's help, avoid the poison of jealousy or envy, and let us preserve the sweetness of charity toward the wicked as well as toward the good. Thus, Christ will not reproach us because of the vice of envy, but will rather praise us and invite us to His reward by saying: 'Come, blessed of my Father, take possession of the kingdom.'[8] Let the divine lesson be in your hands, the Lord's thoughts in your consciousness, constant prayer never cease, and works of salvation continue. As often as the enemy comes near to tempt us, let him always find us busy with good works. Each one should examine his own conscience, and if he sees that he has been struck with the poison of envy because of the good fortune of his neighbor, he should tear out of his heart the thorns and briars. May the Lord's seed be enriched in him as in a fertile field with increased fruit, so that the divine and spiritual seed may abound in the plenty of a rich harvest. Therefore, if anyone is envious, he should cast out this poisonous gall and remove bitter dissensions. With God's help, he should cleanse his mind which has been infected with snakelike malice; the bitterness of all his envy should be alleviated by the sweetness of Christ. He should love those whom he hated before, as also those whom he envied with unjust detractions. Let him imitate the good, and always rejoice in the progress of those who are better. He should not discredit priests or with poisonous slanders ruin his superiors; by a unifying charity he should rather be their support. He will be forgiven if he also forgives; his sacrifices will be accepted when he approaches God in a peaceable spirit. Let each one think of the delights of paradise, and long for the heavenly kingdom to which Christ admits only the harmonious who are in agreement. Let us reflect, brethren, that they alone can be called sons of God who are peace loving,

---

7 Cf. John 8.12.
8 Cf. Matt. 25.34.

according to what is written: 'By this will all men know that you are my disciples, if you have love for one another';[9] and again: 'This is my commandment, that you love one another.'[10] Under His protection may the good Lord bring you to this love by good works: to Him is honor and glory together with the Father and the Holy Ghost world without end. Amen.

Sermon 91

Likewise on Holy Joseph

(1) In blessed Jacob and in his holy son Joseph, dearly beloved, one who notices carefully realizes that God did a very wonderful thing. First of all, I do not think it was without reason that the Lord who had deigned to show Himself so often to blessed Jacob, refused for so many years to indicate to him that his son Joseph was still alive, but allowed him to be consumed with long affliction. Anyone who believes that this happened without a definite, clear reason should consider this: Although situated so near, neither was his son Joseph permitted to send word to his father telling him that he not only was alive, but was even in a position of great honor. For from the place where blessed Jacob was, it is scarcely three hundred miles to Egypt. Many people very frequently hastened from Egypt to the region where Jacob was, and from there to Egypt countless multitudes continually flocked. Perhaps someone will say that blessed Joseph left his father when he was a small child, and for this reason could not have remembered him. This is not true, dearly beloved; a boy of sixteen years could by no means have forgotten his parents. So true is it that he had not forgotten them, that

---
9 John 13.35.
10 John 15.12.

he recognized his brothers as soon as he saw them for the first time.

(2) But someone says that since he served a master in Egypt, he had neither the liberty nor the power to send word to his father. Even if this seems probable, after he was brought out of prison and made the ruler over the whole land of Egypt, during those seven years of fruitfulness and those two years which were spent in the period of famine before his brothers came down to him—during those nine years could he not have sent word to his father those three hundred miles? Doubtless he could have, but in His secret judgment God did not allow it to happen. In fact, he did not even manifest himself to his brothers when they came to buy wheat. Instead, he spoke to them very harshly, kept their brother in chains, and ordered them to return to their father with great grief.

(3) Now notice a still greater wonder and see how blessed Joseph who knew that his father suffered intolerable sorrow on his account, as if what he had endured before were not enough, now causes Benjamin to be taken from him. Surely by this act, he knew that his father would suffer increased grief. I do not believe that all these things happened without the dispensation of the Holy Ghost. God, whose judgments are often hidden but never unjust, and who refused to notify blessed Jacob that his son was living, likewise did not allow holy Joseph to declare his glory to his father. Rather, as was said, by keeping Simeon in bonds and taking away Benjamin, he increased the distress of his father. If we heed these facts devoutly and carefully, dearly beloved, we realize that God acted with great mercy. Since the beginning of the world He has done to His saints what He fulfilled in blessed Jacob with great kindness. However, notice carefully why this happened.

(4) Although servants and friends of God have avoided capital sins and perform many good works, still we do not believe that they have been without slight offenses, because God does not lie when He says: 'Not even an infant one day

old upon the earth is without sin.'[1] Moreover, blessed John the Evangelist, who surely was not inferior to holy Jacob in merits, proclaims: 'If we say that we have no sin, we deceive ourselves, and the truth is not in us.'[2] Furthermore, we read elsewhere: 'The just man falls seven times and rises again.'[3] Therefore, since blessed Jacob could not be without those slight sins, as was already said, God wanted to consume those small offenses in this world by the fire of tribulation. Thus was fulfilled in him what He said through the Holy Ghost: 'As the test of what the potter molds is in the furnace, so in his conversation is the test of a man';[4] moreover: 'God scourges every son whom he received';[5] and: 'through many tribulations we must enter the kingdom of God.'[6] Therefore, in order that our God might present holy Jacob as purified gold at the future judgment, he first removed all the stains of sin from him, so that the other fiery witness might be able to find in him nothing to burn.

(5) This, too, we know happened in the case of blessed Joseph. When the Lord was with him, as the Scripture says, and had granted him favor with his master and the keeper of the prison, he was inspired to ask the man for help. Thus, he said to the chief cup-bearer: 'Think of me when good fortune comes to you, and do me the favor of mentioning me to Pharao, and get me out of this house.'[7] Not yet had it been written: 'It is better to take refuge in the Lord than to trust in man,'[8] and so although in all things he had merited God's grace, still it occurred to him to seek help from man. For this reason two years were added, during which he was still kept in prison, as if God were saying to him: I will show you that you should ask for help from me rather than from man.

---

1 Cf. Job 14.4. Very little of the actual quotation is cited.
2 1 John 1.8.
3 Prov. 24.16.
4 Ecclus. 27.6.
5 Heb. 12.6.
6 Acts 14.21.
7 Cf. Gen. 40.14.
8 Ps. 117.8.

Without any doubt we are to believe that for the punishment of holy Joseph, God did not allow the chief cup-bearer, after he was released from prison, to remember what holy Joseph had asked him. Moreover, since even Joseph, although he was holy, could not be without sin, he was shut up in prison such a long time, in order that there might be fulfilled what we read: 'Those whom I love I rebuke and those whom I esteem I chastise.'[9]

(6) If we notice carefully, dearly beloved, we will realize that Joseph did to his brothers what we believe God did to blessed Jacob. Truly, he was so holy that he could not have hated them. Therefore, we must believe that he wearied them with so many tribulations, in order to arouse them to a confession of their sin and the healing of repentance. Finally, with great grief, they said they suffered those ills deservedly, because they had sinned against their brother, 'whose anguish of heart they witnessed.'[10] Since blessed Joseph knew that his brothers could not be forgiven their sin of murder without much penance, once, twice, and a third time he worried them with salutary trials as with a spiritual fire. His purpose was not to vindicate himself, but to correct them and free them from so grave a sin. Furthermore, before they confessed their sin and consumed the crime which they had committed by mutual reproaches, he did not cause himself to be recognized or give them the kiss of peace. However, when he saw them humbly afflicted for the sin they had committed, he kissed them one by one and wept over each one, moistening their necks as they trembled in fear with the dew of his tears, and washing away the hatred of his brothers with the tears of charity.

(7) Now what God did in the case of blessed Jacob and what Joseph did toward his brothers, this we, too, should do to those who have sinned against us. We should be zealous to hate, not them, but their sins; and according to the merit

---

9 Cf. Apoc. 3.19.
10 Gen. 42.21.

of their guilt we should wish to rebuke them with very severe punishment in such a way that we always are eager to love them in truth. If we do this, dearly beloved; what was written will be fulfilled in us: 'Bear one another's burdens, and so you will fulfill the law of Christ.'[11] Finally, to conclude in a brief word all that I have said, we should forgive those who have sinned against us in the same manner in which we want God to forgive us as often as we offend Him. If we do this, we can say with assurance: 'Forgive us our debts, as we also forgive our debtors.'[12]

(8) It would still give us pleasure to say something to your charity concerning blessed Joseph, but because of the poor people who must hasten to their work, it is better for us to reserve it for you until tomorrow. Therefore, turning to the Lord, let us implore His mercy, so that He may deign to increase and always preserve the desire of hearing the word of God which He has conferred because of His pleasure in us: who together with the Father and the Holy Ghost lives and reigns forever and ever. Amen.

* *Sermon 92*

Again on Holy Joseph

(1) What we saved for your charity from yesterday's sermon on blessed Joseph now attentively hear in quiet and silence, as you usually do.

(2) In order that blessed Joseph might rule the kingdom of Egypt with admirable wisdom, dearly beloved, he first controlled himself. Although he was handsome and imposing in appearance, he did not turn the beauty of his countenance to the injury of another, but kept it for his own credit. He

---
11 Gal. 6.2.
12 Matt. 6.12.

judged that he would be still finer if proven more distinguished in this way, not by the loss of his chastity, but by the cultivation of purity; that true beauty does not captivate the eyes of another or wound weak minds. The sin lay on the side of his mistress who looked at him with evil intent, not with blessed Joseph who did not want to be seen thus. The fault did not consist in his being seen, for it was not within the power of a young slave not to be seen by his mistress. Her husband should have guarded the eyes of his wife. Husbands should guard the eyes of their wives, for men are loved, even those who do not want to be loved. Now Joseph was loved although he despised the one who loved him, and Scripture excuses him well by saying: 'The wife of his master cast her eyes on Joseph.'[1] In other words, he did not display himself or seize her unexpectedly, but she spread her nets and was captivated by seeking him. She extended her snares and was fastened by her own bonds. Then she said to him: 'Lie with me.'[2] The first weapons of the adulteress are those of her eyes, the second are words; however, he who is not captivated by her eyes can also resist the words. He is excused for entering, he is commended for escaping. He did not value bodily clothing more than chastity of the soul. What the adulteress kept in her hands he left as though it was not his, for he thought that what could be seized by the touch of an unchaste woman belonged to someone else. Truly he was a great man, for although he had been sold he did not know a slavish disposition; although loved he did not love in return, when asked he did not consent, and when seized he fled away.

(3) When Joseph was accused by his master's wife, he could be held by his clothing, but was unable to be captivated in soul. He did not even tolerate her words for a long time, considering it a dangerous influence if he delayed any longer, lest through the hands of the adulteress the attractions of

---

1 Cf. Gen. 39.7.
2 *Ibid.*

lust penetrate his soul. Therefore, by removing his garments he shook off all accusation; leaving the clothes with which he was held he fled, robbed, indeed, but not naked, for he was covered still more with the clothing of purity. No one is naked except the man whom guilt has exposed. In earlier times, too, we have the fact that after Adam had disregarded God's command by his transgression and contracted the debt of serious sin, he was naked; for this reason he himself said: 'I heard you in the garden, and I was afraid because I was naked; and I hid.'[3] He asserts he is naked because he has lost the adornment of divine protection; and he hid himself because he did not have the garment of faith which he had laid aside by his transgression. You see an important fact: Adam was naked although he did not lose his tunic; Joseph, who was stripped of his clothing which he left in the hands of the adulteress, was not naked. The same Scripture asserts that the former was naked and the latter was not. Therefore, Joseph despoiled himself rather than become naked when he preserved the garments of virtue incorrupt; he stripped himself of the old man with its actions, in order to put on the new man who is renewed unto knowledge according to the image of the Creator. Adam, however, remained naked because he could not clothe himself again after he was stripped of his singularly privileged virtue: for this reason he took a tunic made of skins, since as a sinner he could not have a spiritual one.

(4) Now when Joseph was accused by his mistress, he refused to say that she was guilty, because as a just man he did not know how to accuse anyone; for this reason the unchaste woman acted with impunity. Therefore, I might say that she was truly stripped even though she held the skirt of his garment in her hand, for she had lost all the adornments of purity and the covering of chastity. I might say further that he was sufficiently adorned and clothed even though his voice was not heard, for his innocence spoke. In this way, Susanna later

---
[3] Gen. 3.10.

spoke better than the prophet even though she was silent at her trial; since she did not seek the help of her own voice she thus merited the defense of the prophet. I might have said Joseph was more blessed when he was cast into prison, for he endured martyrdom in defense of chastity. The gift of purity is a great thing, even when it is preserved without danger, but when it is defended, although at the risk of personal safety, then it is crowned still more fully. While his case was unheard Joseph was thrown into prison as if guilty of a crime, but the Lord did not desert him there. It is not a source of shame for the innocent when they are attacked by false charges and cast into prison because justice is crushed; the Lord visits His own even in prison, and, therefore, there is more help where the danger is greater. What wonder is it that Christ visits His own who are in prison, when He recalls that He has been locked up in prison in the person of His people? As you have it written: 'I was in prison, and you did not come to me.'[4] Where does the divine mercy not penetrate? Joseph found such favor that he who had been shut up in prison rather guarded the bars of the prison.

(5) In him was prefigured what afterwards was fulfilled in our Lord and Savior. Thus, Joseph was thrown into prison upon the plotting and accusations of his mistress, just as Christ was crucified because of the plots and accusations of the synagogue and deigned to descend into hell as if into a prison. Now notice the similarity. Of Joseph it is written that he was free from fetters in prison and had in his power those who were kept there. What, then, is written concerning our Lord and Savior? 'You have plunged me into the bottom of the pit, into the dark abyss.'[5] 'I am a man without strength. My couch is among the dead.'[6] Indeed, this was more truly fulfilled in Christ, for He not only had in His power those who were confined in prison, but He even courageously and

---

4 Cf. Matt. 25.43.
5 Ps. 87.7.
6 Ps. 87.5, 6.

happily recalled from the prison of hell the booty which the devil had seized. 'Ascending on high, he led away captives';[7] that is, He received into life those whom the devil had carried off for death.

(6) Therefore, dearly beloved, let us, with God's help, and following the example of blessed Joseph hasten to avoid as much as we can shameful, suspicious familiarity in order that we may be able to preserve the splendor of chastity. As the Apostle says: 'Flee immorality.'[8] Against other sins we must struggle, but in order to preserve chastity we must flee from it. For this reason let us imitate blessed Joseph in perfect charity and the observance of chastity, in order that we may not wish to return evil for evil to our enemies, and in order that we may so merit to keep the adornments of chastity in this world that we may be freed from eternal shame: with the help of our Lord Jesus Christ, to whom is honor, glory, and might forever and ever. Amen.

* *Sermon 93*

On the Blessed Patriarch Joseph

(1) Sacred Scripture mentions a few facts to us concerning the blessed patriarch Joseph, and we also try to say a few words, as though offering you crumbs from huge loaves. For this reason it is written in the Gospel: 'For even the dogs eat of the crumbs that fall from their masters' table.'[1] Even if crumbs from a great feast do not satisfy, they do feed a man. When we first come to believe, we are fed with the apostolic precepts as with crumbs; but when we have progressed

---

7 Cf. Ps. 67.19; Eph. 4.8.
8 1 Cor. 6.18.

---

1 Matt. 15.27.

in faith, then an abundance of heavenly bread is received so that we may be satisfied with it. In other words, we are to be filled with Him who says in the Gospel: 'I am the living bread that has come down from heaven.'[2] Therefore, let us not refuse the crumbs of doctrine because they are crumbs from a loaf; so, too, we should not conceal them, in order that we may merit to be refreshed with bread.

(2) However, let us now come to holy Joseph, so that we may be fed with the example of his chastity and purity as with a sort of heavenly food. This holy Joseph, then, of whom your charity heard in the present lesson, was handsome in body but more splendid in mind, because he was chaste in body and virtuous in mind. Bodily beauty shone in him, but even more so shone the beauty of his soul. Now although physical beauty is wont to be a hindrance to salvation for many men, it could not harm this holy man because the beauty of his soul governed the splendor of his body. Thus the soul should rule the body, not the body the soul, for the soul is the mistress of the body while the body is the handmaid of the soul. Therefore, unhappy is the soul which is dominated by the body and makes a mistress out of a servant. Truly, the soul which is subject to vices of the flesh becomes the servant of the body, because it loses the faith of its Lord and endures the slavery of sin. The soul of the patriarch Joseph, however, faithfully kept its power, for the flesh could in no way dominate it. Indeed, when asked by his mistress, an unchaste woman, to lie with her, he refused consent because even in his position as a slave he had not lost the dominion of his soul. As a result of this, he was attacked by false accusations and thrown into prison, but the holy man considered that prison a palace, or rather he himself was a palace within the prison: for where there is faith, chastity, and purity, there is the palace of Christ, the temple of God, the dwelling of the Holy Ghost. Therefore, if any man flatters himself because of the splendor of his body, or if any woman boasts about the

---
2 John 6.51.

beauty of hers, they should follow the example of Joseph and that of Susanna. Let them be chaste in body and pure in mind, then they will be beautiful, not only to men, but also to God.

(3) Now there are three models of chastity in the Church, each one of which should be imitated: Joseph, Susanna, and Mary. Men should imitate Joseph, wives Susanna, and virgins Mary. According to a mystical or allegorical interpretation Joseph prefigured a type of our Lord. Now if we consider the actions of Joseph, at least in part, we clearly recognize in him an obvious figure of the Lord. Joseph had a variegated tunic; our Lord and Savior is known to have had one also, since he took the Church which was composed of various nations, like the covering of a garment. The variety of this tunic, that is, of the Church which Christ took is of a different sort; the Church has different, varied graces—the martyrs, confessors, priests, ministers, virgins, widows, and those who perform works of justice. This variety of the Church is not one of colors but of graces; for in this variety of His Church our Lord and Savior shines with a variegated, precious garment. Joseph was sold by his brothers and procured by the Ismaelites; our Lord and Savior was sold by the Jews and acquired by the Gentiles. Moreover, the Ismaelites who bought Joseph carried different kinds of perfumes with them; this was to show that the Gentiles who came to believe would be fragrant throughout the world with the different odors of justice.

(4) Let us notice a great mystery: for Joseph twenty pieces of gold were paid, thirty pieces of silver for our Lord. The servant is sold more dearly than the master; but surely human calculation is deceived in the case of our Lord, for he who is sold is priceless. However, let us explain this same mystery more fully. The Jews offer thirty pieces of silver for our Lord, the Ismaelites twenty gold coins for Joseph: the Ismaelites bought the servant more dearly than the Jews our Lord. The former respected the image of Christ in Joseph, but the latter despised the truth itself in Christ. Therefore, the Jews offered

a cheaper price for the Lord, because they esteemed His sufferings as of less value. How can the Lord's Passion be of little worth, since He redeemed the whole world at the price of it? For the sufferings of Christ did redeem the whole world and the entire human race from death. Listen to the Apostle proving this when he says: 'You have been bought at a great price.'[3] Hear the Apostle Peter giving similar testimony: 'You were not redeemed from your vain manner of life with earthly gold or perishable gold, but with the precious blood of the unspotted Son of God.'[4] If we had been bought back from death by gold or silver, our redemption would be cheap, because man is worth more than gold or silver. However, we have now been bought at an inestimable price, because He who redeemed us by His sufferings is priceless.

(5) If we would also consider other acts of Joseph, we would recognize the image of our Lord prefigured in all of them. Joseph suffers accusation by an unchaste woman, and our Lord was often attacked with accusations by the synagogue of Jews. Joseph endured the penalty of prison, Christ the sufferings of His death. The former is thrown into prison, the latter descends into hell; moreover, frequently Sacred Scripture is wont to call hell a prison. For this reason, it is said in a prophetic spirit: 'Lead me forth from prison';[5] the holy prophet wanted to be freed from hell. Now perceive the mystery in it. After Joseph departed from prison he was made the ruler of Egypt; after our Lord and Savior left prison He obtained dominion over the whole world through the knowledge of faith. Everywhere Christ's name reigns, governs, is believed and revealed; it is honored by nations and adored by kings. To Him is glory and might forever and ever. Amen.

---

[3] 1 Cor. 6.20.
[4] Cf. 1 Peter 1.18, 19.
[5] Cf. Ps. 141.8.

* *Sermon 94*

On What is Written: Joseph Died and the Children of
Israel Increased

(1) We have heard in the lesson which was read, dearly
beloved, that 'When Joseph was dead, the Israelites were
exceedingly fruitful and prolific, and they sprang up like
grass.'[1] What does this mean, brethren? As long as Joseph
lived the children of Israel are not recorded to have increased
or multiplied very much, but after he died they are said to
have sprung up like the grass. Surely, they should have
increased and multiplied more when they were under the
patronage and protection of Joseph. These words were prefigured in that Joseph, dearly beloved; but in our Joseph,
that is, in Christ the Lord, they were fulfilled in truth. Before
our Joseph died, that is, before He was crucified, few people
believed in Him, but after He died and rose again throughout
the world the Israelites, that is, the Christian people, increased
and multiplied. Thus even the Lord Himself says in the
Gospel: 'Unless the grain of wheat falls into the ground and
dies, it remains alone. But if it dies, it brings forth much
fruit.'[2] After the precious grain of wheat died and was buried
through the Passion, from that one grain a harvest of the
Church sprang up throughout the world. Not as formerly
was 'God renowned in Juda' alone, nor is 'his great name'
worshiped only 'in Israel'; but 'from the rising of the sun
unto the going down'[3] His name is praised.

(2) 'Then,' when Joseph was dead, 'a new king, who knew
nothing of Joseph, came to power in Egypt,'[4] and he told his
people to persecute the children of Israel. As long as that

---
1 Cf. Exod. 1.6, 7.
2 John 12.24, 25.
3 Ps. 75.2; 112.3.
4 Exod. 1.8.

king who knew Joseph lived, the children of Israel are not recorded to have been afflicted; they were not tired from working with clay and bricks, their male children were not killed or the females kept alive. However, when that king who did not know Joseph came to power, all those facts are mentioned. According to the words of the Apostle, brethren, these things 'happened' to the Jewish people 'as a type, and they were written for us.'[5] What was prefigured in them carnally is fulfilled spiritually in us. Therefore, if we diligently examine ourselves, we will recognize that this frequently happens to us in the inner man. Our soul is either governed by a legitimate king or ravaged by a tyrant. If, with God's help, we live piously and justly, thinking about chastity, mercy, repentance, and other things similar to these, we are guided by Christ the king even if we are still in Egypt, that is, in the flesh. When He rules us He does not employ us in clay and brick, He does not ruin and afflict us with worldly cares or excessive solicitude. However, if our soul begins to turn away from God and to pursue what is shameful and dishonorable, then by rejecting Christ our king 'the wisdom of the flesh' which 'is hostile to God'[6] subjects our unhappy necks to the tyrant. When this happens he addresses his people, that is, corporal pleasures; after the leading vices have been summoned to counsel there is begun a deliberation against the children of Israel, that is, against thoughts that are holy and pleasing to God. It is planned how to oppress and crush them, how to afflict them with clay and bricks, how to kill the male children and keep the females. In the male children is understood the rational sense; in the females, concupiscence of the flesh. Thus the devil wants to kill the men and keep the women in us, that is, to extinguish in us the rational sense which sees God and to keep whatever belongs to the concupiscence of the flesh.

(3) These truths were not written for us for purposes of

---

5 Cf. 1 Cor. 10.11.
6 Cf. Rom. 8.7.

history, nor are we to suppose that the Sacred Books related the exploits of the Egyptians; but as the Apostle says: 'Whatever things have been written have been written for our instruction and information.'[7] Therefore, you who hear these things and have already received the grace of Baptism whereby you are counted among the children of Israel and have taken Christ as your king within you, if after all this you wish to turn aside and through passion do worldly deeds, realize and understand that there is arisen in you another king who does not know Joseph whenever you perform actions of mud and clay, that is, deeds of wickedness. Indeed, the king of Egypt himself urges you on to his actions, not to serve justice but inquity; he himself makes you work clay and mud for him. By imposing masters and drivers with scourges and whips he leads you on to earthly activity and dissipation; he it is who forces you to hurry through life disturbing the elements of land and sea for the sake of passion. It is the king of Egypt himself who compels you to excite the forum with quarrels and for a small plot of earth to vex your neighbors with contentions. The same one it is who persuades you to plot against chastity through dissipation, to deceive innocence, to commit at home deeds which are abominable, away from home to do what is cruel, and within your conscience to do what is shameful. Therefore, if you perceive that your actions are like this, know that you are serving the king of Egypt, that is, that you are led, not by the spirit of Christ, but by that of the devil.

(4) Now, dearly beloved, we who, before the coming of our Lord and Savior, were the vessels and abode of the devil, by the grace of Christ have merited to be freed from his power. Therefore, with His help, we ought to labor as much as we can that Christ may not be offended by our evil deeds and depart from us, with the devil coming in after His withdrawal. Let not the light be put to flight and gloomy night take possession of our heart, lest there be fulfilled in us what is written in the Gospel: 'When the unclean spirit has gone out

---
7 Cf. Rom. 15.4.

of a man, he roams through dry places in search of a resting place and finds none; then he says, "I will return to my house which I left." And he finds the place swept. Then he takes with him seven other spirits more evil than himself, and they enter in and dwell there; and the last state of that man becomes worse than the first.'[8] This, brethren, is to be understood concerning even a baptized Christian. By the grace of Baptism each one is emptied of all vices, but afterwards, with God's help, he should strive to be filled with all virtues. For if the devil finds anyone free from vices, but without good deeds, he brings with him seven other spirits more wicked than himself, and the last state of that man will be worse than the first. Therefore, where dissipation has been driven out, let chastity be introduced; where avarice is uprooted, almsgiving should be planted; if malice or envy has been expelled, charity should dominate. Since at His coming our Lord bound the strong one, that is, the devil, and freed his vessels, that is, us, from his power, let us with His assistance endeavor as far as we can to serve Him by whom we have been released, with our whole heart and soul until the end of our life. Moreover, after the devil was driven out Christ deigned to make out of us a home for Himself where He might rest and vessels in which He might dwell. Therefore, He should not suffer insult in His home and detect there anything shameful, base, or obscure. May He rather always find the dwelling of our heart full of faith and free from all evils, in order that He may deign, not only to visit us more frequently, but even to continually live within us: who together with the Father and the Holy Ghost lives and reigns world without end. Amen.

---

[8] Cf. Luke 11.24-26.

Sermon 95

On the Birth of Moses and the Bush

(1) We have heard in the sacred lesson which was read to us, dearly beloved, that after holy Moses was born he was put into a basket made of bulrushes and thrown into the sedges of a river because of fear of Pharaoh. If we notice carefully, dearly beloved, we realize that just like blessed Isaac, Joseph, and Jacob, so also Moses represented a type of Christ. Moreover, consider still more attentively and you will see what great mysteries were prefigured in him. Moses was born of a Jewish woman and adopted by the daughter of Pharaoh. Now Pharaoh's daughter prefigured the Church because she left the house of her father and came to wash herself in the water. Pharaoh is accepted as a type of the devil; his daughter, as I said, is understood as the Church. The fact that her father first was the devil, the Lord tells us in the Gospel when He rebukes the Jews: 'The father from whom you are, is the devil.'[1] Therefore, we have had the devil as our father, not through being born of him, but by imitating his wickedness. Pharaoh's daughter, then, left the house of her father; but although she had a wicked father, still it is said to her through the prophet: 'Hear, O daughter, and see; forget your people and your father's house.'[2] The one who says: Hear, O daughter, is her father; however, he whom she is advised to forget is nevertheless also called her father. Thus God the Father admonishes her that she should leave her father, the devil. For this reason this Church which left the house of her father, the devil, and hastened to the water, that is, to the waters of Baptism, to be washed of the sins which she had contracted in the house of her father, finally merited to receive a heart of mercy at once, so that she took Moses who had been thrown

---
1 John 8.44.
2 Ps. 44.11.

into the river by his parents. Therefore, Moses is thrown away by his mother, but is found and picked up by the daughter of Pharaoh. Christ our Lord was rejected by the synagogue of which He was born, but was found and accepted by the Church.

(2) Now after Moses was grown up he went into a distant land and took an Ethiopian woman as his wife. Understand, brethren, that this is not a slight mystery. That Ethiopian woman whom blessed Moses married was from the Gentiles, because Christ also was to unite to Himself the Church from the Gentiles. Moses left his people and was joined to the Ethiopian in distant lands. Christ, too, left the Jewish people and was united to a Church from distant lands, to her who says in the psalms: 'From the earth's end I call to you.'[3] Listen concerning the person of the Church in the Canticle of Canticles. The Church says: 'I am dark but beautiful.'[4] What does this mean, I am dark but beautiful? Dark by nature, beautiful by grace; dark by original sin, beautiful through the sacrament of Baptism.

(3) When Moses was feeding the sheep of his father-in-law in the desert, the Lord appeared to him in a bush and Moses said: 'I must go over to see why the bush burns but is not consumed.'[5] As he approached, the Lord said to him: 'Come no nearer! Remove the strap of your shoe, for the place where you stand is holy ground.'[6] That bush is a genus of thorns, for it burned but was not consumed; in it was signified the synagogue of the Jews. For a long time the heat and fire of the Holy Ghost was in them; however, so rebellious were they always in resisting the Holy Ghost and God's grace, that their sins and evil deeds could not be consumed by the fire of the Holy Spirit.

(4) Then the Lord said to Moses: 'Come, now! I will send

---
3 Ps. 60.3.
4 Cf. Cant. 1.4.
5 Cf. Exod. 3.3.
6 Cf. Exod. 3.5.

you into Egypt.'⁷ And Moses replied: 'Lord, I have never been learned and I am slow to speak.'⁸ But the Lord said to him: 'I will open your mouth and I will teach what you should say.'⁹ Blessed are they whose mouth the Lord opens in order that they may speak. Indeed, all who speak in behalf of truth, justice, chastity, humility, and mercy doubtless have their mouths opened by none but the Lord. So on the contrary those who continually speak of dissipation, avarice, pride, robbery, buffoonery, and wickedness, we do not need to say who opens their mouth, for anyone can recognize it without any difficulty. For this reason, dearly beloved, with the Lord's help, let us constantly think of good things, so that not the cruel adversary but the good God may open our mouth: 'For out of the abundance of the heart the mouth speaks.'¹⁰ Each one of us is wont to utter with his lips the words of him whose presence he has received into his heart. Let our heart be open to Christ and closed to the devil, so that there may be fulfilled in us what is written concerning God and holy people: 'I will dwell and move among them,'¹¹ it says; moreover: 'the Father and I will come to him and make our abode with him.'¹² If a man always speaks what is right, God dwells in him and he in God.

(5) 'Then the Lord said to Moses: "What is that in your hand?" And he said: "A staff." The Lord then said: "Throw it on the ground." When he had thrown it down it was changed into a serpent, and Moses shied away from it.'¹³ That staff, dearly beloved, prefigured the mystery of the cross. Just as through the staff Egypt was struck by ten plagues, so also the whole world was humiliated and conquered by the cross. Just as Pharaoh and his people were afflicted by the power of the staff, with the result that he released the Jewish people to

---
7 Cf. Exod. 3.10.
8 Cf. Exod. 4.10.
9 Cf. Exod. 4.12.
10 Luke 6.45.
11 2 Cor. 6.16. Also cf. Lev. 26.12.
12 Cf. John 14.23.
13 Cf. Exod. 4.2, 3.

serve God, so the devil and his angels are wearied and oppressed by the mystery of the cross to such an extent that they cannot recall the Christian people from God's service.

(6) The fact that Moses put his hand into his bosom and brought it forth leprous, then put it in again and brought it forth sound and like the other flesh, we should not accept with indifference. In that hand was prefigured a type of the synagogue and of the Church. Just as the Jewish people existed first and then afterwards the Gentiles, so the synagogue came before the Church. Moreover, since the Church was chosen and the synagogue rejected, therefore, the hand of Moses became leprous at first and later was like the rest of the flesh. Thus, because of infidelity, the synagogue is left leprous, while the Church like a sound hand is chosen as suitable for every work.

(7) Moses then took his wife Sephora and came into Egypt; and the Lord stood against him and would have killed him. Perhaps at this point we can understand that Moses displeased God because although about to perform such wonders, he wanted to take the hindrance of a wife with him into Egypt. Therefore, we are given to understand that after this time Moses sent his wife back to her father-in-law. Indeed, so true is it that he went down into Egypt without her, that afterwards, as we read, Jethro his kinsman brought his wife to Moses when he was in the desert.

(8) Let us also see what is signified by the fact that the staff which was thrown on the ground was turned into a serpent. As the Lord tells us in the Gospel, the serpent is regarded as wisdom: 'Be wise as serpents,'[14] He says. We have mentioned that the staff prefigured the cross. Therefore, the cross which is considered foolishness by unbelievers—as the Apostle says: 'To the Gentiles foolishness,'[15]—after it was thrown on the ground, that is, prepared for the Lord's Passion, it was turned into a serpent or wisdom. This is that great

---
14 Matt. 10.16.
15 1 Cor. 1.23.

SERMONS 69

wisdom which was to devour all the wisdom of this world.
Finally, it devoured all the serpents which the magicians had
made by their incantations. Now Egypt was scourged by this
staff, just as the world and the devil were completely conquered by the cross. Therefore, let us pray, dearly beloved,
that in His goodness Christ our Lord may deign to overcome
the concupiscence of this world for us, and before His tribunal
bring us a happy victory over the devil and his angels. To Him
is honor and might forever and ever. Amen.

Sermon 96

On the Bush and the Lace of the Shoe

(1) Great, indeed, are the sacraments of God's mysteries,
dearly beloved, and like a kind of covering; although we
cannot explain them all, still we mention briefly to your
charity whatever we can. It was not without reason, beloved
brethren, nor without the signification of some secret that there
was a flame in the bush: 'And the bush was not consumed.'[1]
Indeed, the bush was a genus of thorns; what the earth has
produced for sinful man cannot be put in any kind of praise,
for it was first said to man when he sinned: 'Thorns and
thistles shall the earth bring forth to you.'[2] The fact that the
bush was not burned, that is, was not seized by the flames, is
understood to signify no good. In the flame is recognized the
Holy Ghost; in the bush and thorns is represented the hard,
haughty Jewish people. Doubtless, that flame signified something good, because an angel and the Lord appeared in it;
moreover, when the Holy Ghost came upon the apostles:
'There appeared to them parted tongues as of fire.'[3] If only

---
1 Cf. Exod. 3.2.
2 Gen. 3.18.
3 Cf. Acts 2.3.

that fire would take hold of us, lest it find us hardened and be unable to consume us. Let us rather pray that this fire may burn in us, destroying and annihilating the thorns of our sins.

(2) Now there are two fires: there is the fire of charity from the Holy Ghost and that of passion; the former destroys all that is evil, the latter consumes whatever is good. When the fire of charity burns in a soul, it removes all evil; so on the contrary nothing that is good will remain in a man in whom the fire of passion has been kindled. Therefore, let each one hasten to his own conscience. If a person feels aroused within himself the slightest spark of compunction, he should preserve the grace of divine mercy by good works and further kindle the fire of compunction. That is the fire of which our Lord said: 'I have come to cast fire upon the earth, and what will I but that it be kindled?'[4] However, if anyone knows that the flame of passion burns within him, with God's help, he should labor with all his might to extinguish it and to kindle charity. Whatever good is done by a man in whom passion burns, is bound to perish without any delay. Similarly on the contrary, if a man in whom there exists the fire of charity commits some faults, they are destroyed without delay and are not allowed to dominate at all. Indeed, the Jewish people were consumed by burning jealousy and avarice. For this reason that bush signified the Jewish people who struggled against God, surely a thorny people of whom it is written: 'I looked for the crop of grapes, but it brought forth thorns.'[5] To these people Moses was sent. Now, therefore, the bush did not burn and was not destroyed, because the hardness of the Jews, as I said, struggled against the law; if those people had not been united to thorns, they would not have crowned Christ with them.

(3) Then the Lord exclaimed to Moses: 'Remove the strap

---

4 Luke 12.49.
5 Cf. Isa. 5.4.

of your shoe, for the place where you stand is holy ground.'[6] The same thing which was commanded to blessed Moses is also said to have been told his successor, Josue, when the Lord appeared to him. As he saw a man standing against him with a drawn sword, he asked who he was, and the reply came: 'I am the captain of the host of the Lord and I have just arrived.'[7] Then was added the words: 'Remove the strap of your shoe, for the place where you stand is holy ground.' I beseech you, beloved brethren, according to your holy practice apply yourselves to hear with greater attention what we have learned on this subject from the revelation of the ancient fathers. Since the matter is obscure and difficult to understand, listen patiently; it is necessary for us to repeat some things frequently, in order that we may be able to explain them to your senses more easily.

(4) The Jews were commanded by law that if anyone died without children, his brother should marry the widow. Moreover, as many sons as would be born of them would be considered under the name of the dead brother, not recorded as sons of the man who had begotten them, but of the man whose widow he had married. Therefore, many of the people were unwilling to have their sons called by the name of another, and thus did not consent to marry the widows of their brothers. If anyone wanted to be excused, he was led to the gate of the city where his brother's widow came to remove his shoe and spit in his face, while his house was called that of the unshod. So if a man was not going to be married, the straps of his shoes were removed. If he did agree to it, they were not. I have said this, dearly beloved, so that even if we are unable to understand it all, we may attempt to realize why it was that the Lord said to Moses and Josue: 'Remove the strap of your shoe, for the place where you stand is holy ground.' Why was this said to them except because they were not lawful spouses? The lawful spouse of the Catholic Church

---
6 Cf. Exod. 3.5.
7 Jos. 5.14.

could be no other but Christ of whom the Apostle says: 'I betrothed you to one spouse, that I might present you a chaste virgin to Christ.'[8] Of Him the psalmist had foretold much earlier: 'He comes forth like the groom from his bridal chamber.'[9] Blessed John the Baptist also spoke very clearly concerning Him when he said: 'He who has the bride is the bridegroom.'[10] This he evidently said about Christ; but what did he say about himself? 'But the friend of the bridegroom, who stands and hears him, rejoices exceedingly at the voice of the bridegroom.'[11] Moreover, in order that he might show more clearly that Christ our Lord is the legitimate bridegroom, he says: 'He it is, the strap of whose sandal I am not worthy to loose.'[12] Why did he not dare to loose the strap of His sandal? Because he knew that He was the lawful spouse of the Church. Now Moses and Josue were commanded to remove their shoes because they prefigured the spouse but were not themselves the bridegroom. Finally, see what the Lord said to Moses and Josue: 'Remove the strap of your shoe, for the place where you stand is holy ground.'[13] Can this be understood according to the letter, beloved brethren? How could that ground upon which they trod be holy, since doubtless it was like the rest of the earth? However, notice carefully what was said: 'For the place whereon thou standest is holy ground.' That is to say, Christ whose figure you bear and of whom you seem to be a type, is holy ground. True holy ground is the Body of our Lord Jesus Christ through whom everything heavenly and earthly is sanctified. Of Him the Apostle says: 'Making peace through the blood of his cross with all things, whether in the heavens or on the earth.'[14]

(5) Therefore, as I said above, dearly beloved, the man who refused to marry the wife of his dead brother was deprived

---
8 2 Cor. 11.2.
9 Ps. 18.6.
10 John 3.29.
11 *Ibid.*
12 Cf. John 1.27.
13 Cf. Exod. 3.5
14 Cf. Col. 1.20.

of his shoes and spit in the face; if a man agreed to accept his brother's widow, the sons who were born were not called by the name of the man who had begotten them, but of the one who had died. This fact we see fulfilled in the apostles. When their brother died, that is, when Christ was dead who had said: 'Go, take word to my brethren,'[15] the apostles received His wife, that is, the Church. Thus, indeed, the Apostle Paul says: 'In Christ Jesus, through the gospel, did I beget you.'[16] Now whoever were born of the Church through the teaching of the apostles were not called Petrans or Paulans, but Christians, in order that there might be fulfilled this figure which was anticipated in the law concerning the wife of a dead brother. However, unhappy heretics have not done this. Like exceedingly cruel invaders who seize the wife of their brother, they tear to pieces and split the Church into sects, for although they have all been generated through the sacrament of Baptism, with insolent boldness they want to be called by their own name and not that of Christ. Now in the Catholic Church all who are born are called Christians from the name of the deceased, that is, of Christ; among heretics, however, some are called Donatists, others Manichaeans, others Arians, others Photinians. Since the leaders of the heretics were not the lawful spouses, they did not impose the name of Christ but their own upon the people.

(6) Now I beseech you, brethren, that your holy charity may be indulgent with me. While I have attempted to impress upon you some understanding of what was said to Moses: 'Remove the strap of your shoe,'[17] perhaps I seem to have wearied you with a longer sermon than was necessary. Although there may be nothing in this discourse to please you, still I believe that even our wish and desire should not displease your charity. I have not been able to provide a worthy explanation of such a great subject, but I have striven to indicate

---

15 Matt. 28.10.
16 1 Cor. 4.15.
17 Cf. Exod. 3.5.

a few lines and examples to your pious judgment. As you examine them rather carefully, under the inspiration of Christ, you may be able to reflect upon them even better than we have suggested.

Sermon 97

On the Three Days' Journey in the Desert

(1) In the divine lessons which were read to us during these last days, we heard the Lord command Moses to go a three days' journey into the desert and with all the people to sacrifice to the Lord. Let us see, dearly beloved, what it is that Moses said: 'We will go a three days' journey in the desert, that we may offer sacrifice to the Lord, our God.'[1] Moses truly desired this, but Pharaoh contradicted him and did not want the sons of Israel to go far away. The prince of this world did not want the Lord's army to recognize the engagement of those three days, as that engagement of which the prophet said: 'He will revive us after two days; on the third day he will raise us up.'[2] The first day for us is the Passion of the Savior; the second the day on which He descended into hell; but the third is the day of the Resurrection. So then on the third day God went before them in a pillar of cloud by day, and by night in a pillar of fire, and the people were led through the Red Sea. The three days we can fittingly call the Father, Son, and Holy Ghost: for the Father is a day, the Son is one, and the Holy Ghost is one, and these three are one. That three days' journey by which there was the exit from Egypt is rightly understood as He who said: 'I am the way, and the truth, and the life,'[3] because no one comes to the Father except through Him. He is the way by which the

---
1 Cf. Exod. 5.3.
2 Osee 6.3.
3 John 14.6.

people who are joined to God are led out of Egypt, that is, away from the worship of idols. Through the Red Sea made red by the Blood of Christ and somehow even then mysteriously consecrated as if by the sacrament of Baptism, the people of God are rescued while Pharaoh is drowned. In reality that is what happens, brethren. When Christians are immersed three times in the saving waters as by a three days' journey, the spiritual Egyptians, that is, original sin or actual sins, are buried as if in the Red Sea, and while the sons of Israel cross over to the service of God, only their sins suffer destruction. Moreover, let no one doubt and think that not all of his sins perish through Baptism, but let him realize and understand that, just as none of the Egyptians survived, so nothing at all remains of his sins.

(2) However, before the crossing of the Red Sea, Moses cried out to the Lord. How did he cry out? No word of shouting is heard, and yet God says to him: 'Why are you crying out to me?'[4] I would like to know how the saints cry out to the Lord without any sound of words. The Apostle teaches: 'God has sent the Spirit of his Son into our hearts, crying, "Abba, Father." '[5] He adds further: 'The Spirit himself pleads for us with unutterable groanings';[6] and again: 'He who searches the hearts knows what the Spirit desires, that he pleads for the saints according to God.'[7] So thus by the inspiration of the Holy Ghost in silence, the shouting of the saints is heard in the presence of God.

(3) After this Moses is commanded to strike the sea with his rod. In the rod, as I said before, is recognized the mystery of the holy cross. Moreover, it is true, brethren, for listen and see that, if the rod were not raised over the sea, God's people would not be removed from Pharaoh's power. Thus it is, dearly beloved, that if the holy cross had not been lifted up, the Christian people would have perished forever. But

---
4 Exod. 14.15.
5 Cf. Gal. 4.6; Rom. 8.15.
6 Rom. 8.26.
7 Rom. 8.27.

when the rod was raised, that is, when the cross was lifted up, the sea and its waves drew back, that is, the world and its powers were overcome. Therefore, the waves are driven back to form a wall, because the waters were turned back upon themselves; the expanse of the sea took on a solid footing when its floor dried up into dust. Recognize the goodness of God the Creator: if you obey His will and follow His law, He compels the very elements to serve you, even contrary to their nature. Let us pray then, dearly beloved, that our Lord may effect in our hearts and bodies what He did with regard to the Egyptians in the Red Sea. May He give us the strength and assistance of the Holy Ghost, so that we may be able to destroy the spiritual Egyptians in us. Truly, the man who lives, not carnally, but spiritually, destroys the Egyptian. He destroys the Egyptian who drives unworthy or impure thoughts from his heart or does not even admit them into his heart at all, as the Apostle says: 'Taking up the shield of faith, with which we may be able to quench all the fiery darts of the wicked one.'[8] In this way, then, even today we can see Egyptians dead and lying on the shore, with their chariots and horses drowned. We can even see Pharaoh drowned if we live by such faith that 'God will speedily crush Satan under our feet.'[9]

(4) The three days' journey can also be understood as good thoughts, words, and actions. In reality whoever does this and observes it with all the power of his soul walks, not in the night, but in daylight. He becomes, not the son of darkness, but a son of light, and there is fulfilled in him what the Apostle says: 'You were once darkness, but now you are light in the Lord. Walk, then, as children of light.'[10] When were we darkness, brethren? Surely, when we walked the ways of night, that is, when we had bad thoughts, words, or actions. Later, however, coming to Christ, by His grace we left the works of darkness and by good thoughts, words, and actions, we

---

8 Cf. Eph. 6.16.
9 Rom. 16.20.
10 Eph. 5.8.

hastened to run the way of light. Therefore, these are the three ways by which one attains to heaven, just as those are the three ways by which lovers of the world arrive in hell, namely, bad thoughts, words, and actions. That is the 'wide and broad way'[11] which leads to destruction. By these paths the rich man who was clothed in purple went down into hell, but by those others Lazarus merited to arrive at Abraham's bosom. The former three ways the enemy occupies, as we read of Pharaoh's army: 'The elite of his officers, who were standing three deep, he submerged in the Red Sea.'[12] Who are the elite of his officers? Surely those chosen by the devil for luxury, wickedness, and pride, the source of all evil. Moreover, these, standing three deep, occupy those three ways in order to subvert man to evil deeds, to tempt him to evil speech, or to win him to evil thoughts. Happy is the man who, with God's help, avoids those three ways and by a wholehearted three days' journey withdraws from Pharaoh's society. In this way the enemy would not take any day from him or turn the splendor of his faith into night.

(5) Therefore, brethren, let us fulfill what is written: 'With closest custody, guard your heart.'[13] With God's help, let us consider and keep both our hearts and our consciences. If there is anyone among us whom the enemy tempts to evil thoughts, let him strive, as far as he can, not to sin, at least in word. In other words, if the devil has taken away one day and changed it into night, that he may not be able to obtain a second one in that person. However, if by his very clever subtlety he has been able to obtain even this, that we both think evil in our heart and speak it with our lips, if we have already lost two days, let us, with God's help, keep even the one day. Let not the enemy's wickedness be able to subvert us as far as evil deeds. Still, if even this has happened, let us not then despair of mercy but let us quickly by repentance

---

11 Cf. Matt. 7.13.
12 Cf. Exod. 15.4.
13 Prov. 4.23.

shake our feet free from the mud of dregs, for the Lord does not will 'the death of the sinner, but rather his conversion so that he may live.'[14] Moreover, let us be converted in such a way that we do not look backwards again or perform the evil deeds which we did or return like dogs to their vomit. Rather let us stretch out after a precious and desirable country and by the path of good works arrive at the kingdom, with the help of our Lord Jesus Christ, who lives and reigns world without end. Amen.

Sermon 98

On the Spiritual Struggle of the Israelites and Egyptians which can be Inferred when We Read of the Chaff

(1) Although we should at all times devoutly listen to the word of God with great longing, dearly beloved, in these days especially we should dwell upon the divine lessons and think more carefully of the salvation of our soul. Although the Christian people are harassed throughout the year by many waves of vice through the devil's cunning, still at the approach of the paschal solemnity he is wont to arm himself with even greater violence against the faithful, striving to prick and disturb our hearts with the goads of more serious sins. Just as in those days king Pharao and the Egyptians like the devil and his angels persecuted the children of Israel and brought them to bitterness by afflicting them with mud and bricks, so now at the approach of the paschal solemnity, because the devil grieves that the true Israelites who are to be baptized are leaving his army and possession, he is wont to send greater tribulations and to stir up greater scandals. However, if we follow Moses, that is, if we willingly listen to the law and refuse to look back or long for Egypt, Pharao is drowned

---

14 Cf. Ezech. 33.11.

through the sacrament of Baptism as by the crossing of the Red Sea and we are freed from his power and slavery.

(2) It is most certain, dearly beloved, that just as the Egyptians then led the children of Israel into bitterness by many tribulations, so, as we have already said, at this time the devil and his angels do not cease to attack and disturb devout Christians who are engaged in good works. However, brethren, know that the devil persecutes only the good; he does not usually trouble the wicked, dissolute, avaricious, or haughty, because they are his friends and always do his will. The devil does not pursue them to this extent, that through them he persecutes others, for he is wont to keep the wicked like hammers or whips. Finally, the devil does not persecute the good except through the wicked. Now God has His ministers, and the devil has his helpers. Through good men as His ministers God does everything good; through the wicked as his accomplices the devil exercises all evil. God clothes the naked through the mercy of the good, while the devil robs those who are clothed through the avarice of the wicked. God recalls the discordant to harmony through good men, but the devil incites even those who seem to possess peace to scandals or quarrels through the wicked and haughty. Now it would take too long to go through everything individually so that your charity may know for certain and realize that just as God does good through the just, so the devil is wont to do all that is cruel and impious through the wicked. Finally reflect, brethren, and you will see even with your bodily eyes how the followers of the devil persecute the people of Christ. Adulterers persecute the chaste; drunkards reproach the sober; the proud plot against the humble; the envious, the kind; the avaricious, the generous; and the irascible do not cease to afflict those who observe meekness and patience. Now each one should consider his own conscience. If he sees that in thought, word, and deed he always loves what is good and continually does what is honorable, let him realize that he is God's minister and rejoice. However, if upon examining himself interiorly a man

sees that he not only thinks but even says and does what is evil, he should both understand and grieve that he is a helper of the devil. While the sinful, gloomy soul is still kept shut up in the body, with God's help, a man should try to tear himself away from the devil's power. Otherwise, if sudden death carries him off while he is engaged in evil deeds, he may perchance deserve to hear with the devil whose will he has obeyed: 'Depart from me, accursed ones, into the everlasting fire which was prepared for the devil and his angels.'[1]

(3) No one should deceive himself, dearly beloved. Afterwards in the future life each person will be with the one whose deeds and will he has followed in this life. Therefore, every man is destined either to reign with Christ or to be tortured with the devil in the punishment of hell. So while there is time and with God's help it still lies in our power, if a man knows he is on the left side because of his evil deeds, he should strive to pass over to the right before he departs from this life. Then he will not hear with those on the left: 'Depart from me, accursed ones, into the everlasting fire,' but among the lambs on the right he may merit to hear: 'Come, blessed of my Father, take possession of the kingdom.'[2] In order that, with God's help, we may be able to do all this, let us think more carefully about giving alms. A clear, evident reason shows us how we may cross from the left side to the right: the former drunkard should be sober; the irascible, patient; one who used to seize the possessions of another should begin to give to the poor out of his own goods. The man who habitually cursed should bless; anyone accustomed to commit perjury should refrain altogether from swearing; one who usually committed calumny should try to say what is good. The envious should strive to be kind; the proud, humble. In this way we may always endeavor to cure contraries by their opposites, and hasten to build up virtues when the vices have been destroyed. Thus, then, those who are on the left side may

---

1 Matt. 25.41.
2 Cf. Matt. 25.34.

attempt to cross over to the right in order that before the tribunal of the eternal judge anyone who is willing to do this may merit to hear: 'Well done, good and faithful servant, enter into the joy of thy master.'[3] May the Lord deign to bring you to this, to whom is honor together with the Father and the Holy Ghost world without end. Amen.

* Sermon 99

On the Ten Plagues

(1) When Moses came into Egypt, dearly beloved, and brought a rod to scourge and chastise Egypt with the ten plagues, he is understood as the law. This law was given to the world to punish and correct it with ten plagues, that is, by the ten commandments which are contained in the decalogue. Since, moreover, Moses could be understood as the law, the Lord said in the Gospel: 'They have Moses and the Prophets,'[1] that is, the law and the prophets. However, the rod by which Egypt is subdued and Pharaoh overcome, afforded an image of the cross of Christ. By it this world is overcome and the prince of this world with his principalities and powers conquered. As to the fact that the rod is thrown down to become a dragon or serpent which devours the serpents of the Egyptians, the word serpent is used for wisdom, as it is written: 'Be wise as serpents.'[2] For this reason the rod of Moses, that is, the cross of Christ, after it came down to earth, that is, after it came to the belief and faith of men, was changed into wisdom, and a wisdom great enough to devour all the wisdom of the Egyptians, that is, of this world.

---
3 Matt. 25.21, 23.

---
1 Luke 16.29.
2 Matt. 10.16.

(2) The fact that the waters of the river were changed into blood is quite appropriate. The river in which the children of the Hebrews were cruelly drowned repaid the authors of that crime with a cup of blood, and when they took a drink they were killed by the polluted waters which they had defiled by wicked murder. The second plague, in which frogs were introduced, may figuratively signify the verses of poets who give to this world stories of deception in a sort of lifeless, affected rhythm like the sounds and songs of the frogs. That animal is useful for nothing except to sound like a voice with its harsh and troublesome noise. Next came the sciniphs. This kind of creature is suspended by wings and flies through the air, but it is so small and fine that it escapes being seen by the eye unless a person is watching closely. However, it pierces with a very sharp sting any person that it alights upon, so that even if one cannot see it flying about he is sure to feel it sting. Therefore, this kind of animal can most fittingly be compared to philosophical skill or the cunning of heretics. This pierces souls with the small and fine sting of words, and besets them with such great cleverness that a man who has been deceived does not see or understand how it happened. In the fourth place, we also find the cynomia or dog-fly, which may rightly be compared to the sect of cynics. In accordance with the rest of their wicked deceptions, these men even preach pleasure and the fulfillment of desires as the highest good. Since the world is deceived by each one of these errors, God's word and law comes to censure it with reproaches, so that from the nature of its punishment it may learn the nature of its error. Fifthly, Egypt was scourged by the death of all the animals and flocks. Here is refuted the foolishness and stupidity of men who like irrational herds have bestowed the worship and title of a god upon the images of both men and animals. Therefore, it happened justly that they saw dire punishment inflicted upon the creatures in whom they believed there was a divine nature. After this, in the sixth plague, appeared ulcers and boils along with fever. Now it seems to

me that in the ulcers is rebuked deceitful and putrid malice; in the boils, swollen and infected pride; in the fever, the frenzy of anger and rage. Up to this point punishments are prepared for the world in figures of its errors. However, after these plagues came voices from heaven in the thunder and hail and the lightning accompanying it. Notice the justice of the divine punishment. God does not strike in silence, but utters words and sends instruction from heaven, so that the world may know its guilt from its chastisement. The Lord also sends hail to destroy the still tender shoots of vice, and knowing that there are thorns and briars of sin which flames should feed upon, He also sends fire. As the Lord said: 'I have come to cast fire upon the earth,'[3] for by this means the incentives to pleasure and unlawful desires are destroyed. Eighthly, there is mention of locusts. I think that by this kind of plague is designated the inconstancy of men who are always slandering others or are out of harmony with themselves. 'Although the locust has no king,' as Scripture says, 'he leads his army all in array';[4] but men who have been created rational, neither know how to govern themselves nor how to endure with patience the guidance of their king and God. Darkness was the ninth plague, either to refute the blindness of their minds or to teach them the most obscure plans of the divine dispensation and providence. God, indeed, as the psalmist says: 'made darkness the cloak about him.'[5] Proud souls boldly and rashly want to examine the darkness, and adding one thing after another are gradually enveloped in the dense and tangible darkness of error. The death of the firstborn is recorded last. The firstborn of the Egyptians are fittingly understood to be the leaders and powerful men of this world, that is, the devil and his angels. At His coming Christ is said to have changed them, that is, to have captured them in triumph on the wood of the cross. We can also con-

---
3 Luke 12.49.
4 Cf. Prov. 30.27.
5 Ps. 17.12.

sider the firstborn of the Egyptians all as authors of heresy and inventors of falsehood. All of these errors which exist in the world under the name of religion, together with their authors, the truth of Christ has destroyed.

(3) In order that these words may remain more deeply in your thoughts, and that like fine animals you may spiritually turn them over and chew them in the mouth of your heart, we will summarize them briefly. In the first plague, the fact that the waters were changed into blood signifies the teaching of the philosophers who deceive little ones. The multitude of frogs in the second one indicates the verses of poets which always are utterly useless. In the third plague, sciniphs, that is, very tiny flies, appear and with a painful sting prick people; in these are typified the cleverness of philosophical skill and the poison of unfortunate heretics or most subtle lies. In the fourth plague, comes the dog-fly, to be justly compared with the teaching of the cynics, who among other evils preach pleasure as the highest good. Fifthly, the animals are killed, thereby signifying the foolishness and stupidity of men. In the sixth plague, ulcers, blisters, and boils are produced along with fever. The ulcers rebuke deceitful, putrid malice; the boils, the swelling and infection of pride; the fever, the fury of anger and rage. Then, in the seventh place, comes thunder and sounds from heaven, hail and fire along with it. Heavenly teaching is recognized in the thunder; in the hail, the discipline received by sinners; in the fire, the grace of the Holy Ghost, which consumes the pleasures of unlawful desires and the thorns of sin. In the eighth plague, locusts are introduced, creatures that are harmful because of their bite; in them is signified the arrogance of the wicked who molest each other with false testimony and betrayals. Of these the Apostle says: 'If you bite and devour one another, take heed or you will be consumed by one another.'[6] Ninthly, darkness appears to rebuke blindness of the mind or heart. In the tenth plague, the firstborn are struck, so that in them we may understand

---
6 Gal. 5.15.

spiritual evil or original sin. At the coming of Christ these were very clearly shown to have been destroyed and extinguished by the mystery of the cross and the grace of Baptism. Therefore, let us rejoice and thank God, dearly beloved, because through His mercy these things which we read happened at that time in figures and images we both feel and see have been fulfilled in us: under the guidance of our Lord Jesus Christ, to whom is honor and glory world without end. Amen.

* *Sermon 100*

St. Augustine on the Ten Words of the Law and the Ten Plagues

(1) Beloved brethren, our Lord and Savior like a spiritual physician has provided remedies for our souls by revealing the truths which lie hidden under the covering of words, in order that we may understand what we should love and what guard against. Therefore, consider, dearly beloved, that the number of the precepts of God's law seems to be equalled by the number of plagues whereby Egypt was struck. Just as there are ten precepts of the law by which the people are admonished to worship God, so we read of ten plagues which afflicted the pride of the Egyptians. For this reason, let us consider why ten commandments are mentioned there and ten plagues here. Doubtless, it is because there are remedies in the former for the wounds in the latter; it was necessary for the healing of the ten commandments to remedy the dangerous wounds of the ten plagues. Therefore, I exhort you, brethren, do not receive this with indifference; if, with Christ's help, you diligently pay attention, you can realize that those ten precepts are respectively opposed in order to the ten plagues. Indeed, the first plague is struck by the first

command, the second by the second, the third by the third, and so on to number ten.

(2) The first command of the law concerns one God: 'You shall not have other gods besides me.'[1] In the first plague of the Egyptians, water was turned into blood. Compare the first precept with the first plague: consider the one God who is the source of all things, like the water out of which everything was created. Now to what does the blood refer but to mortal flesh? What does the changing of the water into blood mean except that for people who refuse to believe in God, as the Apostle said: 'Their senseless minds have been darkened; while professing to be wise, they have become fools.'[2] So the water was changed into blood because the feelings of the Egyptians became dark and gloomy. By the just judgment of God it happened that they drank blood from that river in which they had been wont to kill the sons of the Hebrews.

(3) The second commandment is: 'You shall not take the name of the Lord, your God, in vain. For he who takes the name of the Lord his God in vain shall not be cleansed.'[3] The name of our Lord Jesus Christ is truth, for He said: 'I am the truth.'[4] Since the truth purifies while untruth defiles a man, let us see the plague that is opposed to this second command. What is that second plague? An abundance of frogs. In the frogs we understand heretics and philosophers; you have the superficiality of philosophers and heretics fittingly signified if you consider the loquacity of frogs. Indeed, philosophers and heretics who say that everything in Christ is false are frogs shouting in a muddy swamp; by their pride and vain contentions they may have the sound of a voice, but they are unable to instill the teaching of wisdom. All who contradict the truth of Christ and deceive others while they are deceived in their own vanity are frogs bringing disgust to ears but no food to minds.

---

1 Cf. Exod. 20.3.
2 Rom. 1.21,22.
3 Cf. Exod. 20.7.
4 John 14.6.

(4) The third precept is: 'Remember to keep holy the Sabbath day.'[5] In this third commandment is suggested a certain idea of freedom, a repose of the heart or tranquillity of the mind which a good conscience effects. Indeed, sanctification is there because the Spirit of God dwells there. Now look at the freedom or repose; our Lord says: 'Upon whom shall I rest but upon the man who is humble and peaceable, and who trembles at my words?'[6] Therefore, restless souls turn away from the Holy Ghost. Lovers of strife, authors of calumnies, devotees of quarrels rather than of charity, by their uneasiness they do not admit to themselves the repose of a spiritual sabbath. Men do not observe a spiritual sabbath unless they devote themselves to earthly occupations so moderately that they still engage in reading and prayer, at least frequently, if not always. As that Apostle says: 'Be diligent in reading and in teaching';[7] and again: 'Pray without ceasing.'[8] Men of this kind honor the sabbath in a spiritual manner. However, restless souls are continually involved in earthly activity, and of them it is written: 'The burdens of the world have made them miserable.'[9] They are unable to have a sabbath, that is, repose. In reply to their restlessness, it is said that they should have, as it were, a sabbath in their heart and the sanctification of the Spirit of God: 'Be swift to hear,' it says, 'but slow to answer.'[10] Cease your uneasiness, let there not be a tumult in your heart because of phantoms flying about to corrupt you, disturbing and pricking you like flies. You are to realize that God is saying to you: 'Desist! and confess I am God.'[11] By your restlessness you do not want to be still; blinded by the corruption of your contentions you demand to see what you cannot. Notice the opposite third plague which is contrary to this commandment. Sciniphs

---

5 Cf. Exod. 20.8.
6 Cf. Isa. 66.2.
7 1 Tim. 4.13.
8 1 Thess. 5.17.
9 The source of this quotation is unknown.
10 Ecclus. 5.13.
11 Ps. 45.11.

sprang up out of the mud in the land of Egypt, very tiny flies, exceedingly restless, flying around in confusion, rushing into one's eyes, not allowing a man to rest, coming back while they are being driven away, returning again even when expelled. Restless men are like these little flies, when they refuse to observe the sabbath in a spiritual manner, that is, to be zealous for good works and to engage in reading or prayer. Doubtless, such are the phantoms of quarrelsome hearts; just as the human body is tormented by those flies, so their hearts are disturbed and pricked by opposing thoughts. Keep the commandment, but guard against the plague.

(5) The fourth precept follows: 'Honor your father and your mother.'[12] Opposed to this command is the fourth plague of the Egyptians: a fly that is a dog-fly, for it is a Greek word. If a person refuses to honor his parents, a dog-fly, that is, the wickedness of the devil, spiritually afflicts and torments him. Indeed, it is doglike not to recognize one's parents, and nothing is so spiteful as lack of recognition of those who have begotten a man.

(6) Fifth, we find: 'You shall not commit adultery.'[13] The fifth plague is death among the cattle. If a man is intimate with his own wife without any limits or except with a desire for children; if he definitely waits for the wife or daughter of another, his own maid or that of another (which is a very serious sin), he is overcome by bestial passion and becomes like cattle, as though losing his manliness. Such a person is not changed into the nature of cattle but in the form of man bears a likeness to the cattle, for he is unwilling to hear the Lord say: 'Be not senseless like horses or mules.'[14] Moreover: 'Man, for all his splendor, does not abide; he resembles the beasts that perish.'[15] If you are not afraid to be cattle, at least fear to die like them.

---

12 Exod. 20.12.
13 Exod. 20.14.
14 Ps. 31.9.
15 Ps. 48.13,21.

(7) The sixth commandment is: 'You shall not kill';[16] the six plague, boils on the body, swollen blisters causing burning wounds from the ashes of the furnace. Such are murderous men; they burn with anger because through wrath the fraternal spirit of a murderer perishes. Men burn with indignation but also with grace, for both the man who wishes to kill and the one who desires to help his neighbor glows with passion. The former is inflamed with disease, the latter by precept; the one with poisonous ulcers, the other with good works. O if we could see the souls of murders, doubtless we would bewail them more than the decaying bodies of the ulcerated.

(8) Then follows the seventh commandment: 'You shall not steal';[17] the seventh plague is hail on the fruits of the earth. Whatever you take by theft contrary to God's precept you destroy out of heaven, for no one has an unjust gain without a just loss. For example, the man who steals acquires clothing but destroys faith in the judgment of heaven. There is a loss where there is gain, visibly a gain but invisibly a loss; a gain as the result of his blindness, but a loss of the Lord's countenance. Therefore, all who by evil desires steal outwardly are inwardly hailed upon by God's just judgment. O if thieves and robbers could behold the field of their heart, surely they would grieve and mourn when they do not find there what they put into the mouth of their soul, even though in their theft they did find something to swallow in the desire of their gluttony. Greater is the hunger of the soul than that of the body; greater the hunger, more dangerous the plague, and more serious the death. What is worse, many men walk around dead because of this soul-hunger, and though alive carry about their own death. Indeed, some men seem to live physically but by their evil deeds are proven to be dead in heart. Moreover, many who suffer hunger in their soul boast about vain riches. Finally, Scripture says that a good Christian

---
16 Exod. 20.13.
17 Cf. Exod. 20.15.

is inwardly rich: 'The inner life of the heart, which is of great price in the sight of God,'[18] it says; he is not rich before men, but before God, in His sight. Therefore, what does it profit you to steal where man does not see, and to be hailed upon by a just judgment where God sees you?

(9) The eighth commandment is: 'You shall not bear false witness';[19] the eighth plague is locusts, creatures harmful with their bite. What does a false witness desire, except to do harm by biting and to destroy by lying? For this reason the Apostle warns us not to attack each other with false charges: 'If you bite and devour one another, he says, 'take heed or you will be consumed by one another.'[20]

(10) The ninth commandment: 'You shall not covet your neighbor's wife';[21] the ninth plague, dense darkness. If it is a sin to know one's wife except for the sake of children, what kind of an offense do you think it is, not only to sin with one's own wife, but even to desire the wife of another? Truly, the darkness is dense; indeed, nothing causes such pain in the heart of one who suffers it as when his wife is attacked. If a man does this to another, there is nothing that he should not be willing to suffer. Other evils men are wont to accept with patience, but I do not know whether anyone can be found who will bear this calmly. O what dense darkness men suffer when they do and desire such things! Truly, they are blinded with horrible fury, for it is unbridled madness to wish to pollute and defile the wife of another.

(11) The tenth commandment is: 'You shall not covet anything of your neighbor's: neither his sheep, nor his ox, nor anything at all that belongs to him.'[22] Opposed to this precept is the tenth plague, the death of the firstborn. All the possessions which men have they keep for their heirs, and among heirs no one is more dear than the firstborn. When

---

18 Cf. 1 Peter 3.4.
19 Cf. Exod. 20.16.
20 Gal. 5.15.
21 Cf. Exod. 20.17.
22 *Ibid.*

men wish to possess the goods of another as though justly, they seek to become heirs of the dying; indeed, what seems so just as to possess something that has been left to a person? Someone says: It was left to me, I read the will. Nothing seems more just than this word. You praise a man who has possessions, as it were, rightly; God condemns him if he desires them unjustly. See what kind of a man you are if you want to become the heir of another; do you not want him to have his own heirs, among whom no one is dearer than the firstborn? You will be punished in the same manner in your firstborn, if, while desiring the possessions of others, that is, what does not rightly belong to you, you acquire them as though under the semblance of justice. For this reason you kill your firstborn. Surely, it is easy, brethren, physically to kill the firstborn; they are mortal men who are certain to die, whether before or after their parents. This is really difficult, not to kill the firstborn of your heart by this secret and unjust concupiscence. Faith is the firstborn of our heart, for no one does good works unless faith precedes it. All your good works are spiritual sons of yours, but among them faith is the firstborn. Whoever secretly desires the possessions of another destroys interior faith. Doubtless at first he will be an obedient imitator through deceit and not by charity, as if loving him whose heir he wants to become. He says he loves the man he wishes to die, and in order that he may see himself in reality the owner of his goods, he hopes that man will not leave his own heir.

(12) This comparison and sort of opposition of the ten commandments and the ten plagues, brethren, should make us cautious so that we may with assurance keep our possessions in accord with God's precepts; I mean our interior possessions which are stored away in the treasury of our conscience. These are our treasures which no thief or robber or wicked neighbor can ever take away, where no moth or rust need be feared. Indeed, these are true riches, namely, a good conscience, justice, mercy, chastity, and sobriety; anyone who is full of such things is rich, even if he dies naked as the result of ship-

wreck. If you diligently heed these truths and, with the Lord's help, are willing to avoid evil and do good, you will be God's people. Then you will be freed from the unjust persecution of the Egyptians, that is, of spiritual injustice, and will happily reach the land of promise: with the help of our same Lord, to whom is honor and glory world without end. Amen.

* Sermon 100A[1]

On the Agreement between the Ten Plagues of Egypt and the Ten Commandments of the Law

(1) It is not without reason, dearest brethren, that the number of the commands of God's law[2] seems to be equalled by the number of plagues whereby Egypt was struck. Just as there are ten precepts of the law by which the people are admonished to worship God, so we read of ten plagues which afflicted the pride of the Egyptians. For this reason, let us consider why ten commandments are mentioned there and ten plagues here. Doubtless, it is because there are remedies in the former for the wounds in the latter; it was necessary for the healing of the ten commandments to remedy the dangerous wounds of the ten plagues. Therefore, I exhort you, brethren, do not receive this with indifference; if, with Christ's help, you diligently pay attention, you can realize that those ten precepts are respectively opposed in order to the ten plagues. Indeed, the first plague is struck by the first command, the second by the second, the third by the third, and so on to number ten.

---

1 This is another version of the preceding sermon. Although it adds nothing new to the study of Caesarius, Dom Morin has included it because it has never before been edited. Cf. *Sancti Caesarii Arelatensis Sermones . . . editio altera*, II, 407.

2 From here to (2), "What does the changing of the water into blood mean," the previous sermon is repeated.

(2) The first command of the law concerns one God: 'You shall not have strange gods besides me.'³ In the first plague of the Egyptians, water was turned into blood. Compare the first precept with the first plague: consider the one God who is the source of all things, like the water out of which everything was created. Now to what does the blood refer but to mortal flesh? What does the changing of the water into blood mean except that: 'Their senseless minds have been darkened,'⁴ for in their rational mind with which they should have worshiped, venerated, and adored the one God, they have worshiped idols with impious sacrifices? Moreover, in their hearts the purest honoring of the one God has been changed into the bloody worship of different gods.

(3) The second commandment is: 'You shall not take the name of the Lord, your God, in vain.'⁵ The second plague is a multitude of frogs throughout Egypt. For what is said is the truth, as He Himself said: 'I am the way, and the truth, and the life.'⁶ Therefore, whoever preaches rightly concerning God, preaches the truth. But the man who thinks in the light of wicked heresy by his boldness and loquacity murmurs like frogs in the marshes of idolatry, more than he speaks with the authority of the Church. For this reason heretics are compared to frogs, because they murmur about God in empty falsehood more than they speak in the truth of correct faith.

(4) The third commandment is: 'Remember to keep holy the Sabbath day.'⁷ On the sabbath day a kind of rest for faithful souls is indicated. When they are free from worldly desires they rest in the love of God and of neighbor, as it is said: 'Desist! and confess that I am God.'⁸ The exceedingly disordered restlessness of worldly pleasures, which are compared to gnats, is contrary to this most peaceful rest. These gnats

---

3 Cf. Exod. 20.3.
4 Rom. 1.21.
5 Exod. 20.7.
6 John 14.6.
7 Exod. 20.8.
8 Ps. 45.11.

surely were born in the third plague. For worldly cares which settle in the mind blind and confuse the eyes of the heart, turning it aside from freedom for divine contemplation.

(5) The fourth commandment is: 'Honor your father and your mother.'[9] Opposed to this is the fourth plague of the Egyptians, the dog-fly. Nothing is so doglike as not to honor those who have begotten us, or more spiritually, when God the Father and our mother the Church are not venerated with a right faith and worthy honor.

(6) The fifth commandment is: 'You shall not commit adultery,'[10] while the fifth plague is death among the sheep of the Egyptians. What is a man when he does not restrain his unlawful desires with the reason given to him, except an irrational sheep? Of these men it is said: 'Man, for all his splendor, does not abide; he resembles the beasts that perish.'[11] What follows such a man, except an eternal death of torments? Reason was given to man for this purpose, that he might chastise himself and check his carnal impulses and illicit desires. If he labors here in some self-restraint, he will rejoice again at the recompense, for if the work is exhausting the reward is a consolation.

(7) The sixth commandment is: 'You shall not kill,'[12] and the sixth plague is bodily blisters and wounds. Murderous souls decay; they burn with wrath and boil with hatred, for through the anger of murder brotherly love is lost. Just as swelling and a wound burn the body, so the hatred and ill-will of murder burn the soul. Therefore, if we could see the souls of murderers, we would bewail them more than the rotting bodies of the ulcerated.

(8) The seventh commandment is: 'You shall not steal,'[13] and the seventh plague is hail among the crops. For no one possesses an unjust gain without a just loss. For example, the

---
9 Exod. 20.12.
10 Exod. 20.14.
11 Ps. 48.13,21.
12 Exod. 20.13.
13 Cf. Exod. 20.15.

man who steals acquires clothing, but by a heavenly judgment he loses his faith. Where there is gain, there is also loss: visibly a gain, but invisibly a loss. The scarcity of crops because of a hailstorm is compared to it. For through the theft of avarice a scarcity of merits is acquired, and greater is the famine, more dangerous is the plague, and more serious is the death of the interior man than of the exterior.

(9) The eighth commandment is: 'You shall not bear false witness.'[14] The eighth plague is the locust, an animal harmful because of its teeth. Now what does a false witness desire, except to do harm by biting and to consume by lying, as the Apostle testifies when he says: 'If you bite and devour one another, take heed or you will be consumed by one another.'[15]

(10) The ninth commandment is: 'You shall not covet your neighbor's wife,'[16] and the ninth plague is intense darkness. Now what darkness is so dense as when one disrupts the bond of charity in one's neighbor, and violates the laws of chastity in oneself? If a man unlawfully desires the wife of another through adultery, he both repels the Holy Spirit from himself and forces another to suffer from him what he himself is unwilling to endure from another.

(11) The tenth commandment is: 'You shall not covet anything of your neighbor's.'[17] The tenth plague is the death of the firstborn. No one can serve well unless faith has preceded. O man, your firstborn is your reasonable faith, for all of your good works are your spiritual children which come into being in charity. If you secretly desire the property of another, you interiorly lose your faith, and behold, you kill your firstborn. When a man has lost his faith, what more does he have to lose? Just as among children nothing is dearer than the firstborn, with respect to the right of inheritance, so nothing is

---

14 Cf. Exod. 20.16.
15 Gal. 5.15.
16 Cf. Exod. 20.17.
17 *Ibid.*

stronger in gaining the eternal inheritance than faith 'which works through charity.'[18]

(12) We should also know that the ten commandments of the Law are also fulfilled by the two Gospel precepts, love of God and love of neighbor. For the three commandments which were written on the first tablet pertain to the love of God, while on the second tablet seven commandments were inscribed, one of which is 'Honor your father and your mother.'[19] Doubtless, all of the latter are recognized as pertaining to love of neighbor. This it is that we read the Lord said in the Gospel: 'On these two commandments depend the whole Law and the Prophets.'[20] Likewise, we read what the Apostle James said: 'But whoever offends in one point, has become guilty in all.'[21] What does it mean to offend in one point and lose all, except to have fallen from the precept of charity and so to have offended in all the other commands? According to the Apostle, without this nothing in our virtues is shown to avail at all.

(13) These ten precepts are also compared to the psaltery of stringed instruments. The three on the one tablet refer to God, the seven on the other tablet pertain to the neighbor. The first of these is, 'Honor your father and your mother';[22] the second is, 'You shall not commit adultery.'[23] The third is, 'You shall not kill';[24] the fourth, 'You shall not steal';[25] the fifth, 'You shall not bear false witness';[26] the sixth, 'You shall not covet your neighbor's wife';[27] and the seventh, 'You shall not covet anything of your neighbor's.'[28] Add these seven to the first three, in order that you may be able to sing a new

---

18 Gal. 5.6.
19 Exod. 20.12.
20 Cf. Matt. 22.40.
21 James 2.10.
22 Exod. 20.12.
23 Exod. 20.14.
24 Exod. 20.13.
25 Exod. 20.15.
26 Cf. Exod. 20.16.
27 Exod. 20.17.
28 *Ibid.*

hymn of the ten strings. If you touch these strings in order, whichever you are, whether lute-player or hunter, ten exceedingly cruel wild beasts will fall before you. If you touch the first string, whereby one God is worshiped, the wild beast of idolatrous superstition falls. If you touch the second, in which you do not take the name of the Lord your God in vain, the wild beast of the error of wicked heresies falls. You touch the third, where whatever you do, you do in hopes of rest, and the beast which is more cruel than the others, namely, love of this world, is killed. You touch the fourth one in which parents are honored, and the beast of impiety is slain. You touch the fifth string: 'You shall not commit adultery,'[29] and the wild beast which is the impurity of all unlawful desires falls. You touch the sixth string: 'You shall not kill,'[30] and the wild beast of cruelty and wrath is suffocated. You touch the seventh string: 'You shall not steal,'[31] and the wild beast of robbery perishes. You touch the eighth string: 'You shall not bear false witness,'[32] and the wild beast of deception falls. You touch the ninth one: 'You shall not covet your neighbor's wife,'[33] and the wild beast of thoughts of adultery is crushed. It is one thing not to consent to a thought, and another not to commit the deed, and for this reason there are two precepts against fornication: 'You shall not commit adultery,'[34] and here, 'You shall not covet your neighbor's wife.'[35] You touch the tenth string: 'You shall not covet anything of your neighbor's,'[36] and the wild beast of avarice, the root of all evils, is killed. When all the wild beasts fall in this way, you will sing with assurance: 'Blessed be the Lord, my rock, who trains my hands for battle, my fingers for war.'[37] Not only do you kill

---

29 Exod. 20.14.
30 Exod. 20.13.
31 Exod. 20.15.
32 Cf. Exod. 20.16.
33 Exod. 20.17.
34 Exod. 20.14.
35 Exod. 20.17.
36 *Ibid.*
37 Ps. 143.1.

these ten principal wild beasts, but also their young, for there are many heads beneath these. In the individual beasts of the heart, you not only kill the animals one by one, but you kill herds of them. Then, with the love and affection of the ten strings, you will sing a hymn to your Lord and God, who is mercy and a refuge to you, your helper and deliverer, because He frees your soul from the mouth of the lion and from the midst of the lion's whelps.

These are our treasures[38] which no thief or robber or wicked neighbor can ever take away, where no moth or rust need be feared. Indeed, these are true riches, namely, a good conscience, justice, mercy, chastity, and sobriety; anyone who is full of such things is rich, even if he dies naked as the result of shipwreck. If you diligently heed these truths and, with the Lord's help, are willing to avoid evil and do good, you will be God's people. Then you will be freed from the unjust persecution of the Egyptians, that is, of spiritual injustice, and will happily reach the land of promise: with the help of our same Lord, to whom is honor and glory world without end. Amen.

Sermon 101

On the Words: The Lord Hardened the Heart of Pharao

(1) As often as that lesson is read in which we have frequently heard that the Lord hardened the heart of Pharao dearly beloved, it is wont to create anxiety, not only in the laity, but even in some of the clergy. Some people say within themselves: Why is that wickedness imputed to Pharao, when the Lord is mentioned to have hardened his heart? Since on this subject the exceedingly foul Manichaeans with wicked fury are wont to rebuke the writings of the Old Testament,

---
38 This concluding paragraph is a repetition of the conclusion of Sermon 100.

I exhort you, beloved brethren, to listen carefully. Although it is not as much as we should, at least we have wanted to mention briefly to your charity as much as we can concerning how you ought to understand that hardening.

(2) In the first place, let your charity believe devoutly and firmly that God never abandons a man unless He is first deserted by him. Although a man may have committed serious sins once, twice, and a third time, God still looks for him, as He says through the prophet: 'That by his conversion he may live.'[1] However, when he begins to continue in his sins, despair arises from the multitude of them, and hardening is caused by the despair. While careless men at first despise their own sins because they are small, if these slight offenses increase, crimes are even added; they heap up to finally overwhelm them, and when this happens there is fulfilled what is written: 'With wickedness comes contempt.'[2] Of such men the Apostle also says: 'Dost thou not know that the patience of God is meant to lead thee to repentance? But according to thy hardness and unrepentant heart, thou dost treasure up to thyself wrath on the day of wrath.'[3] Moreover, we read elsewhere concerning such hardness: 'A colt untamed turns out stubborn; a son left to himself grows up unruly.'[4] Again Scripture speaks of correcting a son: 'Thrash the sides of your son while he is still small,' it says, 'lest he become stubborn and disobey you.'[5] I have wanted to mention this testimony of the Scriptures to your charity, in order that you might understand that hardening is not effected by the compelling power of God, but is rather produced by His forgiveness and indulgence. Thus, not the divine power, but divine patience must be believed to have hardened Pharao. Furthermore, as often as God's plague struck him the afflicted man repented, but as soon as divine indulgence gave relaxation he was again elated

---
1 Ezech. 33.11.
2 Cf. Prov. 18.3.
3 Cf. Rom. 2.4,5.
4 Ecclus. 30.8.
5 Cf. Ecclus. 30.12.

and lifted up in pride. Therefore, believe very definitely and realize, brethren, that as often as the Lord said: 'I will make Pharao obstinate,'⁶ He wanted nothing else to be understood except: I suspend my plagues, and by removing my scourges, through my indulgence allow him to be hardened against me.

(3) Perhaps someone may say: Why did God cause him to be hardened by sparing him, and why did He remove His scourges? At this point I reply with assurance: God removed His scourges so often because by the immense number of his sins Pharao did not merit to be rebuked as a son for the amendment of his life, but like an enemy he was allowed to become hardened. Such great sins of his had preceded, and he had despised God so often with wicked boldness, that in him was fulfilled what the Holy Ghost said concerning such men: 'They are free from the burdens of mortals, and are not afflicted like the rest of men. So pride adorns them as a necklace; as a robe violence enwraps them. Out of their crassness comes iniquity.'⁷ Behold how a man is hardened if he does not merit to be chastised by our Lord for his correction. Moreover, what is written concerning those whom God's mercy does not allow to become hardened? 'God scourges every son whom he receives';⁸ furthermore: 'Those whom I love I rebuke and chastise';⁹ and again: 'For whom God loves he reproves.'¹⁰ Concerning this hardening the prophet also exclaims to the Lord in the person of the people: 'Why do you harden our hearts so that we fear you not?'¹¹ Surely, this is nothing else than: Thou hast abandoned our heart, that we should not be converted to Thee. This fact we know was fulfilled in the Jewish people because of their many preceding evil deeds.

(4) Now let no one along with pagans or Manichaeans

---

6 Exod. 4.21.
7 Ps. 72.5-7.
8 Heb. 12.6.
9 Apoc. 3.19.
10 Prov. 3.12.
11 Isa. 63.17.

dare to censure or blame the justice of God. It is to be believed as most certain that not the violence of God, but his own repeated wickedness and indomitable pride in opposition to God's commands, caused Pharao to become hardened. What does that mean which God said: 'I will make him obstinate,'[12] except that when my grace is withdrawn from him his own iniquity will harden him? In order that this may be known more clearly, we propose to your charity a comparison with visible things. As often as water is contracted by excessive cold, if the heat of the sun comes upon it, it becomes melted; when the same sun departs the water again becomes hard. Similarly, the charity of many men freezes because of the excessive coldness of their sins and they become as hard as ice; however, when the warmth of divine mercy comes upon them again, they are melted. Surely that is the heat of which it is written: 'Nothing escapes its heat.'[13] This we know was also fulfilled with regard to Pharao. As often as the scourge was removed from him, he became hardened and lifted himself up against God; but whenever he was afflicted, he prayed with humility.

(5) However, why does not our God scourge all men mercifully in such a way that He does not allow anyone to be hardened against Him? Either this is to be ascribed to the wickedness of those who have merited to become hardened, or is to be referred to the inscrutable judgments of God which are often hidden but never unjust. Therefore, it should be enough for us to believe with devotion and humility what the Apostle said: 'Is there injustice with God? By no means!'[14] Moreover, as we are wont to sing in the hymn: 'God is faithful, without deceit.'[15] For this reason, as I mentioned above, we should believe without any doubt concerning Pharao that he became hardened because of God's patience rather than His power. This fact we know clearly from his own admission, for when he was being punished he confessed in this way as justice

---
12 Exod. 4.21.
13 Ps. 18.7.
14 Rom. 9.14.
15 Cf. Deut. 32.4.

compelled him: 'The Lord is just; it is I and my subjects who are at fault.'[16] With what feelings, then, does a Christian complain that God is unjust, when even a wicked king admits that He is just? Indeed, so true is it that God did not harden his heart irrevocably that, after the ten plagues, he not only allowed God's people to leave, but even compelled them to depart. What he is read to have done when he was struck by ten plagues we know could have been fulfilled after the first chastisement. We are wont to do this also with regard to our slaves whom we have reared too luxuriously or rather mildly, when we frequently forgive them after they have offended. When they become worse as a result of their relaxation, we are wont to say to them in reproach: I made you that way, for by sparing you I nourished your boldness and negligence. We do not say this because they have fallen into such pride through our will, but because they have rather become hardened through our goodness and indulgence. So, too, God is recognized to have acted in the case of Pharao; while He suspends His plagues in ineffable kindness, with hardened heart the king proudly raises himself up against God.

(6) By mentioning these truths to you, dearly beloved, I have taken care to include, as it were, a few examples on this very obscure subject. If you piously and faithfully penetrate the mysteries of Sacred Scripture as you usually do, under God's inspiration you will learn more fully the truth of the matter. However, dearly beloved, we know in truth that despair arises from a multitude of sins, and hardness of heart is generated from despair according to what was said above: 'With wickedness comes contempt.'[17] As often as any sins overtake us, let us without any delay hasten to provide the remedy of alms and repentance for the wounds of our souls. A poultice or clamp is applied with profit to wounds when they are still warm, and a wound is quickly restored to health if not allowed to become infected from a long burn. Therefore, whenever we

---
16 Exod. 9.27.
17 Cf. Prov. 18.3.

fail in our duty, let our sins feel us as their judges, not their patrons; let them recognize their accusers, not their defenders, according to what is written: 'I acknowledge my offense, and my sin is before me always.'[18] Acknowledge it and God will forgive it, but how can God deign to pardon what a man disdains to admit in himself? Just as we seek a doctor without any delay and hasten to apply remedies if some blow or wound comes over our body, so we should act with regard to the wounds of our souls. If we are more solicitous for the health of our body than of our soul, by an unfair judgment preferring the servant to the mistress, we may merit to hear the rebuke of the prophet: 'Man, for all his splendor, does not abide; he resembles the beasts that perish.'[19] Indeed, it is necessary for us to think more of the sound condition of our soul than of our body, and to strive to cultivate God's image within us in such a way that before the tribunal of the eternal judge we may merit to receive a recompense rather than confusion: who lives and reigns world without end. Amen.

* *Sermon 102*

On the Manna and the Bitter Water

(1) When the divine lesson was read yesterday, dearly beloved, we heard that after the crossing of the Red Sea the children of Israel came to Mara, that is, to bitter water. The people could not drink the water because it was bitter, and, therefore, the Lord showed blessed Moses a tree which he cast into the water and it became sweet. Certainly, it is strange that He showed Moses a tree which he threw into the water to make it sweet. Just as if God could not have made the water

---
18 Ps. 50.5.
19 Ps. 48.13,21.

sweet without the tree, or Moses did not know the tree, with the result that God showed it to him. Now we must see what the inner sense possesses in these matters that is suitable. The Red Sea signified the sacrament of Baptism; the bitter water designated the letter of the law. In truth, if the law is accepted according to the letter, it is quite bitter. How can that which kills not be bitter, for the Apostle says: 'The letter kills'?[1] What is so bitter as for a boy to receive the wound of circumcision on the eighth day, when his tender infancy suffers the harshness of the knife? So bitter, in fact exceedingly so, is this sort of cup of the law that God's people, not those who 'were baptized in Moses, in the cloud and in the sea,'[2] but Christian people who were baptized in the spirit and in water could not drink of that water. They could not even taste the bitterness of circumcision, or endure the slaughter of victims, or keep the observance of the sabbath. However, if God shows them the tree which is thrown into this bitterness so that the water of the law may become sweet, then the Christian people can drink of it.

(2) What is that tree which the Lord pointed out? Solomon shows us when he says of wisdom: 'She is a tree of life to all who embrace her.'[3] If the tree of Christ's wisdom is put into the law, showing us how circumcision should be spiritually understood and how the sabbath and the law are to be observed, then the bitter water becomes sweet. When the bitterness of the law is changed into the sweetness of spiritual understanding, then the people of God can drink. Therefore, in order that the water of Mara may be drunk, God shows the tree which is to be thrown into it, with the result that anyone who drinks of it will not die or perceive its bitterness. For this reason it is certain that, if a man wants to drink of the letter of the law without the tree of life, that is, without the mystery of the cross, the faith of Christ, or spiritual under-

---

1 2 Cor. 3.6.
2 1 Cor. 10.2.
3 Cf. Prov. 3.18.

standing, he will die because of the excessive bitterness, Paul the Apostle knew this when he said: 'The letter kills.'[4] In other words, the bitter water plainly kills if it is not changed into sweetness by the spirit. For this reason the tree is cast into the water, so that it may be turned into sweetness. It is true, brethren, the bitterness is removed from the water when the tree of the cross is joined to the sacrament of Baptism.

(3) Notice, brethren, that on the Jewish sabbath God never rained any manna at all, nor did the Jews deserve that grace should come down to them from heaven on their sabbath. However, on our Sunday, not only does manna always come to us, but the very beginning of its coming originated on that day. Therefore, God always rains manna from heaven for us: there are those heavenly discourses which are spoken to us, and from God descend those words which are read to us. Thus, when we receive such manna, it is always given to us from heaven. For this reason the unhappy Jews are to be deplored and bewailed, because they do not merit to receive manna as their fathers did. They never eat manna, because they are unable to eat what is small like a seed of coriander or white as snow. The unfortunate Jews find in the word of God nothing small, nothing fine, nothing spiritual, but everything rich and solid; 'For heavy is the heart of this people.'[5] Now an examination of the word tells us the same thing. Manna is interpreted as 'What is this?'[6] See whether the very power of the name does not provoke you to learn it, so that when you hear the law of God read in church you may always ask and say to the teachers: What is this? This it is that the manna indicates. Therefore, if you want to eat the manna, that is, if you desire to receive the word of God, know that it is small and very fine like the seed of the coriander. Indeed, it possesses within itself something of the herb with which a sick man may be nourished and refreshed, because: 'He

---
4 2 Cor. 3.6.
5 Cf. Isa. 6.10.
6 Exod. 16.15.

who is weak, let him eat vegetables.'⁷ It also has some harshness, and in this respect it is like frost. But most of all it contains whiteness and sweetness. What is more shining and splendid than divine knowledge? What is sweeter or more pleasant than the Lord's words, which are: 'Sweeter than syrup or honey from the comb'?⁸

(4) What does it mean that on the sixth day a double measure was gathered for reserve, as much as would suffice for the sabbath? According to our understanding, we ought not pass over this fact with indifference or assurance, but by almsgiving should store away whatever will suffice for a future day. If you amass any good works here, if you store away any justice or mercy or piety, this will be food for you in the future life. The Apostle likewise advises this when he says: 'What a man sows, that he will also reap.'⁹ Therefore, what do we do when we love to store up what is going to be destroyed, not what will remain and endure for tomorrow, that is, for the future life? Avaricious or greedy rich men lay aside these things which will be destroyed in this world or rather with it. However, the good works that are stored up will last until tomorrow. In truth, it is written that those who were unfaithful: 'Kept some of the manna, and it became wormy and rotten.'¹⁰ However, what was put aside for the sabbath: 'Did not become rotten or wormy,'¹¹ but it remained incorrupt. Therefore, if you store up treasures only for the sake of this present life and out of love for the world, worms will at once come forth. Finally, hear what the prophet's words say concerning sinners and those who love the present life: 'Their worm shall not die.'¹² These are the worms which avarice produces; these are worms which the blind passion for riches causes in those who have money and still close their

---

7 Rom. 14.2.
8 Ps. 18.11.
9 Gal. 6.8.
10 Cf. Exod. 16.20.
11 Cf. Exod. 16.24.
12 Isa. 66.24.

hearts when they see their brothers in need. For this reason the Apostle also says: 'Charge the rich of this world not to be proud, or to trust in the uncertainty of riches. Let them rather be rich in good works, giving readily, sharing with others, and thus providing for themselves the true life.'[13]

(5) Someone may say: If you say the manna is God's word, how does it produce worms? It is true, brethren. The worms in us have no other source than the word of God, for thus He Himself says: 'If I had not come and spoken to them, they would have no sin.'[14] If a man sins after receiving the word of God, that same word becomes a worm to him, always digging into his conscience and gnawing at the secrets of his heart.

(6) Therefore, let us now hasten to receive the heavenly manna. Indeed, according as each one receives it, such a taste it creates in his mouth. Moreover, listen to the Lord say to those who approach Him: 'Be it done to thee according to thy faith.'[15] If, then, you receive God's word which is preached in church with all faith and devotion, that same word will do for you whatever you desire. For example, if you are troubled, it will console you by saying: 'A heart contrite and humbled God does not despise.'[16] If you rejoice in hopes for the future, it will increase your joys with the words: 'Be glad in the Lord and rejoice, you just.'[17] If you are angry, it will soothe you by saying: 'Give up your anger, and forsake wrath.'[18] If you are in pain, it cures you with the words: 'The Lord heals all your ills.'[19] If you are consumed with poverty, it consoles you by saying: 'The Lord raises up the lowly from the dust; from the dunghill he lifts up the poor.'[20] Thus, then, the manna of God's word brings to your mouth whatever taste you desire. However, if anyone receives it with infidelity,

---
13 Cf. 1 Tim. 6.17-19.
14 John 15.22.
15 Cf. Matt. 8.13.
16 Cf. Ps. 50.19.
17 Ps. 31.11.
18 Ps. 36.8.
19 Cf. Ps. 102.3.
20 Cf. Ps. 112.7.

not eating but hiding it, worms will come forth from it. Do you think we are to go even so far as to think that the word of God becomes a worm? Let not the sound of this disturb you, but listen to the prophet saying in the person of our Lord: 'But I am a worm, not a man.'[21] Just as He Himself became 'a source of ruin for some, and a means of resurrection to others,'[22] so in the manna He Himself becomes sweet honey to the faithful but a worm to the unfaithful.

(7) Therefore, dearly beloved, with God's help, let us endeavor to apply ourselves to the divine text as much as we can, so that we may merit to learn God's law spiritually. Then the word of God will not become for us a worm which continually accuses and torments our consciences, but there may be fulfilled in us what is written: 'How sweet to my palate are your promises, O Lord! Sweeter than syrup or honey from the comb.'[23] Let us pray that God in His goodness will deign to grant us this grace, to whom is honor and glory forever and ever. Amen.

* Sermon 103

On Raphidim, Amalec, and the Rock Struck in the Desert

(1) 'All who want to live piously in Christ suffer persecution,'[1] says the Apostle, and they are attacked by the enemy. For this reason, with Christ's help, everyone who travels the journey of this life should be armed unceasingly and always stand in camp. So if you want to be constantly vigilant so that you may know you serve in the Lord's camp, observe what the same Apostle says: 'No one serving as God's soldier entangles himself in worldly affairs, that he may please him

---

21 Ps. 21.7.
22 The editor indicates no source for this quotation.
23 Cf. Ps. 118.103.

1 2 Tim. 3.12.

whose approval he has secured.'² If you serve in such a way that you are free from worldly concerns and always keep watch in God's camp, what we heard a little while ago is also said about you. According to the Lord's word, you depart from the desert of Sin and come to Raphidim. Now Sin is interpreted as temptation, Raphidim sound judgment. If a man properly leaves temptation and trial has shown him acceptable, he comes to correct judgment. On the day of judgment he will be safe and will possess soundness, because in the temptations of this present life he has never been wounded by murmuring in the least against God. As we read in the Apocalypse: 'Him who overcomes I will permit to eat of the tree of life, which is in paradise.'³ Therefore, a man will come to sound judgment if he orders his words with judgment after hearing properly the case of another, and does not take bribes against the innocent.

(2) What, then, does Scripture mention in what follows? 'In their thirst for water, the people grumbled against Moses.'⁴ Perhaps this word that he said seems superfluous, that the people thirsted for water; for since he said: "In their thirst,' what need was there to add 'for water'? Thus, indeed, the ancient translation has it. Why did he add this, except because they thirsted for water when they should have thirsted for justice? 'Blessed are they who hunger and thirst for justice';⁵ and again: 'Athirst is my soul for the living God.'⁶ Many people are thirsty, both the just and sinners; the former thirst after justice, the latter after dissipation. The just are thirsty for God; sinners, for gold. For this reason the people thirsted after water when they should have thirsted after justice.

(3) Then the Lord said to Moses: 'Take the staff and strike the rock, that it may produce water for the people.'⁷

---
2 2 Tim. 2.4.
3 Cf. Apoc. 2.7.
4 Cf. Exod. 17.3.
5 Matt. 5.6.
6 Ps. 41.3.
7 Cf. Exod. 17.5,6.

Behold, there is a rock and it contains water. However, unless this rock is struck, it does not have any water at all; but when it has been struck, it produces fountains and rivers, as we read in the Gospel: 'He who believes in me, from within him there shall flow rivers of living water.'[8] When Christ was struck on the cross, He brought forth the fountains of the New Testament; therefore, it was necessary for Him to be pierced. If He had not been struck, so that water and blood flowed from His side, the whole world would have perished through suffering thirst for the word of God. 'Therefore, Moses struck the rock twice with his staff.'[9] What does this mean, brethren? I do not think it is without mystery. What does it mean that the rock was not struck once, but twice, with the staff? The rock was struck a second time because two trees were lifted up for the gibbet of the cross: the one stretched out Christ's sacred hands, the other spread out His sinless body from head to foot. Of this mystery, that is, of the rock that was struck, the Apostle also speaks when he says: 'Our fathers all drank the same drink (for they drank from the spiritual rock which followed them, and the rock was Christ).'[10] Notice carefully, brethren. Since that rock was not spiritual, what was it that the Apostle called spiritual when he even added: 'the rock which followed them'? What was then prefigured corporally certainly was fulfilled spiritually in our Lord. When he said: 'the rock which followed them,' we understand that it had to follow, that is, in the days to come the true rock would appear to offer spiritual drink to the people. Then the people drank from the rock, and immediately after began the war against Amalec. Understand, brethren, that after each one has drunk from the rock, that is, has received the sacraments of Christ, it is necessary for him to go out to battle. As long as a man wishes to perform the works of the devil, he will not feel him fighting in opposition. But if a man leaves him

---

8 John 7.38.
9 Cf. Num. 20.11.
10 Cf. 1 Cor. 10.1,4.

and, drinking from the rock, chooses to follow Christ, he must suffer the hostility of the devil whom he has refused to prefer to Christ by a just decision. Therefore, anyone who is united to Christ should be prepared for battle, not for delights or pleasures, because 'All who want to live piously in Christ suffer persecution';[11] moreover: 'Through many tribulations we must enter the kingdom of God.'[12]

(4) When war threatened the children of Israel, Moses called upon Jesus and said to him: 'Pick out certain men for yourself and engage Amalec in battle.'[13] Up to this point no mention of the blessed name, that is, of Jesus, has been made. Here, for the first time, the splendor of this name shone forth. Moses calls upon Jesus; the law invokes Christ. 'Pick out certain men for yourself.' Moses was unable to choose powerful men; Jesus is the only one who can do so. He it is who said to His apostles: 'You have not chosen me, but I have chosen you';[14] He it is who entered the house of the strong one and plundered his goods.

(5) 'Now Moses climbed to the top of the hill; and it happened that as long as Moses raised up his hands, Israel had the better of the fight.'[15] Notice, brethren. Moses indeed lifts up his hands, but does not extend them. For whom then was it reserved to extend his hands, except for our Lord Jesus Christ? When He was stretched out on the cross as if to embrace the whole world, He spread out the arms of His goodness. Therefore, Moses lifted up his hands. But although he did not extend them, still by raising them, he showed the mystery of the cross. Understand, brethren, that then already opposing nations were overcome by the mystery of the cross. If, with the Lord's help, we lift up our hands, dearly beloved, we, too, conquer the devil. We ought to take our works in

---
11 2 Tim. 3.12.
12 Acts 14.21.
13 Cf. Exod. 17.9. The Old Testament in this passage has Josue, but Caesarius has Jesus.
14 John 15.16.
15 Cf. Exod. 17.10,11.

our hands. If your deeds are such that you are able to lift them on high in the sight of the Lord, you can also destroy your adversaries who are within you. Who properly raises his hands, but the man who continually lays aside treasure in heaven by almsgiving? Who correctly lifts up his hands, except one who constantly supplies food and clothing for the poor? Who properly raises his hands? Surely, the man who fulfills the words of the Apostle: 'Lifting up pure hands, without wrath and contention.'[16] Therefore, since a struggle against hostile powers daily threatens both you and us, if we want to conquer, our hands, that is, our deeds and our conversation, should not be on earth. As the Apostle says, we should have our conversation in heaven even though we walk upon earth. Moreover, it is written: 'Just as a calf licks at the green grass in fields, so the people of Israel will graze upon the people of Amalec.'[17] This seems to indicate that the people of God did not fight with the hand or weapons so much as with the voice and tongue, that is, they poured forth prayer to God, and thus overcame their adversaries. Therefore, you, too, if you want to be victorious, listen to the Apostle say: 'Be assiduous in prayer, being wakeful therein.'[18] This is the most glorious fight of the Christian, not to presume upon his own strength, but always to implore the assistance of God.

(6) If you wish, let these words suffice for your charity. Since it is necessary for us to admonish those who are unable to fast because of bodily infirmity, tomorrow, with God's help, we will advise how they should bend down to their infirmity without offense to their soul: to Him is honor and might forever and ever. Amen.

---

16 1 Tim. 2.8.
17 Cf. Num. 22.4. This bears little resemblance to the Vulgate version.
18 Col. 4.2.

Sermon 104

A Comparison of the Church and the Synagogue when there was a Text in Exodus about the First and Later Tablets

(1) The mystery of the Christian religion, dearly beloved, is not something new or lately discovered by men, but was divinely consecrated from the very beginning of the world and promised throughout all ages by the words of all the prophets. The fact that the synagogue first existed and then later the Church, and that the Church would have greater glory than the synagogue, is very clearly contained in all the books of Scripture. Moreover, this idea is known to have been shown, not once or twice or three times, but very frequently in the writings of the Old Testament. Therefore, even if a man be simple and unlearned, he can recognize it clearly and plainly. At the very beginning of the world, of those two sons who were born of Adam, Abel the younger is chosen, while as a figure of the Jewish people Cain the older one is condemned. Afterwards, in the time of Abraham, the same figure is fulfilled in Sara and Agar. Sara was sterile for a long time as a type of the Church, while Agar as a figure of the synagogue bore a son at once. Hence, it is that the younger son Isaac is received into the inheritance, but Ismael who was older is driven away. This fact also seems to have been fulfilled in those two: Jacob the younger was loved by God, while Esau the elder was rejected according to what is written: 'I loved Jacob, but hated Esau.'[1] This figure is also known to have been fulfilled in those two sisters whom blessed Jacob had as his wives: Rachel who was the younger was loved more than Lia the older. In fact, of the former was born Joseph who was to be sold in Egypt as a type of our Lord and Savior. That Lia was blear-eyed while Rachel was beau-

---
1 Mal. 1.2,3.

tiful in countenance is also significant: in Lia is understood the synagogue, the Church is indicated in Rachel. A man whose bodily eyes are afflicted with inflammation cannot look at the brightness of the sun. Similarly, the synagogue which had the eyes of its heart filled with jealousy and envy against our Lord and Savior as with poisonous fluids, could not gaze upon the splendor of Christ who is 'the sun of justice.'[2] There is the same difference between the synagogue and the Church as that existing between sore eyes and sound ones; for this reason inflamed eyes are tortured by the very light which feeds healthy eyes. Thus it is, dearly beloved, for the synagogue is afflicted by the light of Christ which illumines the Church. This is the light, I repeat: 'That enlightens every man who comes into the world,'[3] the same who said: 'I am the light of the world.'[4] The same light which illuminates the eyes of the heart for all Christians also blinds them for the unhappy Jews. One and the same thing inspires joy in some people and causes torture to others; for truly the light of Christ brings joy to devout Christians but carries punishment for the unfaithful Jews.

(2) In blessed Joseph and his brother, too, we see this same thing fulfilled, for as a type of Christ the youngest was loved more than the other sons by his father. In the sons of this same Joseph, the mystery of the Jewish and Christian people was again demonstrated when blessed Jacob exchanged hands and blessed them, by the mystery of the cross preferring the younger to the older. Indeed, when holy Joseph brought his sons to his father for a blessing, he put the older one at his father's right hand and the younger one at his left; blessed Jacob, however, extended his right hand over the younger and his left hand over the older. Now holy Joseph accepted this action with displeasure and annoyance. Seizing the hands of his father, he wanted to bring the right hand

---

2 Mal. 4.2.
3 John 1.9.
4 John 8.12.

back over the elder son, saying: 'This one is not my firstborn.'[5] But his father said in reply: 'I know, my son, I know. He too shall increase in people; but his younger brother shall be greater than he.'[6] If your charity carefully pays attention, dearly beloved, in this fact of the two peoples there seems to be expressed a figure of the Jews and the Gentiles, as we already mentioned above. Truly, the Jewish people first came to God's notice, but afterwards the younger people of the Gentiles came and received a greater grace of benediction.

(3) A clear comparison of the two peoples of the Jews and Gentiles is recognized in the crossing of the Red Sea and the division of the Jordan. The elder nation of the Jews crossed the Red Sea which has salty and bitter waters to the desert, where they were tried by hunger and thirst. The younger nation which signified the Christian people through the sweet waters of the Jordan entered a land of milk and honey, which was given to them as a perpetual habitation and possession after the defeat of their adversaries. Moreover, in the fact that blessed Moses produced water out of a rock for his thirsting people is clearly recognized as a type of both the Church and the synagogue. When blessed Moses struck the rock the first time, nothing came out of it; but when he had struck it a second time, then abundant water was found to flow from it. What is signified by this, brethren, except that the hardness of the synagogue was prefigured in the first blow and the faith of the Church in the second? Indeed, the observances of the synagogue could supply the dry and faithless Jewish people with no refreshing eternal bliss, but the Church produces fountains and rivers for all who come to her. Thus, in truth, the Lord Himself spoke in the Gospel: 'If anyone thirst, let him come and drink. He who believes in me, as the Scripture says, "From within him there shall flow rivers of living water" ';[7] and again: 'He who drinks of the water that I will

---
5 Cf. Gen. 48.18.
6 Cf. Gen. 48.19.
7 John 7.37,38.

give, in him it shall become a fountain of water, springing up unto life everlasting.'[8]

(4) After the crossing of the Red Sea, as you heard just now when the divine lesson was read, these truths were most clearly shown in those two tablets which were written by the finger of God. Since the earlier people of the Jews were to be rejected, while later by God's grace the Christian people were to be chosen, the first tablets were broken but those which were made afterwards were preserved. Moreover, in blessed Moses and Josue, we also find this comparison completed; the older one, Moses, prefigured the Jewish people and died in the desert, while the youth Josue was commanded to cross the Jordan with the younger people. This we recognize as signified in all the Jewish people: because of their infidelity the older people are destroyed in the desert, but the younger ones enter the land of promise through the River Jordan as the sacrament of Baptism. The same fact seems clear in the case of King Saul and blessed David; Saul who is first and older is condemned, while the younger man David ascends the throne. Moreover, in David and his brothers the same thing is recorded, for through the revelation of the Lord all his older brothers are condemned by blessed Samuel, and David is chosen though still a boy of tender age.

(5) Because I believe that these words which have been spoken should not displease your charity, I want to repeat them in brief so that they may be able to adhere more firmly in your memory. Figures of the two peoples of the Jews and the Gentiles are shown in all the books of the Old Testament, as has often been said. At the very beginning of the world, the younger man Abel was chosen, while Cain the elder was condemned; by God's decree the sterile Sara was preferred to Agar who had been fruitful first. Young Isaac received the inheritance, while Ismael who was older was driven away; Jacob the younger son was loved, while Esau the elder one was hated. The older Lia was despised, but young Rachel was

---

8 Cf. John 4.13,14.

loved all the more; Joseph the youngest was loved more than the others by his father. Ephraim was preferred to his elder Manasses; the younger Moses was elevated above the older Aaron; the crossing of the Jordan is considered more happy than the passage over the Red Sea. Like the synagogue, the rock did not produce water when it was struck just once, but when it was struck a second time, it furnished a river for the thirsty people as a type of the Church. The first tablets were broken on account of the infidelity of the Jewish people, but the second ones were preserved because of the faith of Christians. As a figure of the Jews, the first people were destroyed in the desert, while the younger ones entered the promised land. Although the older man Moses died in the desert to prefigure the Jewish people, the youth Josue as an image of the Gentiles became the leader for the people who went to the land of promise. Saul the elder was condemned, but David ascended the throne though still a boy. If these truths were read once, twice, or three times in the sacred books, dearly beloved, someone could perchance imagine something different from what we said above. But when we read so often that young men were preferred to older ones, who can be found so unlettered or unfaithful as to contend that these things happened by chance rather than that they were divinely arranged by God?

(6) We mention all these facts to your charity, dearly beloved, in order that you may clearly recognize that a figure and mystery of the Catholic Church was shown very frequently in all the books of Scripture ever since the beginning of the world. If you will remember these truths, as we hope, you can clearly explain the mystery of the Christian religion to both Jews and pagans whenever there is an opportunity to do so. For our part, however, we ought to thank God both day and night for our salvation, since we have merited so much blessing without any preceding merits of ours, but solely through the Lord's reward. Even before we were born in this world, we were taught by the Spirit and predestined; thus the Apostle

says: 'He chose us before the foundation of the world.'⁹ We had not yet been created, and we were already chosen before the foundation of the world. For this reason, let us, with God's help, labor as much as we can, so that in return for such great benefits we may possess a reward rather than judgment. If perchance we willingly surrender ourselves to sensuality and other evil deeds, returning evil for good, we make ourselves guilty before the tribunal of the eternal judge. However, may our life be so just that Jews and pagans, according to the Gospel: 'Seeing our good works may give glory to our Father in heaven.'¹⁰ Then, may they desire to have recourse to our faith and imitate the example of our life. Those who wish to give Jews, pagans, or even bad Christians the example of a good life will receive eternal rewards both for themselves and for others. On the contrary, those who show others an example of the worst kind of life by their evil deeds, in such a way that through them, as we read: 'The name of the Lord is reviled,'¹¹ will suffer eternal punishments, not only for themselves, but also for others. Therefore, with the Lord's help, dearly beloved, let us live chastely, soberly, and devoutly, so that we may preserve the image of divine mercy within us and merit to be recognized among his sons by the Father. Let Him not close the doors of eternal life to us and say: 'I do not know you, I do not know you. Depart from me, accursed ones, into the everlasting fire.'¹² In return for our good works, may we rather deserve to hear: 'Come, blessed, take possession of the kingdom.'¹³ May the Lord in His goodness deign to bring us to this, to whom is honor and might forever and ever. Amen.

---

9 Eph. 1.4.
10 Cf. Matt. 5.16.
11 Cf. Isa. 52.5.
12 Cf. Matt. 25.12,41.
13 Cf. Matt. 25.34.

* *Sermon 105*

On Spiritual Blessings

(1) When the sacred lesson was read just now, dearly beloved, we heard the Lord say: 'If you live in accordance with my precepts and are careful to observe my commandments, I will give you rain in due season.'[1] If we faithfully and diligently pay attention to it, brethren, everything which was promised corporally to the Jews is fulfilled spiritually in us; for all the blessings of God which they received on earth, we have obtained in our souls through the grace of Baptism. Therefore, with His help, let us labor with all our strength, so that we may be able to receive God's blessings and avoid His curses.

(2) 'I will give you rain in due season,' says the Lord. Therefore, let us first ask the Jews, and question people who think these words are to be understood directly and materially. If this rain as a reward for labors is given to those who keep His commands, how is the one same rain also given in due season to those who do not observe them, since the whole world enjoys the common rain which God bestows? Because 'He sends rain on the just and the unjust.'[2] But if rain is given to both the just and the unjust, it will not be an exceptional reward for those who have kept the commandments. Therefore, let us ask in Scripture what this rain is that is granted only to holy souls, and concerning which the clouds are commanded not to rain that rain upon the unjust. What this rain is Moses himself may teach us when he says in Deuteronomy: 'Give ear, O heavens, while I will speak; let the earth hearken to the words of my mouth! may my instruction be awaited like the rain.'[3] Behold the nature of the rain

---
[1] Cf. Lev. 26.3.
[2] Matt. 5.45.
[3] Cf. Deut. 32.1,2.

which is given only to the just and denied to sinners. Therefore, the rain is the word of God, but only the just receive it. Lovers of the world, however, who are proud, dissolute, or avaricious, are unwilling to receive the rain of God's word even if it is forced upon them. Why is this? Because they are unwilling to hunger or thirst after justice. Men who are saturated with the filth of dissipation do not deserve to be refreshed with the rain of God's word.

(3) Then there follows as a blessing: 'You will have food to eat in abundance.'[4] I do not consider this as a material blessing, as though the man who observes God's law will obtain that common bread in abundance. Why not? Do not wicked sinners also eat bread, not only in abundance, but even in luxury? Therefore, let us look rather to Him who says: 'I am the living bread that has come down from heaven.'[5] And 'He who eats this bread shall live forever.'[6] As we notice that He who said this is the word with which our soul is fed, we realize of what bread it was said by God in blessing that: 'You will have food to eat in abundance.'[7] Solomon proclaims something similar concerning the just man, when he says in the Book of Proverbs: 'When the just man eats, his hunger is appeased, but the souls of the wicked suffer want.'[8] If this is understood only according to the letter, it seems utterly false, for the souls of the wicked eat more greedily and strive for satiety, while the just sometimes even suffer hunger. Finally, Paul was a just man, and he said: 'To this very hour we hunger and thirst, and we are naked and buffeted';[9] and again he says: 'In hunger and thirst, in fastings often.'[10] How, then, does Solomon say that the just man eats and satisfies his soul? What we understood before concerning the rain we ought to consider at this point also with regard to the bread.

---

4 Lev. 26.5.
5 John 6.51.
6 John 6.59.
7 Lev. 26.5.
8 Cf. Prov. 13.25.
9 1 Cor. 4.11.
10 2 Cor. 11.27.

That heavenly bread, that is, the word of God who said: 'I am the living bread,'[11] none but the just eat, to whom it is said: 'Taste, and see how good the Lord is.'[12] With what kind of a conscience, then, do sinners who are defiled by many sins dare to eat?

(4) 'And you,' it says, 'may dwell securely in your land.'[13] The wicked man is never secure, but is always disturbed and wavering. He is tossed about by every wind of doctrine to deceitful error, by the craft of men. However, the just man who observes God's law dwells in security on his land, because he governs his body in fear of God and brings it into subjection. His understanding is firm when he says to God: 'Strengthen me according to your words, O Lord.'[14] Strengthened, secure, and well-rooted, he dwells on the earth, founded in faith. His house is not built upon sand, but is established on solid ground.

(5) Then follow the words: 'And I will establish peace in your lands.'[15] What peace does God give? The peace which the world possesses? Christ says He does not give that kind of peace, for He declares: 'Peace I leave with you, my peace I give to you; not as this world gives peace do I give to you.'[16] Therefore, He denies that He will give the peace of the world to His disciples. Do you want to see, then, what peace God gives in our land? If the land is good so that it produces fruit a hundredfold, sixty-fold, or thirty-fold, it will receive from God that peace which the Apostle describes: 'May the peace of God which surpasses all understanding guard your hearts.'[17]

(6) 'You may lie down to rest without anxiety.'[18] Moreover, Solomon says in the Book of Proverbs: 'When you sit down,

---

11 John 6.51.
12 Cf. Ps. 33.9.
13 Cf. Lev. 26.5.
14 Ps. 118.28.
15 Cf. Lev. 26.6.
16 Cf. John 14.27.
17 Cf. Phil. 4.7.
18 Lev. 26.6.

you need not be afraid; when you lie down, your sleep will be sweet and you will not be afraid of sudden terror or of the attack of the wicked when it comes.'[19] These words he spoke concerning the just and wise man. Furthermore, it is said in blessing: 'You may lie down to rest without anxiety.' If you are just, no one can frighten you; if you fear God, you will fear nothing else. 'The just man, like a lion, feels sure of himself';[20] and in the words of David: 'I shall not fear the terror of the night,'[21] and so forth. He adds still further: 'The Lord is my light and my salvation; whom should I fear? The Lord is my life's refuge; of whom should I be afraid?'[22] and again: 'Though an army encamp against me, my heart will not fear.'[23] Do you see the courage and constancy of the soul that observes the commandments of God?

(7) After this we read: 'I will rid your country of ravenous beasts.'[24] These material beasts are not entirely evil nor wholly good, but rather in between, for they are mute animals. However, those beasts are spiritual evils, and the Apostle calls them 'spiritual forces of wickedness on high.'[25] That is the evil beast of which Scripture says: 'The serpent was more cunning than all the beasts on earth.'[26] This is the evil beast which God promises to drive out of our land if we keep His commandments. Do you also wish to see another evil beast? Listen to the Apostle Peter: 'Your adversary the devil, as a roaring lion, goes about seeking someone to devour. Resist him, steadfast in the faith.'[27] Under a vision in the desert which he entitled that of the quadrupeds, the prophet Isaia spoke in a prophetic spirit concerning beasts: 'The lion and the young of the lion are in tribulation. Here spring up the

---

19 Cf. Prov. 3.24,25.
20 Cf. Prov. 28.1.
21 Ps. 90.5.
22 Ps. 26.1.
23 Ps. 26.3.
24 Cf. Lev. 26.6.
25 Eph. 6.12.
26 Cf. Gen. 3.1.
27 1 Peter 5.8.

flying basilisks which carry their riches upon asses and camels to a people whose help is futile and vain.'[28] Can these words in any way seem to have been said with regard to corporal beasts, in the minds of those who are very fond of the letter? How can the lion, the young of the lion, or the flying basilisk carry their riches upon asses and camels? However, the prophet enumerates the opposing powers of the most wicked demons, by the Holy Ghost seeing them put the riches of their deceits upon asses and camels, that is, upon souls that are stupid and mindful of nothing else except bodily pleasure. Thus, he designates them figuratively, comparing them to camels and asses. Lest he be delivered to these beasts, the God-fearing soul prays to the Lord: 'Give not to the vulture the life of your dove.'[29]

(8) 'I will rid your country of ravenous beasts, and keep war from sweeping across your land.'[30] There are many fights which pass over our land, if we do not observe the law of God and keep His commands. Let each one return to his own soul or conscience, and examine himself with interior recollection. Let him see how our land, that is, our body, is oppressed at one time by the spirit of fornication, at another by anger or fury. Again it is disturbed by the darts of avarice or struck by the javelins of envy, then it is darkened by the vice of pride. In whatever way the flesh lusts against the spirit or the spirit against the flesh, our land is agitated by exceedingly dangerous battles. Therefore, if a man observes the divine commands, by the Holy Ghost brings his body into subjection, keeps God's precepts and fulfills them, he suffers this fight and war less, or endures them in such a way that he is victorious. Indeed, God takes them away from his land and does not allow them to pass over the land, that is, the soul of the just.

(9) 'You will rout your enemies.'[31] What enemies, except

---
28 Cf. Isa. 30.6.
29 Ps. 73.19.
30 Cf. Lev. 26.6.
31 Lev. 26.7.

the devil himself and his angels? We rout them, not only by driving them from our own hearts, but we repel them far away from others whom they disturb or attack or overcome by our advice or reproof or prayer if we preserve the divine precepts. Thus, through death the enemy falls in our sight. Whose death? I think it is ours when we mortify our members which are on earth, namely, fornication and uncleanness. If we bring this death to our members, that is, to our concupiscences and sins, our enemies, the devil and his angels, will fall in our sight. How will they fall in your sight? If you are just, injustice falls at sight of you; if chaste, lust falls; if devout, you kill the spirit of impiety.

(10) 'Five of you will put a hundred to flight.'[32] Who are those five who can pursue a hundred? The number five is applied to both the praiseworthy and the culpable, for there were five wise virgins and five foolish; so also the number one hundred can be accepted in either way. Therefore, if we belong to the five laudable ones, that is, the five wise virgins, we pursue one hundred of the foolish. If we fight wisely in matters of God's word, if we discuss the law of the Lord prudently, we convince and put to flight a multitude of unbelievers. Similarly, the number one hundred indicates both the faithful and the unfaithful. Under that number of years Abraham is recorded to have believed in God and been justified, while 'The sinner of a hundred years shall be thought accursed.'[33] Now here a hundred unfaithful souls are put to flight by five wise men. Again, a hundred just men who are so designated because of their perfection rather than their number, pursue many thousands of unbelievers. Indeed, devout teachers drive away countless demons, so they will not deceive the souls of believers with their old deceits.

(11) 'Your foes will be cut down by your sword.'[34] Who they are we mentioned above, but let us find out by what

---

32 Cf. Lev. 26.8.
33 Cf. Isa. 65.20.
34 Lev. 26.8.

sword they are said to fall. The Apostle Paul teaches us what this sword is when he says: 'For the word of God is living and efficient and keener than every two-edged sword, and extending even to the joints of soul and spirit, of the members also and the marrow, and a discerner of the thoughts and intentions of the heart.'[35] This is the sword at whose edge our enemies will fall. For it is the word of God which casts down all enemies and puts them under its feet, so that the whole world becomes subject to God. Do you wish to learn from still another epistle of Paul that the sword with which spiritual enemies are overcome is the word of God? Listen to him as he provides arms for the soldiers of Christ: 'Take unto you the helmet of salvation and the sword of the spirit, that is, the word of God. With all prayer and supplication pray.'[36] By these words he declares very clearly that by the word of God which is a two-edged sword our enemies will fall in our sight.

(12) 'I will look with favor upon you, and make you fruitful.'[37] Full of beatitude is the man upon whom God looks with favor. Do you want to understand how great is the salvation of a man upon whom the Lord looks? Peter had once perished, and at the prompting of the devil through the lips of a servant of the high-priest had destroyed the consecration of his apostolic rank. But when the Lord looked at him, he was lifted up at once.

* *Sermon 106*

On What the Lord Said to Moses: Send Men to
Reconnoiter the Land

(1) When the divine lesson was read just now, we heard the Lord say to Moses: 'Send men to reconnoiter the land of

---
35 Cf. Heb. 4.12.
36 Eph. 6.17,18.
37 Cf. Lev. 26.9.

Chanaan, which I am giving the Israelites. You shall send one man from each ancestral tribe.'[1] After they had been sent out, 'They reached the valley of the cluster of grapes,'[2] and looked at it. 'And they cut down a branch and a cluster of grapes, and carried it upon a pole; they took also with them pomegranates and figs,'[3] in order that they might show the fruitfulness of the land and the quality of the fruits. Now although they had brought these things, nevertheless, they disturbed all the people by saying: 'The land which we were sent to reconnoiter is a country that consumes its inhabitants. And all the people we saw there are huge men, veritable giants, before whom we felt like mere grasshoppers.'[4] 'Hearing this all the people shouted and wept aloud that whole night, and grumbled against Moses and Aaron.'[5]

(2) Whatever happened at that time presented an image and shadow of what was to come. Let us see, then, how these things were fulfilled at the coming of our Lord and Savior. Just as those men whom Moses sent were spies of the promised land, so at the coming of our Lord, the Scribes and Pharisees were spies. They were commanded by the law and the prophets to observe and examine the advent of Christ in whom was the land, that is, holy flesh, the kingdom of God, and an abundance of spiritual fruits, in order that they might reach eternal life. Just as the earlier spies instilled despair in the hearts of the people so they would not believe they could take the land from its owner, so also the Scribes and Pharisees caused the Jewish people to despair, lest they might believe in Christ. If anyone wanted to believe in Him, he was driven out of the synagogue as irreligious. Scripture says: 'And they loved the glory of men more than the glory of God.'[6] Thus, they desired to return to Egypt, loving the onions and melons

---

1 Cf. Num. 13.3.
2 Cf. Num. 13.24.
3 *Ibid.*
4 Cf. Num. 13.33,34.
5 Cf. Num. 14.1,2.
6 John 12.43.

of the Egyptians more than the kingdom promised by the Lord. Therefore, let their faithlessness strengthen our faith, and their death avail to our salvation, for the Apostle testifies that these things were written for our edification. What that land of promise signified will be the kingdom of the saints in the future life, for then the divine majesty will be seen by everyone. However, we can also understand the promised land as the Body of our Lord, which by the grace of the Gospel utters honest sweet truths in virtues and promises.

(3) That cluster of grapes which was brought from the land of promise on a lever across the shoulders of two men further prefigured Christ. Just as it was hung on the wood and brought by the services of those two men, so Christ who came from the flesh of a virgin as from the promised land was between both Testaments, between the two peoples of the Jews and Gentiles, and was hung on the wood of the cross. Now of the two men who walked beneath the burden of that cluster of grapes, the first one signified the Jewish people of whom it is said: 'Let their eyes grow dim so that they cannot see, and keep their backs always feeble.'[7] However, the man who came after prefigured our people, that is, the Gentiles who believe and keep Christ before their eyes. They intend always to follow Him as a servant does his master or a disciple his teacher, as the Lord Himself says in the Gospel: 'If anyone wishes to come after me, let him deny himself, and take up his cross, and follow me.'[8] Moreover, this cluster of grapes poured forth the wine of His Blood which was pressed out under the weight of the cross for our salvation, and gave the Church that chalice of His Passion to drink. For this reason it was said to the apostles at the time of the birth of the Church: 'They are full of new wine.'[9]

(4) Not only did they bring a cluster of grapes with them, but also figs as fruits of the earth. Let us briefly show what

---

7 Ps. 68.24.
8 Matt. 16.24.
9 Acts 2.13.

the figs signify. Our Lord testifies in the Gospel that these figs presented an image of the Old Law, saying: 'A certain householder planted a vineyard, and in his vineyard he planted a fig tree.'[10] Who is this father except Christ our Lord, who is the Father of His family? Moreover, the vineyard signifies the Jewish people, as Isaia says: 'The vineyard of the Lord of hosts is the house of Israel.'[11] In His vineyard He planted a fig tree, that is, He planted the law among His people. Now the fig tree throws its first fruits that are dry and useless upon the ground, and brings to full, perfect maturity others that are produced a second time with rich sweetness. Similarly, the law of the Old Testament, which we said the image of the fig tree represented, threw away the first Jewish people who were useless, that is, sinful and wicked. When these sycophants, to use a Greek word, had been rejected, that is, the conceited and worthless Israelites, there was created for Christ through grace as its mother, the rich and fruitful Christian people who were further brought to perfect knowledge of the Gospel. Although there is a genus of fig trees which brings its first fruits to maturity, called double-bearing, it may signify those of whom it is said: 'The Lord loved those figs as his precursors.'[12] The patriarchs are the precursors. Besides, Jeremia the prophet speaks thus concerning the people of Israel and ours: 'The Lord showed me two baskets of figs; one had very good ones, the other had very bad ones.'[13] This fact, as has often been said, presents an image of the two people, for those two baskets prefigured the synagogue and the Church. The basket of very bad fruit mystically designated the people of the synagogue, while the one with very good fruit pointed out the Church of the Christians. Although they proceed from the root of one tree, that is, from one law, as the Apostle says: 'It is not thou that supportest the stem, but the stem thee,'[14]

---

10 Cf. Luke 13.6.
11 Cf. Isa. 5.7.
12 Cf. Osee 9.10.
13 Cf. Jer. 24.1,2.
14 Rom. 11.18.

still they are distinct in fruits. The one kind of fig tree, which first sprang up with leaves but disappeared and did not reach maturity, represents what happened to the Jewish people. They were produced with the leaves of the fig tree, that is, with the very words of the divine law, but could not arrive at perfect maturity, that is, the sweetness of evangelical grace. The other kind, which lost its first fruits but afterwards was restored, is shown to be the basket of very good figs in Sacred Scripture. This is the Christian people who were created after the offense and rejection of the Jews, for they attained the complete protection of divine grace as David says: 'In your goodness, O God, you provided for the needy.'[15] The blessed Apostle further states: 'It was necessary that the word of God should be spoken to you first, but since you rejected it and judged yourselves unworthy of eternal life, behold, we now turn to the Gentiles.'[16] For this reason it ought to be clear to your minds that the fig tree was an image of the law, just as it is certain that the cluster of grapes prefigured the Savior, as the Church declares in the Canticle of Canticles: 'My brother is for me a cluster of henna.'[17] Christ, indeed, cannot exist without the law, nor the law without Christ, for we have said that the law is evidence of the Gospel, and the Gospel is the fulfillment of the law.

(5) Sacred Scripture further adds that pomegranates were brought along with the cluster of grapes and figs. These pomegranates prefigured the appearance of the Church. This fruit has the useful protection of its shell on the outside, which cannot be torn away by the beating of the winds or penetrated by any injury. Similarly, the Church, which is fortified by the strength of the Holy Ghost and in the firmness of its faith raised up and supported by hope in Christ, perseveres against all the storms of the world, firm and steadfast in the nature of its tree, that is, in the wood of the cross. Besides,

---
15 Ps. 67.11.
16 Cf. Acts 13.46.
17 Cf. Cant. 1.13.

although this kind of fruit is enclosed on the outside by a single shell, it contains within a multitude of seeds which are white but with a red glow. So it is, brethren: Baptism makes men white, the Passion makes them red. These fruits further have a sweet taste that is mixed with some sourness; for this reason Christians should be simple as doves and as clever as serpents. This goodness is both sweet and savory, because it possesses in itself both instruction and austerity. The many seeds indicate the multitude of people, as was mentioned, enclosed on the outside by one shell in such a way that they are, nevertheless, distinguished by an inner covering. In the Church, too, although we are all gathered together in the one Body of Christ as His members, still there are different degrees and honors within, diversities of dignities and differences of graces, as the Apostle says. These graces, merits, and duties are divided and distributed in one and the same Church by one and the same Spirit.

(6) Now all these truths were shown to Israel in the figure of the divine law, but they judged themselves unworthy of the gift of this grace and wanted to return to Egypt, that is, to the world. For this reason they did not merit to receive the land of promise which flowed with milk and honey. Let us see what the land is from which Scripture testifies that milk and honey were flowing. If you say Judea, why to this day no one ever remembers that honey has flowed from the rock or milk from the land there. We ought to consider the land from which milk and honey are said to flow as the Body of Christ, for we can say of this teaching: 'How sweet to my palate are your promises, O Lord! Sweeter than syrup or honey from the comb.'[18] This is the flesh of Christ which according to the law was produced from fruitful soil, that is, the body of a virgin as the Apostle says: 'Born of a woman, born under the Law.'[19] All the goods of this land, that is, the inheritance of the heavenly kingdom which was promised

---

18 Cf. Ps. 118.103.
19 Gal. 4.4.

to the Jews, the servants of Christ or the Christian people obtained through faith in Him. Our Lord called these men Israelites when He said to Nicodemus who already believed in Christ: 'Behold an Israelite in whom there is no guile.'[20] Moreover, when the Apostle wrote to the Church he said: 'Peace upon the Israel of God.'[21] These are most of all the Israel of God, because they merited to see our Lord Jesus Christ in the person of a man through faith, believing God in a man, and believing it was God in Him: to Him is honor and might together with the Father and the Holy Ghost world without end. Amen.

Sermon 107

On the Spies and the Cluster of Grapes

(1) When the sacred lesson was read just now, we heard that at the time when the twelve spies were sent to view the land of promise, two of them brought back on a lever to the children of Israel a bunch of grapes of wonderful size. Those two men can be understood in many ways, dearly beloved, for they are not unfittingly believed to have signified both the two testaments and the two precepts whereby God and the neighbor are loved. They can, likewise, be understood both historically and allegorically. That they were a type of the two testaments, we know definitely from the fact that the grapes are read to have been brought between those two men, just as Christ our Lord is clearly recognized in the middle of the two testaments. According to what is written: 'In the middle of the two animals you will be known,'[1] that is, between the Old and New Testaments. When we read, 'in the middle,'

---
20 John 1.47.
21 Gal. 6.16.

---
1 Cf. Hab. 3.2, LXX.

we are not to understand that Christ was between the New and Old Testaments in such a way that He was contained in neither one. This is not true, beloved brethren, but when it says: 'In the middle of the two animals you will be known,' we must realize that He is in the midst of the Old and New Testaments, that is, within in an interior and spiritual sense. This is not according to the letter which is wont to kill all heretics as well as Jews, but according to the spirit which vivifies all Christians who have spiritual understanding. Therefore, 'In the middle of the two animals you will be known,' means in the inner sense of the New or Old Testament.

(2) Thus, then, the grapes were brought by the two men. Those two men who merited to bring the grapes from the land of promise can be further understood as the two precepts of charity, as we already said, that is: 'Thou shalt love God, and thou shalt love thy neighbor.'[2] Consider besides, brethren, that just as those two men brought the grapes hanging down, so too, it is said concerning those two commands of love of God and neighbor: 'On these two commandments depend the whole Law and the Prophets.'[3] Just as those grapes prefigured Christ the Lord, so the land of promise in which He was born seems to have presented an image of holy Mary, for in her was fulfilled the words: 'Truth shall spring out of the earth.'[4] Moreover, how could Mary have failed to be the land of promise, since she was promised by the prophet much earlier? Through blessed Isaia the Lord had promised her many years before when he said: 'The virgin shall be with child, and bear a son.'[5] Indeed, the grapes were brought from the land of promise, for concerning it we read: 'They sucked honey out of the rock and olive oil from the hard, stony ground,'[6] (and of this it is written: 'but the rock was Christ'[7]) 'with the fat

---

2 Cf. Matt. 22.37,39.
3 Cf. Matt. 22.40.
4 Ps. 84.12.
5 Isa. 7.14.
6 Cf. Deut. 32.13.
7 1 Cor. 10.4.

of lambs and the blood of the grape';[8] and again: 'He washes his garment in wine, his robe in the blood of grapes.'[9] These grapes were hung on the wood, I repeat, and carried because of the obedience of those two men. Surely, it was represented to us in the words of the two testaments, as was already mentioned, because it hung on the wood of the cross and in the sufferings of the Passion its wine flowed forth as the price for us.

(3) It is worthwhile for the secrets of the mysteries to be revealed by the ensuing events. Taking a lever, the two men brought those grapes hanging down from it. Those two men may prefigure the Jewish and Christian people. Therefore, they are the two people of the synagogue and the Church, and since the Jewish people came first, the Jew precedes while the Christian follows. The latter kept his salvation before his eyes, the former kept it behind him; the one yields to it, the other shows it contempt. Thus, the prophet testifies concerning the Jews: 'Let their eyes grow dim so that they cannot see, and keep their backs always feeble.'[10] The two men proceed in order under their sacred bundle; the one always sees it, the other leaves it behind. Moreover, the Jew judges that his neighbor is himself and keeps away; therefore, the Christian enjoys the present gift, while the Jew is only weighed down by the burden, for just as Christ is salvation to the believer, so He is a burden to the unbeliever. To the Jews He was, indeed, especially announced, but of them it is said: 'He came unto his own, and his own received him not,'[11] for He became to them a stone of stumbling and a rock of scandal. Since Israel did not recognize Him, the faith of the Gentiles welcomed Him. For this reason the one man followed after but advanced and progressed with his hope before his eyes; the other walked first but deserted and withdrew. The Jew, indeed, carried Christ in the law, but turned away from the

---
8 Cf. Deut. 32.14.
9 Gen. 49.11.
10 Ps. 68.24.
11 John 1.11.

grace which he carried in mystery. He whom the elected received in preaching the unbeliever lost from his heart; although the one despised Him in the law, the other admired Him in the Body. Therefore, the Lord and Redeemer of both is carried by the one who adores Him, but is suspended by the one who turns away from Him. Thus was fulfilled in the Jews the words: 'They turn to me their backs, not their faces.'[12]

(4) Since the former people of the Jews left Christ the Lord behind their backs and crucified Him, we who came after have merited to worship and carry Him. Therefore, in accord with the words of the Apostle: 'Glorify God and bear him in your body,'[13] with His help, let us labor as much as we can not to lay aside from our necks such a sacred load by our evil deeds. Indeed, the burden of Christ is wont to lift up a man and not weigh him down, as He Himself tells us in the Gospel: 'My yoke is easy, and my burden light.'[14] If we humbly lower our neck to receive the yoke of Christ, it will carry us rather than be carried by us; for as the yoke of the world always presses a man down, so Christ's yoke is wont to lift him up. Now since every man is either raised up by carrying Christ or pressed down to lower things by bearing the yoke of the world, each one should examine his own conscience. If a man knows that by his holy thoughts and good works he carries the yoke of Christ, he should rejoice and thank God, endeavoring to persevere with great solicitude and fear. But if he realizes that by his wicked thoughts and evil deeds he is burdened with the very harsh yoke of this world, he should throw off the devil's yoke by prayer, fasting, and almsgiving, in order to merit receiving the yoke of Christ. Let him further faithfully say with the prophet concerning his evil deeds: 'Let us break their fetters and cast their bonds from us!'[15] We will be able to drink with a secure conscience of that spiritual grape from which the wine of joy was extracted

---
12 Cf. Jer. 2.27.
13 1 Cor. 6.20.
14 Matt. 11.30.
15 Ps. 2.3.

by the weight of the cross, provided that dissipation has not defiled us, anger inflamed us, pride inflated us, avarice dimmed our souls, or envy with its viperlike poison struck us. All these things a man should drive out of his heart if he desires and longs to approach the Lord's altar. Now the spiritual vintage, that is, the Feast of Easter, is at hand, the solemnity on which that cluster of grapes which we mentioned before was pressed out through insult and by the weight of the cross. Since we are going to receive the chalice of salvation from such grapes and will drink the wine of joy, let us diligently cleanse the receptacles of our heart and soul with great brilliance by fasting, vigils, prayer, almsgiving, and especially the splendor of chastity. Let us harbor in our hearts hatred for no man, loving not only our friends but also our enemies and adversaries, so that we may say with a clear conscience in the Lord's Prayer: 'Forgive us our debts, as we also forgive our debtors';[16] with the help of our Lord Jesus Christ, to whom is honor and might together with the Father and the Holy Ghost forever and ever. Amen.

* *Sermon 108*

On the Twelve Scouts

(1) As we heard in the lesson which was read to us just now, dearly beloved, twelve scouts from the children of Israel were sent to view the land which had been promised to them. After forty days they returned, bringing back varied reports. Ten of them sent the people into despair, with the result that they wanted to get rid of Moses, choose another leader, and return into Egypt. However, the other two men brought good reports and encouraged the people to remain loyal, saying: 'If the

---

16 Matt. 6.12.

Lord loves us, he will bring us into this land.'[1] Now the Lord said to Moses: 'I will strike them with death, and wipe them out. Then I will make the house of your father a nation, greater and mightier than they.'[2] This threat is not a sign of wrath, but a prophecy. Another nation was to be taken over, that is, the people of the Gentiles, but not through Moses. Moses excused himself, for he knew that the great nation which was promised was not to be called through him, but through Jesus Christ. Those people would not be called Mosaic, but Christian.

(2) The Lord further added: 'Your children must wander in the desert for forty years.'[3] Moreover, He explains the meaning of that mysterious number by saying: 'Forty days you spent in scouting the land; forty years shall you suffer for your sins: one year for each day.'[4] For my part I am afraid to examine the secrets of this mystery, for I see comprehended in it the calculation of sins and punishment. If each sinner is assigned punishment for the sin of one day, and according to the number of days he sins must spend so many years in punishment, I fear that perhaps for us who sin daily and spend no day of our life without offense, even ages and ages will not suffice to pay our penalties. In the fact that for forty days of sin those people were afflicted in the desert for forty years and not permitted to enter the holy land, a kind of similarity to the future judgment seems to be evident. At that time the number of sins will have to be calculated, unless perchance there is the balance of good works or of evils which a man has suffered in his life, as Abraham taught concerning Lazarus. However, it is within the power of no one to know these things perfectly, except Him to whom 'The Father has given all judgment.'[5]

(3) Perhaps someone may deny that it is befitting God's

---

1 Cf. Num. 14.8.
2 Cf. Num. 14.12.
3 Num. 14.33.
4 Cf. Num. 14.34.
5 Cf. John 5.22.

goodness to repay a year's punishment for the sin of one day; in fact, even if He requites a day for a day, He does not seem to be merciful or kind, although just. Therefore, listen to these words, for we may be able to explain the difficult situation by clearer examples. I exhort you, brethren, to pay careful attention. If a wound is inflicted on the body, bones are broken, or the joint of nerves is destroyed, the wounds usually come to bodies within the space of an hour but are cured only with difficulty after a long time of extreme torment and pain. How much infection there is in one place, how much torture is felt! Now if it should happen that in the same wound or fracture a person is wounded repeatedly, with what great penalties and torments can he be cured and healed? In how long a time is he brought back to health, if that is even possible? Scarcely ever will he be cured in such a way that he escapes physical weakness or the ugliness of a scar. Now I pass from an example of the body to wounds of the soul. As often as a soul sins, so many times it is wounded. Lest you doubt that it is wounded by sins as with swords and javelins, hear the Apostle advising us to take up 'The shield of faith, with which you may be able to quench all the fiery darts of the wicked one.'[6] Therefore, you see that sins are the darts or javelins of the wicked one which are directed against the soul. In addition to wounds from darts, the soul also suffers fractures of the feet, because snares are prepared for its feet and its steps are supplanted. In how long a time do you think these wounds and others like them can be cured? O if we could see how our inner man is wounded by each sin, how an evil word inflicts a wound! Have you not read that: 'Swords wound, but not as much as the tongue'?[7] Therefore, the soul is wounded by the tongue, as also by evil thoughts and desires; it is broken and crushed by sinful deeds. If we were able to see all these things and to perceive the scars of a wounded soul, it is certain that we would resist sin

---
6 Eph. 6.16.
7 Cf. Ecclus. 28.22.

even unto death. However, just as those who suffer delirium or have lost their reason do not feel it if they are wounded, because they lack natural sensations, so we cannot feel how great our wounds are and what great misery of soul we have acquired by sin, if we have become mad with worldly pleasures or inebriated with vice. For this reason it follows most naturally that the time of punishment, that is, of cure and remedy, is extended, and for each wound the length of the healing is also prolonged depending upon the nature of the injury.

(4) We have said this, brethren, so that you may know that in the Old Testament God's justice orders a year's punishment to make up for the sin of one day. In other words, the people were tormented in the desert for forty years because of the defection of forty days. What will happen to us if, after receiving the grace of Christ who redeemed us with His own Blood, we still take pleasure in committing not only slight sins but perhaps even criminal offenses? Therefore, as I have frequently advised, if a man knows he has committed some serious sin, he should have recourse to the remedies of repentance while there is still time and it is within his power to do so. Indeed, conversion in the present life and penance that is fruitfully performed bring a swift cure to wounds of this kind, for repentance not only heals a past wound but also guards the soul against further injury through sin. Now I will add something more. For example, if I am a sinner will I suffer the same punishment if I have offended just once, as I will if I sin twice or a third time and even more frequently? Not at all. The amount of punishment is to be measured according to the manner, number, and measure of sin, for God will give us 'the bread of tears and tears to drink,' but 'with ample measure.'[8] Every man will then reap the things he sought in this life by sinning more or less.

(5) These matters, as we said, are in God's hands. Our concern it is to hasten to amend our lives at once, to turn to penance without dissimulation, to grieve over the past, to

---
8 Ps. 79.6.

guard agains future falls, and to invoke God's help. 'As soon as you are converted with groaning, you shall be saved';[9] for you will find an advocate to intercede with the Father on your behalf. This is the Lord Jesus, who is much more excellent than Moses who prayed for the people and was heard. Perhaps Moses is recorded to have intervened for the sins of the first people and to have obtained pardon, so that we might have all the more confidence that Jesus our advocate will give us certain forgiveness from the Father, if only we are converted to Him and do not turn aside our hearts. 'My dear children, these things I say to you in order that you may not sin. But if anyone of us sins, we have an advocate with the Father, Jesus Christ the just, who will intercede for our sins.'[10] To Him is glory forever and ever. Amen.

Sermon 109

On the Spies and the Forty Years Spent in the Desert

(1) Those forty years we heard about when the sacred lesson was read just now, dearly beloved, occurred when the children of Israel lingered in the desert on very long paths of the road, and portrayed the difficult, arduous labors of human miseries in the present life. Because of the numerous sins which abound in this life, no more than two men out of six hundred thousand entered the promised land. As the Lord Himself said to the unbelieving people: 'Since you grumbled against me you shall not enter the land which I promised on oath to your fathers: but your little ones I will bring in to the land you spurned.'[1] Those older people who died in the desert because of their

---
9 Cf. Isa. 30.15.
10 Cf. 1 John 2.1,2.

---
1 Cf. Num. 14.29,30,23,31.

unbelief, dearly beloved, signified the first people of the Jews, while the children or younger people prefigured the Gentiles. Just as the younger people received the promised land after the death of their elders, so the younger people of the Christians obtained the grace of divine benediction after the rejection of the Jews. Now there were two men who proclaimed to the people as they murmured, that if the Lord were favorable He would give them a land flowing with milk and honey. Perhaps they are the same two men whom we read brought the people of Israel grapes of wonderful size hanging on a piece of wood. Nevertheless, dearly beloved, we should not consider in passing or carelessly, but with great fear and trembling, what was said above, that only two men out of six hundred thousand entered the promised land. If anyone wants God to be so merciful that He is not believed just, he should listen to these truths. If we notice carefully, beloved brethren, our God both was merciful toward the six hundred thousand who died in the wilderness, and appeared just to the two men who entered the land of promise. How could He fail to be merciful, when He preserved them for forty years and awaited their repentance? However, not only did they refuse to be converted, but even by their frequent rebellion and murmuring against the Lord added an ever heavier load to the mass of their sins. How does He fail to be merciful, when He waits so long for us to amend our lives? Can His extended mercy take justice away from God, who is a just judge? Indeed, the longer He waits, the more severely He punishes. When we sin for a long time and still suffer no evil from the Lord, it is due to His patience, not His neglect; He has not lost His power, but reserves us for repentance. Therefore, He was merciful to those who died in the desert after He had tolerated them with such longsuffering, and He was also just to those two men whom He brought into the promised land upon the merits of their faith.

(2) Someone may say that even if they had repented they could not have entered the promised land, because God had

passed definite sentence upon them when He said: 'You shall not enter the land which I promised on oath to your fathers, but your bodies shall fall here in the desert.'² This is not true, beloved brethren; if only the sinner would have recourse to repentance as quickly as God is willing to change that fixed sentence. Listen to the Lord Himself through the prophet promise the greatest hope to the human race: 'I will suddenly threaten a nation that I will do evil to them for their sins; but if they repent of their iniquities, I also will repent of the evil which I threatened to do to them, and will not do it.'³ Behold how great is our God's goodness to us, brethren, and learn whether He will refuse His mercy, since He longs to change His sentence if we be converted. Therefore, let us turn to Him, dearly beloved, and not wish to defer our amendment until the end of our life. Let us listen to the prophet when he says: 'Delay not your conversion to the Lord, put it not off from day to day,'⁴ 'for you know not what any day may bring forth.'⁵ O man, why do you delay from day to day, when perhaps today you are going to have your last day? For this reason let us always call to mind with great fear and trembling, dearly beloved, that so great is the justice of our God that, as was already said above, out of six hundred thousand only two men entered the land of promise. If we will continually reflect upon these truths with a humble and contrite heart, instilling into ourselves a salutary fear, we will derive remedies for ourselves from the wounds of others and their death will avail to our salvation. Notice carefully who those two men are that invite the Jewish people to the land of promise, and what they spiritually signify. The two of them represent the New and Old Testaments; under the leadership of those two men, that is, of the Old and New Testaments, the promised land or eternal happiness is reached. Concerning those two Testaments, we read: 'In the middle of the

---

2 Cf. Num. 14.30,23,32.
3 Cf. Jer. 18.7,8.
4 Ecclus. 5.8.
5 Cf. Prov. 27.1.

two animals you will be known';[6] for although the Old and New Testaments in some places differ in the letter, still they agree in truth and both say one thing in a different way. Nevertheless, those two men can be understood in another way. The ascent to the promised land was made under two leaders, because Christ is reached historically and allegorically, by faith and works, by love of God and charity toward the neighbor.

(3) Again and again I beseech and exhort you, brethren, always to reflect with great fear and anxiety upon that severity and just judgment of God whereby the elder people were destroyed for their sin of murmuring in the desert. May we so love the mercy of God that we may, nevertheless, fear His justice. He spares now but is not silent; He is silent now but will not always be so. In His ineffable goodness He not only admonishes us now but also entreats us, in order to recall us from our deadly sins. Let us heed Him while He pleads with us, so that later He may not fail to hear us when He judges. Let us listen to Him say through the prophet: 'Son, have pity on your own soul, pleasing God.'[7] What do you reply to these words, human frailty? God asks you to have pity on your soul, and you will not; He pleads your case with you and cannot obtain it from you. How, then, will He listen to you begging on judgment day, when you have been unwilling to heed Him pleading in your behalf? Indeed, who would not shudder and fear, beloved brethren, at the thought that in return for a space of forty days the Jewish people merited to receive punishment in the desert for forty years? If a year's punishment is to repay the sin of one day, I am afraid that unless the remedies of almsgiving and penance come to our aid, we who daily commit so many sins will be afflicted with eternal, not temporal, punishments.

(4) Since remedies usually more speedily help fresh wounds, whenever we sin let us not with deadly self-assurance wait for

---

6 Cf. Hab. 3.2, LXX.
7 Cf. Ecclus. 30.24.

the wounds to decay, nor again add wound upon wound; but let us immediately have recourse to a spiritual physician and hasten to recover salvation. Thus, when we receive a bodily wound we can quickly recover our health if we seek remedies at once, but if there is a delay it is inevitable that the wound returns to soundness more slowly or that some kind of a scar will remain on the body. If we do this with regard to the body, how much more should we apply in wounds of the soul where we have been made to the image and likeness of God? If we devote so much care to the body which must be reduced to dust whether we will it or not, how much careful solicitude we ought to exert for the salvation of our soul, so that, as the Apostle says, we may merit to appear before the tribunal of the eternal judge without spot or wrinkle. Otherwise, if perchance we come to that marriage feast lacerated with many wounds of sin and covered with the filthy rags of vices, what the heavenly bridegroom said in the Gospel may be said to us: 'Friend, how didst thou come in here without a wedding garment?'[8] May God avert from us what follows: When that sinner heard this and was silent, the head of the family continued: 'Bind his hands and feet and cast him forth into the darkness outside, where there will be the weeping, and the gnashing of teeth.'[9] Behold, what kind of sentence will surely be received by those who show greater solicitude for their body than for their soul, thinking more how their body may live for this very short time in the sight of men, than how their soul may reach the bliss and likeness of the angels, adorned with good works. Therefore, if we will reflect upon these truths with greater attention, as I have begged you before, dearly beloved, we will seek remedies for ourselves in time of need. Then, when the day of judgment comes, we will not be punished with wicked sinners, but along with the just and God-fearing men will happily come to eternal rewards: with the help of our Lord Jesus Christ, to whom is honor

---
8 Matt. 22.12.
9 Cf. Matt. 22.13.

and might together with the Father and the Holy Ghost world without end. Amen.

*Sermon 110

St. Jerome on the Censers of Core and Dathan

(1) When the divine lesson was read just now, dearly beloved, we heard that our Lord told Moses to forge the censers in which those haughty, rebellious men had offered incense, beat them flat, and fasten them to the altar as a sign of the rebellious and proud. 'Because the sinners have consecrated the censers at the cost of their lives,' said the Lord, 'have them hammered into plates to cover the altar, because in being presented before the Lord they have become sacred.'[1] By this figure it seems to have been shown that those censers which Scripture calls brazen represent the sacred writings. Heretics put strange fire in these writings, that is, they introduce a perverse meaning and a sense that is foreign to God and contrary to the truth, thus offering to the Lord an incense that is not sweet but abominable. If we bring these brazen censers, that is, words of the heretics, to the altar of God where there is divine fire, the true preaching of the faith, the same truth will shine all the better in comparison with what is false. For, to mention an example, if I lay down the words of Arians or Manichaeans or any other heretics and refute them with the words of truth and the testimony of Sacred Scripture as the fire of the divine altar, will not the impiety of the former appear all the more evident in comparison with the latter? If the doctrine of the Church were simple and not surrounded by the assertions of heretical doctrines from without, our faith could not appear so clear

---
1 Cf. Num. 16.37,38.

and well-verified. However, due to the fact that the attack of objectors besets Catholic doctrine, our faith does not become paralyzed through inactivity, but is perfected by much exercise. For this reason the Apostle used to say: 'There must be factions, so that those who are approved may also be made manifest among you.'[2] In other words, the altar must be surrounded by the censers of heretics, so that the difference between the faithful and unbelievers may become certain and clear to everyone. When the faith of the Church begins to shine like gold and its preaching glitters to all that behold it like silver that has been tried by fire, then the words of heretics will be despised wtih greater shame and disgrace because of the worthlessness of their dull brass. Concerning the censers of those who were condemned, we have said that when they were commanded to be fastened to the altar, the just appeared more illustrious in comparison with the wicked. Moreover, an example was given to those who followed that no one with the presumption of a haughty spirit should seize the priestly office if it has not been given to him. He should rather yield to one whom no human ambition or favor has corrupted and no profane offer of bribes has chosen, but who has been claimed by a recognition of his merits and the will of God. What those proud Levites suffered because they assumed the priesthood without the Lord's command, will also be endured by men who attempt to install themselves in the office of bishop, priest, or deacon by means of bribes or flattery. Just as the former men were destroyed physically, so the latter are consumed in heart.

(2) Then Moses encouraged the high priest to offer incense in the camp and to pray for the people: 'For the people have already begun to be destroyed.'[3] Moses saw in spirit what was happening, and, therefore, Aaron departed to offer incense for the people. He stood between the living and the dead, and the Lord's fury was alleviated. If you know the course

---
2 1 Cor. 11.19.
3 Cf. Num. 16.46.

of history and have been able to perceive with your eyes, so to speak, the priest standing in the middle between the living and the dead, rise now to the loftier heights of these words. See how the true priest, Jesus Christ, took the censer of human flesh, put fire on the altar which doubtless is that splendid soul with which He was born in the flesh, further added incense which is His pure spirit, stood between the living and the dead, and did not allow death to proceed any farther. As the Apostle said: 'He destroyed him who had the empire of death, that is, the devil,'[4] with the result that anyone who believes in Christ our high priest will no longer die but live forever. Therefore, this was the mystery which the angel who destroyed the people dreaded, even though it was to happen afterwards. He recognized the figure of the censer, fire and incense. He foresaw what kind of a victim was to be offered to God by the true high priest, Christ, who was to be established between the living and the dead. The image which was prefigured saved them at that time, but the truth of salvation has come to us. That destroying angel had not blushed at those garments of the high priest which were purple and woven of wool and fine linen, but he knew what would be the garments of our Lord and Savior, the eminent high priest; moreover, he yielded to them, for every creature is inferior to them.

(3) I believe further that the image was not only completed at the first advent of our Lord and Savior, but will probably also be kept at His second coming. Truly the Son of man will come again, and when He does, doubtless He will find some living and some dead. At this point the dead are not unfittingly understood as those who are proven to have died in their sins because of the excess of their offenses, while the living are those who persevered in the good works of their lives. Nevertheless, somehow this high priest who is our Savior in the future will stand between the living and the dead. Perhaps then He is to be said standing between the living and the dead, when He puts the sheep on His right hand and the

---

4 Heb. 2.14.

goats on His left. To those who are on the right He will say: 'Come, blessed of my Father, receive the kingdom which was prepared for you from the foundation of the world,'[5] and so forth. But to those on the left He will say: 'Depart, you workers of iniquity, into the everlasting fire which my father has prepared for the devil and his angels, for I know you not.'[6] Surely, those who are cast into eternal fire are the dead, while those who are sent into the kingdom are the living. May the good Lord in His kindness deign to bring us to this kingdom: to whom is honor and might together with the Father and the Holy Ghost world without end. Amen.

* *Sermon 111*

On the Rod of Aaron

(1) Every leader of a tribe of people has a rod, for no man can rule people unless he possesses one. For this reason the Apostle Paul who was a leader of the people said: 'What is your wish? Shall I come to you with a rod, or in love and in the spirit of meekness?'[1] Therefore, all the princes of the tribes must have rods, but there is only one true high priest, as Scripture says, of whom the high priest Aaron presented a figure. For this reason his rod blossomed. Just as Aaron's rod sprouted among the Jewish people, so the cross of Christ flowered among the Gentiles. However, since Christ is the true high priest, as we have often said, He is the only one whose rod of the cross not only sprouted but blossomed, and produced the fruit of all believers.

(2) What is the fruit which it bore? 'Ripe almonds.'[2]

---
5 Cf. Matt. 25.34.
6 Cf. Matt. 25.41; 7.23.

1 1 Cor. 4.21.
2 Num. 17.8.

Almonds are nuts, brethren. This fruit is bitter, indeed, in its first covering, is protected and defended by the second, but in the third part feeds and nourishes whoever eats it. Such, then, is knowledge of the law and the prophets in Christ's Church. The first appearance of the letter is quite bitter, because it commands circumcision of the flesh, enjoins sacrifices, and ordains other things which are designated as the killing letter. Throw away all these things as the bitter shell of the nut. In the second place, you will come to the protective covering, in which is indicated moral doctrine or the idea of self-restraint. This is necessary for the protection of what is kept inside, but doubtless must sometimes be broken and destroyed. For example, fasting and chastisement of the body are no doubt necessary as long as we are in this corruptible body which is subject to suffering. However, when it has been destroyed and dissolved at the approach of death, it will become incorruptible at the time of the resurrection when it has been restored from corruption, spiritual after being natural, and without any flattery to the body will dominate, with no difficult suffering or propitiatory fasting but by its own nature. Thus, then, that rather hard covering of the nut seems to be a means of self-control at present that will not be sought later. Thirdly, you will find hidden as in the nut the secret meaning of the mysteries of God's wisdom and knowledge. With these, holy souls are nourished and fed, not only in the present life, but also in the future one. This is that priestly fruit concerning which it is promised to those 'who hunger and thirst for justice, for they shall be satisfied.'[3] In this way, then, the threefold character of this mystery runs through all the Scriptures. Thus wisdom, too, admonishes us to inscribe them 'in our hearts in three manners of ways: to answer the word of truth to those who sent us.'[4] Since the mystery of the priesthood is the rod of the nut, for this reason I think Jeremia, who was one of the priests from Anathoth, saw a rod

---

3 Cf. Matt. 5.6.
4 Cf. Prov. 22.20,21.

made of the root of a nut. Moreover, he prophesied concerning what was written, concerning that rod and the metal vessel or boiling cauldron. By this means he seemed to show that in the rod of the nut was life, death in the boiling cauldron. Indeed, both life and death are put before our countenance. Life is Christ in the mystery of the nut, death is the devil in the figure of the boiling cauldron. Therefore, if you sin you will take your part with the boiling cauldron, but if you live justly your portion will be in the rod of the nut together with the high priest. Moreover, in the Canticle of Canticles the spouse is said to go down into the garden of nuts, where He is recorded to have found an abundance of some sort of priestly fruits together with the nuts.

(3) Notice carefully, brethren, that God promised one thing on the rod but He gave more. It is true, brethren. Our Lord acted as He usually does, for He always gives more than He promises. 'The staff of the man of my choice,' He says, 'shall sprout.'[5] This alone God promised, that the staff of whomever He would choose would blossom. But when it comes to showing the fulfillment of His promise, not only is He said to have done what He promised, but see how much was added. Scripture indeed says: 'Behold the staff of Aaron, representing the house of Levi, sprouted.'[6] Without any doubt this is the only thing that was promised. But others are added, for it is said: 'And it bore leaves and blossoms and nuts.'[7] Therefore, although God only promised a bud, see how much He generously bestowed. Not only did He produce a bud, but also leaves; not only leaves, but flowers too; and not only flowers, but even fruits.

(4) Now let us see what can be gathered and considered from these truths. First of all, we recognize clearly in them the mystery of the resurrection of all men from the dead: the dry staff blossoms, while the dead body begins to come to life

---

5 Cf. Num. 17.5.
6 Cf. Num. 17.8.
7 *Ibid.*

again. Furthermore, what are the four things which will be manifest in the body when it rises again? What was sown in corruption shall rise in incorruption, what was sown in weakness shall rise in power, what was sown in dishonor shall rise in glory, what was sown a natural body shall rise a spiritual body. These are the four things which the dry rod of our body will sprout at the resurrection. However, let us return to what we had begun to say about the staff.

(5) We can still recognize differences in the things which blossomed on the staff. Every man who believes in Christ first dies and then is reborn; this is also a figure that the dry staff afterwards sprouts. Therefore, the first bud is a man's first confession in Christ. Next, it becomes leafy when the man who is reborn receives the gift of God's grace and the sanctification of the spirit. Then, it produces blossoms when he begins to advance, to be adorned with a pleasing character, and to shed the fragrance of mercy and kindness. Lastly, he also brings forth fruits of justice whereby he not only lives himself, but also gives life to others with the assistance of God. When he reaches perfection, of himself speaks the word of faith, the word of knowledge of God, and by his teaching gains others, then he has produced fruits to nourish other men. Thus, then, each one of the faithful blossoms from the staff of Aaron which is Christ. The four differences among them are indicated in other places of Scripture as four ages, and the Apostle John includes them in his epistle with a mystical distinction. He says, indeed: 'I have written to you, little ones; I have written to you, young men; I have written to you, youthful ones; I have written to you, fathers';[8] and in these words he does not indicate physical ages but differences of spiritual progress. Thus, even here, we observe designated the blossom of the priestly staff.

(6) Now all these facts are not considered the same in the staff of Aaron as in the rod which came forth from the root of Jesse, where a flower rose up out of his root and the Spirit

---
8 Cf. 1 John 2.14,13,14,13.

of God rested upon him. In this it is not a matter of indifference that the rod is said to have come forth and the flower to rise up. Although Christ is one, still He becomes different in individual cases, according as there is need for Him to operate. If a man is rather slothful and careless, Christ becomes for him a rod of discipline, and in the rod He is said to come forth and not rise. Truly, the unprofitable, cowardly soul must go out of that condition in which he does not live properly, and cross over to another condition like the staff, under the compulsion or admonition of a more rigid doctrine's severity. However, since the just shall flourish like the palm tree, Christ is said to rise up in this kind of man. Therefore, if a man needs a whipping, the staff goes out to him; but if he progresses in justice, it rises up in him as a blossom. Moreover, it rises as long as a man produces the fruits of the Spirit which are charity, joy, peace, patience, and the other virtues: in Christ Jesus our Lord, to whom is honor and glory forever and ever. Amen.

Sermon 112

On the Brazen Serpent and the Rod of Moses

(1) In the lesson which was read to us, dearly beloved, we heard about the time when the people were destroyed in the desert by serpents or basilisks, because of the pride of the Jews and their murmuring against the Lord. Moreover, the Lord commanded Moses to make a brazen serpent and hang it on a tree, so that anyone who had been struck might look on it and be healed from death. Although this serpent seems to be quite wonderful, dearly beloved, still it prefigured the Incarnation of the Lord. Perhaps this thought might seem difficult to some men, if the Lord Himself had not spoken in the Gospel. Thus He said: 'As Moses lifted up the serpent in the

desert, even so must the Son of Man be lifted up.'¹ That brazen serpent was then hung on a pole, because Christ was to be hung on the cross. At that time whoever had been struck by a serpent looked on the brazen serpent and was healed. Now the human race which was struck by the spiritual serpent, the devil, looks upon Christ with faith and is healed. If a man had been struck and failed to behold that brazen serpent, he died. So it is, brethren: if a man does not believe in Christ crucified, he is slain by the poison of the devil. Then, a man looked at the dead serpent in order to escape the live one; now, if a man wants to avoid the devil's poison, he looks on Christ crucified. Death receives its name from a deadly bite, and it befell the human race because of the bite of the ancient serpent. Moreover, death could not be conquered except by death, so Christ suffered death in order that His unjust death might overcome the just death. By dying for them unjustly, He freed those who were rightly guilty. Whatever the devil did in the case of Adam, he seems to have done justly in the case of that man who sold himself for the pleasure of a single tree. Therefore, in Adam, as in his own servant, he rightly claimed dominion for himself as the master, but in the sufferings of Christ in whom he did not find a stain of sin, he performed his wicked deeds unjustly. As the Lord Himself said in the Gospel: 'Behold the prince of this world is coming, and in me he finds nothing.'² What does this mean, he finds nothing? No sin at all. In the psalms He further says: 'I must restore what I did not take away.'³ For this reason, by suffering death unjustly, Christ payed what Adam justly owed. The latter stretched out his hand to sweet fruits, the former extended them to the bitter cross; the one points out the tree of death, the other the tree of salvation. The one lifted himself up against God and fell; Christ humbled Himself in order to raise up all men. Adam brought death to everyone, Christ

---

1 John 3.14.
2 Cf. John 14.30.
3 Ps. 68.5.

restored life to them all. At that time each one who looked on the brazen serpent was healed of the poisonous serpents. The brazen serpent which was put on a tree overcame the poison of the living serpents; when Christ hung on the cross and died, He suppressed the ancient poison of the devil and freed all men who had been struck by him.

(2) Let us see why that serpent was not made of gold or silver, but of brass. It seems to me that this fact may have two significations: first, because of its durability, since bronze vessels usually last longer; and secondly, because of the clearness of its sound, for among all metals bronze vases are wont to ring louder and resound longer. Instruction could not become known only in the one nation of the Jews, but with the clear sound of salutary preaching reaches throughout the world. Therefore, that brazen serpent was made, so that the doctrine of Christ might be preached more distinctly in the whole world, according to what was written concerning the apostles: 'Through all the earth their voice resounds, and to the ends of the world, their message.'[4]

(3) Furthermore, even according to the teaching of physical doctors who prepare wholesome antidotes out of a dead serpent to be used against the poisons of living snakes, it is not at all improper that a man who desires to be freed from the poisons of living serpents should hold up a dead one. Now we have mentioned all these facts so that anyone who has been struck by the poisons of the serpent, that is, of the devil and his angels, may always devoutly look upon Christ who hung on the cross like that brazen serpent. Then they may be able to say with the blessed Apostle Paul: 'God forbid that I should glory save in the cross of our Lord Jesus Christ, through whom the world is crucified to me, and I to the world.'[5]

(4) Since it is pleasant and salutary to talk more at length about the mystery of the blessed cross, if you wish we will briefly suggest other ideas of it to the ears of your charity.

---
4 Ps. 18.5.
5 Gal. 6.14.

Indeed, what can be mentioned or imagined sweeter or more delightful than the mystery of the holy cross, whereby we have merited, not only to be recalled from hell, but even to be lifted up to heaven? Without any doubt we trust that the members of Christ will follow Him where we believe that He has ascended as our head. A shadow or figures of the wood of the cross were very common even in the Old Testament. Moses performed no sign without the mysterious wood, for he received from the Lord a rod to work wonders and prodigies in Egypt. Moreover, as a sign that he had heard things divinely, it was said to him: 'Lift up your staff.'[6] God, of course, did not need the assistance of a staff; but it was raised so that we might know how great was the mystery of that future wood which was prefigured by the shadow of this staff. When by chance the Red Sea was to be divided, Moses was commanded to lift up his staff. And the sea recognized the figure of the wood to come, immediately extending an unusual path for the people. When the bitter waters of Mara were reached, they would not have become sweet if they had not received the wood of the staff. This fact was a sign that the bitterness of the Gentiles would sometime be changed into a habit of sweetness by the wood of the cross. Furthermore, whenever the people did not have water to drink, a rock was struck with the wood; then it produced by grace what it did not have by nature. When the cruel enemy Amalec came, Josue was commanded to hold the staff in his hand and Moses extended his arms in the form of a cross. Thus, by the figure of the cross, an invincible enemy was overcome. Neither was Eliseus ignorant of the power of this mystical wood, for when an axe fell from its handle into the water, he brought it back from the depths by throwing a piece of wood in the river. This signified the hard hearts and unyielding necks of men which were later to be subdued by the wood of the cross after having been submerged in the abyss of error. O blessed cross which makes men blessed! O cross, from which such great and

---

6 Exod. 14.16.

wonderful fruits are gathered! The fruit of the cross is a glorious resurrection. This fruit of the wood is truly planted 'near running water,'[7] for Baptism is always joined to the cross. However, this wood produced 'its fruit in due season,'[8] at the Lord's Resurrection. It will do so again when He appears from heaven, 'is seen on earth,'[9] and with the dazzling sign of the cross preceding Him, comes from above. Then, the bodies of all men who are buried will rise again, and then, 'The faithful shall exult in glory.'[10] Then those who are not confounded now because of the cross of their King and Lord but rather glory in it, 'shall sing for joy upon their couches.'[11] To Him is honor and glory together with the Father and the Holy Ghost world without end. Amen.

* *Sermon 113*

St. Jerome in the Middle of Lent on Balaam and Balac

(1) When the divine lesson was read, dearly beloved, we heard: 'The children of Israel moved on and encamped in the plains of Moab, near the Jordan over against Jericho, and as Balac the son of Sepphor saw it,'[1] and so forth. All the other details which are recorded concerning Balaam and his ass are historically full of difficulty, but their inner meaning is still more difficult. In fact, I do not know whether it will be easy to explain just the historical ideas. However, with God's help, we will briefly relate whatever we can. A war threatens you, King Balac, the son of Sepphor. Six hundred

---
7 Ps. 1.3.
8 *Ibid.*
9 Cf. Bar. 3.38.
10 Ps. 149.5.
11 *Ibid.*

---
1 Cf. Num. 22.1,2.

thousand armed men are rushing into your borders. There was need for you to prepare arms, collect an army, and think about construction works for battle, in order to meet well-armed the enemy who was still located at a distance. However, you sent to the soothsayer Balaam, offering many gifts and promising still greater ones. You say to him: 'Come, and curse this people that has come out of Egypt.'[2] But Balaam, as the Scriptures inform us, referred the matter to God who forbids him to come. Again, the king sent ambassadors, and neglecting arms put all his hope in Balaam. He wanted him to come and bring words, hurling curses against the people instead of weapons. Perhaps by the words of Balaam the people might be overcome, since the king's army could not accomplish this. Now we have first mentioned all these things in order that we may be able to notice the actions and words of Balaam. Indeed, there are some differences in seers, some are more powerful and others less.

(2) This Balaam was exceedingly famous for his magical art, and very powerful with his harmful verses. He did not possess the power or skill of words in blessing but only in cursing, for the demons are invited to curse but not to bless. As he was experienced in such matters, for this reason he was esteemed by all men in the Orient. Indeed, unless abundant proofs of it had happened before when he had frequently turned back an armed enemy with his curses, the king surely would not have presumed that what could not be accomplished by iron and the sword could be done by words. Therefore, Balac was sure of it and had frequently tried it, for he put aside all instruments and aids of war and sent ambassadors to him saying: 'A people has come here from Egypt, who now cover the face of the earth and are settling down opposite us.'[3] However, I think that something further aroused the king. He seems to have heard that the children of Israel are wont to conquer the enemy by prayer and not by arms, not

---

2 Cf. Num. 22.6.
3 Cf. Num. 22.5.

so much with the sword as with supplications. Truly, Israel moved no arms against Pharaoh, and yet it was said to them: 'The Lord himself will fight for you; you have only to keep still.'[4] Again, against the followers of Amalec, the force of arms was not as powerful as the prayer of Moses, for whenever he lifted up his hands to God Amalec was overcome, but when they were relaxed and let down they caused Israel to be defeated. Surely, Balac the king of Moab had heard this, for it is written: 'The nations heard and quaked; anguish gripped the dwellers in Philistia. Then were the princes of Edom dismayed, trembling seized the chieftains of Moab.'[5] You see that what Moses had predicted in the canticle at the crossing of the Red Sea now happened to them. Therefore, the king of Moab had heard that these people conquered by prayers and fought against enemies with the lips rather than with a sword. Doubtless, for this reason, he thought within himself and said: Since no arms can be matched with the prayers and supplications of these people, I, too, must seek the weapons of words and such prayers as may be able to overcome theirs. Now in order that you may know that the king had any such thought, understand it from the words of Scripture which I learned from a teacher who believed in the Hebrews. Thus it is written: 'So Moab said to the elders of Madian, "Soon the synagogue will devour all the country around us, just as a calf devours the grass of the field." '[6] Thus spoke that teacher who believed in the Hebrews. Why, he says, was such an example used, saying: 'Just as a calf devours the grass of the field'? Doubtless, for the reason that a calf breaks off the grass of a field with her mouth, and cuts whatever it finds with its tongue as a sickle. So these people like a calf fought with their mouth and lips, possessing arms in their words and prayers.

Therefore, the king knew this and sent to Balaam, asking

---
4 Exod. 14.14.
5 Cf. Exod. 15.14,15.
6 Cf. Num. 22.4.

him to bring words to oppose their words, prayers to oppose theirs. Do not wonder if there is such a thing in magical art. Even Scripture declares that this art exists, but prohibits its use. None of the holy spirits obey a seer. He cannot invoke Michael, or Raphael, or Gabriel. Much more so is the soothsayer incapable of invoking Almighty God, His Son our Lord Jesus Christ, or His Holy Spirit. We alone have received the power to invoke God the Father; we alone have the power to call upon His only-begotten Son, Jesus Christ. However, this I say: Whoever has the power of invoking Christ cannot call upon the demons again. Moreover, one who has become a partaker of the Holy Ghost should no longer admit the unclean spirits, for if he does summon them the Holy Ghost will flee from him. Thus, when Balaam received the divine inspiration, although the demons had been wont to approach him, he sees them now put to flight and God coming near. So he says he will question God, because he perceives the demons not at all likely to obey him.

Then God Himself came to Balaam, not because he was worthy to have God come to him, but to rout those who had been wont to approach to curse and do evil. Already God was providing for His people. Therefore: 'God came and said to him: "Why are these men visiting you?" And Balaam answered God, "Balac, son of Sepphor, king of the Moab, hath sent them to me, saying: 'This people that came here from Egypt now cover the face of the earth, and are settling down opposite us. Please come and lay a curse on them for us; we may then be able to strike them and drive them out.'" But God said to Balaam, "Do not go with them and do not curse this people, for they are blessed." '[7]

Now some such objection may be made: Even though Balaam would invoke the demons, curse the people, and the demons, who have been summoned, do what they can; is God unable to defend His people from the demons, and to destroy their force in doing evil? What need was there for Himself to

---

[7] Cf. Num. 22.9-12.

come to Balaam and prohibit him from approaching the usual demons, as if lest they might tempt His people or try to injure them? God anticipates him and forbids him to go and summon the demons to curse, provided that he ceases from passion. But because he persists in the desire for money, God is indulgent to his free will and lets him go again. However, He put His own word into the mouth of Balaam, prohibiting a curse to arise among the demons, in order that it might give place to a blessing. Instead of curses Balaam is made to utter blessings and prophecies, which can edify not only Israel but all other nations. If God's prophecies were inserted in the Sacred Books by Moses, how much more so were they copied by men who then lived in Mesopotamia, for they considered Balaam splendid and certainly were disciples of his art? After his time the profession and instruction of the seers is said to have flourished in parts of the Orient. Possessing copies of everything which Balaam prophesied, they even have it written: 'A star shall advance from Jacob, and a man shall rise from Israel.'[8] The magi kept these writings more among themselves, and so when Jesus was born they recognized the star and understood that the prophecy was fulfilled more than did the people of Israel who disdained to hear the words of the holy prophets. Therefore, only from the writings which Balaam had left they learned that the time was approaching, came and immediately sought to adore Him. Moreover, in order to show their great faith, they honored the little boy as a king.

However, let us return to the subject. Balaam is irksome to God and almost extorts from Him permission to go and curse the children of Israel, and, although God had already come to him, to invoke the demons. He climbed on his ass, and there met him an angel who was vigilant on behalf of Israel; concerning him it is written that the Lord said to Moses: 'My angel will go with you.'[9] Since the seer insists, he is allowed to go. On the way he is crushed by the ass, because

---

8 Cf. Num. 24.17.
9 Cf. Exod. 32.34.

he sees the demons but not the angel whom the ass beholds. Indeed, the latter was not worthy to see the angel, just as she was not worthy to speak, but this happened to confound Balaam. As the Scripture somewhere says: 'A dumb beast of burden spoke with the voice of a man and checked the folly of the prophet.'[10]

Now since many historical facts have already been mentioned, let us briefly relate some of the allegorical ones at the end. If you see the opposing power attacking God's people, you will realize who it is that is sitting upon the ass. If you further consider how men are destroyed by the demons, you will understand what the ass is. Indeed, in the Gospel you will recognize Jesus sending His disciples to an ass which was tied and its colt, so that the disciples might loose and bring her for the Lord Himself to sit upon her. Perhaps this ass, that is, the Church, first carried Balaam and now Christ. She had been loosed by the disciples and released from the bonds which tied her for this very purpose, that the Son of God might sit upon her and with her enter the holy and heavenly city of Jerusalem. Then was fulfilled the Scripture which says: 'Rejoice, O daughter Sion, exclaim, O daughter Jerusalem! See, your king comes to you, meek, and riding on a beast of burden,' that is, an ass (doubtless he is speaking of believers among the Jews) 'or a young colt'[11] (these apparently are those of the Gentiles who believe in Jesus Christ our Lord).

(3) This Balaam who is interpreted as vain people seems to me to represent the scribes and pharisees of the Jewish people. However, Balac is interpreted as a shutting out or devouring, and he himself is to be understood as representing any opposing power of this world which desires to shut out and devour Israel. Therefore, first of all, let us ask Balaam why he is sometimes set forth in Scripture as blameworthy, sometimes as laudable. Indeed, he is blameworthy when he builds altars and places upon them victims to the demons,

---
10 Cf. 2 Peter 2.16.
11 Cf. Zach. 9.9.

seeking divine advice through magic preparations. He is culpable for giving the worst counsel, so that the people are deceived through the Madianite women and the worship of idols. Then again he is shown to be praiseworthy when the Lord's word is put into his mouth, when the Spirit of God comes upon him. Then he prophesies concerning Christ, announces to both Jews and Gentiles future mysteries about His coming, bestows blessings instead of curses upon the people, and by his words extols the name of Israel above all visible glory.

(4) Let these few words out of many more suffice for you at present, dearly beloved. However, keep them all most carefully in your heart, and always turn your hearts to learn spiritual things. Then, since our Lord revealed the whole prophecy to us in the Gospel, we may merit to reach that joy which He promised to those who live piously and justly: with the help of Him who together with the Father and the Holy Spirit lives and reigns world without end. Amen.

Sermon 114

That the Chanaanites were Driven from the Promised Land through the Just Judgment of God

(1) In the lessons which were read to us on Tuesday, we heard that, at the death of Moses, Josue received the rule. After crossing the Jordan, the people of Chanaan were driven out or killed, and their lands given into the possession of the children of Israel. As often as these lessons of the Old Testament are read, dearly beloved, pagans and especially the most wicked Manichaeans are wont to blaspheme and say with impious lips: What was the justice of God in removing the children of Israel from the land of Egypt by force, and after-

wards driving out the people of Chanaan, in order to give their lands into the possession of Israel? So lest this wicked murmuring perchance deceive some simple or ignorant souls, with God's help, I wish as well as I can to briefly show your holiness the most true reason which has been handed down from the ancient fathers. I want to prove that our God is not only merciful but also just, and although His judgments are often hidden, they are never unjust.

(2) Our ancestors tell us that when the sons of Noe divided the whole earth among themselves, at this division of the world, the land which is called Chanaan came into the possession of the elder son of Noe, Sem, and he kept it for a considerable time. However, later the people of Chanaan who were from that son who had been cursed by his father, came to those regions and drove out by force their brethren who were the sons of Sem, holding their land like barbarians. Since blessed Abraham is read to have been of the race of Sem, his sons or the Israelites did not reach a strange land under the guidance of the Lord, but they merely recovered their own country which their fathers had lost through violence. Now the Chanaanites, besides that sin whereby they had attacked the possessions of another, had committed many indescribable and unheard of crimes, even to such an extent that when the Lord destroyed Sodom and Gomorrha we read that He said: 'The wickedness of the Amorrites is not yet complete.'[1] Then the Lord waited for them to be converted and do penance or, if they refused to be converted, adding sin upon sin and filling the measure of sinning, at least that they should suffer the exceedingly just sentence of God. So the divine censure found them doubly guilty for invading the lands of another and afterwards committing sins and unheard of crimes, and, therefore, they are punished by a just judgment when the possessions of their ancient fathers are restored to the Jewish people. We thought these things should be explained to your charity according to the letter, as we find them written in the

---

[1] Gen. 15.16.

books of the saints. Here they are in a plain and simple sermon which everyone can understand, in order that you may have something to reply to the foul and wicked Manichaeans. As was already said, the children of Israel recovered the land of their own ancient fathers, and did not take what belonged to another as though by injustice.

(3) All this is, indeed, recorded as accomplished literally by the just judgment of God. However, since as the Apostle says: 'All these things happened to them as a type, and they are written for us, upon whom the final age of the world has come,'[2] if you notice carefully, as is your custom under God's inspiration, you will also perceive very clearly what they signify spiritually. Before Adam sinned, we were the promised land which the Lord extols so many times as flowing with milk and honey, for then there was nothing in us except what the mercy of the Creator had bestowed. However, after we all sinned in Adam, for the Apostle says: 'In Adam all die,'[3] and again: 'From one man all are unto condemnation,'[4] through the transgression of the first man, the Chanaanites began to take possession of the promised land. The Lord's will did not by nature assign the control of our heart to vices but to virtues, and still after Adam's sin haughty vices like the Chanaanites drove holy virtues out of their own land, that is, from the understanding of a rational mind, and remained there. When through God's grace the possession of our soul is again restored to the virtues, we will be seen to recover our own land, rather than seizing what belongs to another. If, with the Lord's help, our vices are overcome by the people, that is, by the virtues which struggle against them, then chastity will occupy the position which was held in our heart by the spirit of concupiscence or fornication. Patience will possess the man whom fury captivated; salutary joy, which is full of happiness, will keep the soul which had been attacked

---
2 1 Cor. 10.11.
3 1 Cor. 15.22.
4 Rom. 5.16.

by a sadness which effects death. If a man was ruined by the lukewarmness of sloth or carelessness, fortitude will begin to inflame him. If pride crushed him, humility will honor him. The man whom avarice had made obscure will be restored to his former renown by mercy; one who had been struck by the poison of envy will be adorned with kind simplicity. Thus, as each vice is expelled, the contrary virtues will take their position in the passions. The virtues themselves are not undeservedly called the children of Israel, that is, a soul that sees God. Now when, with God's help, they remove all the passions from their heart, they should be thought to recover their own possessions, rather than attacking those of another.

(4) Notice further, brethren, what is especially known to refer to the gift of grace. It was not through any natural good nor through the literal law that the promised land was restored to the Israelites. It was not through Moses, that is, the law of the Old Testament, but through Josue, the successor of Moses. Thus, indeed, the Apostle says: 'The Law brought nothing to perfection.'[5] Therefore, it was not through the letter of the law, but through the grace of the Gospel that the cruel, wicked people, that is, original and actual sins, could be routed from the promised land, that is, the hearts of Christians under the leadership of Jesus. As He Himself says in the Gospel: 'No one can enter the strong man's house, and plunder his goods, unless he first binds the strong man';[6] and again: 'Take courage, I have overcome the world.'[7] Just as the old Adam shut us out of the promised land by consenting to the devil, so on the contrary Christ, the new Adam, restored us to our ancient country by resisting the devil.

(5) Moreover, brethren, understand that the land of promise was not recovered before the River Jordan was crossed in the rule of Josue. So it is, brethren, because the spiritual land of promise, that is, a pure conscience, is not reached except

---
5 Heb. 7.19.
6 Matt. 12.29.
7 John 16.33.

through the sacrament of Baptism. Josue compelled the Israelites to cross through this same river which the true Josue or Jesus later consecrated by His Baptism.

(6) Like clean animals, dearly beloved, spiritually chew over these thoughts which we have suggested to you, as also the words: 'Those whom God loves he rebukes and chastises';[8] and: 'As the test of what the potter molds is in the furnace, so in his conversation is the test of a man.'[9] As often as the Lord's dispensation permits us to be afflicted or to suffer some adversity unjustly, let us, with the Lord's help, bear it patiently and calmly because of what the Apostle says: 'The sufferings of the present time are not worthy to be compared with the glory to come that will be revealed in us.'[10] 'When we are afflicted, we are being chastised by the Lord that we may not be condemned with this world.'[11] We should rather fear if we suffer no tribulations or but slight ones in this world, for if God 'scourges every son whom he receives,'[12] doubtless He does not receive the man whom He fails to scourge. If men calmly endure such great labors and risk such serious dangers for the sake of earthly goods, why are we slothful in behalf of the faith? Why are we fainthearted with regard to heavenly treasure, riches which no shipwreck can take away from us? Indeed, a just man who suffers shipwreck is both rich and naked. Holy Job was full of these riches. Nothing remained in his home, at a single blow everything in which he had seemed to be wealthy a little earlier perished; suddenly he was poor, covered with dung from head to foot. What is more wretched than this misery? What is happier than his inner joy? He had lost all those things which God had bestowed, but he possessed God Himself who had given it. 'Naked I came forth from my mother's womb,' he said, 'and naked shall I go back to the earth. The Lord gave, and the Lord has taken

---
8 Cf. Apoc. 3.19.
9 Ecclus. 27.6.
10 Rom. 8.18.
11 1 Cor. 11.32.
12 Heb. 12.6.

away; blessed be the name of the Lord forever!'[13] Certainly he is poor, for to be sure he possesses nothing. If nothing remains for him, from what treasury are produced those gems of God's praise? Then the tempter approached his flesh; after removing everything else, he left his wife to tempt him. He sent Eve, but this was not Adam. How was he found then? How did he answer his wife who suggested blasphemy? 'Are even you going to speak as senseless women do? We accept good things from the Lord; and should we not accept evil?'[14] O putrid yet innocent man! O filthy yet beautiful creature! O wounded but healthy soul! O you who sit upon dung and reign in heaven! If we love, let us imitate him, and let us strive to follow his example. He who has indicated the struggle will help the soul which fights. God does not watch you fighting in the contest as people do a charioteer. The latter know how to shout but not how to help. They can prepare a crown of straw, but are unable to furnish strength. This is man, not God, and perhaps while he watches he labors more in sitting down than the other who is struggling. When God watches His contestants, He helps those who invoke Him, for the voice of the athlete says in the Psalm: 'When I say, "My foot is slipping," your kindness, O Lord, sustains me.'[15] Therefore, let us not be slothful, my brethren. Let us seek, and ask, and knock. 'Everyone who seeks, finds; and he who asks, receives; and to him who knocks, it shall be opened';[16] with the help of our Lord Jesus Christ, to whom is honor and might together with the Father and the Holy Ghost world without end. Amen.

---

13 Cf. Job 1.21.
14 Cf. Job 2.10.
15 Ps. 93.18.
16 Matt. 7.8.

Sermon 115

Josue Bids the People be Ready to Cross the Jordan; also
Something Concerning Rahab the Harlot and
the Destruction of Jericho

(1) As we have frequently mentioned to your charity, dearly beloved, Moses is understood, not only to have typified Christ, but also to have prefigured the law. In truth, when our Lord was transfigured on the mountain, Moses and Elias were talking with Him, and in those two men were signified the law and the prophets. At the death of Moses, Josue received the rule; and when the law ended, our true Lord Jesus obtained the rule of the whole world. Therefore, Josue who typified the Lord said to the people when he came to the Jordan: 'Prepare your provisions until the third day.'[1] The third day, dearly beloved, we recognize as the mystery of the Trinity. What food should we prepare so that we may come to the third day? It seems to me that this food should be understood as faith; for Christians it is by faith that they believe in the Trinity and arrive at the sacrament of Baptism. Therefore, what Josue then told his people, the true Josue or Jesus now tells the Christian people through His ministers. Indeed, what else does this mean: 'Prepare your provisions until the third day,' except to receive the mystery of the Trinity? After this the Jordan was crossed just as if the mystery of Baptism were completed, and the people of Israel entered the promised land. It is true, brethren; unless a man crosses through the sacrament of Baptism, he will not see the land of true promise, that is, eternal beatitude.

(2) Moreover, Josue sends two spies to the city of Jericho, and they are received by a harlot. Josue sent two spies because the true Josue was going to give two commands of love. In

---
1 Cf. Jos. 1.11.

truth, what else do the men whom the true Josue sends announce to us except that we should love God and our neighbor? For this reason Josue said: 'Prepare your provisions, and be ready for the third day.'[2] Just as they reached the River Jordan on the third day after preparing food, so now in the Catholic Church the mystery of the Trinity and the sacrament of Baptism are reached after receiving the spiritual food of faith, hope, and charity.

(3) Then Josue took twelve stones and put them in the Jordan, and from the Jordan he took twelve others and fastened them in the place of the camp. Those twelve which were thrown into the Jordan seem to me to typify the patriarchs, while those which were lifted out of the Jordan prefigured the apostles. Indeed, after the death of Moses, when the patriarchs were buried the apostles arose as we read in the Psalm: 'The place of your fathers your sons shall have; you shall make them princes through all the land.'[3]

(4) With regard to the fact that when the older people had been buried in the desert the younger people under the leadership of Josue were brought into the land of promise, those older people typified the Jews, while the younger ones prefigured the Gentiles. After crossing the Red Sea the older people were buried in the wilderness; but in addition the younger ones crossed the River Jordan in order to receive their kingdom. It is true, brethren; no one will receive the bliss of the heavenly kingdom, unless he first passes through the sacrament of Baptism. Moreover, of those older people no more than two merited to enter the promised land, and in those two we know that something was indicated. Just as there are two precepts of charity, as was said above, inviting Christian people to receive eternal life, so there were those two men who gave advice to the Jewish people, that if they believed in God they would happily enter the land of promise.

(5) After this they came to Jericho, and the walls of that

---
2 *Ibid.*
3 Ps. 44.17.

city were pulled down to their very foundation at the shouting of the people and with the sound of trumpets. Jericho typified this world, dearly beloved. Just as its walls fell at the playing of trumpets, so now the city of the world, that is, pride with its towers of avarice, envy, and dissipation, together with its people, that is, all evil concupiscence, should be destroyed and perish through the continual preaching of priests. For this reason priests ought not be silent in church; they should rather listen to the Lord saying: 'Cry out fullthroated and unsparingly, lift up your voice like a trumpet blast; tell my people their wickedness.'[4] Therefore, we are commanded to shout, to cry out loudly, and not to spare our voice in order that we may spare our salvation. 'Cry out unsparingly,' He says, that is, the iniquity of the sinner; lest by keeping silent you may perish, and while consulting his sense of shame fail to regard his health. Do not by your silence encourage his wounds for the worse, when you might have removed them by shouting. For this reason we are commanded to cry out, and to cry out loudly, lest anyone say he did not hear it or that the voice of the priest was unknown to him. Moreover, for fear that this might not suffice, He added: 'Lift up your voice like a trumpet blast.' You know that the sound of a trumpet usually inspires terror rather than delight, and engenders fear rather than pleasure. Therefore, the trumpet is necessary for sinners, so that it may not only penetrate their ears but also shake their hearts, not merely delight them with its playing but rebuke them on hearing it. It should both encourage the vigorous in doing good, and frighten the negligent because of their sins. Just as in battle the trumpet dejects the mind of a fearful soldier but kindles the spirits of the brave, so the trumpet of the priest humiliates the mind of a sinner but strengthens the spirits of the just. By one and the same sound, then, this exhortation inspires the man who is quite brave to overcome all fear, and frees the one who is more remiss to sin. Indeed, this is the

---

[4] Isa. 58.1.

usual effect of the trumpet, that it spreads the deeds of sinners and confirms the works of the just.

(6) Now at the trumpets of the priests, the walls of Jericho which contained a sinful people fell to the ground. No army struck them, no military machine destroyed them, but remarkably enough the sound of priests and dread of a trumpet overcame them. Walls which had stood impregnable against weapons collapsed at the sacred sound of trumpets. Who would not be amazed at the fact that rocks were shattered by a sound, foundations shaken by the noise of irrational things? So complete was the destruction that, although the victors damaged nothing with their hands, there remained nothing standing among the adversary. Even though no one touched those walls, still the dwellings of the sinners inside were destroyed by the sound of the just outside; thus by the just judgment of God, a path was opened for the just, but defense was denied the wicked. Doubtless, all these things happened figuratively, for what else do we think the priestly trumpets of that time signified, but the preaching of priests in our day? In terrible words they ceaselessly announce to sinners a severe judgment, preach the gloomy destruction of hell, and with threatening sound assail the ears of the wicked. Just as then the noise of the trumpets reached the depths of the people after the stone walls were destroyed, so now the preaching of priests penetrates the bare soul when wicked thoughts have been removed. Moreover, just as the sound of a consecrated voice destroyed and captured a haughty people, so now the preaching of a priest subdues and captivates sinful people, as the blessed Apostle Paul says: 'The weapons of our warfare are not carnal, but powerful before God to the demolishing of strongholds, the destroying of reasoning—yes, of every lofty thing that exalts itself against the knowledge of God, bringing every mind into captivity to the obedience of Christ.'[5] Therefore, see whether the tongues of priests, according to the words of the Apostle, are not weapons of words which destroy vain

---
5 2 Cor. 10.4,5.

thoughts and capture haughty pride. Seven days the walls of Jericho were surrounded by the trumpets of the priests, as Scripture says, and then they fell to the ground. Therefore, 'combining spiritual things with spiritual,'⁶ we say that now by the number seven one city is not destroyed by God's priests, but the iniquity of the whole world is dispersed. Just as in the naming of a single city the whole world was prefigured, so in the limit of seven days the space of the entire world was designated. Thus, the trumpets of priests' preaching announce destruction and threaten judgment to the world as it is written: 'The world and all that is in the world will pass away, but he who does the will of God abides forever.'⁷ May He grant this who lives and reigns forever and ever. Amen.

Sermon 116

On Rahab the Harlot and the Two Messengers

(1) The lesson which was read to us just now, dearly beloved, does not so much preach to us the exploits of the son of Nun, as depict the mysteries of our Lord Jesus Christ, for He it is who received the rule after the death of Moses. Therefore, Moses died and Josue governed; the old law ceased, and the true Josue or Jesus ruled. Thus, indeed, the evangelist testifies: 'Until John came, there were the Law and the Prophets.'¹ Moreover, that Moses is considered as the law we read in the Gospel: 'They have Moses and the Prophets,'² that is, the law and the prophets; and the Apostle adds: 'down to this very day, when Moses is read,'³ that is, the law.

---
6 1 Cor. 2.13.
7 Cf. 1 John 2.16,17.

---
1 Luke 16.16.
2 Luke 16.29.
3 2 Cor. 3.15.

Therefore, when the law ceased, Jesus our Lord ascended the throne. Now, if it seems right, let us compare the accomplishments of Moses with the rule of Josue. I beseech you, brethren, to notice carefully, because the mysteries which are read are fulfilled in us. When Moses led the people out of the land of Egypt, there was no order among the people, no religious observance among the priests. They crossed the waters of the sea, salty waters which contained no sweetness, came to the wilderness, and for forty years the people were exercised in many labors. Not only were they exercised, but for their continual murmuring were destroyed in the desolation of the desert, and the older people did not merit to enter the land of promise. These events happened under Moses, that is, under the law. However, when Josue who prefigured our Lord and Savior, led the army, notice what was described even at that time concerning the Christian people. The priests walked ahead and the ark of the testament was carried on their shoulders. No sea or salty waters met them, but under the leadership of Josue they came to the Jordan. Not with confusion or violence as before at the Red Sea, not in flight or terrified with fear, but under the command of Josue and together with the priests, they entered the Jordan which was sweet and pleasant water; nor did they do so in furtive silence but with the song of trumpets which played something mystical and divine. Thus, at the preaching of the heavenly trumpet the people followed Josue through the River Jordan as through the sacrament of Baptism, in order that they might merit to enter the land of promise, that is, the happiness of eternal life.

(2) For this reason Josue said to the people: 'Prepare your provisions for the journey.'[4] Today, if you willingly listen, Christ our Lord says to you: If you will follow me, prepare food for the journey. This food is good works which accompany us like faithful viaticum to future bliss. Therefore, consider, brethren, that if each one does not prepare food for himself he cannot follow Josue when he enters the land of

---
4 Cf. Jos. 1.11.

promise. Let us further see what fruits God's people first gathered in the land of promise. 'Then they ate first the produce of the land of palms.'[5] Thus, you see that if we leave the pleasures and concupiscences of this world and rightly follow Jesus, the first palm of victory will come to us.

(3) Now Josue sent spies to Jericho and they were received hospitably by a harlot. That harlot who welcomed the spies sent by Josue, that is, the apostles and doctors, received them for the very purpose of being a harlot no longer. That harlot, dearly beloved, prefigured the Church which had been wont to commit fornication with many idols before the advent of Jesus. However, at His coming Christ not only freed her from fornication, but by a great miracle even made her a virgin, for the Apostle speaks thus of her: 'I betrothed you to one spouse, that I might present you a chaste virgin to Christ.'[6] The soul of each one of us was the harlot as long as she lived in passion and the desires of the flesh; but when she received the spies of Josue what the Apostle said was fulfilled in her: 'You were once darkness, but now you are light in the Lord.'[7] Furthermore, the fact that they were put up on a balcony signifies that the Church does not usually receive the teaching of the apostles in lowly matters but in high ones, for with the Jews she does not follow the killing letter, but she receives the vivifying Spirit which comes down from heaven. In addition, the fact that the harlot covered those men with stalks of flax is fittingly applied to the Christian people, for flax is the covering of a priest and the blessed Apostle Peter says concerning us: 'You, however, are a chosen race, a royal priesthood.'[8]

(4) When that harlot received the messengers of Josue, the king of Jericho immediately became angry at her. It is true, brethren; as soon as a soul begins to take refuge in Jesus, at once the enemy gets angry and begins to rage against her.

---
5 Cf. Jos. 5.12.
6 2 Cor. 11.2.
7 Eph. 5.8.
8 1 Peter 2.9.

As soon as the soul which formerly served vices devotes herself to the highest virtues, she suffers the persecution of the vices. Thus the Lord Himself said: 'If the world hates you, know that it has hated me before you.'[9] Indeed, the king of Jericho, that is, the devil, pursued the spies of Josue, but he could not capture them because they went up through the mountains. They do not walk through low places, nor are they delighted with the valleys, that is, with pleasures, but they follow the mountain tops for they can now say with the psalmist: 'I lift up my eyes toward the mountains; whence shall help come to me?'[10] The prince of this world cannot go up after them because he always loves what is low and fragile, usually commanding those who are delighted with pleasures. He reigns among such men, makes his abode with them, going down even to hell in or with them. Therefore, if we wish to follow Jesus and desire to enter the land of true promise, we must fight against the opposing nations, just as we know the people then fought under Josue the son of Nun.

(5) However, our struggle, beloved brethren, is not to be waged outside but within; for we should fight within ourselves if we want to overcome our adversaries. If we wish to possess eternal life, we ought to follow Jesus as our leader. Let us prepare food for the journey as Jesus advises, dearly beloved. That is, let us trade in alms, so that we may live in perfect charity with Jesus our leader and possess eternal life: with the help of our Lord Jesus Christ, who lives and reigns world without end. Amen.

---

9 John 15.18.
10 Ps. 120 l.

Sermon 116A

On the People of Chanaan[1]

(1) Listen in silence and quiet and with attentive heart to the meaning of those nations which had first ruled in the land of promise. Before Adam sinned our body and soul was a land of promise, but afterwards it became the land of the Chanaanites. What had been the dwelling of virtues became the cave of robbers, for when the virtues were driven out, vices reigned in us. However, now at the coming of our Lord Jesus, let us hasten with His help to expel from us the opposing nations. If we do not remove anger, we cannot give place to patience; similarly, if we do not banish pride, avarice, envy, and dissipation from us, that is, from the land of promise, we are unable to prepare a place in us for holy virtues. Unless with God's assistance you expel in the same way the other vices within you from your land which was sanctified by the grace of Baptism, you will in no wise receive the fullness of the promised inheritance. Indeed, there are within us throngs of vices which continually and ceaselessly assault the soul: spiritual Chanaanites are within us, daily waging an internal war against us. Knowing this, the Apostle said: 'The flesh lusts against the spirit, and the spirit against the flesh.'[2] For this reason consider, dearly beloved, how we must labor and watch, how long we must persevere in good works, in order that all the nations of vice may be routed from us and our land freed from wars.

(2) Let us meditate 'day and night on the law of the Lord,'[3] as the psalmist says, so that we may merit to accomplish this.

---

[1] Some manuscripts have the text of this sermon as a conclusion to the preceding one, without the opening and closing sections (of 116A and 116). Following other textual editors, the material is presented here as a separate entity.
[2] Gal. 5.17.
[3] Ps. 1.2.

Meditation on the divine words is like a trumpet arousing your souls to battle, lest perchance you sleep while your adversary is awake. Therefore, let us meditate on the law of the Lord, not only during the day, but also at night, as the Lord says in the Gospel: 'Watch and pray, that you may not enter into temptation.'[4] If those who watch are scarcely able to avoid temptation, what will those men do who not only sleep all night, but all day devote themselves to worldly occupations, the mad game of draughts which is opposed to the soul, or any other pleasures or carnal desires, but come to church with difficulty in full daylight? Some, indeed, do not come to church even when they arrive, for although they come, they do not devote themselves to the word of God but to idle gossip. Such men the Apostle Paul rebukes, and like a heavenly trumpet admonishes them when he says: 'Awake, sleeper, and arise from among the dead, and Christ will enlighten thee.'[5] Those who continue in the works of death, persevering in their sins and offenses, are here told to rise from the dead; even though their deeds sometimes are not manifest to men, still they are known to God.

(3) We are not mentioning these facts because we think that some of you are such, brethren, but this does not prevent us from admonishing you with paternal solicitude. Let each one examine his own conscience, and if he knows that some opposing nations, that is, leading vices, dominate him, while there is still time let him have recourse to the remedies of repentance. Let him be converted to the Lord with his whole heart, devote himself to prayer, willingly listen to the word of God, and so shudder at his sins and offenses that he may never again return to them. Indeed, what does it avail if we fast for our sins and commit them again? How does it profit us to be cleansed by good works and immediately to wallow in the mire of dissipation? With the Lord's help, let us labor with our whole strength so that all sins and offenses may be

---
4 Matt. 26.41.
5 Eph. 5.14.

removed from us along with the devil their leader. Then Christ, our kind and merciful king, will deign to dwell in us together with the angels and holy virtues. If we want this happiness to come to us, let Christ find in us nothing to offend the eyes of His majesty. May we rather be shining with chastity, adorned with pearls of patience, distinguished in almsgiving, clothed with the light of true charity, and thus merit to hear the Lord say: 'I will dwell among them, and I will be their God.'[6] May He Himself deign to grant this who lives and reigns forever and ever. Amen.

* Sermon 117

St. Ambrose, the Bishop, on Holy Gedeon

(1) Yesterday, dearly beloved, we heard that when Gedeon, the son of Joas, was beating the grain of wheat with a rod under an oak tree, he merited to hear an angel promise that he would deliver God's people from the power of their enemies. It is no wonder that he was chosen for a special grace, when by the predestined mystery of the future incarnation he was even then seated under the shade of the cross of holy and venerable wisdom. He was bringing the tangible grains of a fruitful field out of their concealment, separating choice holy men from the rubbish of useless chaff. Putting aside the superfluities of the old man and his actions by treating them with the rod of experienced truth, they are assembled in the Church as in a winepress. The Church is the winepress of the eternal fountain in which abounds the fruit of the heavenly vine.

(2) When Gedeon heard that through him the Lord was going to free His people from the multitude of the enemy, he offered in sacrifice the kid of a goat whose flesh he put

---
6 2 Cor. 6.16.

with unleavened bread upon a rock according to the angel's commands, pouring over it a broth. At the same time the angel of the Lord touched it with the tip of the rod he held, and fire burst from the rock; thus was consumed the sacrifice which had been offered. It seems clear from this evidence that the rock typified the Body of Christ, because it is written: 'For they drank from the rock which followed them, and the rock was Christ.'[1] Surely, there is more of a reference to His Body than to His divinity in the fact that the hearts of the thirsty people were satisfied by the endless stream of His Blood. Even then it was revealed in the form of a mystery that in His own flesh the Lord Jesus when crucified would do away with the sins of the whole world, not only offenses of commission, but even unlawful desires of the mind. The flesh of the kid refers to the guilt of deeds, the broth to the allurements of desires; as it is written: 'The people were so greedy for meat that they lamented, "Would that we had meat for food!" '[2] The fact that the angel extended the rod and touched the rock from which fire issued, shows that the Body of Christ is full of the divine spirit so as to consume all the sins of human nature. For this reason the Lord says: 'I have come to cast fire upon the earth.'[3]

(3) Now that wise and prophetic man noticed the heavenly mysteries of the future, and for this reason he obeyed the words of inspiration and killed a calf that his father had put aside for the idols, sacrificing to God another of seven years. By this act he very clearly showed that after the Lord's coming all sacrifices of the Gentiles were to be abolished, and only the sacrifice of the Lord's Passion was to be offered to God as the religious observance of the people. Truly that calf was a type of Christ. Furthermore, it was of seven years, because in Christ dwelt the fullness of the seven spiritual virtues, as Isaia said. Abraham also offered this calf when 'he saw' the

---
1 1 Cor. 10.4.
2 Cf. Num. 11.4.
3 Luke 12.49.

day of the Lord, 'and was glad.'[4] Christ it is who was offered at one time in the type of the kid, again as a sheep, then as a calf; a kid, because He was a sacrifice for sins; a sheep, because He was a voluntary victim; a calf, because He was a spotless offering. Thus, holy Gedeon foresaw the mystery. Moreover, he selected three hundred men for battle. This was to show that the world was to be freed from serious assaults of the enemy by the mystery of the cross, not by a numerous crowd; for in the Greek tau, three hundred shows the likeness of a cross.

(4) Now, although Gedeon was brave and confident, still he sought fuller proofs of victory from the Lord, saying: 'If indeed you are going to save Israel through me, as you promised, O Lord, I am putting this woolen fleece on the threshing floor. If dew comes on the fleece, while all the ground is dry, I shall know that you will save the people through me, as you promised. That is what took place.'[5] Afterwards, he added that the second time dew should pour over all the ground and only the fleece be dry; and so it happened. The dew on the fleece was faith in Judea, for the words of God descend as dew; for this reason Moses says: 'May my discourse be awaited like the rain, and my words descend like the dew.'[6] Thus, when the whole world was dried up from the unproductive heat of Gentile superstition, then there was the dew of a heavenly visitation upon the fleece, that is, in Judea. However, after 'the lost sheep of the house of Israel'[7] (foreshadowing, I think, the figure of the fleece of the Jews) refused the fountain of living water, the dew of faith dried up in the hearts of the Jews, and that divine stream turned its path to the hearts of the Gentiles. For this reason, the whole world is now moist with the dew of faith, but the Jews destroyed their prophets and advisers. It is no wonder that they submit to the dryness of faithless-

---

4 John 8.56.
5 Cf. Judges 6.36-38.
6 Cf. Deut. 32.2.
7 Matt. 15.24.

ness, since the Lord God deprived them of the fruitful rains of the prophets, saying: 'I will command the clouds not to send rain upon that vineyard.'[8] Salutary is the rain of the prophetic cloud, as David said: 'He shall be like rain coming down on the meadow, like showers watering the earth.'[9] The sacred writings of the whole world promised us this rain which watered the world at the advent of our Lord and Savior with the dew of the divine spirit. Thus, the dew has already come, and also the rain; the Lord came and brought with Him heavenly showers. For this reason, we who thirsted before now drink, and by an interior drinking absorb that divine spirit. Therefore, holy Gedeon foresaw that by perceiving faith, even tribes and nations would drink the true heavenly dew.

(5) Now Gedeon did not indifferently put the fleece in a field or meadow, but on the threshing floor where there was a harvest of wheat ('The harvest indeed is great, but the laborers are few'[10]), because through faith in the Lord there was to be a fruitful harvest of virtues in the future Church. Nor is it a matter of indifference that he dried the fleece of the Jews and put the dew from it into a basin that it might be filled wih water; and yet he did not wash his feet with that dew. The prerogative of such a great mystery was due to another; Christ was awaited, who alone could wash away the filth of all men. Gedeon was not so great that he would claim this mystery for himself, for not Gedeon but 'The Son of Man has not come to be served but to serve.'[11]

(6) I exhort you, brethren, not to accept as burdensome the fact that we sometimes repeat briefly what has been said for the sake of slower or more simple souls. Those who are experienced and learned through the goodness of God understand without difficulty what is said; but I fear that unless a brief summary is made for the rest who are ignorant and

---
8 Cf. Isa. 5.6.
9 Ps. 71.6.
10 Luke 10.2.
11 Matt. 20.28.

simple, they may grasp too little of what is said. Gedeon was a type of our Lord and Savior, dearly beloved. Since three hundred in Greek calculation forms a cross, so at that time Gedeon with three hundred men freed the Jewish people from very cruel nations, just as Christ later freed the entire human race from the power of the devil through the mystery of the cross. Now the winepress in which he threshed out the harvest typified the Church because of its continuous tribulations. The harvest which was threshed signified the Christian people whom Christ at His coming separated from the chaff, that is, from all sins, by the rod of discipline and the staff of the cross. The angel who came to him is also regarded as a type of our Lord and Savior. The tree under which he stood and the rod which he held clearly indicate the cross. The rock upon which Gedeon offered the holocaust was Christ, for thus the Apostle spoke: 'And the rock was Christ.'[12] The kid which was sacrificed designated the human race guilty of sin. In the fact that the angel touched the rock with the rod and fire came forth to consume the kid, we understand that the cross touched the rock which was Christ, and the fire of charity went forth to consume the sins of the human race. Indeed, Christ the true Gedeon said concerning Himself in the Gospel: 'I have come to cast fire upon the earth, and what will I but that it be kindled?'[13] Moreover, the bull which was killed prefigured our Lord who was offered as an oblation for the redemption of the human race. The fact that he was of seven years seems to signify the sevenfold grace of the Holy Ghost which came to Christ. Then he put the fleece on the threshing floor and asked the Lord that there might be dew only on the fleece and all the ground be dry, and so it happened; again he asked that the fleece might remain dry while there was dew on the entire threshing floor. The fleece represented the Jewish people, but the threshing floor was all the Gentiles in the whole world. At first, the dew of the word

---

12 1 Cor. 10.4.
13 Luke 12.49.

of God was only in Judea, and all the world remained in dryness, just as the dew first came upon the fleece and the floor was dry. But when the Jews later killed Christ the Lord, the fleece was wrung out through the injury of the Passion and the Jewish people remained dry and arid, while not merely dew but even the rain of God's word and the rivers of the apostles came to the whole threshing floor, that is, to the entire world and all nations. Finally, on the entire earth as on the floor, the Church is watered with the dew of spiritual grace, while the unhappy synagogue remains parched and dry of all the moisture and rain of God's word. Now in order that this spiritual rain and the dew of divine grace may continue in us, let us reflect in a salutary manner upon everything that is preached; by talking it over among ourselves, let us chew it like clean animals. Then we may possess a useful fluid upon which our soul can live forever, and satisfied with such delights we may merit to say with the prophet: 'How sweet to my palate are your promises, O Lord!'[14] The sweetness of God's word will then be able to remain in us, provided that we are willing to instill it in others by more frequently mentioning it with full and perfect charity. Then we may be able to procure spiritual profits for ourselves, as the result of both our own salvation and that of others: with the help of Our Lord Jesus Christ, to whom is honor and might together with the Father and the Holy Ghost world without end. Amen.

* *Sermon 118*

St. Augustine, the Bishop, on Samson

(1) Many very obscure sacred mysteries are contained in the lesson which was read to us, dearly beloved, and since they

---

[14] Ps. 118.103.

cannot be explained in brief, for this reason alone we wanted the morning psalms to be finished on time, lest the rather lengthy sermon weary you. Moreover, since you are going to leave church at the usual hour, listen in silence and quiet and with attentive mind to what needs to be said, as you usually do.

(2) The strength which Samson possessed, dearly beloved, came from the grace of God rather than by nature, for if he had been naturally strong his power would not have been taken away when his hair was cut. Where, then, was that most powerful strength, except in what the Scripture says: 'The spirit of the Lord walked with him'?[1] Therefore, his strength belonged to the spirit of the Lord. In Samson was the vessel, but the fullness was in the spirit. A vessel can be filled and emptied. Moreover, every vessel has its perfection from something else, and so in Paul grace was commended when he was called a vessel of election. Let us further see what kind of a parable Samson proposed to the strangers. 'Out of the eater came forth food,' he said, 'and out of the strong came forth sweetness.'[2] This parable was revealed, carried to friends, and solved. Samson was defeated. If he was a just man, the fact is well hidden and the justice of the man is deep down. For since he is read to have been overcome by the flattery of a woman and went in to a harlot, his merits seem to totter in the eyes of those who do not understand so well the secrets of truth. Indeed, he is commanded by a precept of the Lord to take the harlot as his wife. Perhaps we can say that in the Old Testament this was not blameworthy or disgraceful, seeing that whatever was said or done was a matter of prophecy. Therefore, let us find out what the victor and the vanquished mean, also his yielding to the flattery of a woman, the betrayal of the secret of the parable, his going in to a harlot, the seizing of foxes, and the burning of the enemy's fruits with the tails of the foxes to which he had

---
1 Cf. Judges 13.25.
2 Judges 14.14.

fastened torches of fire. Surely, he could have burned the fruits an easier way, if he had not thought there was a mystery in the foxes. Could not the dry stalks burn without the foxes dragging fire through them? Therefore, let us learn the great mysteries which are concealed here.

(3) What was the meaning of Samson? If I say he signified Christ, it seems to me that I speak the truth. However, the thought immediately occurs to anyone who reflects: Was Christ overcome by the flattery of a woman? How is Christ understood to have gone in to a harlot? Then, again, when did Christ have His head uncovered or His hair shaved, Himself robbed of courage, bound, blinded, and mocked? Watch, faithful soul. Notice why it is Christ, not only what Christ did, but also what He suffered. What did He do? He worked as a strong man and suffered as a weak one. In the one person I understand both qualities; I see the strength of the Son of God, and the weakness of the Son of man. Moreover, when the Scriptures extol Him, Christ is entire, both head and body. Just as Christ is the head of the Church, so the Church is His body; and in order that it might not be alone, it is the whole Christ with the head. Now the Church contains within itself both strong and weak members. It has some who are fed on bread alone, and others who must still be nourished with milk. There is a further fact which must be admitted: in association at the sacraments, the imparting of Baptism or participation at the altar, the Church has both just and unjust men. At present the body of Christ is a threshing floor, as you know, but afterwards it will be a granary. While it is a threshing floor it does not refuse to tolerate chaff, but when the time of storage comes it will separate the wheat from the chaff. Thus, some things Samson did as the head and others as the body, but all in the person of Christ. Inasmuch as Samson performed virtues and miracles he prefigured Christ, the head of the Church. When he acted prudently, he was an image of those who live justly in the Church, but when he was overtaken and acted carelessly, he represented those who are sinners in

the Church. The harlot whom Samson married is the Church which committed fornication with idols before knowing one God, but which Christ afterwards united to Himself. However, when she was enlightened and received faith from Him, she even merited to learn the mysteries of salvation through Him, and He further revealed to her the mysteries of heavenly secrets. As to the question implied in the words: 'Out of the eater came forth food, and out of the strong came forth sweetness,'[3] what else does it signify but Christ rising from the dead? Truly, out of the eater, that is, from death which devours and consumes all things, came forth that food which said: 'I am the bread that has come down from heaven.'[4] The Gentiles were converted and received the sweetness of life from Him whom human iniquity loaded with bitterness and offered bitter vinegar and gall as a drink. Thus, from the mouth of the dead lion, that is, from the death of Christ who lay down and slept like the lion, there proceeded a swarm of bees, that is, of Christians. When Samson said: 'If you had not ploughed with my heifer, you would not have solved my riddle,'[5] this heifer is the Church which had the secrets of our faith revealed to her by her husband. By the teaching and preaching of the apostles and saints, she spread to the ends of the earth the mysteries of the Trinity, the Resurrection, judgment and the kingdom of heaven, promising the rewards of eternal life to all who understand and know them.

(4) Then follow the words: 'Samson was angry because a friend married his wife.'[6] This friend prefigured all heretics. It is a great mystery, my brethren. Heretics who divide the Church have wanted to marry the wife of the Lord and carry her away. By departing from the Church and the Gospels, they attempt through adulterous wickedness to seize the Church, that is, the body of Christ, as their portion. For this reason that faithful servant and friend of the Lord's bride

---

3 *Ibid.*
4 John 6.41.
5 Judges 14.18.
6 Cf. Judges 14.19, 20.

says: 'I betrothed you to one spouse, that I might present you a chaste virgin to Christ.'[7] Moreover, through the zeal of faith and a rebuke he touches the person of his wicked companion: 'And I fear lest, as the serpent seduced Eve, so your minds may be corrupted from the truth which is in Christ Jesus.'[8] Who are the companions, that is, the heretical deserters who want to seize the Lord's spouse, unless Donatus, Arius, Manichaeus, and other vessels of error and perdition? Concerning such men the Apostle says: 'I hear that there are strifes among you. Each of you says, I am of Paul, or I am of Apollos, or I am of Cephas.'[9] Now let us see what that mystical Samson did when he was injured by his friend in the person of his wife. He took foxes, that is, adulterous friends of whom it is said in the Canticle of Canticles: 'Catch us the foxes, the little foxes that damage the vineyards.'[10] What does it mean, 'catch'? It means seize, convict, repress them, lest the vines of the Church be destroyed. What else does it mean to catch foxes, except to convict heretics with the authority of the divine law, to fasten and fetter them with the testimony of Holy Scripture as with chains? Samson caught the foxes and put torches of fire on their tails after they were coupled. What do the tails of the foxes tied together signify? What are foxes' tails, except the results of heresy (for their first appearance is flattering and deceitful) bound fast, that is, condemned and dragging fire in their trail? Moreover, they destroy the fruits and good works of those who consent to their seductions. Man is told: Do not listen to heretics, do not consent to them or be seduced by them. He replies: Why? Has not that man or so and so listened to heretics? Has not that other Christian committed such vices, such adultery, or such robbery? And what evil has befallen him? Those are the first appearances of the foxes, and souls that are seduced pay attention; the fire is behind them. Nothing has happened to him now, it is

---

7 2 Cor. 11.2.
8 Cf. 2 Cor. 11.3.
9 Cf. 1 Cor. 1.11, 12.
10 Cf. Cant. 2.15.

said. Since nothing has gone before, will nothing be dragged after? He is sure to come to the fire which follows. Do you think further that the heretics drag along the fire with which to burn the fruits of their enemies, but are not themselves burned? Doubtless, when the foxes burned the harvest they, too, were burned. Thus, judgment will come back upon the heretics; what they do not see now they have behind them. They delight men with their flattery and show themselves at first free from restraint. But at the judgment of God their tails are bound, that is, they drag fire upon themselves afterwards, since wickedness preceded their punishment.

(5) When Samson went in to the harlot, he was impure if he did so without reason, but if he did so as a prophet it is a mystery. If he did not enter in order to lie with the woman, perhaps he did so because of a mystery. We do not read that he was intimate with her, but the story continues: 'His enemies awaited him at the city gate, that they might seize him as he went out from the harlot whom he had visited; but he slept.'[11] See how it is not recorded in Scripture that he was united to the harlot, but it is written that he slept. 'When he arose and left at midnight,' it says, 'he took the city gates with the bolts, and carried them to the top of a hill,'[12] and he could not be held by the strangers. He took away the city gates through which he had gone in to the harlot, and carried them to a mountain. What does this mean? Hell and love for a woman Scripture joins together; the house of the harlot was an image of hell. It is rightly considered as hell, for it rejects no one but draws to itself all who enter. At this point we recognize the actions of our Redeemer. After the synagogue to which He had come was separated from Him through the devil, they shaved His head, that is, they crucified Him on the site of Calvary, and He descended into hell. Then, His enemies guarded the place where He slept, that is, the sepulchre, and wanted to seize Him although they could not see Him. 'But

---
11 Cf. Judges 16.2, 3.
12 Cf. Judges 16.3.

he slept'; this was mentioned here because it was not real death. The words: 'He arose and left at midnight' signify that He arose in secret. He had suffered openly, but His Resurrection was revealed only to His disciples and certain other people. Thus, all saw the fact that He went in, but the fact that He arose just a few knew, remembered, and felt. Moreover, he removed the city gates, that is, He took away the gates of hell. What does it mean to remove the gates of hell, except to take away the power of death? He took it away and did not return it. Furthermore, what did our Lord Jesus Christ do after He had taken away the gates of death? He went up to the top of a mountain. Truly, we know that He both arose and ascended into heaven.

(6) Now what does it mean that Samson possessed strength in his hair? Notice this carefully, too, brethren. He did not have strength in his hand, his foot, his breast, not even in his head, but in his hair. What is hair? If we perceive it, the Apostle answers us after being questioned: 'Hair is a covering';[13] and Christ had strength in a covering, when the shadows of the old law protected Him. For this reason the hair of Samson was a covering, since it was seen and understood in Christ at different times. What does it mean that Samson's secret was betrayed and his head was shaved? The law was despised and Christ suffered. They would not have killed Christ if they had not contemned the law, for they knew that it was not right for them to kill Him. They told the judge: 'It is not lawful for us to put anyone to death.'[14] Samson's head was shaved, the secrets were exposed, the covering was removed; Christ who lay hidden was revealed. Moreover, the hair was restored and again covered the head, because the Jews were unwilling to recognize Christ when He was risen. He was in a mill, blinded, and in a prison house. The prison or mill is the labor of this world. The blindness of Samson indicates men who are blinded by their infidelity and do not

---
13 Cf. 1 Cor. 11:15.
14 John 18.31.

recognize Christ exercising His power or ascending into heaven. Thus, the blindness which they have suffered signifies the blindness of the Jews. Christ was seized by the Jews and put to death, and yet He rather killed those who were slaying Him. 'Therefore his enemies brought him to play the buffoon before them.'[15] Notice here an image of the cross. Samson extends his hands spread out to the two columns as to the two beams of the cross. Moreover, by his death he overcame his adversaries, because his sufferings became the death of his persecutors. For this reason Scripture concludes as follows: 'Those he killed at his death were more than those he had killed during his lifetime.'[16] This mystery was clearly fulfilled in our Lord Jesus Christ, for at His death He completed our redemption which He had by no means published during His life: who lives and reigns forever and ever. Amen.

Sermon 119

On Samson

(1) In the lesson which was read to us, dearly beloved, we heard, and in a way beheld with the eyes of our heart, how Samson in his exceedingly great strength killed a lion alone and unarmed. Then after some time he found honey in the lion's mouth, ate some, and offered it to his parents. Many of the fathers have spoken a great deal about this lion, beloved brethren, and all of them have said what is fitting and in accord with the facts. Some have said that the lion prefigured Christ our Lord. Truly, this is very appropriate, for to us Christ is a lion in whose mouth we found the food of honey after His death. What is sweeter than the word of God? Or what is stronger than His right hand? In whose mouth after

---
15 Cf. Judges 16.25.
16 Judges 16.30.

death is there food and bees, except His in whose word is the good of our salvation and the congregation of the Gentiles? The lion can further be understood as the Gentiles who believed. First, it was a body of vanity, but is now the body of Christ in which the apostles like bees stored the honey of wisdom gathered from the dew of heaven and the flowers of divine grace. Thus, food came out of the mouth of the one who died; because nations which were as fierce as lions at first, accepted with a devout heart the word of God which they received, and produced the fruit of salvation.

(2) Since Sacred Scripture can be understood and interpreted in many ways as a pearl, Christ Himself is not unfittingly regarded as the lion, as was said above. Moreover, Samson prefigured the Jewish people who killed Christ at the very time when He sought desirable union with the Church. Surely, the marriage which was contracted for the Church in Christ could not be confirmed before the lion of the tribe of Juda was killed. Furthermore, our Lord is the same lion which both conquered and was overcome. He was conquered when the Jewish people killed Him, but He was victorious in His triumph over the devil through His death on the cross. Indeed, He is both the lion and the lion's whelp: a lion because equal to the Father; the young of the lion because the Son of the Father who was killed by His own will and rose again by His own power. Of Him it is written: 'Who will disturb him?'[1] Voluntarily offering His Father the sacrifice of His Body for us, He who is most high forever takes up the life which He Himself had laid down, as He testifies. That Samson says: 'Out of the eater came forth food, and out of the strong came forth sweetness,'[2] is fittingly applied to Christ. By His teaching He both chews over the spiritual food of His honey and in His promises gives it to us. In still another way this can be understood concerning Christ. This lion, that is, Christ from the tribe of Juda, victoriously descended into hell to

---
1 Gen. 49.9.
2 Judges 14.14.

snatch us from the mouth of the hostile lion. For this reason He hunts in order to protect, seizes in order to free, leads men captive in order to restore them when freed to their eternal country.

(3) Therefore, let us long to become the booty of this lion, brethren, so that we may not be His enemies. Let us be the food of God lest we become the food of the serpent, for Christ eats us in order that the devil may not devour us. However, by eating us Christ deigns to take from us, as I mentioned, that which could destroy us by eternal death. He exchanges perdition for pardon, sin for justice, infirmity for power, death for life, confusion for glory, the kingdom for exile. We who heard before: 'Dust you are and unto dust you shall return,'[3] have now heard: 'Our citizenship is in heaven.'[4] Now that splendor which was restored in Samson and was covered at his death I think fits every servant of Christ. If a man is overtaken by some sin and in a salutary manner has recourse to the remedies of repentance, with the restoration of grace there returns the face of a good conscience, like the hair which grew again. Thus, it becomes possible for the merits of faith like very strong muscles of courage to attack and overthrow the enemy's pillars which support the hostile house. What are these pillars of the enemy's house, except our sins upon which the house of the devil rests, where he feasts as victor and mocks our minds if they have been captivated? Therefore, we eject this enemy from his house by the destruction and death of our flesh. Our enemy is enclosed within us; he daily wages an internal war inside. As long as we sometimes assent to him, in accord with the evil agreement of our will he gains power over us. With our vices against us as his accomplices within, he attacks our exterior ministry, so that when we hand over to him our members for works of iniquity we are killed by our own sword, as is usually said. However, we ought to remember the agreement which we promised in

---
3 Cf. Gen. 3.19.
4 Phil. 3.20.

return for the grace of Baptism, when we were buried together with Christ in the mystery of the cross: that we would renounce the devil, his pomps, and his works. Let us no longer live in this world as we have been; in fact, let us no longer live ourselves but let Christ live in us. When He has been restored to the honor of the head, the house of the devil will fall, and all our enemies will die with our sins in eternal destruction.

(4) Now when Samson destroyed a thousand men with a jawbone from the body of an ass, the Gentiles were prefigured in the ass; for thus Scripture speaks concerning both Jews and Gentiles: 'An ox knows its owner, and an ass its master's manger.'[5] Before the coming of Christ all the Gentiles were torn to pieces by the devil and lay scattered like dry bones from the ass's body, but when Christ the true Samson came, He seized them all in His holy hands. He restored them to the hands of His power, and with them overcame His and our adversaries. Thus, we who had given our members to the devil before so that he might kill us, were seized by Christ and became instruments of justice unto God. Although we had been dried up because of lack of the dew of God's grace, we merited to be changed into fountains and rivers. At that time Samson prayed and a fountain issued from the jawbone. This fact is clearly fulfilled in us, for the Lord Himself said: 'He who believes in me, from within him there shall flow rivers of living water.'[6]

(5) Behold how much the gentle goodness of our Lord and Savior has conferred upon us. What I mentioned above in this rather lengthy sermon I now repeat in brief to impress it upon your minds. In many ways, as was said above, the lion signified Christ our Lord. Samson prevailed against the lion; the Jewish people overcame Christ. When honey was found in the mouth of the lion, the doctrine of Christ is understood in that honey, for we read concerning it: 'How sweet to my palate are your promises, O Lord! Sweeter than

---
5 Isa. 1.3.
6 John 7.38.

syrup or honey from the comb!'⁷ Indeed, just as bees come to a honey-comb, so swarms of Christians hasten to Christ's doctrine as to the sweetest honey-comb. Furthermore, the fact that after Samson's hair grew again he recovered his former strength and seizing the pillars destroyed the house of his enemies together with its builders, is also seen today in the case of some sinners. If they destroy their vices by repentance and provide a place for virtue, the likeness and figure of Samson is fulfilled in them. Then is accomplished in them what is written concerning Samson: 'Those he killed at his death were more than those he had killed during his lifetime.'⁸ It is true, brethren. A greater number of sins is destroyed by repentance than is known to be overcome at a time when a man seems to be free from offenses. Now we should not notice with indifference that at the death of Samson all his enemies were killed. Thus, may our adversaries also be destroyed at our death. Brethren, the Apostle says: 'Mortify your members, which are on earth: lust, evil desire and covetousness (which is a form of idol-worship).'⁹ Let drunkenness and pride die in us, envy be extinguished, anger appeased, and malice rejected. If we endeavor to kill all these things with God's help, like Samson we can destroy our adversaries by dying to sins and vices. Let us pray to God that as our Savior He may deign to grant this, to whom is honor.

Sermon 120

On the Woman Who Deceived Samson

(1) In the part of the lesson which was read to us at Vespers, beloved brethren, we read how that cruel and wicked woman,

---
7 Ps. 118.103.
8 Judges 16.30.
9 Col. 3.5.

the exceedingly rude and haughty Dalila, through false and poisonous flattery shaved the head of her husband, afterwards handing him over to the Philistines to be mocked. According to history the wickedness of that evil woman was completely vented upon him, but let us be on our guard as far as we can, dearly beloved, lest we suffer spiritually what Samson endured physically. The rational sense in us is understood as the man, while the flesh is accepted as a type of the woman. If a man consents to his body when it gently coaxes him to dissipation, he will suffer from his flesh what Samson bore from his wife. Therefore, in order that we may not endure this, dearly beloved, let us, with God's help, strive as much as we can to fulfill what the Apostle said concerning himself: 'I chastise my body and bring it into subjection.'[1] Thus, with the assistance of God, let us be careful, lest the enemy's razor which shaved the head of the human race when Adam and Eve were deceived by a trick, also go up to our head; for our head is Christ. If we surrender ourselves to a woman, that is, to flattering lust of the flesh or other evil deeds, we are deceived and deprived of spiritual grace, as though stripped of the hair of the Nazarite. Let us rather beg the Lord that our sins, by which we have our soul woven around the hair of our head, may not be cut off in the middle but completely destroyed as with the shave of a razor.

(2) Now there is one razor which cuts in a wholesome manner, another which does so in a harmful way. The razor of healing and beauty for us is Christ our Lord, who cuts wicked, hurtful thoughts out of our heart. He shaves vices of the soul, lightens the head, cares for the beauty of the mind, purifies us like that captive in the old law, frees us from the dreadful hair of wretched slavery, and will make our life holy in chastity and economy when it grows again as the hair of the Nazarite. Behold, we have shown the razor which we ought to desire, just as that other one we should shun and avoid was already indicated above. Thus, the salu-

---
1 Cf. 1 Cor. 9.27.

tary razor is Christ, while the deadly one is the devil. Christ is our head, according to the Apostle. The hair is clearly sometimes virtues and sometimes sins, for when the prophet spoke of his sins he said: 'Those outnumber the hairs of my head.'[2] Therefore, since both virtues and vices are designated in the hair, when we are shaved by Christ we are freed from all vices; but if we are shaved by the devil we are stripped of all virtues. How serious it is to be shaved by the devil is plainly shown by Samson, of whom we spoke a little while ago. As long as he kept his hair he was invincible, but when it was cut he became a captive, again recovering his strength when the hair grew again. Here is shown the fact that virtues can be signified in the hair. Surely, if he had been prudent and guarded against the woman's deceit, he would not have fallen into the hands of his enemies. However, he was conquered by carnal temptation, so that he who had been full of grace and killed a lion before, afterwards sinned by trusting in his own former strength and was overcome by his enemies. Therefore, anyone who does not subject his wife, that is, his flesh, to her husband, that is, to the spirit in God's law, must with wavering mind consent like tender husbands to their spouse who encourages evil. Such men are unworthy of their spiritual teacher, the Apostle Paul, who said: 'I chastise my body, and bring it into subjection.'[3] If a man yields to lust or dissipation, his flesh does to him what Dalila inflicted upon Samson.

(3) Now if we consider all the things Samson suffered when he was deceived by his wicked wife, he physically endured expressly for our instruction the same things which sinners bear in their souls. Indeed, our enemy the devil mocks haughty sinners when Christ's grace has been violated, just as he did Samson when his hair was cut. He takes away the sight of their eyes, put them into prison, and regards them as asses for turning mill-stones. Therefore, lest we fail to subject our

---
2 Ps. 68.5.
3 Cf. 1 Cor. 9.27.

neck to the yoke of Christ and make it worthy of the ass's mill-stone, our Lord admonishes us through the prophet: 'Be not senseless like horses or mules.'[4] Not realizing his honor, that is, the dignity of his nature whereby he dominates the other animals, as the same prophet says elsewhere: 'Man does not abide; he resembles the beasts that perish.'[5] Indeed, man was in a position of honor but he fell back into vice, just as Samson when deserted by the virtue of both wisdom and grace was punished with blindness and a grindstone. A man is worthy of the work of beasts if he deprives himself of the light of reason. One who is subject to his flesh and dissipation through the weakening effect of evil women's flattery, should reflect that the appearance of a beast that is grinding will come to him. As the ass or mule is tied to a grindstone with his bodily eyes weakened or closed with rags, so the dissipated soul has the eyes of his mind put out by the filth of his life, and through the errors of his thoughts is guided, as it were, around the turning mill-stone through laborious compassion, without his own sight and working with that of another. He stands on the road of sinners, fettered with the bonds of his passions. He is his own prison, filled with the darkness of his error, stiff with the squalor of his conscience, enduring within himself the imprisonment of a mill. He turns the rock of his heart which has been hardened by perseverance in iniquity like a grindstone, making flour for his enemy out of the corrupt grain of his soul. Since in the words of Scripture: 'The sinner runs away from his own soul,'[6] the man who is engaged in sinning grinds wheat for the enemy from the marrow of his life in order to feed the devil, and while the soul becomes bread for him it is a source of hunger to itself. However, if a soul does not always proceed to dissipation but sometimes returns by repentance, he recovers his hair, as it

---

4 Ps. 31.9.
5 Ps. 48.13, 21.
6 Cf. Prov. 7.23.

were, that is, he is restored to virtue by the return to blossom of grace.

(4) Nevertheless, if we notice carefully, dearly beloved, we will wonder at the Passion of our Lord sketched in advance in the death of Samson. In the fact that he is written to have destroyed more enemies at his death than he struck before in the whole course of his life, the mystery of the Lord's Passion is shown, for through it the house of the devil fell and the kingdom of death was shattered. Indeed, that house which contained all the princes of the Philistines prefigured the house and kingdom of the devil; and this house is recorded to have rested entirely on two pillars. What are the two pillars which supported the house of the devil? Doubtless, avarice and dissipation, for no evil can be conceived or mentioned or take place without proceeding from the root of avarice as it is written: 'Covetousness is the root of all evils';[7] while concerning dissipation it is said: 'Dissipation makes the body intolerable.'[8] Moreover, Samson prefigured our Lord Jesus Christ, but cruel Dalila typified the synagogue. Samson is ensnared by Dalila, while the synagogue persecuted Christ, crucifying Him on the site of Calvary. Since Samson who represented Christ was blinded, his blindness prefigured bad Christians who would believe in Christ for a time but would not persevere in faith and good works. In the body of Christ, that is, among Christian people, as you know, there are two parts, the good and the bad, humble and proud, dissolute and chaste, drunkards and the sober, the kind and the envious. Therefore, the fact that Samson is read to have been unbecomingly overtaken in certain respects prefigured, as I already said, those in the Church who glory only in the name of Christian but are continually involved in bad actions and wicked deeds. Samson was condemned to prison, while Christ deigned to descend into hell. Samson extended his hands to the pillars, and the house of the Philistines fell with its princes;

---
7 1 Tim. 6.10.
8 Cf. Prov. 11.18.

Christ stretched out His hands to the two beams of the cross as to two pillars, overthrowing and destroying the house or kingdom of the devil and his angels. Furthermore, the fact that Samson is recorded to have killed more men at his death than he had destroyed when alive, signified that few men believed in Christ the true Samson before He was crucified. After He accepted death for the human race, He extinguished the error of unbelief throughout the world, and by His salutary doctrine subjected countless multitudes to Himself.

(5) Each one should watch and guard against his wife as much as he can, brethren. That is, under the yoke of discipline he should rule his flesh and subject it to the spirit by sobriety and moderation, lest he perchance suffer from it what Samson endured from most wicked Dalila. If we do this in a reasonable and spiritual manner, remaining interiorly clean of heart and outwardly chaste of body, when the day of judgment comes we will not be punished with wicked sinners, but with the just and those who fear God we will happily arrive at eternal rewards. May the Lord bring us to this under His protection, to whom is honor and might forever and ever. Amen.

Sermon 121

St. Augustine on David, Isai His Father, and the Unnatural Goliath

(1) In Sacred Scripture, dearly beloved, one and the same person can have a different signification, depending upon the time and situation. When blessed Isaac was offered by his father, as your holiness knows very well, he prefigured Christ the Lord; but when he blessed his son Jacob and sent him to Mesopotamia to find a wife, Jacob typified Christ, while Isaac was an image of God the Father. Then, again, blessed Jacob

who was a figure of Christ, when he took a wife prefigured God the Father in loving blessed Joseph more than all his sons. Moreover, he made him a tunic of damask linen which signified the Incarnation of our Lord and Savior. Just as this happened, then, in the blessed patriarchs, Isaac and Jacob, dearest brethren, so we know it was prefigured in Isai the father of David; for when he sent his son David to look for his brothers, he seems to have typified God the Father. Isai sent David to search for his brothers, and God sent His only-begotten Son of whom it is written: 'I will proclaim your name to my brethren.'[1] Truly, Christ had come to seek His brethren, for He said: 'I was not sent except to the lost sheep of the house of Israel.'[2]

(2) 'And Isai said to David his son: Take an ephi of frumenty, and ten little cheeses, and go see thy brethren.'[3] An ephi, brethren, is a quantity of three measures, and in three measures is understood the mystery of the Trinity. Blessed Abraham knew this mystery well; for when he merited to perceive the mystery of the Trinity in the three persons under the holm-oak of Mamre, he ordered three measures of flour to be mixed. It is three measures, and for this reason Isai gave this amount to his son. In the ten little cheeses we recognize the decalogue of the Old Testament. Thus, David came with the three measures and ten cheeses, in order to visit his brothers who were in battle, because Christ was to come with the decalogue of the law and the mystery of the Trinity to free the human race from the power of the devil.

(3) Now when David came, one of his brothers rebuked him saying: 'Why didst thou leave those few sheep, and camest to the battle?'[4] This elder brother, maliciously chiding David who typified our Lord, signified the Jewish people who jealously slandered Christ the Lord even though He had come for the salvation of the human race, for they frequently chas-

---
1 Ps. 21.23.
2 Matt. 15:24.
3 Cf. 1 Kings 17.17, 18.
4 Cf. 1 Kings 17.28.

tised Him with many insults. 'Why didst thou leave the sheep, and camest to the battle?' Does it not seem to you as though through his lips the devil is speaking in envy of the salvation of men? It is as though he said to Christ: Why did you leave the ninety-nine sheep who had strayed and come looking for the one which was lost, in order that you might call him back to your sheepfold, after freeing him with the staff of the cross from the hand of the spiritual Goliath, that is, from the power of the devil? 'Why didst thou leave those few sheep?' He spoke the truth, although in a wicked and haughty spirit. Jesus intended to leave the ninety-nine sheep, as was already said, in order to seek the one, and to bring it back to His sheepfold, that is, to the company of the angels.

(4) When David had been anointed by blessed Samuel before he came here, he had killed a lion and a bear without any weapons, as he himself told King Saul. Both the lion and the bear typified the devil, for they had been strangled by the strength of David for having dared to attack some of his sheep. All that we read prefigured in David at that time, dearly beloved, we know was accomplished in our Lord Jesus Christ; for He strangled the lion and the bear when He descended into hell to free all the saints from their jaws. Moreover, listen to the prophet entreating the person of our Lord: 'Rescue my soul from the sword, my loneliness from the grip of the dog. Save me from the lion's mouth.'[5] Since a bear possesses his strength in his paw and a lion has his in his mouth, the same devil is prefigured in those two beasts. Thus, this was said concerning the person of Christ, in order that His sole Church might be removed from the hand, that is, the power or mouth of the devil.

(5) As David came he found the Jewish people located in the valley of Terebinth in order to fight against the Philistines, because Christ the true David was to come in order to lift up the human race from the valley of sins and tears. They stood in a valley facing the Philistines. They were in a valley,

---

5 Cf. Ps. 21.21, 22.

because the weight of their sins had pressed them down. However, they were standing but did not dare to fight against their adversaries. Why did they not dare to do so? Because David who typified Christ had not yet arrived. It is true, dearly beloved. Who was able to fight against the devil before Christ our Lord freed the human race from his power? Now the word David is interpreted as strong in hand; and what is stronger, brethren, than He who conquered the whole world, armed with a cross but not a sword? Furthermore, the children of Israel stood against their adversaries for forty days. Because of the four seasons and the four parts of the world, those forty days signify the present life in which the Christian people do not cease to fight against Goliath and his army, that is, the devil and his angels. Moreover, it would be impossible to conquer, if Christ the true David had not come down with His staff which is the mystery of the cross. Truly, the devil was free before the advent of Christ, dearly beloved; but at His coming Christ did to him what is recorded in the Gospel: 'No one can enter the strong man's house, and plunder his goods, unless he first binds the strong man.'[6] For this reason Christ came and bound the devil.

(6) Someone may say: If he is bound, why is the devil still so powerful? It is true, beloved brethren, that he has much power, but those he dominates are lukewarm, careless, not fearing God in truth. He is bound like a dog in chains, and can bite no one except the soul which is willingly joined to him with fatal self-assurance. So now you see, brethren, how foolish a man is if he is bitten by someone in the position of a dog in chains. Do not be joined to him by the pleasures and passions of the world, and he will not dare to bite you. He can bark and annoy you but is unable to bite you at all unless you will it. He does not harm you by force, but by persuasion; he does not wrest consent from us, but asks it.

(7) David came and found the Jewish people fighting against the Philistines. Since there was no one who dared to

---
6 Matt. 12.29.

enter single combat, he who prefigured Christ went out to battle, and carrying a staff in his hand opposed Goliath. In him was surely indicated what was fulfilled in our Lord Jesus Christ, for Christ the true David came and carried His cross with the purpose of fighting against the spiritual Goliath, that is, the devil. Notice where blessed David struck Goliath, brethren: on the forehead where there was no sign of the cross. Just as the staff typified the cross, so the stone with which he was struck prefigured Christ our Lord, for He is the living stone of which it is written: 'The stone which the builders rejected has become the cornerstone.'[7] The fact that without a sword David stood over Goliath and killed him with his own sword, shows that at the coming of Christ the devil was defeated with his own sword. Indeed, by the wickedness and unjust persecution which he practiced toward Christ, the devil lost his power over all those who believed in him. David put the arms of Goliath in his tent, and we were the arms of the devil, for thus the Apostle speaks: 'As you yielded your members to sin as weapons of iniquity, so now yield your members to God as weapons of justice';[8] and again: 'Do not yield your members to sin as weapons of iniquity.'[9] Christ, indeed, put the arms of our enemy in His tent when we who had been the house of the devil merited to become the temple of God through His grace, for we are known to dwell in Christ and He lives in us. The Apostle proves that Christ dwells within us when he says: 'Have Christ dwelling through faith in the inner man';[10] and the same Apostle shows again that we live in Christ by saying: 'All you who have been baptized into Christ, have put on Christ.'[11] Our Lord further tells His disciples in the Gospel: 'I am in my Father, and you in me, and I in you.'[12]

---

7 Ps. 117.22.
8 Cf. Rom. 6.19.
9 Rom. 6.13.
10 Cf. Eph. 3.16, 17.
11 Gal. 3.27.
12 John 14.20.

(8) The fact that Goliath was not struck in any other member but the forehead signifies something that happens in our own case. When a catechumen is signed on the forehead the spiritual Goliath is struck, the devil is routed. Since we both know and feel that through Christ's grace the devil has been thrust from our hearts, with His help, let us endeavor as much as we can, not to wilfully invite him to us again by our evil deeds and wicked or dissolute thoughts. In that case, although may God forbid it, there would be fulfilled in us what is written: 'When the unclean spirit has gone out of a man, he roams through dry places in search of rest, and finds none. Then returning to his house which he left, he finds it swept. Then he takes with him seven other spirits more evil than himself, and the last state of that man will be worse than the first.'[13] Now since by the grace of Baptism we have been rid of all evils without any preceding merits of our own, with God's help, let us strive to be filled with spiritual goods. As often as the devil wants to tempt us, may he find us always filled with the spirit of God and engaged in good works. Then will be fulfilled in us what is written: 'He who has persevered to the end will be saved.'[14] May He deign to grant this, who lives and reigns forever and ever. Amen.

Sermon 122

St. Augustine, Bishop, on the Plague of God

(1) When the lesson from the Book of Kings was read just now, we heard about the plague of God which raged among the Jewish people. As the angel of the Lord who was striking them stood near the threshing floor of Areuna the Jebusite, the Lord said to him: Stretch out your hand over Jerusalem,

---
13 Cf. Matt. 12.43-45.
14 Matt. 10.22.

so that I may destroy it. 'And when the angel had stretched out his hand, the Lord had pity on the affliction, and said to the angel that slew the people: It is enough: now hold thy hand';[1] and the plague desisted from the people. Areuna, dearly beloved, was king of the Jebusites, and was seen to possess part of Jerusalem. Although all the nations in the surrounding country were subject to King David, still God did not allow the Jebusites to be destroyed entirely, as He Himself says elsewhere: 'I for my part will not clear away for them any more of the nations. Through them the Israelites were to be made to prove whether they would fear me.'[2] For this reason the prophet said to David: 'Go up, and build an altar to the Lord in the threshing floor of Areuna the Jebusite.'[3] That pagan king represented the people of the Gentiles. Notice, brethren, that no place in the land of the Jews was found worthy for the altar of the Lord to be built; but in the land of the Gentiles a place is chosen where the angel is seen and the altar of the Lord is built, and thus the wrath of the Almighty Lord is appeased. Then already was prefigured the fact that in the hearts of the Jews no worthy place could be found to offer spiritual victims; the land of the Gentiles, that is, the conscience of Christians, is chosen as the place for the Lord's temple. This the Apostle clearly indicates when he rebukes the Jews and says: 'It was necessary that the word of God should be spoken to you first, but since you have judged yourselves unworthy of eternal life, behold, we now turn to the Gentiles.'[4] This means: Because you have rejected Christ and have not prepared a worthy place on which to set the Lord's altar, we will put it in the land of the Gentiles, that is, in the hearts of all the people. For this reason the same Apostle exclaims to us: 'Holy is the temple of God, and this temple you are.'[5] Now notice, dearly beloved, that the land

---

1 2 Kings 24.16.
2 Cf. Judges 2.21, 22.
3 2 Kings 24.18.
4 Acts 13.46.
5 1 Cor. 3.17.

of the Gentile king was chosen at the time when the Jewish people were struck by God's plague. This we see fulfilled in the Lord's Passion; for when the Jewish people rejected the Lord and crucified Him, then His altar was consecrated on the threshing floor of the Gentiles, that is, on every land. That is why the angel of the Lord stood on the threshing floor of the Gentile king; the true angel, Christ, visited the people of the Gentiles.

(2) Therefore, the king himself offered blessed David the threshing floor and oxen for a holocaust, but King David refused to accept them without first paying a price. This, too, was fulfilled at the coming of our Lord and Savior, for He refused to take the hearts of the Gentiles for Himself without first giving His precious Blood for them. What, then, did he give? 'Fifty sicles of silver,'[6] it says. In the number fifty the grace of the Holy Ghost is understood and the remission of sins is designated. Indeed, on the fiftieth day the Holy Ghost was sent to the apostles, and in the Old Testament the fiftieth year was dedicated to forgiveness and pardon. That David, to be sure, gave silver; our David, whose type the other prefigured, shed His precious Blood. Thus, in order to buy the pagan king's threshing floor David offered fifty sicles; in order to build an altar to Himself on the threshing floor of the Gentiles Christ, the true David, gave the grace of the Holy Ghost and forgiveness of sins on the fiftieth day. Therefore, brethren, since He has deigned to make a temple for Himself in us and out of us, let Him not suffer any insult in His home. If He does suffer injury because of our sins, He quickly withdraws, and woe to the unhappy soul from which He departs. Doubtless, if a man is deserted by the light he will be seized by darkness. For this reason let us with His aid endeavor so to live that we may merit to have the good Lord not only as our guest but as a perpetual inhabitant: with the help of our same Lord Jesus Christ, to whom is honor and glory

---

6 2 Kings 24.24.

together with the Father and the Holy Ghost world without end. Amen.

* Sermon 123

St. Augustine, the Bishop, on the Judgment of Solomon and the Two Harlots

(1) The lesson to be read at Vespers, dearly beloved, concerns the two harlots who came for the decision of Solomon; one of them who was not only dissolute but also cruel and wicked, shouted to the king that he should command the infant to be cut in two. Now if you willingly listen, we would like to mention to the ears of your charity what the holy fathers have explained about the matter. The woman who cried out that the boy should be kept whole represented a type of the Catholic Church; the other cruel and impious woman who shouted that the boy should be divided signified the Arian heresy. The Catholic Church like a most devoted mother exclaims to all heretics: Do not make Christ less than the Father; do not divide His unity; do not divide the one God in various degrees and fashion, as it were, idols of the pagans in your hearts. Keep Him with you entirely; if you want to have peace, do not divide His unity. Indeed, if you have the whole, everything remains yours. So great is the omnipotence of God that all possess Him entire, and each one possesses all of Him. However, the impious, cruel heresy exclaims: 'No, but divide him.'[1] What does this mean, divide him, except that the Son is not equal to the Father? If a man takes equality from the Son, he denies that the Father is good and omnipotent. If God the Father could beget a Son like Himself but would not, He is not good; if He would but could not, He is not almighty. Be assured, brethren, that none

---

1 3 Kings 3.26.

of the Arians can answer this statement; but whenever they are limited by the truest reason, like a slippery snake they take refuge in some sort of clever and involved inquiries.

(2) Therefore, dearly beloved, I show you a testament, I speak the words of the one who is making the will: If there is something to be divided, I will find it; if not, I will resist them with the testament itself. O unhappy heretic, listen to the testament He has: 'Peace I leave wih you, my peace I give to you.'[2] This is the inheritance of Christians. Moreover, who is the one who makes the will? Read the testament and you will find out. When the prophet spoke of the Lord he said: 'His greatness shall reach to the ends of the earth; he shall be peace.'[3] 'Glory to God in the highest, and on earth peace among men of good will';[4] not to those who divide holy unity, but 'among men of good will.' He Himself is both our inheritance and the testator; do you seek to divide Him? Why will you divide what is one? If you divide the one, you have nothing whole.

(3) Blush for shame, O cruel and impious Arian heresy. When Solomon was judge the harlot did not allow her son to be cut in two lest she betray him, regardless of whence he was conceived and already born. Will you, then, divide your God? Moreover, although a harlot she was, nevertheless, good because she was a mother; you, heresy, are wicked because you are not a mother. You choke what you bring forth, you gather what you do not produce; your heart has become hardened, hers trembled. What does she say who represented a type of the Catholic mother? 'Give her the child, and do not divide it.'[5] He is my son, but it is better for my son to be given to her whole, for let my maternal affection still remain with me. 'Give her the child,' let not my prayers be removed; let not the integrity of His members be divided, let not my piety be taken from me. What she says: 'Give her the child,

---
[2] John 14.27.
[3] Mich. 5.4, 5.
[4] Luke 2.14.
[5] Cf. 3 Kings 3.26.

and do not divide it,' behold I also say: Possess Him entirely, and do not divide God. No, she says, if you want to have peace, divide the inheritance; I speak without prejudice. And how do I have to divide Him? Listen: The Father is greater, the Son lesser, the Spirit a creature. O portions! O justice! O equity! Do I divide, since I do not divide peace? If peace is broken, there will no longer be any peace. How can peace be unimpaired for you if your faith is not entire? Therefore, although you want to possess it with me, you still want to divide peace but are unwilling to divide the inheritance.

(4) Finally, if according to your custom you are eager for treachery and not peace, go, question Christ the judge; let us see what He will tell you. Say to Him what we read in the Gospel: 'Lord, tell my brother to divide the inheritance with me.'[6] Doubtless He will reply to you: 'Friend, who has appointed me a judge or arbitrator?'[7] You want to divide peace and you seek to have peace as your judge? I do not want to be your judge; I am peace, I assist those who are in harmony, but fly from those who quarrel. If I enable all my Christians to have one heart through unity of will, how can I divide the unity between my Father and me, since I give all my faithful people one heart and one charity? What does the Lord say to Philip? 'Have I been so long a time with you, and you have not known me, Philip?'[8] I have come to join you to my Father; do not separate me. Why do you, as it were, seek another besides me? 'He who sees me sees also the Father.'[9] So great is the likeness, unity, and charity in us, that I am in the Father and He is in me. Through this unity may the Lord deign to join us to Himself and keep us: with the help of our same Lord Jesus Christ, who with the Father and the Holy Ghost lives and reigns world without end. Amen.

---

6 Luke 12.13.
7 Luke 12.14.
8 John 14.9.
9 *Ibid.*

Sermon 124

St. Augustine, the Bishop, on Blessed Elias and the Widow Gathering Two Sticks of Wood

(1) I have frequently admonished you, beloved brethren, that in the lessons which are read to us on these days we should not follow the killing letter and leave the vivifying spirit, for as the Apostle says: 'The letter kills, but the spirit gives life.'[1] If we want to understand only what is literally said, we will derive little or almost no edification from the sacred lessons. Indeed, all the things which are read were a type and image of the future; they were prefigured in the Jews, and fulfilled in us by the gift of God's grace. Blessed Elias typified our Lord and Savior. Just as Elias suffered persecution by the Jews, so our Lord, the true Elias, was condemned and despised by the Jews. Elias left his own people and Christ deserted the synagogue; Elias departed into the wilderness and Christ came into the world. Elias was fed in the desert by ministering ravens, while Christ was refreshed in the desert of this world by the faith of the Gentiles. Truly, those ravens which took care of blessed Elias at the Lord's bidding prefigured the Gentiles, for on this account it is said concerning the Church of the Gentiles: 'I am dark and beautiful, O daughter of Jerusalem.'[2] Why is the Church dark and beautiful? She is dark by nature, beautiful by grace. Why dark? 'Indeed, in guilt was I born, and in sin my mother conceived me.'[3] Why beautiful? 'Cleanse me of sin with hyssop, that I may be purified; wash me, and I shall be whiter than snow.'[4] Why dark? The Apostle says: 'I see another law in my members, warring against the law of my mind and making me prisoner

---
1 2 Cor. 3.6.
2 Cant. 1.4.
3 Cf. Ps. 50.7.
4 Ps. 50.9.

to the law of sin.'[5] Why beautiful? 'Who will deliver me from the body of this death? The grace of God through Jesus Christ our Lord.'[6] Truly, the Church of the Gentiles was like a raven, when she despised the living Lord and before receiving grace served idols as dead bodies.

(2) After this, Elias was commanded to set out for Sarephta of the Sidonians, in order that he might be fed there by a widow. Thus, the Lord spoke to him: 'Go to Sarephta of the Sidonians: I have commanded a widow there to feed thee.'[7] How and by whom did God command the widow, since there was almost no other prophet at that time except blessed Elias, with whom God spoke quite plainly? Although the sons of some of the prophets lived at that time, they feared the persecution of Jezabel so much that they could scarcely escape even when hidden. 'I have commanded a widow,' said the Lord. How does the Lord command, except by inspiring what is good through His grace within a soul? Thus, God speaks within every man who performs a good work, and for this reason no one should glory in himself but in the Lord. Were there not many widows in Judea at that time? Why was it that no Jewish widow merited to offer food to blessed Elias, and he was sent to a Gentile woman to be fed? That widow to whom the prophet was sent typified the Church, just as the ravens which ministered to Elias prefigured the Gentiles. Thus, Elias came to the widow because Christ was to come to the Church.

(3) Let us further see where blessed Elias found that widow, dearly beloved. She had gone out to get water and to pick up sticks of wood. Let us now consider what the water and the wood signify. We know that both are very pleasing and necessary for the Church, as it is written: 'He is like a tree planted near running water.'[8] In the wood is shown the mystery of the cross, in the water the sacrament of Baptism. Therefore,

---
5 Cf. Rom. 7.23.
6 Rom. 7.24, 25.
7 3 Kings 17.9.
8 Ps. 1.3.

she had gone out to gather two sticks of wood, for thus she replied to blessed Elias when he asked her for food: 'As the Lord liveth, I have nothing but a handful of meal and a little oil in a cruse; and behold I am going out to gather two sticks that I may make food for me and my son, and we will eat it and die.'[9] That widow typified the Church, as I said above; the widow's son prefigured the Christian people. Thus, when Elias came the widow went out to gather two sticks of wood. Notice, brethren, that she did not say three, or four, nor only one stick; but she wanted to gather two sticks. She was gathering two sticks of wood because she received Christ in the type of Elias; she wanted to pick up those two pieces because she desired to recognize the mystery of the cross. Truly, the cross of our Lord and Savior was prepared from two pieces of wood, and so that widow was gathering two sticks because the Church would believe in Him who hung on two pieces of wood. For this reason that widow said: 'I am gathering two sticks, that I may make food for me and my son, and we will eat it and die.' It is true, beloved brethren; no one will merit to believe in Christ crucified unless he dies to this world. For if a man wishes to eat the Body of Christ worthily, he must die to the past and live for the future.

(4) As we mentioned, that widow prefigured the Church, and her son was a type of the Gentiles. The son of the widow lay dead because the son of the Church, that is, the Gentiles, were dead because of many sins and offenses. At the prayer of Elias, the widow's son was revived; at the coming of Christ, the Church's son or the Christian people were brought back from the prison of death. Elias bent down in prayer and the widow's son was revived; Christ sank down in His Passion and the Christian people were brought back to life. Why blessed Elias bent down three times to arouse the boy I believe that the understanding of your charity has grasped even before I say it. In the fact that he bowed three times is shown the mystery of the Trinity. Not only the Father without

---

9 Cf. 3 Kings 17.12.

the Son, nor the Father and Son without the Holy Ghost, but the whole Trinity restored the widow's son or the Gentiles to life. Moreover, this is further demonstrated in the sacrament of Baptism, for the old man is plunged in the water three times, in order that the new man may merit to rise.

(5) After this blessed Elias presented himself to the king: 'Went up to Mount Carmel, and put his head between his knees,'[10] praying the Lord to send rain upon the earth. 'And he said to his servant: Look toward the sea.'[11] When the boy reported that he saw nothing at all, he told him: 'Go, and look seven times.'[12] The seventh time he returned and said: 'I see a little cloud rising out of the sea like a man's foot. And suddenly the heavens grew dark, and there fell a great rain.'[13] For this reason, as we said, Elias prefigured our Lord and Savior. Elias prayed and offered sacrifice; Christ offered Himself as a spotless sacrifice for the whole world. Elias prayed on Mount Carmel, Christ on Mount Olivet. Elias prayed for rain to come upon the earth; Christ prayed that divine grace might come down into the hearts of men. When Elias told his servant: 'Go, and look seven times,'[14] he signified the sevenfold grace of the Holy Ghost which was to be given to the Church. When he declared that he saw a little cloud rising out of the sea, it prefigured the Body of Christ which was to be born in the sea of this world. Therefore, lest perchance anyone doubt, he said that the cloud had the foot of a man, surely of that man who said: 'Who do men say the Son of Man is?'[15] After three years and six months, rain came down from heaven at the prayer of Elias, because at the coming of our Lord and Savior the rain of the word of God happily watered the whole world during the three years and six months in which He deigned to preach. Just as then, at the coming

---

10 Cf. 3 Kings 18.42.
11 Cf. 3 Kings 18.43.
12 *Ibid.*
13 Cf. 3 Kings 18.44, 45.
14 3 Kings 18.43.
15 Matt. 16.13.

of Elias all the priests of the idols were killed and destroyed, so at the advent of the true Elias, our Lord Jesus Christ, the wicked observances of the pagans were destroyed.

(6) By briefly suggesting these truths to the minds of your charity, we have shown to the eyes of your faith a few paragraphs as examples by which your holy desires may be aroused to examine the divine mysteries in a salutary manner. Now in order that by our wholesome advice we may provide spiritual food for your holy souls to chew over continually, so that they may not by chance disappear from your memory, we will, if you desire it, make a summary of what was said. Thus, as we mentioned above, understand holy Elias as a type of our Lord and Savior. Just as our Lord arose and ascended into heaven after He had exercised much power and suffered His Passion, so Elias was taken up into heaven in a fiery chariot after the many miracles which God had worked through him. The fact that Elias deserted Judea signified that Christ left the synagogue; the ravens which ministered to Elias, as was already said, prefigured the Gentiles. The widow who received Elias in Sarephta typified the Church, while the two sticks she was gathering showed the mystery of the cross. Now if, as we trust, you receive these truths with sincere kindness, dearly beloved, like clean animals chewing them over in your hearts by continual reflection, there will be fulfilled in you what was written: 'Precious treasure rests in the mouth of the wise';[16] with the help of our Lord Jesus Christ, to whom is honor and might together with the Father and the Holy Ghost world without end. Amen.

---

16 Cf. Prov. 21.20.

Sermon 125

On Holy Elias and the Two Captains

(1) As often as the lesson of blessed Elias is read to us, dearly beloved, see to it as well as you can that no spark of doubt or reproach arouses you and consumes the field of your heart with evil suspicion, by instilling some unfortunate error of the Manichaeans. These wretched men are wont to censure the writings of the Old Testament saying: How was it just for blessed Elias to burn two captains with their soldiers by means of fire brought down from heaven? How justly and mercifully this was done, dearly beloved, we want to indicate briefly to your hearts. In the days of the Old Testament, any crimes or offenses committed among the people were ordered to be physically punished. Thus it is written: 'Eye for eye, tooth for tooth.'[1] Indeed, some were punished in order that the rest might fear bodily punishment and refrain from sins and offenses. Now, in the time of the prophet blessed Elias, all the Jewish people had abandoned God and were sacrificing to idols, not only refusing to honor God's prophets, but even very frequently trying to kill them. For this reason blessed Elias was aroused with zeal for God and caused some to be punished physically, so that those who had neglected the salvation of their souls might be healed in heart by fearing bodily death. We should consider that not so much blessed Elias as the Holy Ghost did this. We know that the same thing was done through blessed Peter in the case of Ananias and Sapphira, for through him they incurred the destruction of death themselves in order that an example might be given to the rest. Thereupon, as it is written: 'Great fear seized all who heard of this.'[2] Examples are given to everyone whenever punishments are inflicted upon sinners. Because the unfor-

---
1 Exod. 21.24.
2 Cf. Acts 5.11.

tunate Jews thought only of their body and refused to be solicitous for the salvation of their soul, with God as judge they suffered punishment in the very body to which they had devoted so much care.

(2) Now if you consider well, dearly beloved, you will realize that not only the Jewish people fell through pride, but also those two captains perished from the same weakness. With great pride and arrogance but lacking any humility, the latter came to blessed Elias and said: 'Man of God, the king summons thee.'³ Because they did not give him honor as an old man nor reverence as a prophet, the Holy Ghost spoke through the mouth of the prophet and they were struck down by a blow sent from heaven. The third captain, however, coming with great humility and contrition, as was proper, pleaded in a tearful voice and not only merited to escape punishment but even induced blessed Elias to condescend to go to the king. All this, dearly beloved, happened for the salvation of all the people, since the good and merciful Lord struck a few people in order that He might heal them all. He justly inflicted death upon a few in order to confer salvation on everyone, and because none of them feared the future judgment or learned to fear the destruction of souls through present death of the body. Finally, blessed Moses, of whom it is written that he 'was a man meek above all men,'⁴ when he came down from the mountain ordered twenty-three thousand people to be killed for their sin of the golden calf, in order to free all the people from God's wrath. The priest Phinees, too, killed two adulterers together with his own hand, thereby pleasing God so much that he lessened the Lord's wrath which had been aroused against the people. Therefore, since we see that both in the Old and the New Testaments punishment even to death has been inflicted by holy men, no one should dare to censure blessed Elias with impious mouth or assert he is unjust or cruel. Moses and Elias in the Old Testament and the blessed

---

3 Cf. 4 Kings 1.9.
4 Cf. Num. 12.3.

Apostle Peter in the New similarly punished a few people under divine inspiration rather than presumption, in order to impose discipline upon all.

(3) I have mentioned these facts to your charity, dearly beloved, so that none of you may presume to agree with the wretched Manichaeans and censure the Old Testament, in a devilish spirit discrediting the patriarchs and prophets. As you have always kept everything devoutly through the goodness of God, believe that all the things written in the Old Testament under the inspiration of the Holy Ghost went before as a type or figure; in the words of the Apostle: 'They were written for us, upon whom the final age of the world has come.'[5] Therefore, it is necessary that none of you lack confidence in any part of the Old Testament or murmur against Sacred Scripture in the presence of the foul Manichaeans. Turning to the Lord let us implore His assistance, that He may sanctify our hearts with heavenly blessing and visit us with His continual presence. To Him is honor and glory forever and ever. Amen.

Sermon 126

On Holy Eliseus and the Spring which was Changed into Sweetness

(1) I have frequently suggested to your charity that in the lessons which are read in church we should not only heed what we have heard read according to the letter, but should rather consider what is to be understood spiritually. Now, since the text which was read is about blessed Eliseus, through the goodness of God your piety knows that blessed Eliseus himself represents a type of our Lord and Savior. This fact

---
5 1 Cor. 10.11.

is proven by many evident testimonies of the wonders which we read he performed, while your charity has heard it also in the text which was just read. The sons of the prophets said to blessed Eliseus: 'Lord, the situation is very good, but the waters are barren and bitter.'[1] In reply blessed Eliseus said to them: 'Bring me a new vessel, and put salt into it. And when they had brought it, he cast that vessel into the spring, and said: Thus saith the Lord: I have healed these waters, and there shall be no more in them barrenness or bitterness.'[2] And so it was done.

(2) Let us see what these facts mean, dearly beloved. Eliseus, as I have frequently suggested, is the type of our Lord and Savior. That bitter spring seems to signify Adam, from whom the human race has sprung. Before the coming of the true Eliseus, that is, our Lord and Savior, the human race remained in barrenness and bitterness through the sin of the first man. Although that new vessel in which salt was thrown represents a type of the apostles, still we can fittingly accept in it the mystery of the Lord's Incarnation. Now salt is put there as wisdom, for we read: 'Let all your speech be seasoned with salt.'[3] Moreover, since Christ is not only 'the power of God' but also 'the wisdom of God,'[4] the Body of Christ like a new vessel was filled with the salt of divine wisdom when the Word was made flesh. Furthermore, the new vessel with salt was thrown into the bitter waters by Eliseus, and they were changed into sweetness and fruitfulness. Similarly, the new vessel, that is, the Incarnate Word, was sent by God the Father to recall the human race like bitter flowing waters to sweetness, to lead it to pure charity from evil habits and sterility of good works, and to restore it to the fruitfulness of justice. Truly, brethren, does it not seem to you as though the new vessel full of the salt of divine wisdom was put into the water when Christ the Lord went down into the river to

---
1 Cf. 4 Kings 2.19.
2 Cf. 4 Kings 2.20, 21.
3 Col. 4.6.
4 1 Cor. 1.24.

be baptized? Then all the waters were changed into sweetness and were sanctified by that new vessel, that is, the Body of Christ. As a result, not only were the waters not sterile, but throughout the world by the grace of Baptism they have produced a countless number of Christians like abundant fruit and an exceedingly rich harvest.

(3) Although we believe that this truth is fulfilled in things which are seen, still we know that it also takes place spiritually in all people. The fact that the waters signify the people is mentioned in the Apocalypse: 'The waters that thou sawest are peoples and nations.'[5] Moreover, that the vessel with salt which was put in the water represents the apostles is very clearly indicated by our Lord in the Gospel when He says: 'You are the salt of the earth.'[6] Therefore, by His grace He made new apostles out of old men and filled them with the salt of His teachings and divine wisdom, sending them to the whole world as to the spring of the entire human race, to remove its barrenness and bitterness. Finally, from the time that the salt of divine wisdom is afforded to human hearts, all bitterness of relations or sterility in good works is known to be removed.

(4) Therefore, dearly beloved, as we mentioned above, understand Christ our Lord in blessed Eliseus, and the human race in that spring. Recognize clearly the malice of the devil, which served the first man in what was bitter and sterile. In that new vessel which was put in the spring full of salt, devoutly think of Christ's teaching seasoned with the salt of divine wisdom, and through the apostles directed to the human race.

(5) We, too, dearly beloved, without any preceding good merits have received such great goods from the Lord through His generous graces, and have merited to be changed from bitterness to sweetness, summoned from barrenness to the fruitfulness of goods works. Therefore, let us, with God's help,

---

5 Apoc. 17.15.
6 Matt. 5.13.

prepare our minds for every good work, considering what the Apostle preaches when he says: 'I entreat you, brethren, not to receive the grace of God in vain.'⁷ What does it mean to receive the grace of God in vain, except to be unwilling to perform good works with the help of His grace? What does it mean, except to defile with impious thoughts and pollute with dissolute words what He has cleansed? What, except to destroy what He has built up and to kill what He has animated? Therefore, dearly beloved, let not the divine benefits be destroyed in us by succeeding evil deeds, lest vices overtake us and virtues be excluded from our hearts. Then would be fulfilled in us what is written: 'If a man again touches a corpse after he has bathed, what did he gain by the purification?'⁸ If virtues are driven away and we are willing to accept vices, we should fear that there will be fulfilled in us the words: 'When the unclean spirit has gone out of a man, he roams through dry places in search of a resting place, and finds none. After this he returns to the house which he left and finds it unoccupied; then he takes with him seven other spirits more evil than himself, and the last state of that man will be worse than the first.'⁹ However, as we mentioned above, brethren, let us who have merited to be freed from all evils by the grace of Baptism, with its assistance strive to be filled with spiritual goods. Then, when the heavenly farmer comes and begins to fan his threshing floor, we will not be burned by unquenchable fire along with the chaff, but may deserve to be stored away like wheat in the heavenly barn: with the help of our Lord Jesus Christ, to whom is power and might forever and ever. Amen.

---

7 2 Cor. 6.1.
8 Ecclus. 34.30.
9 Cf. Matt. 12.43-45.

Sermon 127

On What Is Written Concerning Holy Eliseus: Go Up, Thou Bald Head

(1) When the divine lesson was read, we heard that as blessed Eliseus passed, boys mocked him shouting: 'Go up, bald head';[1] and for this reason at the prayer of Eliseus 'there came forth two bears out of the forest, and tore of them two and forty boys.'[2] As enemies of God and of their own souls, the exceedingly foul Manichaeans, who not only refuse to accept the writings of the Old Testament, but even presume to blaspheme with raging lips, are wont to say: What great cruelty that was in Eliseus, to cause forty-two boys to be torn to pieces on account of the jesting words of children! Therefore, we will briefly tell your charity how their madness is to be answered. At the time when blessed Eliseus was in Judea, he and the other prophets not only were not honored by the majority of the people, but they were even held in derision and disgrace, considered as madmen possessed by the devil. So true was this that at the time when blessed Eliseus sent one of the sons of the prophets to anoint Jehu as king, the captains who were sitting with Jehu said: 'Why came this mad man to thee?'[3] They saw the prophet of the Lord and blasphemed him as one possessed by the devil. Indeed, at that time the holy prophets were held in such great contempt and disgrace, that even to blessed Eliseus who performed such great wonders, as we said above, undisciplined boys shouted: 'Go up, thou bald head; go up, thou bald head.'[4] They are believed to have done this at the instigation of their parents, for clearly those boys would not shout like that if it displeased

---

[1] 4 Kings 2.23.
[2] 4 Kings 2.24.
[3] 4 Kings 9.11.
[4] 4 Kings 2.23.

their parents. Therefore, blessed Eliseus grieved over the ruin of the people, or rather the Holy Ghost through blessed Eliseus wanted to check the pride of the Jews, and caused two bears to come and tear to pieces forty-two boys. The reason for this action was so that when their children were struck their elders might be disciplined, and the death of their sons might mean the training of the parents. Then, they might learn at least to fear the prophet they refused to love when he was working miracles. However, the Jews had continued in their evil so long that they wounded themselves with the remedies, and acquired death where they might have obtained salvation; for they changed light into darkness, and sweetness into bitterness. Indeed, there was fulfilled in them what is written: 'I struck your children; the correction you did not take.'[5] Therefore, let no one with viper-like mouth dare to discredit blessed Eliseus, because what happened to those boys is not to be believed the action of his own power but the Holy Ghost working through him. This was arranged in great goodness and ineffable mercy, as I said, so that since the Jews refused to believe in God when the prophets preached with humility, they should fear him when inflicting punishment with severity. By thus fearing physical death, they might seek the salvation of their souls. We read that this happened, not only in the Old Testament, but even in the New, through the blessed Apostle Peter in the case of Ananias and Sapphira; for the sentence of Peter condemned them in such a way that no one dared lie to the Holy Ghost in their offerings and gifts.

(2) Now according to the letter, dearly beloved, we are to believe, as we mentioned above, that blessed Eliseus was aroused with God's zeal to correct the people, rather than moved by unwholesome anger, when he permitted the Jewish children to be torn to pieces. His purpose was not revenge but their amendment, and in this fact, too, the Passion of our Lord and Savior was plainly prefigured. Just as those undisciplined children shouted to blessed Eliseus: 'Go up, thou bald

---

5 Jer. 2.30.

head; go up, thou bald head,'⁶ so at the time of the Passion the insane Jews with impious words shouted to Christ the true Eliseus: 'Crucify him! Crucify him!'⁷ What does 'Go up, thou bald head,' mean except: Ascend the cross on the site of Calvary? Notice further, brethren, that just as under Eliseus forty-two boys were killed, so forty-two years after the Passion of our Lord two bears came, Vespasian and Titus, and besieged Jerusalem. Also consider, brethren, that the siege of Jerusalem took place on the paschal solemnity. Thus, by the just judgment of God the Jews who had assembled from all the provinces suffered the punishment they deserved, on the very days on which they had hung the true Eliseus, our Lord and Savior, on the cross. Indeed, at that time, that is, in the forty-second year after the Passion of our Lord, the Jews as if driven by the hand of God assembled in Jerusalem according to their custom to celebrate the Passover. We read in history that three million Jews were then gathered in Jerusalem; eleven hundred thousand of them are read to have been destroyed by the sword or hunger, and one hundred thousand young men were led to Rome in triumph. For two years that city was besieged, and so great was the number of the dead who were cast out of the city that their bodies equalled the height of the walls. This destruction was prefigured by those two bears which are said to have torn to pieces forty-two boys for deriding blessed Eliseus. Then was fulfilled what the prophet had said: 'The boar from the forest lays it waste, and the beasts of the field feed upon it';⁸ for as was indicated, after forty-two years that wicked nation received what it deserved from the two bears, Vespasian and Titus.

(3) Since the unhappy Jews merited to be rejected, despised, and scattered throughout the world on account of their pride, let us to whom the divine goodness has granted so many benefits keep an upright faith with all humility. In order that

---
6 4 Kings 2.23.
7 Luke 23.21.
8 Ps. 79.14.

pride may find no place in us, let us observe perfect charity toward all men, and to the end of our life endeavor to serve the Lord with a clean heart and chaste body. Then, after the labor of good works, we may merit to hear that desirable word: 'Well done, good and faithful servant; enter into the joy of thy master';[9] because you managed well your life in time, receive eternal life; since you guarded the price of my blood, accept a share in my kingdom. May the divine goodness deign to bring us to his kingdom, who lives and reigns forever and ever. Amen.

Sermon 128

On Blessed Eliseus

(1) Just as we said concerning blessed Elias that he typified our Lord and Savior, dearly beloved, so we assert with confidence and assurance that holy Eliseus was an image of our Savior. As you heard in the sacred lesson, a certain widow cried to blessed Eliseus, beseeching him with tearful voice: 'My husband is dead, and behold the creditors are come and want to take away my sons.'[1] Thereupon, he asked her what she had in the house. The woman replied: 'As the Lord liveth, I have nothing but a little oil, to anoint me.'[2] Then Eliseus said: 'Borrow vessels of thy neighbors and pour out of that oil into all the vessels, and when the vessels are full, sell, and pay thy creditors.'[3] This widow typified the Church, beloved brethren, just like the one who merited to receive blessed Elias. This widow, that is, the Church, had contracted a heavy debt of sins, not of material substance. She had a debt and she

---

9 Matt. 25.21.

---

1 Cf 4 Kings 4.1.
2 Cf. 4 Kings 4.2.
3 Cf. 4 Kings 4.3, 4, 6, 7.

endured a most cruel creditor, because she had made herself subject to the devil by many sins. Thus, indeed, the prophet foretold: 'It was for your sins that you were sold, for your crimes that your mother was dismissed.'[4] For this reason the widow was held captive for such a heavy debt. She was a captive because the Redeemer had not yet come, but after Christ our Lord the true Redeemer visited the widow, He freed her from all debts. Now let us see how that widow was freed; how, except by an increase of oil? In the oil we understand mercy. Notice, brethren: the oil failed, and the debt increased; the oil was increased, and the debt disappeared. Avarice had grown and charity was lost; charity returned and iniquity perished. Thus, at the coming of the true Eliseus, Christ our Lord, the widow or the Church was freed from the debt of sin by an increase of oil, that is, by the gift of grace and mercy or the richness of charity.

(2) Let us now consider what blessed Eliseus said to her: 'Borrow many vessels of thy neighbors and thy friends, shut thy door, and pour out of that oil into the vessels of thy neighbors.'[5] Who were those neighbors, except the Gentiles? Although that widow typified the Church, she was still a widow, and so those neighbors from whom she borrowed vessels prefigured the Gentiles. They offered empty vessels in order that they might merit to receive the oil of mercy, because before obtaining the gift of grace all the Gentiles are known to have been without faith, charity, and good works. Finally, all who are offered to the Church to receive salutary Baptism receive the chrism and oil of benediction, so that they may no longer merit to be empty vessels but full of God as His temples.

(3) Notice, dearly beloved: as long as that widow had oil in her own vessel, it was not enough for her and she could not pay her debt. It is true, brethren. If a man loves only himself he does not suffice for himself and he does not pay the

---

4 Isa. 50.1.
5 Cf. 4 Kings 4.3, 4.

debt of his sins; but when he begins to pour out the oil of charity upon all his friends and neighbors and in fact upon all men, then he is able to suffice for himself and can free himself from all debts. Truly brethren, such is the nature of holy love and true charity that it increases by being spent, and the more it is paid out to others, the more abundantly it is accumulated in oneself. If you want to give bodily food to the needy, at present you cannot keep what you have given him; but if you offer the bread of charity to one hundred men, it still remains whole. Even if you give it to a thousand, it stays undiminished for you. In fact, if you want to lavish it upon the whole world, you will still lose nothing of it; or rather, not only does it not decrease, but the gain of all those upon whom you bestowed it increases manifold for you. For example, you had a single loaf of charity; if you had given it to no one you would have it alone, but if you gave it to a thousand you would have acquired a thousand loaves. So great is the possession of charity that it remains entire for each individual, and still can be undiminshed for them all. Therefore, if you have given to others, you have lost nothing at all; or rather, not only did you not lose anything but, as I already said, whatever you have conferred upon others you have acquired a hundredfold. For this reason, beloved brethren, realize that the widow was freed from her creditors by nothing else than oil; know also that the Catholic Church has been freed from her offenses by no other means than the oil of God's mercy.

(4) Understand still further, brethren, that as long as the woman had vessels in which to pour the oil it kept on increasing. Indeed, she said to her son: 'Bring me yet a vessel. And he answered: I have no more.'[6] Moreover, Scripture says that the oil stood when she found no more place to pour it. Thus, as long as charity is bestowed, dearly beloved, so long it increases. Therefore, we should of our own accord seek vessels in which to pour oil, for we have shown that as long as we

---
6 4 Kings 4.6.

pour it upon others we will have all the more. Men are the vessels of charity, and if we want to abound in the oil of charity we ought to love the wicked as well as the good; the good because they are good, and the evil that they may become good. Indeed, the oil of charity has this power of making the good better, and of restoring the wicked to the light of truth from the darkness of their sins.

(5) The fact that Scripture says the widow poured oil into the vessels with the door shut signifies that each one should give alms with his door closed, that is, for love of God alone; not in such a way that he may be praised by men, but that he may merit to find grace with God. If a man gives alms for the sake of human praise, he does it with his door open, because it is open to the view of all men. However, if a man performs good works only for the sake of eternal life and the remission of his sins, even if he does so publicly he does it with his door shut, because he does not seek what is seen through his almsgiving but what is unseen. Now human praise is seen, but an eternal reward is not seen; furthermore, listen to what the Apostle says: 'For the things that are seen are temporal, but the things that are not seen are eternal.'[7] Therefore, let each one with assurance practice almsgiving even publicly, provided that he does not seek human glory in return.

(6) We have heard that after this blessed Eliseus passed by Sunam, where a certain woman received him and said to her husband: 'I perceive that this is a man of God: let us make him a chamber and put a bed in it for him, and a table, and a stool, and a candlestick, that when he cometh, he may abide there.'[8] Now, that woman was sterile, but at the prayer of Eliseus she bore a son. So, too, the Church was sterile before the coming of Christ; but just as that other bore a son at the prayer of Eliseus, so the Church bore the Christian people when Christ came to her. However, the son of that woman died during the absence of Eliseus; thus also, the

---

7 2 Cor. 4.18.
8 Cf. 4 Kings 4.9, 10.

Church's son, that is, the Gentiles, died through sin before Christ's advent. When Eliseus came down from the mountain, the widow's son was revived; and when Christ came down from heaven, the Church's son or the Gentiles were restored to life. However, let us see how this happened.

(7) After the death of her son, that woman went out and prostrated herself at the feet of holy Eliseus, but the blessed man gave his staff to his servant and said to him: 'Go, and lay my staff upon the face of the child. If any man salute thee, return not the greeting.'[9] At this point, brethren, see to it that no wicked thought overtake anyone by saying that blessed Eliseus wanted to practice augury, and that for this reason he commanded the boy not to return the greeting if anyone should salute him on the way. We read this frequently in Scripture, but it is said for the sake of speed, and is not a command of something superfluous or a wicked practice. It means in effect: Walk so quickly that you may not presume to busy yourself on the way or retard yourself with gossip. Therefore, the servant departed and laid the staff upon the face of the child, but the boy did not rise at all. That servant typified blessed Moses, whom God sent into Egypt with a staff; without Christ Moses could scourge the people with the staff, but he could not free or revive them from original or actual sin. As the Apostle says: 'For the Law brought nothing to perfection.'[10] It was necessary that He who had sent the staff should Himself come down. The staff without Eliseus availed nothing, because the cross without Christ had no power.

(8) Thus, blessed Eliseus came and went up to the chamber, because Christ was to come and ascend the gibbet of the cross. Eliseus bent down to revive the child; Christ humbled Himself to lift up the world which lay in sin. Eliseus further put his eyes upon his eyes, his mouth upon his mouth, and his hands upon his hands. Consider, brethren, how much that man of

---
9 Cf. 4 Kings 4.29.
10 Heb. 7.19.

full age drew himself together, so that he might fit the little child who lay dead; for what Eliseus prefigured in the case of the boy, Christ fulfilled in the entire human race. Listen to the Apostle say: 'He humbled himself, becoming obedient to death.'[11] Because we were little children, He made Himself small; since we lay dead, the kind Physician bent down, for truly, brethren, no one can lift up one who is lying down if he refuses to bend. In the fact that the boy gaped seven times is shown the sevenfold grace of the Holy Ghost which was bestowed upon the human race at Christ's advent in order to restore it to life. Concerning the Spirit Himself the Apostle says: 'If anyone does not have the Spirit of Christ, he does not belong to Christ.'[12] Our Lord gave the same Spirit to His disciples when He breathed upon them and said: 'Receive the Holy Spirit.'[13] Truly, in a way He put His mouth on theirs when He breathed upon them and gave them the Spirit. Therefore, let us thank our most kind Redeemer who restored us to life without any preceding merits of ours, and not only snatched us from endless death, but even with the help of His grace promised us eternal rewards if we live well. May He deign to grant this, who together with the Father and the Holy Ghost lives and reigns world without end. Amen.

Sermon 129

On Blessed Eliseus and His Servant Giezi

(1) We have frequently mentioned to your charity, beloved brethren, that blessed Eliseus typified our Lord and Savior; moreover, his disciple Giezi is not unfittingly understood to have prefigured the traitor Judas or the Jewish people. Just

---
11 Phil. 2.8.
12 Rom. 8.9.
13 John 20.22.

as Giezi served blessed Eliseus in such a way that he might acquire money, so Judas kept close to our Lord and Savior in order that he might commit fraud and amass earthly riches. Indeed, it is written in the Gospel concerning him: 'He was a thief, and holding the purse, used to take what was put in it.'¹ Now Giezi, who could have merited the favor of his master just as his lord had obtained that of blessed Elias, was overcome by avarice and deserved to be covered forever with cruel leprosy; Judas lost the grace of apostleship through his love for money, and ended his life with a noose. Thus, we understand that all greedy, avaricious men are covered within in their soul with the leprosy of sin.

(2) Now Naaman, the general of the army, who was a leper but at the suggestion of a servant-girl came to blessed Eliseus to be cured, prefigured the Gentiles. That girl had been led from Judea as a captive, and told her mistress that if her master would go to blessed Eliseus, he would recover his health. She was an image of prophecy, for although at that time the grace of prophecy flourished in Judea alone, still it was inevitable that the blessed knowledge of it would reach the neighboring nations also. Therefore, Naaman listened to the girl and came to Eliseus; the Gentiles heard the prophet and came to Christ. Upon coming to Eliseus, Naaman was healed of his leprosy; and upon coming to Christ, the Gentiles were cleansed from all the leprosy of their sins.

(3) However, Giezi can also prefigure the Jewish people, as I already said, because they were struck with the leprosy of sin at the very time when the Gentiles were freed from it. Finally, the unhappy Jews exclaimed thus during the Lord's Passion: 'His blood be on us and on our children.'² Then they, indeed, deserved to be covered with the leprosy of sin, when with impious lips they shouted against the heavenly Physician: 'Away with him! Away with him! Crucify him!'³

---
1 John 12.6.
2 Matt. 27.25.
3 John 19.15.

For this reason the leprosy remained in them at the time when grace passed over to us. Finally, the Apostle Paul also spoke to them as follows: 'It was necessary that the word of God should be spoken to you first, but since you have judged yourselves unworthy of eternal life, behold, we now turn to the Gentiles.'[4] When the teaching of the apostles passed over to the Gentiles, then the leprosy of sin remained in the wretched Jews.

(4) Let us further see what blessed Eliseus commanded Naaman the Syrian. 'Go,' he says, 'and wash seven times in the Jordan.'[5] When Naaman heard that he was to wash seven times in the Jordan, he was indignant and did not want to comply, but accepting the advice of his friends, consented to be washed and was cleansed. This signified that before Christ was crucified the Gentiles did not believe in Christ when He spoke in His own person, but afterwards devoutly came to the sacrament of Baptism after the preaching of the apostles. For this reason Eliseus told Naaman to wash seven times in the Jordan. See, brethren: Eliseus sent Naaman to the River Jordan because Christ was to send the Gentiles to Baptism. Moreover, the fact that Eliseus did not touch Naaman himself or baptize him showed that Christ did not come to the Gentiles Himself but through His apostles to whom He said: 'Go, and baptize all nations in the name of the Father, and of the Son, and of the Holy Spirit.'[6] Notice further that Naaman who prefigured the Gentiles recovered his health in the same river which Christ later consecrated by His Baptism. However, when Naaman heard that he was to wash seven times in the Jordan, he became angry and said: 'Are not the waters of my region better, the rivers of Damascus, the Abana, and the Pharphar, that I may wash in them and be made clean?'[7] When he had said this, his servants advised him to agree to the counsel of the prophet. Carefully notice what this

---

4 Acts 13.46.
5 4 Kings 5.10.
6 Cf. Matt. 28.19.
7 Cf. 4 Kings 5.12.

means, brethren. Holy Eliseus, as we said, typified our Lord and Savior, while Naaman prefigured the Gentiles. The fact that Naaman believed he would recover his health as the result of his own rivers indicates that the human race presumed on its free will and its own merits; but without the grace of Christ their own merits cannot possess health, although they can have leprosy. For this reason if the human race had not followed the example of Naaman and listened to the advice of Eliseus, with humility receiving the gift of Baptism through the grace of Christ, they could not be freed from the leprosy of original and actual sins. 'Wash seven times,'[8] he said, because of the sevenfold grace of the Holy Ghost which reposed in Christ our Lord. Moreover, when our Lord was baptized in this river, the Holy Ghost came upon Him in the form of a dove.

(5) When Naaman descended into the river as a figure of Baptism, 'His flesh became like the flesh of a little child.'[9] Notice, beloved brethren, that this likeness was perfected in the Christian people, for you know that all who are baptized are still called infants, whether they are old men or young. Those who are born old through Adam and Eve are reborn as young men through Christ and the Church; the first birth begets men unto death, the second one unto life. The former produces children of wrath, the latter generates them again as vessels of mercy. The Apostle says: 'In Adam all die; in Christ all will be made to live.'[10] Therefore, just as Naaman, although he was an old man, became like a boy by washing seven times, so the Gentiles, although old by reason of their former sins and covered with the many spots of iniquity as with leprosy, are renewed by the grace of Baptism in such a way that no leprosy of either original or actual sin remains in them. Thus, following the example of Naaman, they are renewed like little children by salutary Baptism, although they have always been bent down under the weight of sins. Then may be fulfilled

---

8 4 Kings 5.10.
9 4 Kings 5.14.
10 1 Cor. 15.22.

in them what the Apostle tells the Church concerning Christ: 'That he might present to himself the Church not having spot or wrinkle.'[11]

(6) When Naaman later was cleansed and offered blessed Eliseus gifts which he refused to accept, understand in this a prefiguring of the grace of Christ. It is called grace because it is freely given. Thus, indeed, Christ told His disciples in the Gospel: 'Cure the sick, raise the dead, cast out devils. Freely you have received, freely give.'[12] Since we see all the mysteries of our Lord which were prefigured in the Jews fulfilled in us, let us thank God as much as we can, even if it is not as much as we should. Without any preceding merits of ours He has deigned to confer such great blessings upon us. For the sake of our salvation He not only sent His disciples but even came down Himself, patiently bearing for us the scourges, reproaches, and other insults of which we read. He was wounded to heal our wounds; He died to free us from eternal death. He descended into hell to rescue us from the jaws of the most cruel dragon. He arose from the dead to inspire us with the hope of a resurrection; He ascended into heaven to show us where we should follow Him. What, then, will we give the Lord in return for these gifts which we cannot imagine or express in words? Let us continually thank Him as much as we can, as I already said, and with His help strive that His gifts and benefits may avail to our progress, not judgment. Let us endeavor to fulfill His precepts, so that when the day of judgment comes we may be freed from the evil hearing. Then, there may be directed to us that desirable word: 'Come, blessed, receive the kingdom which was prepared for you from the foundation of the world.'[13] May the Lord bring us to this under His protection: to whom is honor and glory together with the Father and the Holy Ghost world without end. Amen.

---

11 Eph. 5.27.
12 Matt. 10.8.
13 Cf. Matt. 25.34.

Sermon 130

On Eliseus and the Axe Which Fell into the Water; This Ought to be Read as Instruction on the Creed

(1) When the divine lesson was read now, dearly beloved, we heard that as blessed Eliseus was going to the River Jordan with the sons of the prophets to cut some wood, an axe fell into the water, and the man from whose hand it slipped cried out to blessed Eliseus: 'Alas, my lord, for this was borrowed.'[1] After this blessed Eliseus threw a piece of wood into the place where the axe had fallen, and the iron swam. Eliseus typified our Lord and Savior, dearly beloved, as we have frequently mentioned to your charity. Moreover, in the boy who was from the sons of the prophets and from whose hand the axe slipped, we not unfittingly understand Christ our Lord. That axe which fell seems to signify Adam or the whole human race. Therefore, the son of the prophets held the axe in his hand, because our Lord and Savior had in the hand of His power the human race which He had created. Just as the axe fell out of the prophet's hand into the water, so the human race through pride shook itself free from the hand of Almighty God, fell, and plunged itself into the river of dissipation and the waters of every sin. So the axe lay in the water, because the human race had fallen into the abyss of all vices in miserable ruin. As it is written: 'I am sunk in the abysmal swamp'; and again: 'I have reached the watery depths; the flood overwhelms me.'[2] That river where the axe fell signifies the pleasure or dissipation of this world which is passing, fleeting, and descending into the abyss. A river derives its name from the idea of flowing; now since all sinners are said to flow along clinging to transitory pleasures, for this reason that axe lay sunk in the river and mud.

---
1 4 Kings 6.5.
2 Ps. 68.3.

(2) At his coming Eliseus threw in a piece of wood, and the iron swam. What does it mean to cast the piece of wood and bring the iron to light, except to ascend the gibbet of the cross, to lift up the human race from the depth of hell, and to free it from the mud of all sins by the mystery of the cross? After the iron floated, the prophet put in his hand to recover it, and it returned to the useful service of its master. Thus, it also happened to us, dearly beloved brethren. We who had fallen from the Lord's hand through pride, merited to return again to His hand and power through the wood of the cross. Therefore, with His help, let us strive as much as we can not to fall again from His hand through pride. Without any preceding good merits of ours we have been brought from darkness to light, recalled from death to life, and brought back to the right path from many errors. For this reason let us run while we still possess the light of life, and not neglect the passing times of salvation. Let not the unwholesomely sweet and exceedingly dangerous joy of this world delight us, lest we again fall away from good works and the path of justice as from the hand of the Lord, and hasten to the wicked river of this world. Let us not be submerged again in the mud of all sins in unhappy destruction, but let us listen to the Apostle say: 'If you have risen with Christ, mind the things that are above, where Christ is seated at the right hand of God. Seek the things that are above.'[3] Why does he say: 'If you have risen,' unless because we had fallen? Elsewhere the same Apostle says: 'Awake, sleeper, and arise from among the dead, and Christ will enlighten thee.'[4] Does it not seem to you as though he is shouting to the axe which is lying in the mud? Awake, he says, you who sleep in the deep waters, and Christ will enlighten you through the mystery of the cross.

(3) All these truths have already been fulfilled in us, beloved brethren, through the sacrament of Baptism. For this reason, with God's help, let us strive to the best of our ability

---

3 Cf. Col. 3.1, 2.
4 Eph. 5.14.

so to act that the grace of our Lord may produce progress in us and not judgment. Let us observe the sweetness of charity, purity of heart, and chastity of body in such a way that the sacraments of God may suffer no injury in us. If it is true, or rather since what the Apostle says is true, that we are the temple of God and the Spirit of God dwells within us, as often as we commit some sin by thought, word, or action we destroy the temple of God and inflict insults upon Him who abides in us. Therefore, if anyone has defiled God's temple in himself by shameful thoughts, profaned it by dissolute words, or perchance destroyed it to its very foundations by any offenses, with God's help, he should strive while there is time to restore what was ruined, to lift up what fell, to build up what was destroyed. Then, when judgment day comes, even though he does not merit to receive a crown, such a man will merit at least to obtain forgiveness of his sins. However, when I said at least the remission of sins, I seem to have suggested this because of humility which is quite necessary for us. Indeed, the heavenly Physician is wont to repay, not only with pardon but even with a crown, penitents who are full of compunction and rather generous in almsgiving.

(4) For my part, dearly beloved, although I am careless, still I have been appointed by the Lord as some kind of herald of the truth. Therefore, to the best of my ability, if not as well as I should, I suggest, proclaim, and admonish what you ought to hear and I must say. If anyone despises the herald, let him fear the Judge. Before the tribunal of Christ, no one of you will be able to excuse himself by saying that he was not admonished to resist all vices with God's help, and to devote himself to virtues. Since you have frequently been shown what you ought to shun and avoid, and it has been declared by continual preaching what you should do and desire, with the assistance of God, live in such a way that our advice may avail unto reward rather than judgment before the tribunal of the eternal judge.

(5) Since the time is approaching when we should teach the Creed to the catechumens, do you who will receive them as sons and daughters in Baptism know that we will be responsible for them before God. Therefore, teach them now to learn the Creed in such a way that those who are older may answer it by themselves, and have it answered through yourselves or others for the little children who will receive it. If anyone does otherwise, he should know that he will suffer greater shame. After those whom you receive are baptized, always correct them so that they may live chastely and soberly, love justice, avoid stealing, not bear false witness, shun deceitful weights and false measures as poison of the devil, disregard omens, refrain from swearing as well as perjury, observe chastity until marriage, and flee from lying and drunkenness as the pit of hell. All these truths and similar ones, brethren, you should very frequently teach the children who are born of you or whom you receive in Baptism. However, if you want to teach them well, then, with God's help, observe this yourself, for a man truly teaches well if he shows what he teaches not only in word but by his example. Above all teach your entire household as well as your children to memorize the Creed, because if a man does not arrange for his family to learn the Creed, he shows himself to be a tepid and careless Christian. Let no one excuse himself by saying he has no memory to learn. Since many men and women (so much the worse!) remember dissolute songs to their own destruction and that of others, with what boldness do they not blush to say that they are unable to learn the few words of the Creed? However, we trust in the mercy of God that you deign to observe what you are taught by us and to provoke your children by example as well as by words to what is commanded, so that you may not incur guilt through neglect, but attain to eternal happiness by a holy and just life. May He deign to grant this, who together with the Father and the Holy Ghost lives and reigns forever and ever. Amen.

* *Sermon 131*

On Holy Job

(1) In the lesson which was read to us, dearly beloved, we heard that God's most glorious athlete fought admirably against the very cunning enemy. According to what the Apostle says, we have merited not without great wonder to hear and in a way to behold with the eyes of faith a worthy 'Spectacle to God, to his angels, and to men.'[1] Indeed, we saw blessed Job bravely and happily struggling, not only against the happiness of the world, but also against poverty, exceedingly harsh sufferings, and the loss of his children. When he was wealthy, he despised no man; when he suffered want, he blasphemed no one nor dared to murmur against the dispensation of God. As a rich man he said: 'I opened my house to all wayfarers,'[2] 'and the shoulders of the infirm were warmed with the fleece of my sheep.'[3] However, when later he was oppressed with poverty, he spoke thus in his distress: 'The Lord gave and the Lord has taken away; blessed be the name of the Lord!'[4] The devil fought steadfastly, but was unable to overcome God's athlete; he emptied the quiver of his arrows, but could not wound the exceedingly brave warrior. He stirred up huge waves, but was unable to move the firm rock; he applied his machinations, but could not overthrow the strong tower. He shook the tree, but was not able to knock off the fruit; he even broke the branches, but did not harm the root. He pierced the wall, but could not carry away the treasure. Now this treasure I am mentioning is not one of gold or silver, but the faith of the just man, for this treasure the devil hastened to destroy when he tormented Job with

---
1 Cf. 1 Cor. 4.9.
2 Cf. Job 31.32.
3 Cf. Job 31.20.
4 Job 1.21.

an intolerable plague after stripping him of all wealth. You saw the waves increased, the exceedingly firm rock, the impregnable tower. You beheld God glorified and the devil confounded. Therefore, I do not know by what title to call this just man. Am I to call him an athlete? But he excels in such a number of crowns. Shall I call him a rock? I see he is much firmer than that. A soldier? I perceive he is much stronger in constancy. Am I to call him a tower? But he stands out in wisdom. Shall I call him a tree? He is found much more handsome. Fruit? He is shown to be more beautiful than that. A treasure? He is recognized as more wealthy than this. And so I do not find a title by which to name the holy man.

(2) Both the rich and the poor should listen how this blessed man in times of wealth and good fortune was a kind steward of his riches, and in trials of poverty endured it with patience and fortitude. Therefore, you see that it is not impossible to be rich in good works, and for a poor man to be blessed through patient endurance of his poverty. I do not want you to tell me: I am afraid of poverty. You fear poverty, and do you not fear sin? I do not want you to fear poverty, but fear iniquity which is the mother of torments. Our Lord asks tribute from you, and you are unwilling to give to Him. If when you hear Him say: 'As long as you did it for one of the least of these,'[5] you give to the poor, you lend to Christ. If you close your hand to the poor, how and with what confidence will you ask the Lord for mercy on that day? Will He not rebuke you by saying: You saw me naked, and did not cover me; hungry, and did not feed me? What will you reply to such words, and what pardon will you entreat? Will not your conscience make you guilty, so that you become speechless? Indeed, sometimes you are satisfied even to excess with costly, choice dainties, while you refuse to give the poor simple food to drive away hunger. You walk about covered with exceedingly costly clothes, but do not give even the cheapest garment to the naked poor. You strive to arrange

---
5 Matt. 25.40.

and adorn your home in every kind of pomp; perhaps you do not receive a stranger or poor man in even a corner of it. When the irrevocable end approaches for such men, if repentance does not save them, they will go to hell without good works, while their home remains with all its adornments as a testimony of their avarice. Every passerby will say: This was the home of that robber, plunderer, and miser. How many widows he afflicted, how many orphans he robbed, how many men he made miserable, in order to erect this home at the price of great expenses incurred through sin.

(3) Someone may say: I am noble and in a position of honor. No one censures nobility, no one argues about the dignities which are given by God for the benefit of men. Therefore, if men who are rich or in positions of honor live in chastity, justice, and mercy, no one should censure them. However, sad and pitiable men are if they are so inflated with pride in their dignities that they think they will be immortal because of that honor, and do not consider their true condition as coming from the earth, and that some day they will be reduced to ashes. In return for the short joy of this life, if indeed it can be called joy or even life, they will endure endless torments. You look at a man and despise him, not realizing that he is a man like yourself, a man who is dear as a friend and possession of God. For the sake of this man heaven was established, the sea spread abroad, the earth founded; for him the sun rises and sets, the moon waxes and wanes, the sparkling stars arise. Thus, you despise a poor man for whom God arranged such wonders. Finally, to speak still further, a man for whom the Son of God assumed human flesh, endured reproaches and scourging, bore the cross, felt the bitterness of the scourging, tasted death, descended into hell, and at the price of His own Blood freed those who were held in subjection by the devil. Behold, how many great favors the divine goodness has bestowed upon the human race. See whether it is just, then, for us to despise a poor man upon whom the divine goodness has lavished so many benefits.

(4) For this reason let us love and not despise the poor or strangers, dearly beloved, lest He also despise us: 'Who, being rich, became poor for our sakes.'[6] Consider, brethren, and carefully notice that from the beginning God has wanted us to despise no poor man. As you have frequently and diligently heard in Sacred Scripture, in order to check the pride and vanity of the world God did not choose as teachers the eloquent, officials, the wealthy, or the powerful, so that He might entrust to them the secrets of His word. Instead, He selected shepherds like the patriarchs and blessed David, or fishermen like blessed Peter and the other apostles, so that through the weak He might bring to naught the strong, and through the humble cast down the lofty and proud. Therefore, let us love the poor, in order that we may have a part with Him who said: 'Learn from me, for I am meek and humble of heart.'[7] Since the human race incurred a mortal wound through pride, Christ offered the remedy of humility. For this reason do not despise the humble poor who can make you rich even though he is poor in himself. Moreover, the rich should imitate blessed Job by giving generous alms with humility. Let them not be elated in prosperity; and if, with the Lord's consent, they suffer some adversity let them not be depressed by it, in no way murmuring against the judgments of God, but saying with a humble and devout conscience: 'The Lord gave and the Lord has taken away; blessed be the name of the Lord!'[8] to Him is honor and might forever and ever. Amen.

---

6 Cf. 2 Cor. 8.9.
7 Matt. 11.29.
8 Job 1.21.

Sermon 132

The Bishop St. Augustine on Blessed Job the Prophet and on the Verse of a Psalm: Break into Song, Sing Praise[1]

(1) So holy was blessed Job, concerning whom yesterday's lesson was read to us, dearly beloved, that in him was fulfilled what the Holy Ghost said in a psalm: 'Sing praise to the Lord with the harp and melodious song.'[2] Do not assume words alone, but also works; so that we should not only sing, but also work with our hands. If a man both sings and works, he sings praise on the psaltery and the harp. One who sings on the psaltery sings divine words from heaven, while the one who works with his hands performs human works. Extend your hands and give to the poor: clothe the naked, receive the stranger with hospitality. However, when you observe this, do so devoutly and cheerfully. Remember that you are doing it to Him who will tell you: 'I was hungry and you gave me to eat,'[3] and so forth. See what kind of instruments are added in the comparison: 'With trumpets,'[4] it says. Blessed Job was so full of the Spirit of God, beloved brethren, that he sang the praises of the Lord sweetly like a long trumpet. The noise of such men is 'With trumpets, and the sound of the horn.'[5] Instruments of brass are long and are extended by beating them. Now when are they extended? If, when we suffer the persecution of wicked men, we do so with patience and never murmur against the Lord's dispensation, by being attacked we will be long trumpets extended to the praise of the Lord. If we advance in perfection through tribulation, adversity is the striking and our progress is the extending. Blessed

---
1 Ps. 97.4.
2 Ps. 97.5.
3 Matt. 25.35.
4 Ps. 97.6.
5 *Ibid.*

Job was a trumpet when he in no way murmured against the Lord, even though he was struck with so many sufferings by the devil and was even afflicted with the loss of his children. By the striking of such great distress he became a trumpet. Therefore, let us hear whether that trumpet sounds well. Listen: 'The Lord gave and the Lord has taken away; blessed be the name of the Lord!'[6] See, brethren, how sweetly it sounded, how pleasant a sound it produced. This alone did not suffice, but he was afflicted still further: he had the opportunity of having his body struck. He was struck, and began to rot so much that swarming masses of worms dug into him. Now although blessed Job was a just man, he was not without sins, for he was no better than St. John the Evangelist who said: 'If we say that we have no sin, we deceive ourselves.'[7] So by this exceedingly cruel punishment his slight offenses were cleansed. Realizing this fact, Job thanked God and like a very severe judge of his negligences, scraped the corrupt matter with a potsherd instead of soft linen.

(2) Of all his possessions, the devil left Job only his wife. His wife, Eve, was placed near him as a seduction. It was necessary that his wife be kept for him, not indeed as comfort to her husband but as a minister of the devil. The woman suggested blasphemy, but Job refused and did not obey. Adam did not reject Eve in paradise, but Job did on the dunghill. Job was sitting on dung, covered with worms and rotting; but Job full of wounds on the dung was better than Adam unharmed in paradise. Truly, Eve was still his wife, but he was no longer Adam. What, then, did his wife say? 'Curse God and die.'[8]

(3) Behold, we have heard how the trumpet was sounded: the devil struck Job with a serious wound from head to foot, and he sat on a dunghill rotting and covered with worms. We have heard how he was struck; let us also listen to the sweet sound of the brass, if you wish. He replied to his wife: 'Are

---

6 Job. 1.21.
7 1 John 1.8.
8 Cf. Job 2.9.

you going to speak as senseless women do? We accept good things from the Lord; and should we not accept evil?'⁹ O loud sound! O sweet sound! Whom would that sound not arouse, even though he be asleep? Who would not be aroused by boldness in the Lord, to go forth to battle against the devil with assurance, not expecting to obtain it by one's own strength but under the protection of God's help? Indeed, He who allowed Job to be tempted also gave him aid. The devil would not strike him of his own accord; he could do nothing unless the divine dispensation permitted it. Concerning the punishment of the devil, a future prophet said in retrospect: 'The hammer of the whole earth has been shattered!'¹⁰ This hammer of the whole earth God wants to be understood as the devil. With this hammer placed in the Lord's hand, that is, in His power, trumpets or holy souls are struck in order that they may reecho God's praises.

(4) Both the just man and the sinner are struck with this hammer. The former as a trial, the latter for punishment; or at least that the just man may increase in virtues and the sinner be corrected of his vices. Under this hammer which is placed in the hand or power of the Lord, not only the humble but also the proud are struck; but the humble are beaten like gold, while the proud are crushed like glass. One and the same striking brings the good to glory and reduces the wicked to ashes, so that there is fulfilled in them what is written: 'He is like chaff which the wind drives away.'¹¹ As often as holy souls are struck with the hammer through the dispensation or with the permission of God, they in no way murmur or contradict, but with humility exclaim like a long trumpet: 'You are just, O Lord, and your ordinances are right';¹² we still suffer less than we deserve. This, indeed, is what holy souls say. But souls that are proud and guilty of sins, in a rebellious spirit dare to murmur against the Lord whenever

---
9 Cf. Job 2.10.
10 Jer. 50.23.
11 Ps. 1.4.
12 Cf. Ps. 118.137.

they are struck with some adversity, saying: O God, what have I done to you? Why do I suffer such great evils? To these men divine justice replies: You say well, O God, what have I done to you? It is true that you have done nothing for me but everything for yourself. If you had done some good you would have done it to me, but since you have committed sins and offenses, you have done everything for yourself and not for me. Moreover, since 'What a man sows, that he will also reap,'[13] it is not unjust that a man gathers the thorns and brambles of sin if he sowed iniquity. For our part, beloved brethren, let us listen to the Apostle who says: 'Let us sow what is good to all men, but especially to those who are of the household of faith.'[14] Let us fear that perhaps if according to the Apostle we sow in the flesh, of the flesh we shall reap corruption. Upon his testimony let us rather sow in the spirit, so that of the spirit we may reap life everlasting. May the Lord deign to lead us to this under His protection: to whom is honor and might forever and ever. Amen.

* *Sermon 133*

On the Verse of Psalm XLIX Which Says: You Sit Speaking Against Your Brother

(1) Dearly beloved, with the psalmist we frequently chant the verse in which detractors are struck with a spiritual sword; for thus he speaks: 'You sit speaking against your brother; against your mother's son you spread rumors.'[1] When he says 'you sit,' he wants to show that the slander was not in passing, nor was he overtaken by surprise and thus spoke evil

---
13 Gal. 6.8.
14 Cf. Gal. 6.10.

---
1 Ps. 49.20.

of his neighbors. 'You sit,' that is, at leisure, as if unoccupied for the very purpose of discrediting your neighbor. 'When you do these things, shall I be deaf to it?'[2] Let no one deceive himself with false assurance, dearly beloved, thinking that he will not come before the tribunal of Christ to render an account of his deeds. Truly, 'May' the Lord 'our God come and not be deaf to us!'[3] Indeed, now He is said to be silent, because he still seems to suspend punishment. 'When you do these things, shall I be deaf to it?'[4] What does this mean, 'shall I be deaf to it?' except I did not pass judgment, I postponed my severity, I prolonged my patience for your benefit, for a long time I awaited your repentance? 'When you do these things, shall I be deaf to it?' Although I looked for this very thing, that you should repent, you still despised me and refused to heed the Apostle; but 'According to thy hardness and unrepentant heart, thou dost treasure up to thyself wrath on the day of wrath and of the revelation of the just judgment of God.'[5]

(2) 'Think you that I am like yourself?'[6] It is not enough that your wicked deeds please you, you think they also please me. Since you do not suffer God as an avenger at once, you want to keep a partner and to have a companion of your plunder as a corrupt judge. Of the many goods you have seized, you give little alms and still do not desert your sins, thinking you can redeem yourself, as it were, by bribing the judge. Since you do not abandon your sins, you would deceive yourself even if you gave away everything, by losing your money and not redeeming your sins. 'Think you that I am like yourself? I will correct you.'[7] Indeed, when our Lord and God comes, He will not be silent. 'I will correct you.' What will I do to reprove you? What will I do to you? Now you do

---

2 Ps. 49.21.
3 Ps. 49.3.
4 Ps. 49.21.
5 Rom. 2.5.
6 Ps. 49.21.
7 *Ibid.*

not see yourself, but I will make you behold yourself; because if you saw yourself and displeased yourself, you would please me. Since you do not see yourself, you are satisfied with yourself and will displease both me and you: me when you will be judged, yourself when you will burn in hell. Indeed, what will I do to you, someone says?

(3) 'I will draw you up before your eyes.'[8] In the fact that you want to be concealed from yourself, you are behind your own back and do not see yourself. I will make you see yourself by placing before your face what you put behind your back. You will see your hideousness, not in order to correct it, but to blush at it. Truly, beloved brethren, all lovers of dissipation who commit sin with delight, now throw their sins behind them. But if by chance on some occasion they do something good, they put it before themselves and continually boast of it saying: I freed that man, I did good to him, I gave him so much. While they thus attribute to themselves the good which God did through them, by their vanity they destroy what they seem to acquire by almsgiving. Therefore, before the tribunal of Christ, since they have lost the good things which they kept before them, the sins which they had thrown behind their back will be summoned before their face. Then they will suffer punishment without end, because they refused to procure a remedy for themselves while they lived. This is the case with men who love present things more than future ones. However, men who think more attentively about the salvation of their soul act in a contrary manner; they throw the good which they do behind their back, and place before their eyes the evil which has overtaken them. In the present life they blush over their sins, striving with all the devotion of faith to heal what was wounded, to revive what was dead, and to cleanse what was defiled. When these men come before the tribunal of Christ on judgment day, the evil which they had placed before their face and redeemed by good works will be

---

8 *Ibid.*

taken away, and the good deeds which they had cast behind their back because of vanity will be set before their eyes, and they will merit to hear: 'Come, blessed of my Father, receive the kingdom.'[9] Although this is true, we should not despair of those who are still unwilling to correct their vices and do not even blush to defend them. In a similar way hope was not abandoned for that city of which it is written: 'Three days more, and Ninive shall be destroyed';[10] yet in those three days it was able to be converted, pray, bewail, and merit mercy from the threatened punishment. Therefore, let all who are such listen to God while it is possible to hear Him in His silence, that is, not punishing at present; for He will come and will not be silent, and will then reprove when there is no chance of amendment. 'I will draw you up before your eyes.'[11] Therefore, do you, whoever are like this, as was already said above, do what the Lord threatens to do to you. Remove yourself from behind you where you do not want to see yourself, hiding your deeds, and put yourself before you. Ascend the tribunal of your mind, be your own judge. Let fear torment you, a confession of your guilt result, and say to your God: 'For I acknowledge my offense, and my sin is before me always.'[12] Let what was behind you come before you, and when it is before you, let it be punished by you, lest afterwards you be put before yourself by God the judge and have no place where you may flee from yourself.

(4) Now 'Consider this, you who forget God.'[13] You did not think about your evil life; understand yourself, you that have forgotten the Lord: 'Lest I rend you like a lion and there be no one to rescue you.'[14] What does it mean, 'like a lion'? Like someone powerful and strong, whom no one can resist. Those lovers of the world whom we mentioned above seem

---

9 Matt. 25.34.
10 Cf. Jona 3.4.
11 Ps. 49.21.
12 Cf. Ps. 50.5.
13 Ps. 49.22.
14 *Ibid.*

to praise God with their mouth, but they are proven by their deeds to do far otherwise. According to what the prophet says: 'This people honors me with their lips, though their hearts are far from me.'[15] To them the Holy Ghost exclaims: 'But to the wicked man God says: "Why do you recite my statutes, and profess my covenant with your mouth?"' [16] It is as if He were saying: It does you no good to praise God. It is profitable for those who live well to praise Him, but if you praise Him and do not abandon your sins, it avails nothing. Why do you praise me? Listen to the Scriptures say: 'Unseemly is praise on a sinner's lips.'[17] If you live a wicked life and say good things, you do not yet praise God. Again, if when you have begun to live well you attribute it to your own merits, you do not yet praise God. I do not want you to be a robber deriding the cross of our Lord, but neither do I want you as His temple to throw away His merits in you and conceal His wounds. If you are wicked and persevere in that evil, I will not tell you: Your praise will not profit you, but: You do not praise me, because I do not consider it as praise. Again, if you seem just, that is, humble and good, but go along puffed up with your justice, despising others in comparison with yourself or exalting yourself in a boasting way because of your merits, you do not praise me. Neither he who lives a wicked life nor he who lives well as though by his own merits praises me. Was that Pharisee such by himself when he said: 'I thank thee that I am not like the rest of men'?[18] He thanked God that he had some good in himself. Therefore, even if there is some good in you, do not acknowledge it as proceeding from yourself, but admit that you received what is good from God. If you extol yourself above another who does not possess this good, in this you will be considered proud and not yet one who praises me. First of all, then, be corrected from your very wicked path. Begin to live well, and realize that you cannot

---

15 Cf. Isa. 29.13.
16 Ps. 49.16.
17 Ecclus. 15.9.
18 Luke 18.11.

amend your life except by the gift of God; for 'By the Lord are the steps of a man made firm.'[19] When you have understood this, help other men so that they may also be what you are; for you once were what they are. Assist them as much as you can, and do not despair. God is not rich only as far as you are concerned, and believe that what He has given to you, He both will and can bestow upon others. Therefore, a man does not praise God if, when he has begun to live well, he thinks it is by himself that he lives well and not something received from God. Nor does a man praise Him if, although he knows the fact that he lives well is a gift from God, still he wants God to be rich only to himself and does not want Him to be merciful to others. For this reason could not the Pharisee who said: 'O God, I thank thee that I am not like the rest of men, dishonest, robbers, adulterers, or even like this publican,'[20] also say: O Lord, give also to this publican what you have given to me, and fill me with what you have not yet given? Instead he vomited, as though he was satiated. However, what did that poor man or publican say? 'O Lord, be merciful to me the sinner!'[21] Therefore, 'The publican went back justified rather than the Pharisee.'[22] Now listen, both you who live well and you who lead a wicked life: 'He that offers praise as a sacrifice glorifies me.'[23] No one offers this sacrifice to me and is wicked. I do not say: Let not the wicked offer it, but: No wicked man offers it. The man who praises me is good, because if he praises me he lives well. If he praises me, not only his tongue does so, but his life agrees with his tongue.

(5) Therefore, I exhort you, dearly beloved. With God's help, let us endeavor as much as we can to praise God by a good life just as we do with words, for it would be better to be silent and do good than to praise Him and commit sin.

---
19 Ps. 36.23.
20 Luke 18.11.
21 Luke 18.13.
22 Cf. Luke 18.14.
23 Ps. 49.23.

If a man praises God at the same time by his life and his tongue, equally with words and good deeds, he calls forth the grace of God doubly upon himself. Indeed, if he is unable to praise Him with words, let him do so by good works, continual prayer, and holy thoughts. If we diligently do this, we can both praise the Lord with a secure conscience in this world and happily reach eternal joy in the life to come.

* *Sermon 134*

On a Section of Psalm L, that is, On the Sin of David

(1) As often as you know that some of our sons under vain persuasion or harmful love run to mad, bloody, or shameful spectacles, as if to something good, dearly beloved, you who through the goodness of God despise dissolute and cruel amusements ought to rebuke them and pray to God for them more often. Truly, you know that they are going to vanity and false mad desires, neglecting that to which they have been called. If perchance they shudder at the circus for some reason, they immediately sign themselves, and bearing the cross on their forehead stand there whence they would depart if they carried it in their heart. If a man happens to strike his foot while hurrying to some evil deed, he signs his mouth. He does not know that he shuts in the devil, rather than excludes him. He would sign himself properly and drive the devil out of his heart if he recalled himself from that evil deed. Therefore, I beseech you again and again, beloved brethren, pray for these men with all your strength, so that they may merit understanding to condemn such things, the desire to avoid them, and mercy for their pardon. Thus, fittingly for the sake of continual compunction, we daily chant for you the fiftieth penitential psalm. However, let us address those who are

frequently drawn away from the congregation in church by wicked spectacles. I exhort you, dearly beloved, as often as you see them do something like that, reprove them most severely in our stead. Let our words be your reminder to them: correct them by a rebuke, comfort them by speaking to them, show them an example by your life. He who was with you will also be with them, for the bridge of God's mercy was not cut off after you had passed those dangers. Where you have come, they will come; where you crossed, they will do so, too. Indeed, it is burdensome, exceedingly dangerous, and certainly destructive for them to keep on sinning, not in ignorance but in knowledge, after having been frequently admonished by us. One man runs to these vanities because he despises the word of Christ; another does so not knowing why he is fleeing. However, not even of such men should we despair, as is clearly shown by the greatness of divine mercy which 'Has no pleasure in the death of anyone who dies, but rather in the wicked man's conversion, that he may live.'[1] Even in blessed David we know that this was most clearly fulfilled. Indeed, it is with grief and trembling that we mention his sin, and yet God did not want to pass over in silence what He desired recorded. Therefore, I will say what I am compelled to speak, not what I want. I will say it, not to exhort you to imitation, but to instruct you unto fear.

(2) Blessed David was captivated by the beauty of another man's wife, and committed adultery with her, even though he was both the king and the prophet of whose seed according to the flesh our Lord was to come. He further ordered the husband of this woman to be killed in battle, thus augmenting the adultery with murder. After this deed Nathan the prophet was sent to him by our Lord to rebuke him for the great sin he had committed. We have said what men should guard against, but let us also hear what they should imitate if they fall. Many, indeed, want to fall with David, although they are unwilling to rise with him. We are not proposing an ex-

---
1 Cf. Ezech. 18.32.

ample of falling, but if you should fall, a model of rising again. See to it that you do not fall. Let not the fall of older men be a source of pleasure to the younger ones, but let the fall of their elders cause fear and trembling to the young. This is why it is mentioned, is written, and chanted so often in church. Those who have not fallen should listen so as not to fall; those who have fallen should listen that they may rise again. The sin of such a great man is not passed over in silence, but is preached in church; those who listen with evil intent hear it and seek for themselves defense of their sin. They look for a means of defending what they are ready to commit, not for protection against what they have committed, saying to themselves: If David committed adultery, why not I? Due to the fact that the soul is more wicked if it commits evil because David did so, it does something worse than David did. I will explain this more clearly, if possible. David proposed no one to himself as an example, as you do; he fell through a slip of passion, not under the defense of holiness. You, however, propose to yourself the fact that you are sinning as something holy; you do not imitate his sanctity, but his ruin. You love in David what he hated in himself; you prepare and dispose yourself to sin. You look at the book of God in order that you may sin. You listen to God's writings for the very purpose of doing what displeases God. David did not do this. He was rebuked by the prophet, but did not fall through him.

(3) Good men, sons of the Church who are perfect in the love of Christ, heed the fall of this holy man and fear their own weakness. Desirous of avoiding what God condemns, they restrain their eyes, do not fasten them on the beauty of another's body, and are not self-confident in wicked simplicity. They do not say: I directed my attention to that body with a good spirit, in a kindly fashion, and I looked at it a long time out of charity. They propose to themselves the fall of David, and seeing that such a great man fell, like little children they do not want, or rather do fear, to see something

that might occasion their fall. They curb their eyes from wantonness, do not easily become attached, do not mix with strange women, and do not readily lift their eyes to the dwellings and balconies of another. From afar David saw that woman by whom he was captivated. The woman was far away, but lust was close at hand. Therefore, this weakness of the flesh must be watched, and the words of the Apostle recalled: 'Do not let sin reign in your mortal body.'[2] He did not say: Let sin not exist, but: 'Let it not reign.' Sin is within if you take delight in it; it reigns if you consent to it. Carnal pleasure, especially when it proceeds to what is unlawful or belongs to another, must be curbed and not relaxed; it must be subdued by power, not placed in control. Pay attention, you who are self-assured, see whether you have not something in which you might be aroused. However, you reply: I hold on firmly. Are you stronger than David? Indeed, I have said that you cannot be stronger than David or wiser than Solomon. If careless familiarity with women and dangerous allurements overcame such holy men, what do men think of themselves when they neither fear nor blush to both live and stay in the same house with strange women, frequently or always feasting with them? Of such men there can and should be said what the Apostle asserted concerning the widow who lived in pleasures, that although living they are dead. Such an example also warns that no one should extol himself in prosperity. Many men fear adversity but not prosperity, although success is more dangerous for the soul than distress is for the body. Prosperity first corrupts men, in order to find something for adversity to shatter. We must watch more alertly against good fortune, my brethren, and for this reason see how the word of God removes self-assurance from us in times of success. 'Serve the Lord with fear,' it says 'and rejoice before him with trembling.'[3] There is exultation, that we may give thanks; trembling, lest we fall. David did not commit adultery

---

2 Rom. 6.12.
3 Ps. 2.11.

and murder at the time he endured Saul as his persecutor. When holy David tolerated Saul as his enemy, was troubled by his persecutions, and fled in different directions lest he fall into his hands, he did not desire the wife of another or kill a man after committing adultery with his wife. The more miserable he seemed, the more intent upon God he was in the infirmity of his tribulations. However, after the enemy was overcome, he became self-confident. Then, the weight of his flesh and the swelling of pride sprang up. Therefore, this example should be able to make us fear success. 'I fell into distress and sorrow,' he said, 'and I called upon the name of the Lord.'[4]

(4) Those who have not committed this evil should listen to these truths, in order that they may be vigilant to preserve their purity, and since they notice that a great man fell, they should fear like little children. If someone who has fallen hears this, and oppressed with the weight of his great crime has begun to despair, he should, indeed, pay attention to the magnitude of his wound, but still not despair of the power of the Physician. Sin along with despair means certain death. Therefore, let no one say: If I have done some evil I am already condemned, because God does not forgive such sins; why shall I not add sin upon sin? I will enjoy life in wanton pleasure and wicked passion. Since all hope of repair is lost, let me have what I see, if I cannot have what I believe. Now just as our God makes men who have fallen cautious, so He does not want those who have fallen to despair. If any of you have sinned and hesitate to do penance for your offenses, despairing of your salvation, listen to what David did. Nathan the prophet was not sent to you; David himself comes to you. Listen to him shout and cry out with him; hear him groan and join him. Listen to him weep and break out into tears; hear him corrected and rejoice with him. If sin could not be kept from you, at least let not the hope of pardon be prevented. Indeed, Nathan the prophet was sent to King David. The latter

---

4 Ps. 114.3, 4.

did not consider the loftiness of his kingdom, and in a meek and humble spirit did not reject the words of his teacher. He did not say to the prophet: Since you are poor and lowly, how have you dared to address me, a king? The lofty king listened to the prophet; let humble man listen to Christ.

(5) Therefore, if any of you have committed some serious offense, listen to these words and say with David: 'Have mercy on me, O God, in your goodness.'[5] If a man prays for great mercy, he admits his own great misery; let those who have sinned through ignorance seek your slight mercy. 'Have mercy on me, in your goodness'; remedy my serious wound according to thy great healing. What I have done is grave, but I have recourse to one who is almighty. I would despair of such a deadly wound, if I did not find such a great Physician. 'Have mercy on me, O God, in your goodness; in the greatness of your compassion wipe out my offense.'[6] When he says: 'Wipe out my offense,' it means, 'have mercy on me'; and 'in the greatness of your compassion' signifies 'in your goodness.' Your abundant pity arises from your great mercy. You pay attention to those who despise you in order to correct them. You heed the ignorant to teach them; you care for those who confess their guilt so that you may forgive them. A certain man did wrong unknowingly and what does he say? He had done some things and had committed many sins. 'I obtained mercy,' he says, 'because I acted ignorantly, in unbelief.'[7] David could not say: 'I acted ignorantly,' for he was not ignorant of the seriousness of his sin in touching the wife of another, and killing her husband who knew nothing about it and certainly was not angry. Therefore, those who have done wrong ignorantly obtain mercy, but those who do so knowingly obtain, not any kind of mercy, but great mercy. For this reason say again and again: 'Have mercy on me, O God, in your goodness.'[8]

---
5 Ps. 50.3.
6 *Ibid.*
7 1 Tim. 1.13.
8 Ps. 50.3.

(6) Now consider whom you invoke. You are calling upon the just one who hates sin, and if He is just He punishes offenses. You cannot take away from the Lord God His justice. Implore mercy, but heed His justice. He is mercy insofar as He forgives the sinner; He is justice when He punishes sin. What then? You seek mercy, and will the sin remain unpunished? David and others who have fallen can reply. They can answer with David that like him they merit mercy, and say: Not unpunished, O Lord will my sin be; I know the justice of Him whose mercy I seek. It will not be unpunished, but I do not want you to punish me, because I punish my own sin. Therefore, I beg you to forgive me, because 'I acknowledge my offense, and my sin is before me always.'[9] I have not placed what I did behind my back; I do not look at others and forget myself. I do not strive to cast the straw out of my brother's eye, when there is a beam in my own eye. My sin 'is before me,' not behind me. Indeed, it was behind me when the prophet was sent to teach me the parable of the poor man's sheep. Nathan the prophet said to David: 'There was a certain rich man who had very many sheep; but his poor neighbor had one little ewe lamb which he nourished in his bosom with his own food. A stranger came to the rich man: he took nothing from his own flock, but desired the lamb of his poor neighbor and killed it for his guest. What did he deserve?'[10] In anger David passed sentence. Clearly, the king did not know at the time how he was ensnared, for he said the rich man deserved death, and the ewe should be restored fourfold. He judged most severely and very justly. But his sin was not yet before him; what he had done was behind his back, and not yet realizing his own iniquity, he did not forgive that of another. However, the prophet who was sent for this purpose took the sin from behind him and put it before his eyes, so that he might see that the exceedingly severe sentence was passed against himself. In order to cut and heal the wound

---

9 Cf. Ps. 50.5.
10 2 Kings 12.1 ff.

of his heart, God made an instrument of iron out of his tongue.

(7) Let us acknowledge our iniquities, beloved brethren, and struggle against our evil concupiscences as much as we can. By fasting, vigils, prayers, and more generous almsgiving, let us redeem the evil we have done and, with God's help, let us strive to pursue good works in such a way that our evil inclinations may not draw us back again to our former sins. Let us rather persevere in every good work, and with the prophet return thanks to God by saying: 'You have loosed my bonds. To you will I offer sacrifice of thanksgiving':[11] with the help of our Lord Jesus Christ, who together with the Father and the Holy Ghost lives and reigns world without end. Amen.

* *Sermon 135*

On a Verse from Psalm LXXV: Make Vows to the Lord Your God and Fulfill Them

(1) The divine word admonishes us through the prophet, dearly beloved: 'Make vows to the Lord, your God, and fulfill them.'[1] Therefore, each one should vow and pay what he can. Do not vow and then not pay, but let each one vow and pay what he can. Do not be slothful in vowing, for then you will not fulfill it with all your strength. You will fail if you trust in yourself, but if you rely on Him to whom you vow, vow and you will pay with assurance. 'Make vows to the Lord, your God, and fulfill them, all of you' together. What should we vow and pay, brethren? Belief in Him, hope of eternal life from Him, and a good life according to a common standard. There is, indeed, a common standard for all men. Not to commit adultery is a precept for married people as well as for

---
11 Ps. 115.16, 17.

---
1 Ps. 75.12.

religious; it is a command in common for both religious men and women. Not to steal is a precept for all men. Not to love drunkenness, in which men plunge themselves and destroy the temple of God within them, is equally commanded to everyone. Not to be proud is a precept alike for all men. Not to commit murder, to hate a brother, or to plan ruin for anyone, is a command in common for everyone. Therefore, we all ought to vow whatever belongs to faith, justice, chastity, or mercy, and with the help of Him to whom we vow it we will pay. One man will vow to God conjugal chastity, so that he may not know any woman but his wife; so, too, his wife, in order to know no other man but her husband. Others will vow not to suffer or desire or endure any such thing in the future, even though they are now without a spouse; and these people vow something greater than the former ones. Still others will vow this virginity from the very beginning of their life, so that they never will experience anything like those others tried and left; and these vow the most. Some people will vow to keep their home hospitable to all holy men who approach; they will make a great vow. Another will vow to leave all his possessions for distribution among the poor, and go live a common life in company with the saints; he will vow something great.

(2) 'Make vows to the Lord, your God, and fulfill them.' Each one should vow what he wants to promise, but he should see to it that he pays what he has vowed. It is wrong for a man to look back from what he has vowed. A certain religious wanted to marry. What did she want? To be a virgin. What did she want? To be a mother also. Did she desire something evil? Very much so. Why? Because she had already married her Lord and God. Indeed, what does the Apostle Paul say about such people? Although he says that 'the younger widows should marry'[2] if they wish, still he says somewhere else: 'but she will be more blessed, in my judgment, if she remains as

---

2 Cf. 1 Tim. 5.14.

she is.'³ He shows that she will be more blessed if she remains as she is, and yet is not to be condemned if she wishes to marry. However, he says concerning some who vowed and did not pay: 'They are to be condemned because they have broken their first troth.'⁴ What does this mean: 'They have broken their first troth'? They made a vow and did not keep it.

(3) Therefore, let no one who is situated in a monastery say: I am leaving the monastery; not only those in a monastery are going to reach the kingdom of heaven, and do not those who are there belong to God? To him we reply: But they did not make a vow; you vowed, and then looked back. What does the Lord say when He threatens the day of judgment? 'Remember Lot's wife.'⁵ This He said to all men. What did Lot's wife do? She was freed from Sodom, and while on the way looked back. Where she looked back, there she remained; she became a statue of salt, to preserve men by the contemplation of her. Let them take heart and not be foolish or look back, lest after giving a bad example they should remain there to preserve others. Now we say to those of our brothers whom we happen to see shaken in their good resolve: Do you want to be such men as they are? We present to them certain men who looked back; then those who are foolish may fear the example of those who were turned into salt, in a way be seasoned by them, and become wise so as not to look back.

(4) For this reason: 'Make vows to the Lord, your God, and fulfill them,'⁶ because Lot's wife refers to all men. Although married, that woman wanted to commit adultery; from the position to which she had come, she looked back. If a widow who has vowed to remain so wishes to marry, she wants what is lawful for a married person, but it is not lawful for her since she is looking back from her position. A virgin who is a religious already dedicated to God should also possess other

---
3 1 Cor. 7.40.
4 1 Tim. 5.12.
5 Luke 17.32.
6 Ps. 75.12.

qualities which truly adorn virginity, and without which virginity itself is shameful. What does it profit to be bodily chaste but corrupt in mind? What have I said? What if no one has touched her body, but she is perhaps a drunkard, proud, contentious, or loquacious? God condemns all these things. If she had married before making a vow, she would not be condemned. She chose something better, overcoming what was lawful; but if she is proud, she does things that are unlawful. For this reason I say: It is permissible to marry before making a vow, but it is never lawful to be proud. O virgin of God, you refused to marry as you might have; you extol yourself, which is not right. A humble virgin is better than a humble married woman, but a humble bride is better than a proud virgin. A woman who looks back at marriage is not condemned because she wants to marry, but because she had already gone beyond that. Thus, she becomes Lot's wife by looking back.

(5) Do not be slothful, you who have the ability and whom God inspires to take a higher rank, because we are not mentioning these truths so that you will not vow, but that you may make a vow and fulfill it. 'Make vows to the Lord, your God, and fulfill them.' Perhaps you wanted to make a vow, but since we have discussed these matters you do not now wish to do so? Pay attention to what the psalm tells you. It does not say: Do not vow, but 'Make vows and fulfill them.' Are you unwilling to vow because you heard 'fulfill them'? Therefore, you wished to vow, but not to keep it? Rather do both. Let the one result from your own profession, and the other will be accomplished with the assistance of God. Look upon Him who leads you, and do not look backwards whence He brought you. He who leads you walks before you; whence He brought you is behind you. Love your Leader, so that He may not condemn you for looking back. For example, someone resolves to observe conjugal chastity; from that time on justice begins. He withdraws from fornication and unlawful impurity; when

he turns to fornication, he looks backward. Through God's gift another vows something greater: he determines not to enter upon marriage. He would not be condemned if he had married, but if he marries after the vow which he made to God, he will be condemned. Although he does the same thing as a person who made no promise, the latter is not condemned but the former is. Why, unless because the one looked back? The one who vowed is in front, while the other had not yet arrived there. Thus, if a virgin married she would not sin, but if a religious does so she will be considered an adulteress of Christ, because she looked back from the place to which she had come. Now some people are glad to leave all worldly hopes and earthly activity, and to enter the society of the saints—that common life where nothing is called one's own, but everything is in common and 'They have one heart and one soul in God.'[7] If anyone wants to withdraw from such a life, he is not considered the same as one who never entered it. The latter did not approach it as yet, while the former looks back.

(6) Therefore, beloved brethren, 'Make vows to the Lord, your God, and fulfill'[8] whatever each one can and as he is able. Let no one look backwards or take delight in former things; let no one turn aside from what is in front to that which is behind, but let him run until he arrives. Not with our feet do we run, but with our desires. However, let no one say that he has arrived in this life. Indeed, can anyone be as perfect as Paul? Nevertheless, he says: 'Brethren, I do not consider that I have laid hold of it already. But one thing I do: forgetting what is behind, I strain forward to what is before, I press on towards the palm of God's heavenly call in Christ Jesus.'[9] Do you see Paul still running, and think that you have already arrived? Who are those that hasten? Those who turn to the Lord, since they do not find here the rest they were seeking

---
7 Cf. Acts 4.32.
8 Ps. 75.12.
9 Cf. Phil. 3.13, 14.

and the joys which were promised, but then, as it were, faint on the way, believing a long time remains until this world or this life is ended. Seeking here some rest, which is false even if it is had, they look backwards and fall away from their resolve, not noticing with what terror it is said: 'Remember Lot's wife.'[10] Indeed, why was she made a statue of salt, if she does not preserve men so they may be wise? For this reason her bad example becomes good for you if you avoid it. 'Remember Lot's wife.' She looked back to the place where she had been freed from Sodom and remained there where she looked back, destined to remain in that place to preserve others who would pass by. Therefore, since we have been freed from the Sodom of our past life, let us not look back to it. This is what it means to hasten, not to heed what God promised because it is afar off, but to look back at what is very close, that from which you were freed. What does the Apostle Peter say about such men? 'What the true proverb says has happened to them, "A dog returns to his vomit."' [11] Indeed, the consciousness of sins weighed down your heart. By receiving pardon you vomited, as it were, and your heart was relieved. Your conscience became good from a bad one; why do you return again to your vomit? If a dog that does this causes your eyes to shudder, what will you be in the sight of God? When a man leaves the place on his journey to which he had arrived in his progress, and which he had vowed to God, brethren, then he looks backward.

(7) For this reason I exhort you and advise you with pure charity, beloved brethren and most holy women. If anyone knows he has vowed something to God, or under His inspiration is preparing to do so and considering it, with God's help, let him strive by devout perseverance to continue his glorious and salutary resolve to the end. Then, he will merit to say with assurance along with the Apostle: 'I have fought the good fight, I have finished the course, I have kept the faith. For the rest, there is laid up for me a crown of justice, which

---
10 Luke 17.32.
11 2 Peter 2.22.

the Lord, the just Judge, will give to me in that day; yet not to me only, but also to all who love His coming.'[12] Moreover, we ought to guard against what the same Apostle declares with some warning for our precaution: 'Art thou freed from a wife? Do not seek a wife. Art thou bound to a wife? Do not seek to be freed.'[13] He further declares what he is advising according to his own counsel: 'It is good to marry, but better not to marry.'[14] For this reason I exhort and entreat you with humility, both frequently and in many ways, that each one of you may consider his vocation, and whomever our Lord and God has called, as it is written: 'Let every man remain in the state in which he was when called.'[15] Hence, let each one of you make his vow for the salvation of his soul in the name of God and the strength of His power, beloved brethren, so that with His help it may be fulfilled. If anyone who knows he has already made a vow keeps it to the end with the cooperation of our Lord and pays it undiminished, he will escape the sentence of damnation for his transgressions, and through the remuneration of Christ will receive eternal rewards in return for his obedience. However, since I have no confidence in merits of my own, if you condescend to pray for me because of the admonitions of my office, our Lord Jesus Christ will at least deign to grant the remission of my sins: to whom is honor and glory forever and ever. Amen.

---

12 2 Tim. 4.7, 8.
13 1 Cor. 7.27.
14 Cf. 1 Cor. 7.38.
15 1 Cor. 7.24.

Sermon 136

Concerning What Is Written:
The Sun Knows the Hour of Its Setting

(1) Dearly beloved, that psalm which is recited at about the twelfth hour throughout the world, both in churches and monasteries, is so well known to almost all men that the majority of them keep it in mind. However, because this is not to be understood according to the letter, we wish, as far as possible, to make known briefly to the ears of your charity what the ancient fathers thought about it.

(2) As you know, that psalm contains the words: 'The sun knows the hour of its setting. You bring darkness, and it is night.'[1] What man, though unlettered, does not understand and know that when the sun reaches its setting, immediately night and darkness appear? Why, then, was it necessary for the prophet to say what is evidently understood by everyone? Likewise what follows: 'Then all the beasts of the forest roam about. Young lions roar for the prey and seek their food from God.'[2] Can there be found anyone who does not know this? Truly, it is known to everyone that when night comes all the beasts roam about everywhere. Since, as you see, we ought not receive this according to the letter, listen attentively, as is your custom, to their spiritual significance.

(3) Now what the psalmist said: 'The sun knows the hour of its setting,' is not to be taken concerning the sun, but with regard to Him of whom the prophet says: 'For those who fear your name there will arise the sun of justice with its healing rays.'[3] Of Him we read in Solomon that the wicked will say: 'The sun did not rise for us.'[4] Therefore, Christ is the true

---

1 Ps. 103.19, 20.
2 Ps. 103.20, 21.
3 Cf. Mal. 4.2.
4 Wisd. 5.6.

sun of justice. He knew His setting when He yielded to His Passion for our salvation; for when He was crucified, night and darkness took hold of the souls of His disciples. Truly, brethren, how was there not darkness in those who did not believe Christ was risen from the dead? Finally, when the women reported that they had seen the Lord: 'This tale seemed to the apostles to be nonsense, and they did not believe the women.'[5] Moreover, on another occasion the two disciples spoke thus to the Lord who was talking to them: 'But we were hoping that it was he who should redeem Israel.'[6] When the apostles spoke these words, then was fulfilled those others: 'The sun knows the hour of its setting. You bring darkness, and it is night.'

(4) There follows: 'Then all the beasts of the forest roam about.'[7] Those beasts are understood, not as material but as spiritual, concerning whom the blessed Apostle Peter says: 'Your adversary the devil, as a seizing and roaring lion, goes about seeking someone to devour.'[8] At the crucifixion of Christ, when the darkness of unbelief took possession of the souls of the apostles, those spiritual beasts began to go about, seeking to devour souls. However, while they went about: 'The sun rises, and they withdraw.'[9] What does this mean: 'The sun rises, and they withdraw,' unless that Christ arose and all the spiritual beasts were gathered together? 'And they couch in their dens.'[10] Indeed, when at the sun's rising the splendor of faith again began to shine in the apostles, those spiritual beasts lay down in their dens, that is, in the hearts of the Jews. Truly, brethren, the hearts of the Jews who crucified the Lord of majesty, how were they not dens of spiritual beasts? In order that you may be able to understand this more clearly, consider what is said about Judas: 'The devil having already

---

5 Cf. Luke 24.11.
6 Luke 24.21.
7 Ps. 103.20.
8 Cf. 1 Peter 5.8.
9 Ps. 103.22.
10 *Ibid.*

put it into his heart to betray the Lord.'[11] If the devil was in the one who took the money, how did he not also remain doubly in those who gave money for the shedding of innocent blood?

(5) After this the psalmist proceeds to say: 'Man goes forth to his work and to his tillage till the evening.'[12] That man who shall go forth to his work is understood as the Church, that is, the Body of Christ, which then was only in the disciples. Indeed, before Christ rose again Peter, the chief of the apostles, at the questioning of a single maiden denied the Lord three times. However, when the sun rose, that is, at the Lord's Resurrection, he was strengthened so as to be willing to be scourged and killed for the name of Christ. Therefore, upon receiving the grace of the Holy Spirit the man went forth to his work, that is, Christ's Church began to do its work. And not merely began it, but even completed it: 'To his tillage till the evening,' that is, until the end of the world. Moreover, in order that this may be attributed more to God's grace than to human industry, this follows: 'How manifold are your works, O Lord!'[13] Surely, they are His works, not our merits. The psalmist continues to say: 'In wisdom you have wrought them all,'[14] that is, Thou hast accomplished everything through Christ who is your power and wisdom. Further: 'The earth is full of your creatures.'[15] Now see, dearly beloved, whether this can be fittingly understood according to the letter. What man, indeed, does not see that the whole earth is full of God's creatures? What need was there, then, for the prophet to mention this, since no man can be ignorant of it? 'The earth is full of your creatures.' This was said of Christians who are holy and fear God, for they persevere in constant good works. With regard to these the Lord says that they will bring forth fruit, some a hundredfold, some sixtyfold, and some thirtyfold.

---

11 John 13.2.
12 Ps. 103.23.
13 Ps. 103.24.
14 *Ibid.*
15 *Ibid.*

(6) After this the prophet added the words: 'The sea also, great and wide, in which are schools without number of living things.'[16] The sea is understood as the world which is full of storms and dangerous waves, even full of bitterness and saltiness. It also has quite large fish which do not cease to devour the smaller ones. There are numberless creeping things, so-called because they creep over the earth. For this reason carnal men and those who are too fond of the world, because they think only of the present life and continuously apply themselves to its pursuits out of love for it, are not unfittingly called creepings things. Furthermore, the words: 'The sea also, great and wide, where ships move about,'[17] are not to be understood relative to the ships of wood which are carried over the sea by the force of the wind, but to the Catholic Church. While the latter desires to reach the port of paradise by holy, just works, she is beaten by many waves of tribulation and the winds of various storms. Moreover, although she is tossed by the violent beating of the winds, she is so well directed by the oars of holy discipline, so well driven by the breath of the Holy Spirit, that she is carried to eternal life by the very adversities which oppose her. In this sea there is also that dragon of which it is written: 'This sea dragon which you formed to make sport of it.'[18] That dragon is understood as the devil. He is wont to play in the wicked in such a way that, not only does he persuade them to sin, but using them as his ministers he does not cease to persecute even those who are holy and just. This dragon was made a good angel by God, but since he exalted himself against God by pride and fell from that happy angelic state, deceiving himself by pride, through God's hidden but just judgment he is permitted to deceive with his cunning careless men.

(7) Now then, dearly beloved, we ought to consider, not indifferently but with great fear and trembling, what was

---
16 Ps. 103.25.
17 Ps. 103.25, 26.
18 Cf. Ps. 103.26.

said of those spiritual beasts. For when we hear: 'Then shall all the beasts of the forest roam about,'[19] it is thus: 'Young lions roar for the prey and seek their food from God.'[20] As the Lord said in the Gospel: 'Look at the birds of the air: they do not sow, or reap, yet your heavenly Father feeds them';[21] and this: 'He gives food to all flesh.'[22] If every creature seeks food for itself, do not the spiritual beasts, then, seek theirs? What are spiritual beasts, except those that we mentioned above, that is, the devil and his angels? And what kind of food do they seek from the Lord, except careless and tepid men, the bloodthirsty, proud, sensual, and avaricious? They, indeed, are the food of spiritual beasts, for by their wicked deeds they compensate the devil for the loss of his soul. Just as the life of the saints refreshes Christ, so on the contrary the actions of the wicked feed the devil. Why do the spiritual beasts seek for food for themselves from God? Because when Adam sinned, as it was said to him: 'Dust you are and unto dust you shall return,'[23] so it was said to the devil: 'dust shall you eat.'[24] Is it the earth that we tread under foot that the devil eats, brethren? No, but men who are earthly-minded, sensual, and proud, who love the earth and place all their hopes in it. They labor entirely for carnal advantages, nay rather for such pleasures, and think little or nothing of the salvation of their souls. Men like these, then, the devil seeks. He seems to do so justly, for they were assigned to him at the beginning of the world when it was said to him: 'Dust shall you eat.' Therefore, let each one look to his own conscience. If he sees that he has greater care for his body than for his soul, let him fear that he will become the food of the serpent. As far as possible let him strive to fulfill what the Apostle says: 'But our citizenship is in heaven.'[25] Moreover, when the priest

---

19 Ps. 103.20.
20 Ps. 103.21.
21 Cf. Matt. 6.26.
22 Ps. 135.25.
23 Cf. Gen. 3.19.
24 Cf. Gen. 3.14.
25 Phil. 3.20.

says: 'Lift up your hearts,'[26] let him reply with perfect security that he has turned to the Lord. If, then, you do not want to be the food of a serpent, do not be earth. In other words, do not place all your hopes and efforts in the earth. Indeed, if the devil sees you occupied too much with worldly pleasure, he seeks you from God as food for himself. Moreover, God cannot deny what he asks, for He Himself commanded him to eat dust all the days of his life. Since our God is not only merciful but also just, if anything is asked justly He cannot deny it. Therefore, let us continually beg the mercy of God to snatch our soul from the sword, to save our only soul from the dog's power, to free us from the lion's mouth. Let us, then, hasten to free ourselves from the snare of earthly desires, so that the devil may not be able to seize us for his food. Still more, with the Lord's help, may we deserve to have spiritual wings and to say with the prophet: 'We were rescued like a bird from the fowlers' snare; broken was the snare, and we were freed. Our help is in the name of the Lord, who made heaven and earth.'[27] May He deign to bestow this, who lives and reigns world without end. Amen.

* *Sermon 137*

On A Verse of Psalm CXVIII: I See That All Fulfillment Has Its Limits

(1) We have frequently sung with your charity, dearly beloved, the psalm in which the Holy Ghost through blessed David makes known to us a remarkable end. Thus, indeed, he speaks: 'I see that all fulfillment has its limits; broad indeed is your command.'[1] What did he see? Are we to think

---
26 This is one of the prayers of the priest before the Preface of the Mass.
27 Ps. 123.7, 8.

---
1 Ps. 118.96.

he ascended the top of a very high mountain, looked with very keen eyes and saw the orbit of the earth and the globe of the whole world, for this reason saying: 'I see that all fulfillment has its limits'? If this is praiseworthy, let us ask the Lord for bodily eyes. Do not go far, behold I say to you: Ascend the mountain and see the end. Christ is the mountain; come to Him, and from there you will see the end of all perfection. What is the end? Ask Paul: 'Now the purpose of this charge is charity, from a pure heart and a pure conscience and faith unfeigned';[2] and in another place: 'love is the fulfillment of the Law.'[3] What is so finite and limited as a fulfilling? Therefore, whatever you do, do it for the love of Christ, and let the intention or end of all your actions look to Him. Do nothing for the sake of human praise, but everything for love of God and the desire for eternal life. Then you will see the end of all perfection, and when you have reached it you will wish for nothing more. When the psalm is read and you hear: 'Unto the end, a psalm of David,'[4] do not understand it except as Christ, for the Apostle says: 'Christ is the consummation of the Law unto justice.'[5] If you come to anything else, pass beyond it until you reach the end. What is the end? 'But for me, to be near God is my good.'[6] Have you adhered to God? You have finished your journey, and will remain in your true country.

(2) Direct your attention, then, brethren. You seek money; let it not be an end for you, but pass by it as a pilgrim. Look for the means to pass over necessities, but not to remain there through passion. If you love it through avarice, you will become entangled in it. Avarice will be fetters for your feet, and you will not be able to go any farther. Therefore, pass by it, seek the end. You look for bodily health; still do not remain there. What is this health of body which death destroys and

---

2 1 Tim. 1.5.
3 Rom. 13.10.
4 Cf. Ps. 4.1.
5 Rom. 10.4.
6 Ps. 72.28.

sickness weakens? It is worthless, mortal, and uncertain. Seek God, search for Him and do so freely; seek Him for His own sake, not yours. It is a true and chaste love which loves Him, not because He gives us some earthly good, but because He reserves Himself for us. There is the end. You seek honors? Perhaps you want some good done, so that by so doing you may please God? Do not love honor itself, lest you remain there. You seek praise? If you are looking for God's you do well, but if you seek your own you do wrong and remain on the road. But behold, are you both loved and praised? Do not congratulate yourself when you are praised in yourself, but be praised in the Lord and you may sing with assurance: 'Let my soul glory in the Lord.'[7] You speak a good word, and is your speech praised? Let it not be extolled as your own, for that is not the end; if you put the end there, you are finished. In that case you are not finished as though perfected, but finished in order to be destroyed. Therefore, let not your words be praised as proceeding from yourself, as your own. But how should they be extolled? As the psalm says: 'Let my soul glory in the Lord,' 'In God, in whose promise I glory, in God I trust without fear; what can flesh do against me?'[8] When your mind and all your possessions are praised in God, there is no reason to fear that your praise will perish, because God does not fail. Therefore, pass over even your own praise.

(3) Notice how many things we pass over, brethren, because there is no end in them. We use them, as it were, on the road and so we may be refreshed as at an inn, provided that we do not remain there. Therefore, love God; this will be our eternal happiness. You labor on earth, but come to the promised fruit. Indeed, who can take away from you the God whom you love? You sleep in security, or rather you watch in security, lest by sleeping you destroy what you love. Not in vain is it said: 'Give light to my eyes that I may not sleep in

---
7 Ps. 33.3.
8 Cf. Ps. 55.11.

death.'⁹ If men close their eyes against charity, they go to sleep in the concupiscences of carnal delights. Therefore, watch. Indeed, to eat, drink, be dissolute, play, and hunt are pleasures, but all vices follow upon these vain pomps. Do we not know that they are delights? Who denies that they give pleasure? But the law of God is to be loved still more. Cry out against such advisers: 'The proud have dug pits for me; this is against your law, O Lord.'¹⁰ This kind of pleasure abides; it not only remains where you are, but even recalls you from flight, lest you perish.

(4) Love of God is true, if we observe His commandments. You have already heard what these precepts are: 'On these two commandments depend the whole Law and the Prophets.'¹¹ On what two precepts? 'Thou shalt love the Lord thy God with thy whole heart,'¹² and 'Thou shalt love thy neighbor as thyself.'¹³ Upon these two commands the whole law and the prophets depend. Therefore, observe charity and rest assured. Why do you fear that you might injure someone? Who injures someone he loves? It is impossible to love, unless you do good. But perhaps you reprove? Love does this; it is a matter of discipline, not severity. Maybe you strike? You do it for purposes of correction, not cruelty, because the affection of this love does not allow you to neglect one who is undisciplined. Thus, it sometimes happens that the results are contrary and opposite when hatred flatters and love is severe. Someone hates his enemy but feigns friendship for him. He sees the other person do some evil, praises and encourages him. He wants him to be rash, to go blindly through the precipices of his passions from which he may not return. He extols him: 'For the wicked man glories in his greed.'¹⁴ He applies to him the unction of his flattery, concerning which the prophet says:

---
9 Ps. 12.4.
10 Cf. Ps. 118.85
11 Cf. Matt. 22.40.
12 Matt. 22.37.
13 Matt. 22.39.
14 Ps. 9B.3.

'It is oil for the head, which my head shall not refuse.'[15] Behold, he hates and praises. Another man sees his friend do wrong and calls him back; he utters words of reproach, reproves, and pleads with him. Sometimes, it even gets to the point of requiring pleading. Behold, hatred flatters while love pleads. Do not pay attention to the words of the flatterer and the seeming severity of the reproof; look at the vital part, consider the root whence it proceeds. Why does the one flatter? In order to deceive. The other pleads in order to correct.

(5) Now there is no need for our heart to be expanded of itself, brethren. Obtain from God that you may mutually love all men, not only your friends but also your enemies. Do not love them because they are your brothers, but in order that they may become so. Always burn with fraternal charity both toward one who has become your brother, and toward your enemy so that he may become your brother through love. Whenever you love a brother, you love a friend; because he is with you, joined to you in Catholic unity. If a man lives well, you love him as one who became a brother from an enemy. You may love someone who does not yet believe in Christ, or if he does believe in Christ, in order that he may believe in the devil; for behold, he may believe in Christ and still not love Him. Do you love even such a man, and do so with fraternal affection. He is not yet your brother, but love him in such a way that he may become your brother because of your attention. Therefore, all our love ought to be fraternal.

(6) I beseech you, brethren, consider and behold this spiritual sweetness. Strength, fruits, flowers, beauty, pleasantness, pasture, drink, food, a chaste embrace are not true without the association of charity. If it delights us so while we are still pilgrims, how will it please us when we come to our country? If the dew thus feeds us, how will the river satisfy us? Therefore, since our Lord and Savior through the sweetness of His love gave us a taste of it from our country, let us through His assistance strive with all our strength to observe perfect

---
15 Ps. 140.5.

charity. Then, when we come to our principal country after the pilgrimage of this world, we may merit to be satisfied more fully with the delights of charity: with the help of our Lord Jesus Christ, who together with the Father and the Holy Ghost lives and reigns world without end. Amen.

* Sermon 138

An Admonition to the People on the Valiant Woman and the Church

(1) I beseech you, dearly beloved, that according to your custom you devoutly receive in silence and repose the words which are preached to you. When, with God's help, my mind is able to conceive some thoughts in explanation of Sacred Scripture, it desires to find a spiritual nest in your hearts. Therefore, with fervor strive like most pious turtle-doves to foster the divine words of the Holy Ghost in the nest of your heart. Do not allow the seed of God's word to freeze in you through the coldness of your sins, according to what is written: 'Iniquity will abound, charity will grow cold.'[1] Instead, as the Apostle says: 'Be fervent in spirit.'[2] Now just as pigeons and turtle-doves will lose their young if they allow them to become cold, so you, too, will not be able to bear desirable fruit if you permit God's word which you have received to grow cold through forgetfulness. As I already said, our mind is anxious and seeks a place in your ears and minds to bring forth its thoughts. Provide a nest in you for these holy words, according to what is written: 'Even the swallow finds a nest in which she puts her young.'[3] The writings of Solomon commend to us a great woman who had a great husband, saying: 'Who shall

---
1 Matt. 24.12.
2 Rom. 12.11.
3 Ps. 83.4.

find a worthy wife?'⁴ On this subject we desire to suggest to your ears a few thoughts which God deigns to supply according to the meaning of the text.

(2) 'Who shall find a worthy wife?' It is difficult to find her, but it is also difficult not to know her. Is she not the city on a mountain which 'cannot be hidden'?⁵ Why, then, is it said: 'Who shall find,' when it should have been said: Who will not find? Surely, you see a city that is placed on a mountain. Moreover, she was found in order to be put on the mountain, for she was like the sheep that was lost. Now truly, brethren, who does not see the Catholic Church after she has been made known? Who found her when she was hidden? As has been said already, she is the city and that one sheep which the shepherd sought when it was lost, and after it was found carried on his shoulders rejoicing. The shepherd himself is the mountain; the sheep on his shoulders is the city on the mountain. It is easy for you to see her when she is set on the mountain, but when would you find her if she were hidden in the brambles and thorns, as it were, of sin? It is a great wonder that someone sought and found her there. This difficult discovery is commended when it is said: 'Who shall find a worthy wife?' that is, the Church. Who does not see her? Why, she was found by Christ and now stands out visible, glorious, admirable, clear, and, to describe her quickly, universal. Understand that woman, as was already said, as the Church; the one who sought and found her is recognized as Christ. Now after He found her, not only did He rescue her from the thorns of sin, but He even adorned her with precious stones. For this reason it is said of her: 'She is more precious than precious stones.'⁶ Why is it wonderful that this woman is more precious than precious stones? Let us only think of human avarice. If precious stones are taken into possession, why is it remarkable if the Church is found more precious than stones? There is no com-

---
4 Cf. Prov. 31.10.
5 Matt. 5.14.
6 Prov. 31.10. Although cited by the editor as a quotation from Prov. 31.10, there is no connection between that and the words here quoted.

parison, although there are precious stones in her. In fact, so precious are they that they are said to be alive. Therefore, there are precious stones adorning her, but she herself is still more precious. I want to mention something to your charity as well as I understand and you do, too, namely, how much I fear and how much you ought to fear for those precious stones. There are and always have been precious stones in the Church, the learned who abound in knowledge, eloquence, and all instruction of the law. They plainly are precious stones; among them were Cyprian, Ambrose, and others like them. Some of their number have wandered from the adornment of this woman, as far as pertains to the eloquence of doctrine, for which the Church is distinguished.

* *Sermon 139*

That the Church Was Pointed Out Before the Coming of Our Lord As Well As After It

(1) The Catholic Church was not only preached after the coming of our Lord and Savior, beloved brethren, but from the beginning of the world, it was designated by many figures and rather hidden mysteries. Indeed, in holy Abel the Catholic Church existed, in Noe, in Abraham, in Isaac, in Jacob, and in the other saintly people before the advent of our Lord and Savior. Truly, Solomon says of her: 'Who shall find a worthy wife?'[1] What does he mean: 'Who shall find'? Here, we should understand the difficulty, not the impossibility, of finding her. That valiant woman is the Church. How can she fail to be valiant, since from the beginning of the world she is troubled by such great tribulations and still is not overcome? 'Who shall find a worthy wife?' This means, who else except Christ? Indeed, He did not find her valiant, but made her so by finding

---

1 Cf. Prov. 31.10.

her. In fact, to find her he left the ninety-nine in the mountains and searched for the one which had wandered, putting her upon His shoulders and carrying her back to her own sheepfold. For this reason Solomon says of her: 'Who shall find a worthy wife?'

(2) Next, he explains what work that woman did, that is, the Church. 'She obtains wool and flax and makes cloth with skillful hands.'[2] The sacred word describes that woman as working in wool and linen. Perhaps you will ask us what the wool and linen are. The wool signifies something carnal; the linen, what is spiritual. This interpretation is given because in the order of clothing inner garments are of linen, outer ones are of wool. Therefore, the wool signifies something carnal, because it is produced from a mingling or union, while the linen is brought forth from the earth without any carnal pleasure and for this reason seems to be an image of chastity. So true is this that by command of the law, priests of the Old Testament used linen bands as an indication of chastity. Therefore, something carnal is signified in the wool, something spiritual in the linen. If you practice almsgiving with the intention of pleasing God, a carnal thing is properly joined to the spiritual; but if you do it for the sake of human praise, only the flesh works instead of the spirit. However, only to work with the spirit and not with the flesh is characteristic of the slothful. You find a man extending his hand in alms to the poor and yet not thinking about God but desiring to please men by this act; his garment may seem to be of wool, but he has no linen inside. You find another one tells you: It is enough for me to worship God in my own conscience, to adore Him there; what need is there for me to go to church, or to mingle visibly with Christians? He wants to have the linen without a tunic. That woman neither knows nor commends such works. She found wool and linen and 'makes cloth with skillful hands.' The wool is found in Sacred Scripture. Many find it but are unwilling to work it with their hands,

---

2 Cf. Prov. 31.13.

whereas that woman found and worked it. When you willingly listen, you find it; if you live well, you work it. 'She obtains wool and flax and makes cloth with skillful hands.'

(3) 'She puts her hands,' but 'to useful things, and her arms ply the spindle.'[3] I will speak of the spindle which the Lord gave, for those woolen works are not foreign to men. Listen to what is meant in 'her arms ply the spindle.' He might have said a distaff, but he mentioned a spindle and probably not without purpose. Although it may seem so, it is not to be foolishly understood that works in wool are signified in the spindle, but in the woolen works good works as proper to a chaste woman who is a diligent, careful wife. Notice, furthermore, that there are two instruments in woolen work, the distaff and the spindle. On the distaff is rolled the wool which is to be spun as thread and pass over onto the spindle for weaving. When it is wrapped on the distaff, it is still on the left side and not yet on the spindle. When it is gathered on the spindle, it is already worked. Now let your work be on the spindle, not on the distaff. What you are going to do is on the distaff, what you have finished is on the spindle. Therefore, see whether you have anything on the spindle and let your arms take hold. There your conscience will be strong and you can say to God with assurance: Give, because I have given; forgive, because I forgave; do as I have done. Indeed, you do not ask for a reward unless work has been done, not while it is in process. Therefore, whatever you do, let your whole soul be put to the spindle, for what hangs on the distaff must be transferred to the spindle. However, what has been collected on the spindle is not to be recalled to the distaff. Therefore, see what you are doing, so that you may have something on the spindle and your arms may take hold of it. This will console and strengthen you, giving you confidence in prayer and hope.

(4) What follows? 'She reaches out her hands to the needy.'[4]

---
3 Cf. Prov. 31.19.
4 Cf. Prov. 31.20.

Well then, brethren, let us not be ashamed to practice holy works of wool. If anyone has a full storeroom or granary, all those things are on the distaff; let them pass over to the spindle. They are on the left side as long as you do not give to the poor, but as soon as you begin to practice almsgiving, they are transferred to the right side and become a work from which a garment may result. Finally, let us mention how these things are done. 'She reaches out her hands to the needy, and extends her fruits to the poor.'[5] The poor is understood as anyone who needs food and clothing, or the needy servant of God who despises the world and continually serves God. When you exercise mercy toward a beggar, the poor man receives food. When you offer some gift to God's servant, the needy receives fruit, and of this the Apostle says: 'Not that I am eager for the gift, but I am eager for the profit.'[6]

(5) In that work of wool we can observe something more plainly. 'All her charges are clothed.'[7] If a man stays anywhere, will he be solicitous about the nakedness of his servants when he has such a wife? Who is this man except Christ? Or who is the wife except the Church? They are clothed and in the best way. Do you want to know how they are clothed in the best manner? 'As many as have been baptized into Christ,'[8] are clothed, both the good and the wicked servants. The just who have put on Christ are clothed, not only according to the form of the sacrament, but also in exemplary deeds, following the footsteps of God. The others who are clothed in accord with the sacrament will have to render an account of their garment. However, that woman does not cease to clothe everyone, so that no one may complain and say: I have not worked well because I was not clothed. Therefore, see how you are clothed, you who 'have put on Christ.'[9] Let us also perform deeds in

---

5 *Ibid.*
6 Phil. 4.17.
7 Prov. 31.21.
8 Gal. 3.27.
9 *Ibid.*

accord with our garments, 'for all her charges are clothed.'[10]

(6) Does this woman who clothes her servants do nothing for her husband? 'Her husband is doubly clothed.'[11] I think you know what the double toga is which the Church makes for Christ her spouse. The togas which she makes for Him are praises: praises of faith, of confession, of preaching. Why double ones? Because you praise Christ as God and as man. Praise Him doubly and simply; doubly because He is both God and man, simply that you may not be false. A certain woman, that is, the Photinian heresy, followed Photinus, and for this reason the heretics are called Photinians. She followed him as a precious stone removed from her adornments, although now it is cheap and despicable. She chose to make, as it were, a simple cloak for her husband: she believed Christ was man, but refused to believe Him God. Another detestable woman wove, as it were, a cloak for her husband, but she wove ragged tales. She said: Christ is only God and possesses nothing at all of man. This is what the Manichaeans assert. The Photinians say He is only man; the Manichaeans say He is only God. The former admit nothing divine in the Lord; the latter declare that He is all divine, and so falsely that there is nothing at all human in Him. If Christ was not man He did not die, He was not crucified, and surely did not rise again; however, He could rise again because He was dead. For this reason He showed His deceiving scars to the doubting disciple. Indeed, without a doubt, these scars were false if true wounds did not precede them, but if real wounds preceded, His flesh was true, His death was real, the cross was genuine, He was truly man, all truth, and abundant praise. Behold, what precious garments come from the distaff of the Church, and for this reason it is written of her that she made double cloaks for her husband. Men who have feared to make double garments in a praiseworthy manner have remained false in their deceit. 'Her husband is doubly clothed.' Again, she made

---

10 Prov. 31.21.
11 Cf. Prov. 31.22.

double cloaks by confessing God in a Man and a Man in God. Therefore, the Church first wove that exceedingly precious mantle of praise: 'In the beginning was the Word, and the Word was with God; and the Word was God. He was in the beginning with God.'[12] She also wove another garment by her daily life among men. 'And the Word was made flesh, and dwelt among us.'[13] For this reason that woman, that is, the Church, made double cloaks for her husband, but she prepared 'for herself' spiritual 'garments of fine linen and purple';[14] of fine linen, by a candid confession of faith; of purple, by the glorious Passion. When we acknowledge God we recognize her fine linen; in the martyrs we praise her purple.

(7) Now for our part, brethren, God has deigned to confer upon us so much good that we were not born of Jews or heretics, but merited to be children of the Catholic Church. Therefore, let us thank God as much as we can, because He vouchsafed to inspire and instill in our hearts a faith that is right and pleasing to Him. Since faith without works cannot save us, let us strive with all our might, according to what we mentioned above in a figure of the Church, to prepare our souls for spiritual work with wool. Whatever God has deigned to give us in our granary, cellar, or storehouse is, as it were, now wrapped on the distaff. Therefore, let us hasten to draw it from the distaff to the spindle by continually giving alms, thus bringing it from the left side to the right. By almsgiving to the poor each one of us may prepare for himself a garment for eternity, so that when we are brought in to that heavenly nuptial feast, as the Apostle says: 'We shall be found clothed, and not naked.'[15] Let it not be said to us: 'Friend, how didst thou come in here without a wedding garment?'[16] but let us rather happily be separated from those people who are to be condemned for the barrenness of their good works. May we be

---
12 John 1.1, 2.
13 John 1.14.
14 Cf. Prov. 31.22.
15 2 Cor. 5.3.
16 Matt. 22.12.

freed from that evil hearing which they will hear, and happily merit to hear the desirable word: 'Come, blessed of my Father, receive the kingdom which was prepared for you from the foundation of the world.'[17] May He deign to grant this who, together with the Father and the Holy Ghost, lives and reigns world without end. Amen.

* Sermon 140

St. Augustine on the Words: Happy the Rich Man Who Turns Not Aside After Gain. That If a Man Finds Anything He Should Restore It to the One Who Lost It Without Delay. On the Man Who Found Two Hundred Gold Coins. That a Wolf Came to the Sheepfold and Departed

(1) We read in Sacred Scripture, dearly beloved, that: 'Happy the rich man who turns not aside after gain!'[1] 'He could have sinned but did not, could have done evil but would not.'[2] Well, then, brethren, let us question our own consciences and see whether we despise avarice in such a way that we may be sharers in that beatitude. Perhaps someone will reflect and say: I do not steal or commit acts of violence; I never commit robbery or keep what belongs to another. Maybe you never did so because no one was willing to entrust anything to you, or if they did it was under witness. Tell me whether you returned something that you received alone from a single person when only God was between you? If you returned it then, or if, the person who entrusted it to you having died, you restored it to his son who did not know about it, then I will praise you. In that case you did not go after gold; you could

---

17 Matt. 25.34.

---

1 Ecclus. 31.8.
2 Ecclus. 31.10.

have transgressed and did not do so; you might have done evil, but did not. Again tell me, if you happened to find a bag of gold coins belonging to another on a road where no one saw you, did you without any delay return it to its owner? Return to yourself thus, brethren, question yourself, observe yourself, answer the truth about yourself, and 'Judge not' yourself 'according to your person, but give just judgment.'³ Behold, you are a Christian, you go to church often, willingly listen to the word of God, and are moved with great joy at the reading of His word. You praise the person who discusses it, while I am looking for someone who fulfills it; you, I repeat, extol the man who speaks it, but I am seeking one who does it. You are a Christian, you often go to church, you love the word of God, and willingly hear it. Behold, examine yourself in what I suggest, weigh yourself in it. Ascend the tribunal of your mind, place yourself before you, and judge yourself. If you find yourself perverse, correct yourself. Consider what I am proposing. In His law God says that anything found must be returned. In that law which He first gave to the people when Christ had not yet died for them, God said that if anyone should find something belonging to another, he should return it at once. Doubtless, if that man had lost it himself he would have wanted to be treated thus, too, by another according to what is written: 'All that you wish men to do to you, even so do you also to them in like manner.'⁴ For example, if anyone finds a bag of gold coins belonging to another on the road, he should return it. Does he not know to whom? Let him not excuse himself because of ignorance, lest avarice master him.

(2) Now there are gifts of God, and among God's people there are some who do not hear the word of God in vain. I will tell your charity what a certain exceedingly poor man did at the time St. Ambrose was bishop of Milan, when Augustine was also present although not yet a bishop. So poor was this man of whom we are speaking, that he was the assistant of a

---
3 Cf. John 7.24.
4 Matt. 7.12.

grammarian. However, he was plainly a true and perfect Christian; he who stood at the curtain was better than the one who sat in the chair. Now this poor man found a bag with two hundred pieces of gold, but mindful of the divine law, he publicly posted a notice. He realized that it had to be returned, but did not know to whom he should restore it. He publicly posted a notice: Whoever lost the gold coins should come to that place and question the man. A certain man who bewailed his loss and was wandering all around found and read the notice, then came to this man. Lest perchance he might be seeking what belonged to another and not his own, proof was sought. He was asked the quality of the bag and the number of gold coins. When the man answered all these facts faithfully, the poor man returned what he had found. Filled with joy and desirous of repaying him, the other offered him as tithes twenty gold coins; the poor man refused to accept them. Ten were offered, and he refused again. He was asked to accept at least five, but still refused. Furious, the other man threw down the bag. I have lost nothing, he said; if you will not take anything from me, I did not lose anything. What a contest, my brethren, what a struggle, fight, and conflict! The world is its theatre, God the spectator. Overcome, the poor man took what was offered and immediately gave it all to the poor; not a single coin did he take to his own home.

(3) Consider, brethren, whether such a glorious example and so admirable a deed has done something in your hearts, whether the word of God reposes in your souls. Do this, brethren. Do not think you suffer a loss if you return whatever has been found by you. Rather believe it is a great gain if you have done what I suggest. Perhaps someone has lost some gold coins upon coming into your house. It is common ground, you are together in one house; you are both travellers in this world, you have entered the single habitation of this life. He put that down, forgot it, it fell away from him. You found it and you have read the law that anything found must be re-

turned. Who found it? You praised the word of God when you heard it; you have found it. Therefore, if you praised it honestly, return what you found. If you fail to do so, when you extolled it you gave testimony against yourself. Be faithful finders and then censure unjust robbers. Truly, if you have found anything and did not return it, you have robbed: you did as much as you could and did not take more because you found no more. If a man keeps what belongs to another, he would take more if he could.

(4) Fear prevents you from taking that. You do no good but fear evil. A robber also fears evil, and when he cannot, does not do it; and still he is a robber. Indeed, God does not question the hand but the heart. A wolf comes to the sheepfold, seeks to attack it, tear to pieces and devour the sheep. The shepherds are watching, dogs bark; he is powerless and does not carry off or kill the sheep. However, the wolf still came and the wolf still went away. Since he did not carry off the sheep, did he come as a wolf and leave as a sheep? The wolf came growling and left trembling; however, it is still the wolf when both growling and trembling. Therefore, examine yourself, whoever wants to judge others, and if you do no evil when you can and are not punished by men, then you fear God. No one is there except yourself and the man you might injure, and God who sees you both; fear this. When I say fear evil there it is not enough; also love good there. Even though you do no wrong out of fear of hell, you are not yet perfect. I dare say that if you do no evil because you fear hell, there certainly is faith in you since you believe in the future judgment of God. I rejoice at your faith, but still fear for your wickedness. What have I said? That if you do no evil through fear of hell, you will do no good through a love of justice.

(5) It is one thing to fear punishment, but quite another to love justice. There ought to be pure love in you, so that you may desire to see, not heaven and earth, the clear expanse of the sea, frivolous spectacles, or the glitter and splendor of

gems; but that you may behold your God and love Him. What is written? 'Beloved, we are the children of God, and it has not yet appeared what we shall be. We know that, when he appears, we shall be like to him, for we shall see him just as he is.'[5] Behold, on account of this vision, do good and refuse to do evil. If you love to see your God, sigh for Him with all your heart during this sojourn, and long for Him. Do what your Lord wants you to esteem, so that it may be clear why you love Him, whether for Himself or for the earthly goods which He confers upon you. Then He may tell you: Do what you will, fulfill your desires, increase your wickedness, consider whatever you like is lawful. I will not punish you for this or send you to hell, only you will never see my face. If you dread this sentence exceedingly, then you have loved. If your heart trembles at what was said, that God will deny His countenance to you, since you have considered it a great punishment not to behold your God, you freely love.

(6) We have mentioned this, brethren, because there are some men so negligent, tepid, and (what is worse) so unfaithful that they say: If only God would give me all good things in this world! It makes no difference to me what He wants to happen to me in the future life. O unhappy soul! Even if God would not cast you into punishment, provided that He merely would not allow you to see His face, would it not be better for you not to have been born? However, since it cannot happen that a man who merits not to behold His face may escape eternal fire, why do you love the pleasure of this present life so much that you do not dread the flame of eternal fire? Therefore, if my sermon finds in your hearts any spark of spontaneous love, nourish it. Arouse yourself to increase it by humble prayer, the sufferings of penance, delightful justice, good works, sincere groaning, a praiseworthy life, and devout friendship. Blow upon this spark of virtuous love, nourish it within you, for the Lord said concerning it: 'I have come to cast fire upon the earth, and what will I but that it be

---
5 1 John 3.2.

kindled?'⁶ Then, when it has grown and formed a most suitable flame, it will consume the wood of all carnal desires. May He deign to grant this, who together with the Father and the Holy Ghost lives and reigns forever and ever. Amen.

* Sermon 141

Another Homily on the Words: Happy the Rich Man Who Turns Not Aside After Gain, and So Forth

(1) We have read, dearly beloved, that: 'Happy the rich man who turns not aside after gain!'¹ 'He could have sinned but did not, could have done evil but would not.'² 'Who is he, that we may praise him? he, of all his kindred, has done wonders.'³ Now at this point someone may reflect and say: Who can be found like this? Far be it from us to despair that there is such a man, or rather not such a man but such men. However, men who are inexperienced and ignorant of God's justice cry out and say: Behold many evils arise from gold; let it be removed from human life. Rather let the gold remain and men's lives be examined. If you say: Let gold be taken away because through it many evils arise in the world, I say in turn: Let the human tongue be cut out because of blasphemers against God, and then how will there be men to praise Him? Remove the eyes which look with impurity upon the wives or daughters of another; take away the hands by which property of another is stolen; remove feet which go to a brothel; take away the ears which not only willingly but even frequently desire to hear shameful, dissolute words; and now what will remain in man? You tell me concerning gold,

---

6 Luke 12.49.

1 Ecclus. 31.8.
2 Ecclus. 31.10.
3 Ecclus. 31.9.

let it be taken away, and I mention the human members by which men often offend God. If a good music master touches an instrument properly, does the instrument play by itself? Your members are your instrument. Let your mind be good and all is well. Indeed, our mind at one moment is a king, at another a tyrant. It is a king when it governs itself properly and thinks right thoughts; but when it begins to love dissipation and seize the property of another, it passes over to that detestable title, becoming a tyrant instead of a king.

(2) Again, you may criticize and say: How evil gold is. Look at it. Let a wicked man take it, and what do you think he will do with it? Listen: He oppresses his inferiors, bribes judges, overthrows laws, and puts human affairs into a state of confusion. Why is this? Because a wicked man has the gold. Let a good man have it: what will he do with it? Listen: He feeds the poor, clothes the naked, frees the oppressed, ransoms captives. How much good arises from gold which a good man possesses! Give also a good tongue and mind; do you see what great good things are spoken with the tongue? The discordant are brought into agreement, the sad are consoled, the dissolute corrected, the irascible restrained; God is praised, Christ glorified, the mind aroused to love what is divine, not human, the pure rather than the dissolute. The tongue performs these good works because the mind which uses this tongue is good. On the contrary, how does an evil mind use the tongue? It is blasphemous, intriguing, contentious, and accusing. Does your tongue do such evil? Truly, all the members of the body are good, but they look for good men. Gold, silver, possessions, and honors are all good things, but they are common alike to the good and the bad. Moreover, there are other things that are really good, for no one except good men can have them: piety, faith, justice, chastity, prudence, modesty, charity, and other virtues of this kind only good men possess. Again, it may be said: Why did God give those good things to wicked men? I will tell you how much God deigns to give. You

murmur because God gives these earthly goods to wicked men? If you would understand, it is for your instruction, not perversity on the part of God. Now listen, you who censure and accuse God by saying: God should not give those good things to wicked men, but only to the just. This is why that deadly impiety overtakes some people, because they think God is entirely ignorant of human affairs. Truly, they argue within themselves and say: If God paid attention to human affairs, would that wicked man possess such great riches? Would that cruel individual enjoy such great honors and such power? God does not care about human affairs, for if He did He would give these blessings only to good men.

(3) Return to your heart, man, and thence to God. Indeed, when these facts offend you, you have gone out of yourself. If these temporal advantages were not given to wicked men, they would be considered as goods by the just. Therefore, when you see that these benefits are given to evil men by God, do you consider what great benefits are reserved for you in eternal bliss since you are just. For this reason reflect and say: If our just God confers such great blessings upon those who blaspheme Him, what kind of benefits do you suppose He reserves for those who worship Him? Behold, our Lord now addresses you as a kind father does his son. Place God before your mind: O son, why is it that you daily arise and pray, cast yourself upon your knees, strike your forehead, shed tears, and say to me: O my God, give me riches? If I grant them you will think you have obtained something good, because you asked for and received them. Behold, I will give them, but do good with them. Before you had them, you were humble; look, now you have become proud. Before possessing them you saw a man in want and said: Oh, if only I had something to give him! Those men and others have possessions but do not give. Now, after you have begun to possess riches, you despise the poor. How can gold truly be a good, since you have become worse by it? Even then you were wicked when you deceived

yourself, and you did not know that riches would make you worse.

(4) God says to you: Before when you were poor you shed tears in my sight, you hurried to church. You have begun to possess riches; now you disturb the theater and the circus with your noisy words. Behold, I gave to try you; you found riches and have been discovered. When you did not possess them, you were unknown. I am telling you this to correct you. Throw away avarice, despise vanity; condemn the world, and love God. You think that what you ask of God is great. Look, your God replies to you: Do you who ask me for worldly riches not see to whom I have given them? If the gold which you ask of me were something great, would this robber possess it? This traitor? This murderer? This man who blasphemes me? Finally, if gold were a great good, would this exceedingly notorious individual possess it? This shameless harlot? If a pious senator requests without success what a very infamous man has, how can it be profitable? If a virtuous woman asks me for something that a shameless harlot possesses, what great benefit does she seek?

(5) Now you say to me: Therefore, is gold not a good? It is, but wicked men do evil with good gold. Moreover, since you see to whom I give these things, ask me for better ones. And yet evils arise in the world, you say. If there are evils in the world, depart from it and surrender yourself to God. If you had a house falling into ruin, would you not leave it before consulting an architect? For this reason depart from the world and return to God. Men say: The world is evil; still it is difficult both to leave the world and to rest with Christ. When mothers or nurses see their children grow, they cover their breasts with something bitter, so the children will not suck too much milk and will not seek it any more. If a small child thus shuns bitterness, why do not you who are a Christian flee from the bitterness of the world? God has filled the world with bitterness, and will you not avoid what a child flees from its

mother? What if the world were sweet? How would it then be loved? Behold, the world rushes on and you follow. How would you cling to it if it were beautiful, since you embrace it thus when it is ugly? What would you do with its flowers, if you do not withdraw your hand from its thorns?

(6) For our part, beloved brethren, when we recognize our kind Redeemer and reflect upon our price, let us not love 'the world, or the things that are in the world';[4] but according to the Apostle, 'having food and sufficient clothing, with these let us be content.'[5] Let us seek the use of what is necessary, but not have desires of avarice. If we lack riches, let us not seek them in the world by evil deeds or unjust gains. However, if we have them, let us transmit them to heaven by good works, so that there may be fulfilled in us what is written: 'Lavishly he gives to the poor; his generosity shall endure forever';[6] with the help of our Lord Jesus Christ, who lives and reigns forever and ever. Amen.

* Sermon 142

On What Is Written Concerning Our Lord and Savior:
He Grew Up Like a Sapling, Like a Shoot from
the Parched Earth

(1) Many times before, beloved brethren, it has been prophesied concerning our Lord and Savior: 'He grew up like a sapling, like a shoot from the parched earth.'[1] Why like a root? Because 'there was in him no stately bearing.'[2] He suffered, was humiliated, and spit upon, He had no beauty. He appeared as a man, although He was God. Now in the

---

4 1 John 2.15.
5 Cf. 1 Tim. 6.8.
6 Ps. 111.9.

---

1 Isa. 53.2.
2 Ibid.

same way, a root is not beautiful, but possesses within it the force of beauty. . . Listen, brethren, and consider the mercy of God. You notice a beautiful tree that is pleasing, green with foliage, rich in fruits, and you praise it. It gives pleasure to pick some of its fruit, to sit under the shade of it, and to rest from the heat; you praise its whole beauty. If the root is shown to you, there is no beauty in it. Do not despise what is lowly, for from it proceeds what you admire. 'Like a shoot from the parched earth.' Now notice the splendor of the tree.

(2) The Church grew, nations came to believe, princes of the earth were conquered under the name of Christ. In order that they might be victorious in the world, they placed their neck under the yoke of Christ. Formerly, they persecuted the Christians for the sake of idols; now, they persecute idols for the sake of Christ. In all tribulations and trials everyone has recourse to the Church's aid. That grain of mustard seed has grown up and become greater than all herbs; birds of the air who are the proud of this world come and rest under its branches. Whence is this great beauty? It arose from some root. Moreover, this beauty is in great glory. Let us seek the root: He was spit upon, humiliated, scourged, crucified, wounded, and despised. Behold, there is no beauty in Him, but the glory of the root is powerful in the Church. For this reason the bridegroom is described as despised, without honor, abject. However, now you have to behold the tree which arose from that root and filled the whole world. 'A shoot from the parched earth.'

(3) 'There was in him no stately bearing to make us look at him, nor appearance of beauty.'[3] 'Is not this the carpenter's son?'[4] He lacked comeliness to such an extent that it was said: 'Are we not right in saying that thou hast a devil?'[5] At His very name the demons fled, and still He was accused of having a devil. Why is this? 'There was in him no appearance of

---
3 Cf. *ibid.*
4 Matt. 13.55.
5 John 8.48.

beauty to make us look at him.'⁶ What beauty did He possess within, where it could not be seen? 'In the beginning was the Word, and the Word was with God; and the Word was God.'⁷ What is this beauty of His? 'Though he was by nature God, he did not consider being equal to God a thing to be clung to.'⁸

(4) When was He seen to possess neither beauty nor comeliness? 'And he had no beauty; but his look was downcast, and his position unseemly to all men: a man in wounds.'⁹ He was a man in His wounds, God before them, and the Man-God after them. 'A man in wounds, who was accustomed to infirmities.'¹⁰ Whose infirmities? The infirmities of those from whom He suffered. The Physician bore the infirmities of madmen, and when He was crucified He prayed: 'Father, forgive them, for they do not know what they are doing.'¹¹ Listen, let us love our bridegroom. The more ugly He is presented to us, the dearer, the sweeter He becomes to His spouse. 'Therefore he turned away.'¹² He turned away so that those who crucified Him might not know Him. 'His face was outraged, and we held him in no esteem.'¹³

(5) 'It was our infirmities that he bore, our sufferings that he endured, while we thought of him as stricken, as one smitten by God and afflicted. But he was pierced for our offenses, crushed for our sins; upon him was the chastisement that makes us whole, by his stripes we were healed. We had all gone astray like sheep and the Lord delivered him for our sins.'¹⁴ Is this the Gospel or a prophecy? What do the Jews say to this? Is it not strange that they hear these words, have them and read them, find no one concerning whom they could be said except Him who is preached throughout the

---

6 Cf. Isa. 53.2.
7 John 1.1.
8 Phil. 2.6.
9 Cf. Isa. 53.2, 3.
10 Cf. Isa. 53.3.
11 Luke 23.34.
12 Cf. Isa. 53.3.
13 *Ibid.*
14 Cf. Isa. 53.4-6.

world in the Gospel—and still they are not Christians, but are so blind before the exceedingly clear words of the prophets? Do not wonder at the blindness of the Jews concerning Christ. Behold, it comes to pass that what is said of the bridegroom begins to be true of the bride also. Just as you were astonished at the blindness of the Jews in the case of the bridegroom, so now you will be amazed at the blindness of heretics before the bride.

(6) Let us now wonder at just the blindness of the Jews. 'The Lord delivered him for our sins; and although he was harshly treated, he opened not his mouth. Like a lamb led to the slaughter or a sheep before the shearers, he was silent and opened not his mouth. In his humility judgment was taken away.'[15] Do not despise Him, for 'Who would have thought any more of his destiny?'[16] What destiny? 'Before the daystar, like the dew, I have begotten you.'[17] Behold, the single generation, 'before the daystar'; before everything that was created, before all the angels and every creature. Why? Because 'all things were made through him.'[18] Perhaps His second generation is described. Who mentions it? He is conceived through faith, without the approach of man, and the womb of the virgin swells. He comes 'like the groom from his bridal chamber.'[19] Wonderful is this birth. The human one is extraordinary because it is without a father; the other is remarkable because it is without a mother. 'Like a lamb led to the slaughter or a sheep before the shearers, he was silent and opened not his mouth. In his humility judgment was taken away. Who would have thought any more of his destiny? He was cut off from the land of the living.'[20] His Resurrection is foretold. You see that the Lord said this in truth (just as if truth could say anything but what is true): 'These things are

---

15 Cf. Isa. 53.6-8.
16 Isa. 53.8.
17 Ps. 109.3.
18 John 1.3.
19 Ps. 18.6.
20 Cf. Isa. 53.7, 8.

written in the Law and the Prophets and the Psalms concerning me.'[21] Indeed, you have heard: 'Christ should suffer, and should rise again,'[22] for you now heard: 'He was cut off from the land of the living.'[23] 'Repentance and remission of sins should be preached in his name to all the nations, beginning from Jerusalem';[24] this you will also hear from this prophet. However, we should not prefer the prophet to our Lord; the herald preceded, the Judge followed. The herald did not utter his own words but those of the Judge, and the Judge coming afterwards confirmed His words in the herald. 'He was cut off from the land of the living, and smitten for the sins of his people.'[25] You heard Him now telling them: What have I done to you? If you have found sin in me, prove it. But they answered: 'Crucify him! Crucify him!'[26] They thought He was a man, even though an innocent one. For this reason: 'He was smitten for the sins of his people.'[27]

(7) Therefore: 'A grave was assigned him among the wicked.'[28] What does this mean: 'A grave was assigned him among the wicked and a burial place with evildoers'?[29] A grave among the wicked, a burial place with evildoers. When our Lord hung on the cross, that rich man, Joseph of Arimathea, went in to Pilate and asked for the Body of Christ; Pilate agreed, in order that the burial might take place. The rich were given for His death: Joseph buried the poor man in whom he sought riches. For this reason: 'A burial place with evildoers.' What was mentioned last, happened first; what was said first, occurred afterwards. 'A grave among the wicked.' Where do we prove this? 'The Jews went in to Pilate saying, "Sir, we have heard how that vagrant (that is, that imposter)

---

21 Luke 24.44.
22 Luke 24.46.
23 Isa. 53.8.
24 Luke 24.47.
25 Cf. Isa. 53.8.
26 John 19.6.
27 Cf. Isa. 53.8.
28 Isa. 53.9.
29 *Ibid.*

said to his disciples that he would rise again after being killed. Give orders that the sepulchre be guarded, or else his disciples may come by night and steal him away; and the last imposture will be worse than the first." Pilate said to them, "You have soldiers; go, guard it as you wish." '[30] So they took soldiers and placed them there. These men are wicked; they are given as a guard for his burial. How do we prove that they are wicked? They were sent as very innocent soldiers; the judge gave them a command, they came to the sepulchre, and guarded it. Hear that they are wicked: read the Gospel. After our Lord arose and they saw the angel, they were terrified and frightened exceedingly. When they were told: 'Do not be afraid,'[31] they were struck with fear because they were not supported by faith. Now although they knew these truths, they came to the Jews and told them everything. The Jews said: 'We will give you money.'[32] For this reason they were wicked: they concealed the truth and sold a lie. How did they sell a lie? It is no wonder that they did so, for the blind sold a lie to the blind. They were told: 'Say, "His disciples came and stole him while we were sleeping." '[33] O vanity selling untruth to the vain who will hear and believe it! Today, this same word holds among the Jews, the same story prevails, and how vain, how false, how empty it is! They are unwilling to hear the testimony of the martyrs that they may live; they listen to the testimony of those who sleep and perish. If the guards were asleep, how could they know who took Him from the sepulchre? Either you were watching, wicked soul—O evil man of whom the prophet said with good reason: 'A grave was assigned him among the wicked'[34]—O wicked men, the worst of all, either you were watching and should have been guarding; or you were asleep and do not know what happened. Truly, what the Holy Ghost

---

30 Cf. Matt. 27.62-65.
31 Matt. 28.5.
32 Cf. Matt. 28.12.
33 Cf. Matt. 28.13.
34 Isa. 53.9.

foretold much earlier through the psalmist was fulfilled: 'Devising plots, they cannot succeed.'³⁵

(8) Let us for whose salvation all these truths were foretold and fulfilled, beloved brethren, thank the divine mercy and labor as much as we can with all our strength, so that God's benefits may not avail us unto judgment but unto perfection. Then, when the dreadful day of judgment and the time for rendering an account comes, our Lord and Savior who was judged may find what He conferred upon us unharmed as He comes to judge us. When He comes He will surely pay what He promised, but He will also require what He ransomed: at His second coming He will demand what He bestowed at the first. Although we ought to trust much in God's mercy, still we should not fear His justice with indifference, for He who redeemed you with mercy will judge you with justice. The fact that we have sinned so long and He still spares us is not due to His neglect, but His long-suffering. He has not lost His power, but He reserves us for repentance. Therefore, let us fear His justice, since we long for His mercy. He spares us now but is not silent; and yet even if He is silent, He will not always be so. For this reason let us listen to God while He is not silent in His commands, if we want Him to spare us when He will not be silent at the judgment. At present, indeed, His mercy is conferred upon us, but then justice will be demanded of us and 'He will render to everyone according to his conduct.'³⁶ Then will take place what the Apostle mentioned: 'Judgment is without mercy to those who have not shown mercy.'³⁷

---

35 Ps. 20.12.
36 Matt. 16.27.
37 James 2.13.

* Sermon 143

On the Repentance of the Ninivites

(1) At the time when blessed Jona preached destruction to the city of Ninive, dearly beloved, what kind of feeling do you suppose that holy man had at the sight of those people with perfect compunction hastening to the remedies of repentance and so devoutly trusting in the mercy of God? No doubt, the more he rejoiced over the Assyrians, the more he was troubled at his own people. As often as he praised the Ninivites, he presently mourned for the sons of Abraham. The race of Chanaan advanced, while the seed of Jacob strayed; what foolish circumcision lost there, the uncircumcision of the Gentiles found here. Among the Jews only the sabbath was kept; among the Gentiles the whole command was fulfilled. Indeed, who revealed God's mystery to the Ninivites, with the result that they could pay a fixed penalty by fasting? They received advice from both God and man, for in not considering Jona a liar or God cruel, they believed the prophet and trusted God's mercy. What might not be obtained by such torments, whereby the thirsty lips of children were kept from the breast and herds stood hungry before an empty manger? According as nature suffered there arose prayer, or the lowing of animals, or the crying of infants. There the dryness of hunger abounded, as also the ugliness of ashes, continually moist eyes, and a crying tongue. Everywhere was charity, chastity, and love; peace among men, silence among women, either no difference or an agreeable one between servants and free women. Both the rich and the poor had but one manner of life, and abandoning all rivalry there was one mode of dress for all who were placed under the same yoke. Since one redemption was to be gained for all, there was one kind of labor for everyone. The pale crowd stood around the gates of hell; if day appeared they

did not expect to see evening, and if they again reached evening they did not hope for the coming of dawn.

(2) 'Jona went out, awaiting what would happen to the city.'[1] He outwardly counted the days, while they interiorly numbered their sins. Moreover, six weeks they served in vigils, fasting, and weeping. Meanwhile, Jona feared that the results of their tears might make him guilty of falsehood. He could not stand the heat of the sun; they were unable to endure their burning anxiety. He sought a covering of grass and a shade of ivy; they extinguished the fire of their sins with their cooling tears. Behold, the green shelter over the head of Jona withered, while mercy flourished and piety sprang up above the cruel Ninivites. Now God saw the Assyrians repent, and the conversion of Ninive pleased Him more than Jerusalem. Jona stood afar fearing he would suffer the charge of lying, but gradually his anxiety was exchanged for security and indignation for mercy. Thus, that dead city rose again and escaped the destruction which he had announced to it. Do you imagine that the citizens then went out to the prophet and addressed to him words of this sort? Rejoice with us, O blessed prophet, because when miserable through you we found a new life; through you we received the key of repentance. Exult, O doctor, because the one you took care of has been healed. You did not lie to us at all, believe it, for you brought us to life from the danger of death. Who would think you deceitful, since if you had not been believed surely no one would have done penance? Behold, pray for the little children who were saved by your preaching, and may your spirit console you, friend of God. May this day likewise be sacred to us, for on it we have begun to acknowledge your God. Now the angels rejoice in heaven because of you, since through you men are saved on earth.

(3) Let us likewise, dearly beloved, imitate the repentance of the Ninivites. Let us, with God's help, renounce our sins in such a way that we may never return to excessive lusts. May

---
1 Cf. Jona 4.5.

there be in us no false or feigned love, but let us with great roaring and groaning be eager to apply the remedy for our past sins that we may always be careful of future ones. Indeed, if with a humble and contrite heart we devoutly take refuge in the haven of repentance, we will happily arrive at eternal joys. May the Lord in His kindness deign to grant this, who lives and reigns world without end. Amen.

* Sermon 144

On Prayer, Repentance, and the Ninivites

(1) When the Gospel passage was read, dearly beloved, we heard: 'Repent, for the kingdom of heaven is at hand.'[1] The kingdom of heaven is Christ, who is generally acknowledged to be the judge of good and evil, the discerner of all motives. Therefore, let us anticipate God in the confession of sin, and before the last judgment let us correct all the errors of our soul. Indeed, there is the risk of danger if a soul does not know how to amend its sin by some kind of remedy. We ought to do penance, especially when we realize that we will have to render an account for the causes of our negligences. Understand, dearly beloved, how great is the goodness of God toward us, so that He wills the guilt of an offense that has been committed to be appeased by penance before the last judgment. In this way our judge, who is always just, advises us beforehand, so that He may never have to exercise the justice of severity. It is not without profit, dearly beloved, that God demands of us a fountain of tears, so that repentance may restore what our negligence lost. For He knows that man does not always continue with a pure intention; frequently, he sins in his body or fails in his speech. For this reason God has shown

---

1 Matt. 4.17.

the path of repentance by which man can straighten what was crooked and restore what was lost. Since he is assured of pardon in this way, man should always sigh over his transgressions. Even if human nature labors under many wounds, still no one should ever despair, because the Lord is generous enough willingly to bestow the graces of His mercy upon all who are weak.

(2) Perhaps someone may say that he has nothing to bewail. Let each one have recourse to his own conscience, and he will find sin disturbing him within his heart. One struggles over wounds in his heart, another with attacks against his body; pride dominates one, while harmful dissipation shames another. Drunkenness disgraces one man, lust inflames another; lying accuses one, and because of avarice the property of his neighbor rebukes still another. One man is defiled by the shedding of human blood, and another is polluted by love for a despicable woman. How can there be anyone who does not groan over these great and principal attacks of either mind or body and pour forth humble tears to the Lord? Therefore, no one should be ashamed to offer his wounds to God; if a man blushes to be cured, he never has recourse to a remedy. With all kinds of sickness some are easier to heal and others are difficult. However, no sick person is in a more grave condition than one who does not want his illness cured. Sacred Scripture teaches this same truth: no one who sought a remedy has perished, and no one who despised it has escaped destruction. The city of the Ninivites was destined to perish within three days unless there was recourse to repentance. Now what did the prophet say? 'Three days more and Ninive shall be destroyed. When the news reached the king of Ninive, he rose from his throne, laid aside his robes, covered himself with a hairshirt, and sat on ashes.'[2] Great was his repentance, dearly beloved; he cast away his royal robes and clothed himself in a hairshirt. Indeed, he preferred to escape in a hairshirt, rather than to perish in purple garments. Where, then,

---

2 Cf. Jona 3.4, 6.

was the loftiness of his power? In order to escape punishment for his pride, he had recourse to the help of humility. Thus, we may understand, dearly beloved, that lowliness avails more than power. For the whole kingdom of the Ninivites would have perished at that time, if repentance, like a patron, had not saved him.

(3) In that repentance of the Ninivites, there is further added the fact that at the same time infants and animals also fasted. Now why should the little children, who had committed no sin, fast? Evidently, the innocent fasted in order that sinners might escape punishment; the little child cried out that the older man might not perish. But even if the fasting of infants was necessary, why the further fasting of flocks and herds? Surely, in order that the hunger of even the animals might manifest the repentance of men. By their roaring to God beneath their burden, what was committed by a few men was to be redeemed by all creatures. Therefore, dearly beloved, we, too, ought to cry out to the Lord, our God, with harmonious hearts and united faith. Those others cried out after they had offended; let us do so in order that we may not sin. They shouted, indeed, after their guilt; let us cry out in order that we may not become guilty. Blessed is the man, dearly beloved, whose fear is like a scourge; such a man is corrected, not by punishment, but by discipline. The man who fears that he may some day suffer torments never suffers them.

(4) But perhaps someone among the people may say: Why should I be afraid, since I do no evil? Listen to the Apostle John preaching about this: 'If we say that we have no sin,' he says, 'we deceive ourselves, and the truth is not in us.'[3] Therefore, let no one deceive you, dearly beloved; not to know one's sins is the worst kind of sin. All who admit their offenses can be reconciled to the Lord by means of repentance, but no sinner is more worthy of lamentation than one who thinks he has nothing to lament. For there are many kinds of sins, dearly

---

[3] 1 John 1.8.

beloved, and some of them are more dangerous because of the very fact that they are believed to be quite slight. Those which some men think are not even sins at all are all the more harmful, for no evil is more deceptive than what is not understood to be an evil. Therefore, I am not now speaking about murders, adultery, or wicked counsel, for far be it from a Christian to commit these sins. If, perchance, he does commit them he bewails the fact that he has fallen and did not at once resist. But I am rather talking about those things which are believed much smaller and slighter. Now who of you is there, dearly beloved, whom drunkenness has not defiled, or ambition carried away, or jealously consumed, or lust inflamed, or avarice wounded? Therefore, I advise you, dearly beloved, according to what is written, that you 'Humble yourselves under the exceedingly mighty hand of God.'[4] Since no one is without sin, no one should be without penance; for by this very fact a man becomes guilty if he presumes that he is innocent. A man may be guilty of lesser sin, but no one is guiltless. Surely, there is a difference among men, but no one is safe from guilt. For this reason, dearly beloved, those who have sinned more grievously should seek forgiveness all the more devoutly, while those who have not been defiled by the more serious sins should pray that they may not become so: with the help of our Lord Jesus Christ, who lives and reigns with the Father and the Holy Spirit forever and ever. Amen.

---

4 Cf. 1 Peter 5.6.

Sermon 145

An Admonition of St. Augustine on What Is Written: 'Come to Terms with Thy Opponent While Thou Art with Him on the Way.'[1] Also on the Mote of Anger Which Is Nourished by False Suspicions and Becomes a Beam

(1) Your charity has frequently heard in Sacred Scripture, beloved brethren, in what danger priests are situated if they are unwilling to fulfill what the Apostle enjoins: 'Preach the word, be urgent in season, out of season; reprove, rebuke, entreat with all patience and teaching.'[2] So heavy a weight hangs over our necks, to whom it is said: 'If you do not dissuade the wicked from his wicked conduct, I will hold you responsible for his death.'[3] For this reason it is necessary for us to rebuke, either in secret or in public, those who are careless. Now if the man whom we reprove is wicked, when we do so he will notice by whom he is rebuked, and he will more readily recognize what is being corrected in the one who is reproving him than in himself. And if he actually finds something to say against the one by whom he is corrected, he rejoices. How much better it would be for him to rejoice over his own cure when he has been reproved, than over the weakness of another when he has been rebuked! Now consider that what you say is true, that you have found something in the man by whom you have been corrected. Nevertheless, truth was speaking to you through him; through a wicked, unjust instrument truth was speaking to you. You are looking for something to blame in a man; instead, find something blameworthy in truth. Whether you will it or not, that is your adversary, in which you find nothing to rebuke. Make it your friend if you can. Your adversary is the word of God; whether the sinner or the just man

---
1 Matt. 5.25.
2 2 Tim. 4.2.
3 Cf. Ezech. 3.18.

utters it, it is the word of God, it is blameless. This is your adversary: 'Come to terms with him while thou art with him on the way.'⁴ The way is that manner of life; the opponent of all the wicked is the word of God. Is it of little account to you that, although truth was remaining in its most blessed and hidden abode, it came to you to be with you on the way? It wanted to accompany you, so that when you walk and have it in your power, you may settle and plead your case when you are about to finish your journey. And when you have finished your journey, there will be no one with whom you can rest your case, for: 'Thy opponent will quickly deliver thee to the judge, and the judge to the officer, and the officer will cast thee into prison. Thou wilt not come out from it until thou hast paid the last penny.'⁵ The word of God is with you as an opponent on the way; you have it in your power, come to terms with it. What does that opponent ask of you? That you live in harmony with it. What is that, except your salvation? It walks with its opponents and tells them to live in harmony with it. Let this be done: the journey is not yet ended. What was not done yesterday may come to pass today. The journey is not yet ended; why do you wait until it is ended? When it is finished there will be no other, where you will be in harmony with your opponent. The judge remains, as also the officer and the prison. This has been the way for many: although they promised themselves many more years in it, suddenly it was ended. Now just because your way will be long, always make your opponent walk with you; do you not blush that you have been in disagreement with such an opponent for so long a time? The word of God is your friend as much as it can be; you yourself make it your opponent. Truly, it wishes well to you, but you, on the contrary, do the opposite. It commands, Do not steal—you steal; it orders, Do not commit adultery—you commit adultery; it says, Do not perpetrate deceit—and you do it. It forbids you to swear—you

---

4 Cf. Matt. 5.25.
5 Cf. Matt. 5.25, 26.

take a false oath; you do everything contrary to what it says, and thus you yourself make the word of God your enemy. And it is no wonder, when you are even an enemy to yourself for: 'The lover of violence he hates.'[6] If, then, you hate your own soul by loving iniquity, do you wonder that you hate the word of God which wishes well to your soul?

(2) Shall we be silent, then, and rebuke no one at all? Let us openly reprove, but first let us rebuke ourselves. You wish to correct your neighbor; nothing is closer to you than you yourself. How is it far away? You have yourself before you. For what does the Lord say through the Scriptures? 'Thou shalt love thy neighbor as thyself.'[7] Therefore, if you do not love yourself, how do you love your neighbor? You have taken the measure of love for your neighbor from yourself. I do love him, you say. For this reason I say, first love yourself and talk to yourself. Now, if you truly speak out of love, it is evident that the word which is spoken has had some effect within you. But it is to be feared that you do not love yourself and would like to blame someone else, and that you do this out of hatred. Moreover, if you hate your brother, you are accusing him of lesser faults than you are committing. 'Everyone who hates his brother is a murderer.'[8] You heard the Epistle of John read today. Scripture says that men should not make little account of what they have interiorly in their hearts while they make accusations of what is done through the body, for it says: 'Everyone who hates his brother is a murderer.' Although the hand is not yet armed, the throat strangled, the treachery prepared, the poison sought, a man is considered guilty in the sight of God as soon as hatred is conceived. The person whom a man seeks to kill is still alive, and the man is already judged to have committed the deed. Therefore, if you rebuke a man out of hatred, do you as a murderer dare to blame anyone? Just because men do not bind

---

6 Ps. 10.6.
7 Matt. 22.39.
8 1 John 3.15.

you and bring you to a judge, do you not recognize your fault in the eyes of God, the supreme judge? If you are unwilling to admit your sin, you will recognize your punishment, for He does not spare murderers. But I do correct myself, you say, when I am on the way. Therefore, rebuke yourself and then you will be able to correct your brother. You accuse him of slighter faults, while you commit more grievous ones: 'Thou dost see the speck in thy brother's eye, and yet dost not consider the beam in thy own eye.'[9] This, indeed, the Lord said because of men who blame others out of hatred. Do you rebuke one who is angry and perish yourself through hatred? Weigh in the balance of your thought anger and hatred. What is anger? A kind of heated spirit. At present it displeases you. Already within you that anger has become of long standing, and for this reason it has aroused hatred. Anger is a mote, destined to be a beam as the result of continuous growth, because just as a mote grows into a beam, so inveterate anger becomes hatred. Already you hate, and you blame one who is angry. Now the mote in him displeases you, while the beam in you still causes you pleasure. Do you want to know the difference? We often find that fathers become angry at their sons, but you will find that it is difficult for a father to hate his son. A father can become angry at the son whom he loves; we might say that he is angry and he loves. It cannot be said that he hates and loves. I have said this because of the fact that men, who punish lesser offenses in others, do not punish greater sins in themselves.

(3) Therefore, as we think about these matters in a salutary fashion, dearest brethren, let us conclude friendship with our opponent while we are on the way with him. In other words, let us consent to the word of God as long as we are still in this life, because afterwards, when we have passed out of this world, no agreement or satisfaction will be possible. The judge remains, and the officer, and the prison. For this reason let us love with our whole heart, not only our friends, but also our

---
9 Matt. 7.3.

enemies, in order that with the Lord's help we may be able to fulfill all these commands. Thus, there may be realized in us what is written: 'The whole Law is fulfilled in one word: Thou shalt love thy neighbor as thyself';[10] and further: 'Charity covers a multitude of sins.'[11] May He who is true charity deign to grant this to us, who lives and reigns with the Father and the Holy Spirit forever and ever. Amen.

Sermon 146

On the Excerpt of the Gospel Where It Says: 'Do Not Let Thy Left Hand Know What Thy Right Hand Is Doing':[1] Also on Prayer

(1) It seems to me that the Gospel lesson which was read to us just now, beloved brethren, cannot be understood according to the letter. Therefore, with God's help, let us ask how we may arrive at the spiritual meaning of it. For thus the Lord speaks: 'Take heed not to do your good before men, in order to be seen by them';[2] and again: 'When thou givest alms, do not let thy left hand know what thy right hand is doing, so that thy alms may be given in secret.'[3] How can we accept this according to the letter, when the Lord Himself says again: 'Even so let your light shine before men, in order that they may see your good works and give glory to your Father in heaven'?[4] How does He say: 'Do not let thy left hand know what thy right hand is doing,' when He says elsewhere, 'So let your light shine before men, in order that they may see your good works'? Listen carefully, brethren, and ask for an

---
10 Gal. 5.14.
11 1 Peter 4.8.

---
1 Matt. 6.3.
2 Matt. 6.1.
3 Matt. 6.3, 4.
4 Matt. 5.16.

understanding of the divine writings with humility and wisdom, for the Lord cannot contradict Himself in the Gospel lesson. The fact that He Himself both said that alms should be given in secret and advised that they be given publicly demands prudent understanding, in order that His precepts may not seem to contradict each other. One who gives alms out of the desire to be praised by men gives them publicly, even if he bestows them in secret, since he seeks praise from men. However, one who gives alms solely out of love for God, in order that other men may imitate him in this good work and that God, not himself, may be praised, gives them in secret even if he does so in public. In return for those alms this man desires, not that which is seen, but what is not seen; he does not long to receive praise from men, but a reward from God.

(2) This we also ought to understand concerning fasting. For although the Lord Himself says: 'Anoint thy head and wash thy face, so that thou mayest not be seen fasting by men,'[5] do we act contrary to the precepts of Christ when we publicly announce our fasting by doing it with all the people looking on at the same time? This, too, ought to be understood in the same sense, that no one should fast for the sake of human praise, but rather to obtain the forgiveness of sins and the divine mercy. Therefore, let each one examine his own conscience, and if he gives alms solely out of love for God, he can do so with assurance, even in public. Then people who see him may imitate him, too. As for the fact that the Lord says: 'Do not let thy left hand know what thy right hand is doing,'[6] this is recognized as applying to what we said before. For love of God is understood in the right hand, vanity or worldly desires in the left hand. If you give alms for the sake of human praise, the left hand does it all and the right hand does nothing at all. However, if you give it to obtain the remission of sins and out of love for eternal life, the right hand does it all. Therefore, what is meant by: 'Do not let thy left hand know

---
5 Matt. 6.17, 18.
6 Matt. 6.3.

what thy right hand is doing,' except that whatever the love of God does should not be spoiled or destroyed by vanity or worldly desires? Now if someone believes that he can fulfill this according to the letter, what will he do if his right hand suffers pain? Should he not give any alms at all with his left hand? Or if he wants to ransom a captive, how can he either untie his purse or open his coffer if he does not join his left hand to his right hand? Moreover, if he wishes to receive a stranger and, in accord with the precept of the Lord, to wash the feet of the saints, I do not see how he can fulfill this without the knowledge of his left hand.

(3) What the Lord said also applies to this: 'When you pray, do not pray at the street corners,' He says; 'but go into thy room, and closing thy door, pray to thy Father in secret.'[7] Look, and you yourselves will realize very well that this cannot always be fulfilled literally. Both we ourselves and all the people, not only pray in our rooms, but also come to the church publicly and bend our knees together with all the people. When we do this are we in contradiction to the precepts of Christ who told us that we should close the door and pray in our rooms? That is not the case. Listen carefully to the way in which this meaning is appropriate to the former thought and how it, therefore, ought to be understood. Whenever you pray to God and seek from Him what is visible, you are praying in public with the door open, because you want to receive from God what is seen. However, if you want to beg for the forgiveness of sins and for eternal life, even if you pray in public, you are praying with your door closed, because you do not seek what is visible but what is unseen. 'For the things that are seen are temporal, but the things that are not seen are eternal.'[8] If you seek temporal things, as I already said above, you pray publicly and with your door open. If you ask for eternal things, your prayer is secret, because you long to receive, not the things which are seen, but those which are

---

7 Cf. Matt. 6.5, 6.
8 2 Cor. 4.18.

not seen. Now the man who seeks in truth for the things which are not seen will also receive the things which are visible. This happens through the gift of the Lord, because He does not lie when He says: 'But seek first the kingdom of God and his justice, and all these things shall be given to you.'[9] We are not saying this, brethren, in order that we may not pray to God for temporal things, that is, for bodily health, or peaceful times, or an abundance of fruits. These things, too, we ought to ask from God, but in the second or third place; the first place in every intention of our prayer ought to be held by love of the soul and a desire for eternal life. Let us, then, pray for the body, but without any comparison, let us pray still more for the soul. Therefore, dearly beloved brethren, as often as this Gospel lesson is read to you, you ought to have an understanding of it in the order which we mentioned above. Thus, whether in almsgiving, or in fasting, or in prayers, we ought to observe this with regard to the right and left hand, that whatever we do we should do out of love for eternal bliss, and not out of vanity or worldly desires.

(4) May these thoughts now suffice for your charity. When you assemble rather early tomorrow morning according to your custom, through God's gift you will hear more fully what we ought to say and you should hear.

* *Sermon 147*

An Explanation of the Lord's Prayer

(1) You have recited what you believe, you have heard for what you should pray. Surely, you could not invoke one in whom you did not believe, as the Apostle says: 'How are they

---
[9] Matt. 6.33.

to call upon him in whom they have not believed?'¹ For this reason you first learned the Creed. Here is a rule of your faith which is both short and long: short in the number of words, long because of the weight of thoughts. Moreover, this prayer, which you received today to be kept and recited for eight days, was spoken by our Lord Himself to His disciples, as you heard when the Gospel was read. From the disciples, then, it has come to us, since: 'Through all the earth their voice resounds.'²

(2) Now, having found a Father in heaven, do not cling to earthly possessions, for you are about to say: 'Our Father who art in heaven.'³ You have begun to belong to a great race, for under this Father, both master and servant are brothers; so also the general and the soldier, the rich man and the pauper. All devout Christians have different fathers on earth, some noble ones, others of ignoble birth; but they call upon one Father who is in heaven. If our Father is there, an inheritance is there prepared for us. Moreover, such is the nature of that Father that with Him we possess what He gives. For He gives an inheritance, but does not leave it to us at His death; He did not die in order that we might succeed Him, but He continues to live in order that we may approach Him. Therefore, since we have heard from whom we should ask, let us also know what we should seek, lest perchance we offend such a Father by asking for what is evil.

(3) What, then, did the Lord Jesus teach us to ask of the Father who is in heaven? 'Hallowed be thy name.'⁴ What kind of a favor is it that we ask of God, that His name should be hallowed? The name of God is always holy. Why, then, do we ask that it be hallowed, except in order that we ourselves might be sanctified through Him? For this reason we pray that what is always holy may be sanctified in us. The name of God is hallowed in you when you are baptized. Since you have

---

1 Rom. 10.14.
2 Ps. 18.5.
3 Matt. 6.9.
4 *Ibid.*

been baptized, what will you pray for in this, except that what you have may continue in you?

(4) There follows another petition: 'Thy kingdom come.'[5] Whether we ask it or not, the kingdom of God is destined to come. Why, then, do we ask, except in order that what is going to come to all the saints may also come to us? Thus may God count us in the number of His saints, to whom His kingdom is going to come.

(5) We say in the third petition: 'Thy will be done on earth, as it is in heaven.'[6] What does this mean? That just as the angels serve Thee in heaven, so may we also serve Thee on earth. Moreover, the holy angels obey Him, do not offend Him, and carry out His commands by loving Him. Therefore, we say this prayer so that we may fulfill the precepts of God out of love. Again these words: 'Thy will be done on earth, as it is in heaven,' are also understood in a different way. Heaven is the soul within us, the earth is our body. In this sense what does it mean: 'Thy will be done on earth, as it is in heaven'? Just as we have heard thy precepts, so may our flesh be in harmony with us, lest we be unable to fulfill the precepts of God when our flesh and spirit are in conflict.

(6) There follows in the prayer: 'Give us this day our daily bread.'[7] Whether we ask the Father for necessary provision for the body, signifying in the bread whatever is needful for us, or whether we understand it as that daily bread which you are about to receive at the altar, we ask rightly that He give it to us. For what do we pray, except that we may commit no sin by which we may be separated from such bread? And the word of God which is preached every day is bread; because it is not bread for the stomach it does not, therefore, cease to be bread for the mind. Now when life passes away we will not seek that bread which our hunger desires, nor will we have to receive the Sacrament of the altar since we will be there

---
5 Matt. 6.10.
6 *Ibid.*
7 Matt. 6.11.

with Christ whose Body we now receive. Neither do these words have to be said, as we are now saying them to you, nor do the Scriptures have to be read, when we will see Him, because He is the Word of God. Through the Word all things were made, on It the angels feed, are enlightened and become wise. They do not seek words of involved speech, but they drink in the admirable Word, and, filled with it, pour forth praises and do not cease to utter words of praise. For: 'Happy,' says the psalmist, 'are they who dwell in your house! continually they praise you.'[8]

(7) Now we ask in this life for what follows: 'Forgive us our debts, as we also forgive our debtors.'[9] In Baptism all of our debts, that is, all of our sins, are immediately forgiven. But no one can live here without sin, even though not the serious faults whereby man is separated from that bread. Since no one can be on this earth without sins and we cannot receive Baptism a second time but only once, we have in this prayer the means whereby we may be cleansed daily. Thus, our sins may daily be forgiven, but only if we do what follows: 'As we also forgive our debtors.' Therefore, my brethren, I advise you as my sons in God's grace and my brothers under God the Father. Whenever anyone offends or sins against you, then comes and confesses it, seeking pardon from you, I urge you to forgive him and to do so promptly with all your heart, so that you may not hinder God's pardon from coming to you. For if you yourself do not forgive, neither will He forgive you. Therefore, we also ask for this in the present life, since sins can be forgiven here where they can be retained; in that life they are not forgiven, because they are not committed.

(8) There is a final petition when we say: 'Lead us not into temptation, but deliver us from evil.'[10] This, too, it is necessary for us to ask in this life, that we may not be brought to temptation, because there are temptations here. Moreover, may we be

---

8 Ps. 83.5.
9 Matt. 6.12.
10 Matt. 6.13.

delivered from evil, because there is evil here. Now in this prayer there are these seven petitions, three pertaining to eternal life, four to the present one. 'Hallowed be thy name'; it always will be. 'Thy kingdom come'; this kingdom will always exist. 'Thy will be done on earth, as it is in heaven'; and this will happen. 'Give us this day our daily bread,' because it will not always be present. 'Forgive us our debts'; this, too, will not always be. 'Lead us not into temptation,' for this will not always be the case. 'But deliver us from evil,' which will not always be so. Where temptation is, there is evil, and there it is necessary for us to pray. For this reason Almighty God must be entreated by us in such a way that, whatever human weakness is unable to shun and avoid, this our Lord Jesus Christ may graciously deign to bestow upon us, who lives and reigns with the Father and the Holy Spirit forever and ever. Amen.

Sermon 148

On Prayer, On What Is Written in the Gospel According to Matthew: 'Do Not Judge, That You May Not Be Judged,'[1] and So Forth

(1) When the Gospel was read just now we heard the Lord say: 'Do not judge, that you may not be judged. For with what judgment you judge, you shall be judged.'[2] What does this mean, brethren, when the Lord Himself said in another place of the Gospel: 'Judge not by appearances, but give just judgment,'[3] and elsewhere it is said: 'render true judgment'?[4] The divine lesson cannot contradict itself, but it requires prudent understanding. In human life, dearly beloved, there are some

---
1 Matt. 7.1.
2 Matt. 7.1, 2
3 John 7.24.
4 Zach. 7.9.

things which are reasonably criticized, but there are certain things which are not judged without sin. For obvious evils ought to be judged and rebuked, but those about which we are ignorant or cannot know whether they were done with a good or bad intention we should not judge at all. For example, do you see a man fasting rather frequently? Rejoice greatly, but do not praise excessively, because this might also be done for the sake of human glory. However, do not blame, because he may be fasting for the sake of God and as a remedy for his soul. Have you seen another man fail to observe a prescribed public fast and willingly partake of a meal? Admonish him with charity. If he says that he is unable to fast because of a weak stomach, believe him and do not judge him, because both may be the case, that he wants to eat because of gluttony or dissipation and cannot fast because of illness. Did you see still another impose discipline upon his subjects with severity and very reluctantly show indulgence? Do not judge him to be cruel, because perhaps he does not do this through disorderly anger but out of a zeal for discipline and a love of justice, on account of what is written: 'Zeal for your house consumes me.'[5] Perhaps a neighbor or friend of yours has greeted you but slowly or more slowly than he should have, because his mind has been occupied with matters of the utmost concern to him? Do not judge him to be proud and do not believe he is malicious. Think that it was done through forgetfulness or thoughtlessness, rather than through spite or pride. Perhaps it has also frequently happened to you, since human nature is frail, that when you were too intent upon other matters, you seemed to have acted rather incautiously and carelessly; and still you would not have wanted to be judged ill-intentioned because of this. Therefore, in these and similar instances where we cannot know whether things are done with a good or bad intention, it is better to incline our soul toward the right side. For it is more tolerable for us to be overcome in this respect, that we believe those who are

---
5 Ps. 68.10.

evil to be good, rather than to suspect what is evil even of the good as a result of our habit of judging others. Therefore, in those matters which are known to God but unknown to us, we judge our neighbors hazardously, for the Lord has said of such people: 'Do not judge, that you may not be judged.'[6] However, evils which are open and a matter of public knowledge we can and ought to judge and rebuke, but still with charity and love. We hate, not the man, but the sin; not the vicious, but the vice, detesting the disease rather than the sick man. For if the public adulterer, robber, continuous drunkard, traitor, and proud are not judged and corrected, there will be fulfilled in them what the most blessed martyr Cyprian said of such people: 'He who flatters the sinner with fawning words, supplies fuel for the sin.'[7]

(2) Pertinent to this matter, too, beloved brethren, is what we heard in the same Gospel lesson: 'Why dost thou see the speck in thy brother's eye, and yet dost not consider the beam in thy own eye?'[8] You have seen a man suddenly get angry; do not immediately judge him, but wait a little. Perhaps as quickly as his anger is aroused, so quickly it is appeased. Let us further see what the speck and the beam signify. Sudden anger is a speck, but when it is drawn out over a long period of time and is nourished with hatred by false suspicions, it becomes a beam. Therefore, to get angry quickly and to be calmed swiftly is a speck, but anger which is kept in the heart for a long time is a beam. Anger of long standing, then, is changed into a beam. Now with what boldness does the man who keeps hatred in his heart presume to judge the person in whose eye he discerns, not a beam, but a speck? For a speck clouds the eye of the heart, but a beam blinds it. What I have said, brethren, I should prove by the testimony of the Scriptures. Listen to the psalmist tell how anger clouds the eye of the heart: 'My eyes are dimmed,' he says, 'with sorrow.'[9] More-

---
6 Matt. 7.1.
7 Cyprian. *De lapsis* 14.
8 Matt. 7.3.
9 Cf. Ps. 6.8.

over, John the Evangelist testifies how hatred blinds the eye of the heart: 'He who hates his brother,' he says, 'is in the darkness, and walks in the darkness, and he does not know whither he goes; because the darkness has blinded his eyes.'[10] According to this evidence, then, the eye of the heart is clouded by sudden anger, but the light of charity is extinguished by hatred.

(3) For this reason, beloved brethren, I am inserting certain headings and notes as to how you ought to understand and receive these matters, for through the goodness of God you can accept and observe them better. In order that the things which I have said may be kept more closely in your hearts, I am briefly repeating what I mentioned. Therefore, in these matters, as I already said above, we judge others dangerously when it is doubtful whether they are acting with a good or bad intention in fasting, keeping vigils, bestowing alms, abstaining or not abstaining from wine and meat, and other similar matters. These things can be done for the sake of God and for human praise, and because we do not know with what motive they are done, we should not judge at all. In matters of this kind the Lord said: 'Do not judge, that you may not be judged,'[11] but in a matter of open sin it is said: 'Reprove, entreat, rebuke with all patience and teaching.'[12] Moreover, there is what we already mentioned above: 'Render just judgment.'[13] Now if we are willing to consider these words carefully as we believe, brethren, and, with God's help, to observe them with great solicitude, we are freed from not a little sin. For by their indiscreet judgment, the majority of the human race are proven to be prompt and ready to criticize, although they are not so willing to be judged by others as they are to judge them. Because of this fact Sacred Scripture admonishes us, saying: 'Before investigating, find no fault; examine first,

---
10 1 John 2.11.
11 Matt. 7.1.
12 2 Tim. 4.2.
13 Cf. Zach. 7.9

then criticize.'¹⁴ Every man first wants to be questioned, and then, if he is guilty, he patiently endures reproof. Now since we all want this to happen to us from others, it is just that we strive to fulfill the same thing toward them. Let us first inquire with patience and solicitude. Then, when we have learned something quite certainly, we should be willing to give reproof if it is evil and to defend it if it is good, because of what is written: 'All that you wish men to do to you, even so do you also to them in like manner; for this is the Law and the Prophets.'¹⁵ And so let us turn to the Lord and implore His help, so that He Himself may deign in His goodness to grant us true discretion and perfect charity: to whom is glory and might together with the Father and the Holy Spirit forever and ever. Amen.

Sermon 149

On the Two Paths, the One to be Desired,
and the Other to be Feared

(1) When the Gospel was read, beloved brethren, you heard the Lord mention two paths: the one terrible and to be feared, the other very desirable and to be followed. By the one, the just are lifted up into heaven after short labor, while on the other, lovers of the world after brief pleasure are dragged into hell. 'Enter by the narrow gate. For wide is the gate and broad is the way that leads to destruction, and many there are who enter that way. How close the gate and narrow the way that leads to life! And few there are who find it.'¹ Behold, beloved brethren, God has placed in the sight of the whole human race what we should seek and what we should avoid, what we should desire and what flee, what to fear and what to love with

---
14 Ecclus. 11.7.
15 Matt. 7.12.

---
1 Matt. 7.13, 14.

our whole heart. As He Himself said earlier through the prophet: 'Before man are life and death, whichever he chooses shall be given him,'² and again: 'Behold before you are fire and water, death and life; choose life, that you may live.'³ Everything that we mentioned above, that is, good and evil, is contained in these two. For heaven and hell, Christ and the devil, height and depth are proposed to us in them. Through His grace God has put it into the power of each one to choose and to stretch out his hand to whatever he wishes.

(2) Christ presides over the straight and narrow way, while the devil commands the wide and broad way. The former invites man to heaven, the latter moves him toward hell; the one raises him on high, the other presses him down into the depths. The devil shows a false sweetness, in order that he may attract man to true bitterness; Christ invites him to brief difficulty, in order to lead him to long blessedness. If we open only our bodily eyes, the wide and broad way deceives us, but if we listen with the eyes of our heart, the rough and difficult way makes us safe.

(3) Therefore, let us admonish each other, dearly beloved, and continually encourage each other with true charity that we ought rather to choose the short and narrow way by which we may merit to arrive at the celestial expanse of paradise. However, with God's help, we ought to reject and despise as much as we can that way which, after a short expanse, is wont to plunge its lovers into the depths of hell. If, then, we contemn the path on the left whose end brings us into hell and follow the one on the right which leads to eternal life, we will merit to reach Him who is 'The way, and the truth, and the life.'⁴ And it is no wonder if we happily come to Him through whom we faithfully walk, for since He Himself is the way, we run through Him, and since He is our true country, we will reach Him when we have finished our course. Although He is

---

2 Ecclus. 15.18.
3 Cf. Ecclus. 15.17; Deut. 30.19.
4 John 14.6.

rest and the land of the angels in accord with His Divine Nature, He became the way of pilgrims through His human nature. What is the true country and the repose of the angels or of all the faithful? 'In the beginning was the Word, and the Word was with God; and the Word was God.'[5] What is the way of pilgrims? 'The Word was made flesh, and dwelt among us.'[6]

(4) When through the sin of the first man we were all cast out of paradise into this world as into a valley of tears, we lost at the same time both the way and our true country. 'We journeyed through impassable deserts, but the way of the Lord we knew not.'[7] But the kind and merciful King of our true country, not only was eager to send His servants to us frequently, but He even deigned to come down Himself and to prepare the way by which we might return to our country. O man, since you were slow to seek the way, the Way itself has condescended to look for you, and because you were sluggish in coming to the way, the Way itself came to you. 'Arise, and walk':[8] flee from the wide and broad way of the world which delights you for a time but will torment you in eternity. Run on the path of Christ in which you will labor for a very short time but afterwards will rejoice forever with the angels.

(5) Perhaps you may say: How should I run on the path of Christ? If you have both of your feet in good condition, you run happily. Now what are these two feet, except: 'Thou shalt love the Lord,'[9] and 'Thou shalt love thy neighbor. On these two commandments depend the whole Law and the Prophets'?[10] If you love the Lord and do not love your neighbor, you have only one foot and cannot run; if you love your neighbor but do not love the Lord, you have remained lame

---

5 John 1.1.
6 John 1.14.
7 Wisd. 5.7.
8 Matt. 9.5.
9 Matt. 22.37.
10 Cf. Matt. 22.39, 40.

and useless. Therefore, run on the way of Christ, or rather run through Christ, the Way, for He Himself is the Way. Through this way of love even the Lord Himself ran when He hung on the cross and prayed for His enemies, saying: 'Father, forgive them, for they do not know what they are doing.'[11] On the same way blessed Stephen also was so anxious to run manfully that he deserved to see the heavens opened and Christ standing there as if to meet and assist him.

(6) But because you ought to run with humility if you want to arrive swiftly and happily, see that you run in Him, and through Him, and to Him who said: 'Learn from me, for I am meek and humble of heart.'[12] Do not despise poverty or the poor, since Christ deigned to be poor. Condescend to be humble where Christ was humble, and if you want to be lofty, remain there where Christ remains exalted. Therefore, as we said above, let not the lowly disdain to run on the way which the ruler deigned to walk. Labor for Christ in the world, so that you may merit to reign with Christ in heaven, for as John the Evangelist says: 'He who says that he abides in Christ, ought himself also to walk just as he walked.'[13] For this reason let the Christian not disdain to live in the same way in which Christ deigned to live, since every Christian wants to ascend to the place where Christ has been exalted. And so I beseech you, beloved brethren, with God's help, let us labor as much as we can that the fleeting and deceitful shadow of this world may not deceive us, but let us think more carefully about the salvation of our soul than about bodily pleasure. Behold, as far as the Lord has deigned to inspire us, we have shown to the eyes of your faith the ways of death and of life and the ends to which they lead their lovers. Therefore, love the Lord and despise the world; long for heaven and fear eternal punishment. Reject transitory joy, in order that you may happily reach heaven; despise the devil and follow Christ

---

11 Luke 23.34.
12 Matt. 11.29.
13 1 John 2.6.

who even in this world always deigns to guide you in your good actions and afterwards to happily lead you to your eternal country; to Him is honor and glory forever and ever. Amen.

Sermon 150

This Admonition Explains How We Were Cast into the Hell of this World because of the Sin of the First Man, and that We Should Not Deserve to Come to the Lower Darkness on Account of Our Sins, but Should Strive with All Our Strength to Ascend to Our Chief Country by Good Works as by Certain Steps

(1) I am sure, dearest brethren, that your holy charity cannot be ignorant of the fact that our father, Adam, was placed in the midst of the delights of paradise. Under the devil's persuasion, however, he despised the precepts of God and was cast into the miseries of this world, as though from a higher place to a lower one. For this reason paradise is celestial, while this world is hell; but a different hell is the one in which sinners and the wicked are plunged after death. For that there are two hells the prophet clearly indicates when he says: 'O God, you have rescued me from the depths of the nether world.'[1] Surely, he would not say the lower hell unless he knew that there is a higher one. Moreover, our God is 'Merciful and gracious, slow to anger and abounding in kindness,'[2] and when by His just judgment He cast us from the height of paradise into the hell of this world in the person of our father, Adam, in His ineffable goodness He did not want us to reach the lower hell in irrevocable destruction. Thus, He somehow put us between paradise and the lower hell as though in a middle place. In this way, if we are willing to do penance, we may

---
1 Cf. Ps. 85.13.
2 Ps. 102.8.

merit to ascend to the height of our principal country, but if we want to remain continually in that tyranny of pride whereby we fell beneath the persuasion of the devil, we are pressed down under the weight of sin into the depths of the lower hell from which there can no longer be any return.

(2) As we consider these facts, dearest brethren, not in a transitory fashion, but with great fear and trembling, let us realize that we have been placed in this higher hell through the mercy of God for a purpose. It is in order that we may long to return to Him who created us by the steps of good works, rather than to go down to the depths of the lower hell with him who deceived us. Now since we have been placed, as it were, between water and fire, as between the highest good and the greatest evil, between the destruction of the lower hell and the height of paradise, let us hear the Lord crying out to us in Scripture with wonderful goodness: 'I have set you between death and life,' He says, 'choose life, that you may live.'[3] Concerning these two ways the Lord admonished us in the Gospel when He said: 'Wide and broad is the way that leads to death, and many there are who enter that way. How close the gate and narrow the way that leads to life! And few there are who find it.'[4] The return to paradise is through that close and narrow way, while in the lower hell the descent is through that broad way. Therefore, while we still can and it is within our power with God's help, as we already mentioned above, let us try to ascend to the joy of paradise through the close and narrow way, rather than to arrive at the punishments of hell through that wide and broad way.

(3) But perhaps someone will say: I would like to know who are the ones who descend on the broad way with perilous joy, and who are the ones who rise with labor on the close and narrow road. All lovers of the world, the proud, the avaricious, robbers, the jealous, drunkards, those who commit

---

3 Cf. Deut. 30.19.
4 Cf. Matt. 7.13, 14.

adultery, those who use deceitful balances and false measures, all who harbor hatred in their hearts, those who return evil for evil, men who love bloody or furious or disgraceful spectacles, these are proven to descend on the wide and broad way. But the chaste and the prudent, the merciful, those who observe justice, all who give alms with a prompt and cheerful spirit according to their means, those who keep hatred for no man in their hearts, these ascend to heaven on the close and narrow road. Even though these people seem to still live here on earth in the body, nevertheless, according to the Apostle, their 'Citizenship is in heaven.'[5] Thus when the priest says: 'Lift up your hearts,'[6] they may reply with assurance that they have lifted them up to the Lord. Think it over, I beseech you, brethren, and rebuke with fear as well as with grief those who are hurrying along on the wide and broad way. Tell them and show them that after brief joy they will have to endure endless punishment. On the other hand, rejoice greatly with those who are trying to ascend on the close and narrow way. Faithfully unite yourself with them, and together with them hasten to reach the height or blessedness of eternal life. Do not be afraid because you will have labor on the way, but rejoice because you will find a great reward in your true country. Therefore, I beseech you again and again, beloved brethren, let us consider the eternal joy of the just after short labor, and let us fear the endless punishment of sinners after fleeting pleasure. We may further consider that those who go down on the broad way cannot rejoice very long, while those who seem to ascend laboriously on the close and narrow road are seen not to labor a very long time. Just as those who serve avarice or dissipation in unhappy pleasure are destined to burn in hell along with the devil when their journey on the broad way is ended, so on the contrary those who despise the false joys of the broad way or a wicked life will merit to enter

---
[5] Phil. 3.20.
[6] These are words of the priest before the Preface of the Mass.

the company of the angels in heaven when they have finished the course of the narrow road with some difficulty.

(4) Now we have spoken about the higher place of paradise where true blessedness exists and about the two hells, and we have also briefly shown what we ought to avoid or what to desire according to the power which God has given us. There are three further matters which pertain to the same subject, and we wish to suggest them to your charity. They are three things about which we can and should think with advantage and devotion, and which we frequently recognize even with our bodily eyes as taking place in human life. For there is the doctor, the sick man, and the disease. If the sick man allies himself with the doctor there remain only two, for the illness is conquered. If the sick man prefers to ally himself with the disease rather than the doctor, there, too, because two are together, the doctor is overcome. However, as a result of this victory whereby the doctor is overcome the sick man dies, for if he consented to the doctor the disease would perish and the sick man survive, since nothing at all can win if two fight against it. Listen carefully to the reason why I have made this comparison. God is the doctor, the sick person is man, and sin is the disease. If the sinner allies himself with God, who is the true doctor, the disease immediately perishes and the sick man is set free. However, if the unhappy sinner loves his sickness so that he would like to ally himself with his sins as with deadly illness, rather than cling to the heavenly doctor, he not only fails to admit his illness, that is, his sin, but he even strives with the most shameless boldness to defend it. As long as he wills to unite himself to his sins, he seems, as it were, to overcome the heavenly physician, but by that unhappy victory, he descends into hell on a wide and broad path. If he had been willing to yield to the physician, his sin would have perished like a most cruel disease, and he would have deserved to ascend into heaven on the close and narrow road.

(5) Let us, then, devoutly think over these truths, dearest brethren, while it is still within our power to do so with the

help of God. As we shudder at the wounds of our sins as at deadly poisons, let us apply ourselves to almsgiving, prayer, and fasting. Above all, by a charity which loves not only friends but even enemies, let us have recourse to the mercy of that heavenly physician to recover the health of our souls as if by spiritual remedies. For He Himself said: 'I take no pleasure in the death of the sinner, but rather in the wicked man's conversion, that he may live';[7] and again: 'When you groan and are converted, you shall be saved.'[8] In His goodness may He lead us to this salvation, who together with the Father and the Holy Spirit lives and reigns forever and ever. Amen.

Sermon 151

On the Earthly Sojourn of Christians, and also on the Easy Way Which Leads to Death and the Rough Road Which Leads to Life; Further on the Fact That Paradise is Our True Country Where All the Saints, Who Have Traveled Out of This World, Await Us with the Extended Arms of Charity

(1) We have a sermon for you, beloved brethren, on what you heard in the Gospel: 'Close and narrow is the way that leads to life; wide and broad the way that leads to death,'[1] or in other words, on the earthly sojourn of Christians.

If temporal necessities permitted it, beloved brethren, we would want to visit you, not only once a year, but even a second or a third time, in order that we might satisfy at the same time both your and our longing for the sight of you. However, what our wills desire temporal necessities do not allow. And yet nothing prevents you and us from always

---

7 Cf. Ezech. 18.32; 33.11.
8 Cf. Isa. 30.15.

---

1 Cf. Matt. 7.14, 13.

being united in love and charity, even though we see each other bodily but seldom. For in the sojourn of this world we could not always be together, even if we could be in the same city, for that is a different kind of city, where good Christians are never to be separated from each other.

(2) There are two cities, dearest brethren: the one is the city of the world, the other the city of paradise. The good Christian ever journeys in the city of the world, but he is recognized as a citizen of the city of paradise. The former city is full of labor, while the latter is restful; the one is full of misery, the other blessed; in the one there is labor, in the other repose; if a man lives wickedly in the one, he cannot arrive at the other. We ought to be pilgrims in this world, in order that we may merit to be citizens in heaven. If a man loves the world and wants to be a citizen of it, he has no place in heaven, for by the fact that we long for our true country we prove that we are pilgrims. Let no one deceive himself, beloved brethren; the true country of Christians is not here, but in heaven. The city of Christians, their blessedness, their true and eternal happiness is not here. If a man seeks happiness in the world, he will not possess it in heaven. Our true country is paradise, our city of Jerusalem is that heavenly one; the angels are our fellow-citizens, our parents are the patriarchs and prophets, the apostles and martyrs, and our king is Christ. May we, therefore, so live in this earthly sojourn that we may be able to long for such a country as long as we are here, for if a man wills to lead a wicked life he will not be able to long for that true country.

(3) Now to that country there has preceded us the multitude of patriarchs and prophets, also the glorious army of the apostles and martyrs, many thousands of confessors and virgins, and a considerable number of the faithful. All of these who have already been established in blessed rest daily await us with the extended arms of their charity. They equally long and pray that they may receive us with triumph and exultation in that land of paradise after we are victorious in the

combat of this world, where we must fight against the devil. If we do well, despising diabolical sins and deadly pleasures in this world, we bring joy to all those in heaven. However, if we reject God and love the world, embracing sins and offenses, we make all those people sad, as we mentioned above, the angels, apostles, and martyrs in heaven, and at the same time we prepare an eternal fire for ourselves. Therefore, I beseech you, brethren, if we do not grieve for our own sakes, we ought to grieve at least for the sake of those whom we sadden when we lead a wicked life.

(4) Behold, Christ with His angels awaits us in heaven, as we resist the devil and his angels. Let us not be afraid, brethren, because Christ not only waits for us, but He also helps us. Do not fear or fall into despair; the devil indeed rages, but Christ extends His consolation. He watches you fight. He assists you in difficulty, He crowns you when you are victorious, so do not despair or give up hope. Such a ruler you have over you, and are you afraid? Consider what it is that the devil promises you, and what it is that Christ is going to give you. The devil promises false pleasure, Christ true blessedness; the devil inspires useless worldly joys, Christ the true bliss of paradise. By means of adultery the devil affords lustful pleasure for an hour, in order that he may kill an immortal soul; Christ commends chastity to you for the few days in which you live in the world, in order that He may make you like the angels in heaven. The devil tempts a man to hell on the wide and broad path of wickedness, while Christ invites him to heaven on the close and narrow way of chastity and mercy.

(5) Behold, man, you have before you 'Water and fire, life and death, good and evil,'[2] heaven and hell, the legitimate king and a cruel tyrant, the false sweetness of the world and the true blessedness of paradise. Power is given to you through the grace of Christ: 'Stretch forth your hand to whichever you

---

2 Cf. Ecclus. 15.17, 18.

choose.'³ 'Choose life, that you may live';⁴ leave the broad way on the left which drags you to death, and cling to the narrow path on the right which happily leads you to life. Do not allow the wideness of that road on the left to keep you or give you pleasure. To be sure, it is spacious and level, adorned with different kinds of flowers; but its flowers quickly fade and even between the flowers poisonous serpents frequently lie hidden, so that when you hurry on to these false joys you are struck by their deadly venom. This way is spacious, but it is not long. You pay attention to the kind of road you are walking, and do not notice what kind of a land you are reaching. If you listen to me, you withdraw yourself from death, for if you do not believe in Christ you will perish in hell, as the Lord Himself said in the Gospel: 'Wide and broad is the way that leads to death, and many there are who enter that way.'⁵ Truly, it gives pleasure for a time, but it deceives for all eternity. On the other hand, the road on the right should not sadden or frighten you: it is indeed narrow, but it is not long. The rejoicing on the wide path does not last long, and neither does the labor on the narrow way; after a short, broad path the former drags one into eternal straightened circumstances, while after brief difficulties the latter leads to endless bliss.

(6) Let us, then, strive to labor with God's help, beloved brethren, and by rejecting sin adorn ourselves with good works so that Christ our king, our fellow-citizens the angels, our parents the patriarchs, prophets, apostles, martyrs, confessors, and virgins who have happily preceded us to our true city, that heavenly Jerusalem, may receive us with joy and exultation. May we so live, brethren, that through our good deeds there may be 'Joy in heaven over one sinner who repents,'⁶ as the Lord Himself deigned to say before. If, then, we cause joy in heaven when we do penance, surely we bring sadness when we return to the pleasure of our sins.

---

3 Ecclus. 15.17.
4 Deut. 30.19.
5 Cf. Matt. 7.13.
6 Luke 15.7.

(7) Therefore, dearest brethren, in order that, with God's help, we may be able to avoid all sins, let us endeavor to preserve our charity intact, loving not only friends but also enemies, wishing well to everyone, and praying for all men. For if you do to all men what you yourself would like them to do to you, you close the door entirely to vices. There will be no room for sin to enter your soul, if you are willing to love, not only your friends, but also your enemies with your whole heart.

(8) I beseech you, brethren, let us live in this world just as strangers and pilgrims. By almsgiving let us store up for the eternal country whatever we acquire as the result of some work or a fair business transaction or service in a just war. With the exception of daily nourishment and simple clothing, what is left should not be consumed by dissipation in this exile and earthly sojourn, but should be transmitted to our true country through the exercise of mercy. We are traveling a journey, brethren, and directing our course toward our true country. Let us not indulge in excess on the journey of this life, and let us never be over-confident. Ever vigilant, careful, and solicitous, let us not prepare for ourselves pleasures on the way, in order that we may be able to bring whatever is best to our true country. If in this land we spend whatever we are able to earn for dissipation, gluttony, or drunkenness, how will we come to that eternal country? With what boldness will we be able to enter among the angels and archangels if we are naked of good works, wrapped in the filthy swaddling clothes of sins, wounded by evil deeds? For this reason let almsgiving store up whatever avarice was burying on earth. Then, when our soul leaves this dead body, it may be adorned with splendid garments and the pearls of chastity, mercy, patience, humility, and brotherly love, so that we may merit to hear from the Lord: 'Well done, good and faithful servant; enter into the joy of thy master.'[7] We ought to long for this word, brethren, and to dread that other one which will be heard by the soul which

---
7 Matt. 25.21.

is naked of good works and wrapped in the filth of sins. For our Lord in the Gospel speaks about such a soul when He says: 'Friend, how didst thou come in here without a wedding garment?'[8] And when that man is silent He says to His servants: 'Bind his hands and feet and cast him forth into the darkness outside, where there will be the weeping, and the gnashing of teeth.'[9] May God avert from us this sentence which will be heard by those who indulge in any kind of wickedness and are adorned with most precious ornaments for the sake of vanity and worldly pomp. Such men seize the property of another, are filled even to the point of vomiting with many delicacies, bury themselves in excessive drinking, and store up by almsgiving little or nothing for heaven. Concerning these men the Apostle says: 'The soul which gives herself up to pleasures is dead while she is still alive.'[10] When such men die they are not lifted up by the angels into the bosom of Abraham along with Lazarus, but with the rich man in purple garments they are plunged into the depths of hell. Therefore, as we consider these truths, let us curb our food and clothing as much as we can while we are in this world. Then, after our death, we may deserve to be adorned in heaven with the most precious and splendid garments of our charity, and to hear that desirable word: 'Well done, good and faithful servant; because thou hast been faithful over a few things, I will set thee over many; enter into the joy of thy master.'[11] May the good Lord bring us to this joy under His protection, who lives and reigns.

---

8 Matt. 22.12.
9 Cf. Matt. 22.13.
10 1 Tim. 5.6.
11 Matt. 25.21.

Sermon 152

On What Is Written in the Gospel: 'Where Two or Three Are Gathered Together for My Sake.'[1]

(1) Our Lord has deigned to give us a great assurance, beloved brethren, when He says in the Gospel: 'Where two or three are gathered together for my sake, there am I in the midst of them.'[2] If He condescends to be present among two or three, how much more so when all the people are gathered in church with pious devotion, the body of the Church united with Christ its Head in a society of harmonious members? 'Where two or three,' He says, 'are gathered together for my sake.' Now since a congregation pertains to many people, we must perceive how the Divine Word has judged that we should talk about two or three. I believe that it can be said about one individual, because he can be collected in the house of God, that is, in order to pray to God a man should enter wholly, not only with the exterior senses, but also the interior ones, with holy desires, faith, and good works. For if anyone is kept inside of a church with his body only, while he is occupied outside of church with all his heart, he enters with his exterior separated and distinct from his spirit. Then, what is the more precious part of man travels far away from the divine service; while only his earthly part is kept in the presence of God, his soul is captivated by passing delights and is distracted by manifold preoccupations. Therefore, whenever any one of us comes to commend his eternal welfare before his Judge, let him not appear one thing interiorly and be another exteriorly. Let no part of a man be absent. For if God has said: 'Where two or three are gathered together,' how will a man be proven to be gathered together if he is scattered

---
1 Matt. 18.20.
2 *Ibid.*

away from himself by the wandering of his thoughts? Or how will God be in the midst of you if you yourself are not there? If the one who is asking is missing, how will the one to whom you are praying be there? How will the judge be aroused if the advocate is asleep? For this reason it is imperative that affectionate zeal obtain what the sound of the voice entreats. Call your anxious mind back within you, for it is proper to offer every sacrifice through it; it is not right for the priest to be missing from the temple of God.

(2) Therefore, as we consider these truths, dearest brethren, and as often as we chant the psalms or prostrate in prayer, let us continually meditate on what the Apostle says: 'Be assiduous in prayer, being wakeful therein';[3] and again: 'I will sing with the spirit, but I will sing with the understanding also.'[4] For if while we sing or are engaged in prayer worldly thoughts divert the attention of our soul from the meaning of divine contemplation, they captivate our senses and make us run here and there without any fruit of the soul. With the help of Christ we will be able to avoid this condition at once if we are willing to think rather carefully about the multitude of our sins. For if we make supplication for our sins, that is, whatever evil thoughts we have had or whatever we have spoken unjustly, and do so with much crying and groaning as we should, useless thoughts either do not occur to us or, if they do insinuate themselves, they immediately blush and depart when we do not give consent to them. For what should be the object of man's thought when he speaks with God, except to look intently at His mercy with all the attention of his mind? And because it is difficult not to have other thoughts steal upon us, at least they should not be allowed to linger within us. For a thought which arises from passion or dissipation is the same as if someone seizes burning coals in his hands: if he immediately throws them away without delay, the burning fire will not be able to hurt him, but if he allows

---

[3] Col. 4.2.
[4] 1 Cor. 14.15.

any delay at all, they will not be thrown away without a wound. Now as a result of our many negligences, not only slight faults like flitting flies continually torment us, but even serious offenses frequently urge us to commit some kind of sin. Therefore, we ought to fight with courage, as I already mentioned above, striving with all our heart and soul both day and night against the snares of the enemy, for it is written of them that they are: 'A thousand names, a thousand ways of inflicting harm.'[5]

(3) Now if we carefully examine our consciences, we recognize that spiritual battles take place there, and in accord with the thought of the Apostle Paul, we are: 'A spectacle to God and to His angels.'[6] Moreover, we feel that in the arena of this world we are continually fighting against all sins and faults as against the most cruel beasts. If a man carefully pays attention to this he is present as his own examiner, and in his anxiety he will see certain distractions of his soul and opposing wills and doubtful struggles as useful, considering with the interior eye what is proper for him. I entreat you, brethren, look and notice carefully, because we have within ourselves a spiritual amphitheater, and the wild forest which is depicted in spectacles we daily experience in the movement of our heart. For my part, brethren, I do not wish to injure anyone, and I mention no one by name; let each one see what he finds in his own conscience. For in our life I see the wrath of lions, in our affections the cruelty of bears, in our minds the fickleness of panthers, in avarice the greed of wolves, in lust the thirst of wild asses, in our senses the filthiness of vultures, in our memory the forgetfulness of stags, in lying the deceitfulness of foxes, in envy the poison of snakes, in fasting the slowness of oxen, in our hearts the ignorance of steers, in pride the necks of bulls, in shamelessness the boldness of rams, in frivolity the agility of roebucks, in the flesh the hardness of boars, in evil thoughts the swamps of pigs, in the tongue the

---

5 Vergil. *Aeneid* VII, 337.
6 Cf. 1 Cor. 4.9.

teeth of wild boars, in a bad conscience the spots of tigers, in wrath the swollen necks of serpents, and in sins the huge bulk of elephants. For this reason I entreat that since we recognize that we are surrounded by such great dangers, we should pray more devoutly to the Lord for each other. O blessed brothers and helpers and fellow-servants in the Lord, may our hands come to the Lord, that is, holy prayers along with good works. Then, when we are brought to the exceedingly dangerous contest in the theater of this world, in which: 'No one is crowned unless he has competed according to the rules,'[7] we may afford a joyous spectacle to God and the angels. After our adversaries have been overcome and laid low with the help of God, we may journey in triumph to the eternal land and merit to hear that happy and desirable word: 'Come, blessed of my Father, receive the kingdom which was prepared for you from the foundation of the world.'[8]

(4) In order that we may deserve to obtain this through the grace of God, as we indicated above, when we either bow our head in prayer or genuflect, let us strive with the whole attention of our mind and with all our strength, so that no useless or wicked thought may steal upon us and be able to withdraw our mind from a perfect and contrite prayer. And since, when we pray humbly on behalf of our sins we know that we are speaking to the Lord, we ought to fear that if we are thinking of something else than what we are asking we may offend the Divine Majesty before whom we seem to stand. For we ought to be certain and to trust with all our devotion that what we are uttering with our lips we also have in our hearts when we either chant the psalms or pray; then our whole prayer is heard by the Lord. May He Himself deign to grant this, who together with the Father and the Holy Spirit lives and reigns forever and ever. Amen.

---

7 Cf. 2 Tim. 2.5.
8 Cf. Matt. 25.34.

* *Sermon 153*

St. Augustine on the Gospel where It Says: 'If Thou Wilt Enter Into Life, Keep the Commandments.'[1]

(1) When the Gospel was read, dearest brethren, we heard the Lord say: 'If thou wilt enter into life, keep the commandments.' Who is there, brethren, who does not want life? And yet who is there who wishes to keep the commandments? If you are unwilling to keep the commandments, why do you seek life? If you are slothful in the work, why do you hasten to the reward? That rich young man said that he had kept the commandments, and he heard still greater commands: 'If thou wilt be perfect, one thing is lacking to thee: sell all that thou hast, and give to the poor.' You will not lose it, but 'Thou shalt have treasure in heaven; and come, follow me.'[2] For how does it profit you to do this and not follow me? What that man heard, most beloved, we, too, have heard; the Gospel of Christ is in heaven, but it does not cease to speak on earth. Let us not be dead to it, for He thunders; let us not be deaf, for He shouts. But if you are unwilling to do the greater things, do the lesser ones. These are the greater ones: 'Sell all that thou hast, and give to the poor; and come, follow me.' The lesser ones are these: 'Thou shalt not kill, thou shalt not commit adultery, thou shalt not seek false witness, thou shalt not steal, honor thy father and mother, thou shalt love thy neighbor as thyself.'[3] If you are unwilling to observe the greater commands, at least do these. Spare yourself, have pity on yourself. This life still allows you to put it off, but do not reject reproof. You were a thief yesterday? Do not be one today. Perhaps you have already been one today, too? Do not be one tomorrow. Now at last put an end to evil, and exact

---
1 Matt. 19.17.
2 Cf. Matt. 19.21; Mark 10.21.
3 Cf. Matt. 19.18, 19.

the good in exchange. You want to have good possessions, and you are not willing to be good; your life is contrary to your wishes. If it is a great good to possess a fine farm, how great an evil is it to have a wicked soul?

(2) When he had heard this command, the rich man 'Went away sad,'[4] as you have heard, and the Lord says: 'With what difficulty will they who have riches enter the kingdom of God!'[5] At length the disciples became very sad when they heard this and they said: 'If this is so, who then can be saved?'[6] Rich and poor, listen to Christ: I am speaking to God's people. Most of you are poor, but do you also listen with understanding. And listen still more, if you glory in your poverty. Beware of pride, lest the humble rich surpass you; beware of wickedness, lest the pious rich confound you; beware of drunkenness, lest the sober rich excel you.

(3) Therefore, listen to the Apostle when he calls you rich: 'Charge the rich of this world not to be proud.'[7] Pride is the first worm of riches; it is a harmful gnawing worm which gnaws at everything and reduces it to ashes. 'Charge the rich of this world not to be proud, or to trust in the uncertainty of riches,'[8] lest perchance you go to sleep as a rich man and arise a poor man. Perhaps someone will take your gold away from you: will anyone be able to take God from you? What does a rich man have if he does not possess God? And what does a poor man not have if he possesses God, for He says: 'Charge them not to trust in the uncertainty of riches, but in God, who provides all things'?[9] For this reason the rich: 'Should give readily, sharing with others, and thus providing for themselves a good foundation against the time to come, in order that they may lay hold on the true life.'[10] I have admonished the rich, but do you who are poor also listen. Do you also spend out of what

---

4 Matt. 19.22.
5 Cf. Mark 10.23; Matt. 19.23.
6 Cf. Matt. 19.25.
7 1 Tim. 6.17.
8 *Ibid.*
9 *Ibid.*
10 Cf. 1 Tim. 6.18, 19.

you possess, and do not be covetous; give your wealth, and curb your passions.

(4) Let us now meditate more carefully, brethren, on the unique and singular medicine of almsgiving. If we have given to the poor in either food or clothing as much as our strength allows, we will deserve to obtain, not only the forgiveness of sins, but even an eternal reward. Then will be fulfilled in us what the Lord said in the Gospel: 'Nevertheless give alms, and behold, all things are clean to you.'[11] Moreover: 'Water quenches a fire, and alms atone for sins';[12] and what is written elsewhere: 'Store up almsgiving in your treasure house, and it will save you from every evil.'[13] May He deign to grant this, to whom is honor and might together with the Father and the Holy Spirit, forever and ever. Amen.

Sermon 154

On What Is Said in the Gospel: 'Woe to Those Who Are with Child, or Have Infants at the Breast.'[1]

(1) We ought to know and to understand, dearest brethren, that for Christians tribulation can never be lacking as long as they live in this body. For thus the Apostle also attests, as you have heard, when he says: 'All who want to live piously in Christ suffer persecution';[2] and again: 'Through many tribulations we must enter the kingdom of God.'[3] Days of tribulation, and of even still greater tribulations are going to come. They will come, as Scripture says, and as the days pass trials will be increased. Let no one promise himself what the

---
11 Luke 11.41.
12 Cf. Ecclus. 3.33.
13 Ecclus. 29.15.
1 Matt. 24.19.
2 2 Tim. 3.12.
3 Acts 14.21.

Gospel does not promise, for just as when the end of the world approaches, as the Gospel says: 'Iniquity will abound, charity will grow cold,'[4] so because of our iniquities adversity will never be lacking. It is necessary for us to prepare our souls, not only for penance, but also for patience. I exhort you, my brethren, pay attention to Sacred Scripture and see whether it has deceived in any way, or whether it has said anything and afterwards it turned out otherwise than it had said. Thus it is necessary that even to the end everything will happen just as is indicated. The Scriptures promise us nothing in this world except tribulations, afflictions, difficulties, additional griefs, an abundance of temptations, as the Lord Himself says in the Gospel: 'In the world you will have affliction.'[5] Again we read: 'The world shall rejoice, and you shall be sorrowful, but your sorrow shall be turned into joy.'[6] For this in particular let us prepare ourselves, so we will not faint on the way if we are not ready.

(2) Now concerning the tribulations themselves you heard when the Gospel was read: 'Woe to those who are with child, or have infants at the breast.'[7] Those with child are all who are puffed up with expectation, while those who have infants at the breast, that is, nursing mothers, are those who have already obtained what they had desired. Truly, the pregnant mother swells in expectation of her child when she does not yet behold him; the woman who already nurses her child embraces what she was hoping for. The pregnant woman is like one who covets the possessions of another; the nursing woman is one who has carried away what she had desired. Now in order that even simple souls may be able to understand this more clearly, let us propose an example. Someone longs for the farm of another and says: That farm of my neighbor is a good one, Oh, if only it were mine! Oh, if only I could annex it and make one estate out of this one and that! Avarice also

---
4 Matt. 24.12.
5 John 16.33.
6 Cf. John 16.20.
7 Matt. 24.19.

loves oneness; what it loves is good, but it does not know when it is to be loved. If perchance that neighbor who possesses the fine farm is a rich man and this one suspects that he cannot take it away from him because he is a powerful man, able to defend himself against the man, he neither covets the land nor is impregnated with the thought. Since he expects nothing and does not covet, he is not pregnant in spirit. But if the neighbor next door is a poor man who is in a position of want so that he might sell, or who can be oppressed and forced to sell, his eye is cast upon him and he hopes that he can take away the farm or the farmer's house of that poor neighbor. So he sends some kind of tribulations to that man; for example, he deals secretly with men who have power so that the tax-collectors will implicate the man or keep him bound in some public and harmful affair. As a result of the many debts contracted, the unhappy man finds it necessary to sell the very small house which was a means of support for himself and his children. Compelled by necessity, then, he comes to the man through whose wickedness he is oppressed and afflicted, and not knowing that he suffers through his instigation he says to him: Give me, I beseech you, my lord, a few coins. I suffer want, and am oppressed by a creditor. And that man says: I do not have anything in my hands now. He says that he has nothing in his hands for this reason, in order that the other man, overwhelmed by slander, will have to sell. When at length he has told him that he is compelled by his excessive affliction to divide the farm, the other man immediately replies: Although I do not have any money of my own from which I am anxious to lend to you in order to help you, since you are my friend, if it is necessary to do so I will divide even my little bit of silver, in order that you may suffer no harm. When a favor was being sought he admitted that he did not have any money at all, but when he said that he would sell his possessions he says that he will help him, as though his friend. Although he has brought him to this necessity he tells him that he ought to make the sale. For the little farmer's house for which he first offered perhaps one hundred coins, for example, he does not agree to give even a moderate price when he sees the man oppressed. To such men, then, as was already said above, the evangelist proclaims: 'Woe to those who are with child, or have infants at the breast.' Indeed, it will be woe for them on the day of judgment, and they will not be able to be freed from the evil hearing; on the contrary they are going to hear: 'Depart from me, accursed ones, into the everlasting fire which was prepared for the devil and his angels. For I was hungry and you did not give me to eat; I was thirsty and you did not give me to drink.'[8] At this point let your charity pay careful attention. If the man who did not give away his own goods is sent into the fire, where do you think a man is to be sent if he attacks the property of another? If the man who has not clothed the naked has to burn with the devil, where do you think the man who has robbed him is going to burn?

(3) Therefore, as often as the Gospel lesson is read to you where it is said: 'Woe to those who are with child, or have infants at the breast,'[9] do not believe it only about women who have lawful husbands. For what evil has a woman done if she has conceived a child of her own husband? Why will it be evil for her on judgment day if she has done what God commanded? For this reason this is not to be believed concerning women who rightly conceive and bear children, but rather concerning those whom we mentioned above, who seem to be pregnant because they unjustly desired the possessions of their neighbor. Of such men we read that it is written: 'He was pregnant with mischief, and brings forth failure.'[10] Now every man conceives, and no one can exist without conception, but some conceive of Christ and others of the devil. Of those who conceive through the devil it is said: 'He was pregnant with mischief, and brings forth failure,' while of those who

---

8 Matt. 25.41, 42.
9 Matt. 24.19.
10 Ps. 7.15.

conceive through the Holy Spirit it is written: 'We conceived and writhed in pain, giving birth to the spirit of your salvation.'[11]

(4) If a man carefully pays attention to the things which we have said, dearest brethren, let him immediately correct himself if he recognizes that the aforementioned evils have existed in him or perhaps are still there. Past sins do not harm us if they do not please us, for there is still room for repentance and amendment. The separation of some on the right hand and others on the left has not yet been made; not yet are we in hell where that thirsting rich man is who longs for a drop of water. Let us listen and be corrected while we still live; let us not desire the goods of another and be puffed up with pride as though pregnant. Let us not want to approach those possessions and in obtaining them kiss them as sons. When a man covets the goods of his neighbor, as was already said, his soul seems as though it has conceived; but if he has been able to obtain what he desires through some cleverness or wickedness, he is recognized as kissing and nursing, as it were, his son who has been born. Therefore, let us not love these earthly possessions in such a way, brethren, that we lose the heavenly ones. The heart must be changed and lifted up, so that we no longer live here in spirit. Love of the world is an evil land; let it be enough that we still seem to be here in the flesh. Let us listen to the Apostle when he says: 'If you have risen with Christ, mind the things that are above, seek the things that are above, not the things that are on earth.'[12] What has been promised to you does not yet appear; it is already prepared, but it cannot be seen. Do you want to be puffed up with covetousness? Be impregnated with this: desire eternal life to which God invites you. Let this be your hope and it will be a sure begetting, not an abortion. You may not embrace in time what you have begotten, but you will possess it in eternity.

(5) Doubtless, what has been promised must be given, but

---
11 Cf. Isa. 26.18.
12 Col. 3.1, 2.

it is still in reverse order: it will not be given now, but later. Consider what great things are given, brethren, for who is even able to count them? Now of all things which were promised to us in Sacred Scripture only one has remained. If God has spoken the truth to us in such great matters, does He deceive us in this one? It is written concerning the Church that it will exist, and it is evident that it does; it is written of idols that they will not be, and it is seen that they are not. It is written that the Jews would lose their kingdom, and it is evident that they did; it is written of heretics that they were destined to exist, and it is obvious that they do. We also read about the day of judgment, the rewards of the good and the punishment of the wicked. Let no one deceive himself, brethren, because just as all those things which were promised came to pass so also the day of judgment, the punishment of sinners and the rewards of the just, without any doubt will come to be. Therefore, while it is possible and with God's help it still rests in our power, let each one of us strive to avoid sin and do what is good. Then when that terrible and dreadful day comes, we may not be burned in endless fire with wicked sinners, but together with the just and those who fear God, we may deserve to arrive at an eternal reward. May He deign to grant this, to whom is honor and might forever and ever. Amen.

Sermon 155

On the Ten Virgins

(1) In the lesson which was read to us, beloved brethren, we heard the Lord say: 'The kingdom of heaven is like ten virgins who took their lamps and went forth to meet the bridegroom and the bride.'[1] If we understand this only literal-

---

1 Matt. 25.1.

ly, it seems to be too harsh and difficult. Far be it from our thoughts that out of the household even of the Christian poor so small a number reaches eternal life. Because this should by no means be understood according to the letter, since in reality the Lord Himself said it was a parable, let us ask why five were called foolish and five wise. Now those five prudent virgins signify all the saints who are destined to reign with Christ. Those five foolish virgins, on the contrary, seem to prefigure wicked Christians who glory only in the title of Christian but are completely without good works. Moreover, they are called the five foolish and wise virgins because there are shown to be the five senses in all men: sight, hearing, taste, smell, and touch. Now through these senses, like certain kinds of doors or windows, either death or life approaches our soul, and concerning them the prophet also said: 'Death has come up through our windows.'[2] For this reason, then, five virgins are called wise, since they use their senses well, and five are called foolish, because through those five senses they receive more death than life.

(2) Let us further diligently inquire how those five senses like the five virgins either preserve virginity or subject it to corruption. If any man or woman sees the son or daughter of another, a servant or a handmaid, and looks closely upon her with unlawful desire, one virgin is corrupted, because through the eyes or bodily windows the poison of death has entered the depths of the heart. Moreover, if anyone, either religious or lay, willingly listens to men who gossip or speak idle words and sing wicked or shameful songs, and when he calmly hears it accepts it with pleasure, another virgin is corrupted. And if a man is not satisfied with food in moderation but looks for extravagant delicacies, always striving for them through evil speech, by this evil sense of taste a third virgin is corrupted. Moreover, if unfamiliar scents are diligently sought in order to be able to please men in dissipation, a fourth virgin is violated. And if through lust a man is willing to touch with

---
2 Jer. 9.21.

his hands the sons or daughters of another in pleasure, and with motives of pleasure seeks exceedingly soft garments, a fifth virgin has now been corrupted. In this way the five senses in man, like the five virgins, are corrupted. On the contrary, when holy souls curb those five senses from everything unlawful, that is, the sight, hearing, taste, smell, and touch, they preserve the chastity of their five senses, piously and chastely releasing them for things that are lawful and legitimate. Thus, five of the virgins signify good men, and the other five typify those who are wicked.

(3) Truly, dearest brethren, of what profit is it for a man or woman, whether cleric or monk or religious, if bodily virginity is preserved, as long as purity of heart is violated by evil desires? Of what benefit is it to show chastity in one member and to keep corruption in all the rest? For if you notice carefully, those virgins who follow the lamb do not do so merely because of the fact that they have preserved only bodily virginity. Finally, when He had said: 'These are they who did not defile themselves with women,'[3] He continued and added: 'and in their mouth there was found no lie; they are without blemish.'[4] Listen carefully that if anyone boasts about bodily virginity alone, as long as he loves deceit he will not be able to follow Christ along with those holy virgins. For this reason let no virgin presume only upon her physical virginity, because if she is disobedient or gossiping she knows that she will have to be excluded from the bed-chamber of her Heavenly Spouse. Although a virgin possesses a hundredfold and a married woman the thirtyfold, still a chaste and humble married woman is better than a proud virgin. For that chaste woman who serves her husband in humility possesses her thirtyfold, while not even one will remain for the proud virgin; in both of them is fulfilled what the psalmist says: 'Lowly people you save, but haughty eyes you bring low.'[5]

---

3 Cf. Apoc. 14.4.
4 Apoc. 14.5.
5 Ps. 17.28.

(4) Since the blessed Apostle has called the entire Catholic Church a virgin, considering not only the physical virgins in her but desiring the minds of all to be incorrupt, for this reason he says: 'I betrothed you to one spouse, that I might present you a chaste virgin to Christ.'[6] Therefore, the souls, not only of religious, but of all men and women do not doubt that they are spouses of Christ if they are willing to preserve both bodily chastity and virginity of heart in those aforementioned five senses. For Christ is to be understood as the spouse of souls, not of bodies. Therefore, dearest brethren, let both men and women, boys and girls, preserve their virginity until their marriage by a wise use of those five senses, that is, sight, hearing, taste, smell, and touch, not corrupting their souls. Then, when the doors are opened on judgment day, they will happily deserve to enter the eternal bed-chamber of their Spouse. However, those who both corrupt their bodies by adulterous union before their marriage and afterwards throughout their whole life do not cease to defile their souls by evil sight, hearing, and speech, if the fruit of worthy repentance does not come to their aid, when the doors are closed such people will shout to no avail: 'Sir, sir, open the door for us!'[7] Then they will deserve to hear: 'Amen I say to you, I do not know where you are from.'[8] Now if all of us, brethren, whether clerics or the laity or monks or religious or those in the married state, faithfully and diligently pay attention to these truths, with the Lord's help preserving purity of heart as well as bodily chastity, we will not be cast out with the foolish virgins 'Into the darkness outside, where there will be the weeping, and the gnashing of teeth.'[9] Instead, we will be admitted to the spiritual nuptials and merit to hear: 'Well done, good and faithful servant; enter into the joy of thy master.'[10] May He deign to grant this.

---

6 2 Cor. 11.2.
7 Matt. 25.11.
8 Matt. 25.12; Luke 13.25.
9 Matt. 22.13.
10 Matt. 25.21.

Sermon 156

Likewise a Sermon on the Ten Virgins

(1) In the Gospel passage which was read to us concerning the ten virgins, beloved brethren, it is said: 'All the virgins trimmed their lamps.'[1] Now the foolish virgins did not have oil ready with their lamps: 'While the wise did take oil in their vessels. Then as the bridegroom was long in coming, they all became drowsy and slept. And at midnight a great cry arose, "Behold, the bridegroom is coming, go forth to meet him!" Then all those virgins arose and trimmed their lamps.'[2] When the lamps of the foolish virgins were extinguished, they asked the others who had oil in their vessels to give them some of theirs, but they said: ' "Lest there may not be enough for us and for you, go rather to those who sell it, and buy some for yourselves." Now while they were gone to buy it the bridegroom came; and those who were ready went in with him to the marriage feast, and the door was shut. Afterwards there came the other virgins, who said, "Sir, open the door for us!" '[3] The answer was given to them: 'I do not know where you are from.'[4] Now what these facts signify, dearest brethren, we briefly suggest to your charity according to what we read in the exposition of the ancient fathers. They were not called five virgins because there was to be so small a number in eternal life, but because of the five senses through which either death or life enters our soul. If we use them badly we are corrupted, but if we steadfastly use them well we preserve the purity of our soul. When it was said: 'As the bridegroom was long in coming, they all became drowsy and slept,'[5] that sleep

---

1 Matt. 25.7.
2 Matt. 25.4-7.
3 Matt. 25.9-11.
4 Luke 13.25.
5 Matt. 25.5.

signified death. Finally, the Apostle also speaks in the same way: 'I would not, brethren, have you ignorant concerning those who are asleep.'[6] When a great cry arose, the middle of the night typified the day of judgment. It is called the middle of the night on account of ignorance, since no one knows when or at what hour the day of judgment will come.

(2) It is a fact that all the virgins trimmed their lamps, and that those foolish virgins had some oil but it was so little that it could not be enough for them and eventually they began to be extinguished. Therefore, we ought to strive as much as we can, with God's help, beloved brethren, to store up in the vessels of our souls as much as will be enough for us in eternity, since mercy or charity is understood in the oil. A little is sufficient for no one, dearest brethren, unless a man is unable to give more because of poverty. The lamp of the soul must be full, so that through the oil of charity our light may shine forever. If God has given a man considerable wealth, he should open his hands in almsgiving as much as he can, and not believe that just a little can be enough for him. Each one ought to think of how much he owes for every evil thought which he has formed since the time when he reached the age of reason, every evil word he has spoken, and every wicked deed he has performed. He should notice the multitude of his sins and carefully weigh the price for each one of them. Let him see how much he owes for lying, false oaths, perjury, slander or detraction, drunkenness, gluttony and dissipation, lust, envy and pride, filthy thoughts, and idle words. Now let each one meditate on all these and similar things which cannot be counted, and then he will realize how much almsgiving he ought to practice. Even if we should give everything we have, unless the mercy of God weighs it down, we are not able to redeem all of our sins. However, let us do as much as we can in humility, with a contrite and repentant heart, and let us not do it for the sake of human praise but out of love for God and the thought of eternal life.

---

6 Cf. 1 Thess. 4.12.

(3) When the foolish virgins said to the wise: 'Give us some of your oil,'[7] and the wise virgins replied: 'Lest there may not be enough for us and for you,'[8] this was said with humility and out of fear. So great will be the fear and investigation on the day of judgment, that even those who know that they have prepared the oil of mercy quite abundantly will be afraid that it cannot suffice to redeem all of their sins. But when it is said: 'Go rather to those who sell it, and buy some for yourselves,'[9] this can be understood concerning the poor. For they are the business men who sell the necessary oil for the lamps of souls, and through them Christ is wont to exercise this trade. In their person He accepts earthly goods in order that He may repay heavenly ones; He takes fleeting possessions because He will repay eternal goods. Finally, He Himself has said: 'As long as you did it for one of these, the least of my brethren, you did it for me.'[10] Now the lamps are understood as souls, but the vessels in which oil is kept are typified as good consciences. For what does it mean to have oil in vessels, except to store away good works within one's conscience? Now some men do good deeds out of love for God, while others do them through the desire for human praise. For this reason, although those foolish virgins were chaste in body and engaged in vigils, psalmody, spiritual reading, and prayer, they did all of these things wholly through a desire for human praise and not for God or eternal bliss. Therefore, when death came upon them and the praise of men withdrew from them, their oil also failed them at the same time. What was said to them: 'Go rather to those who sell it, and buy some for yourselves,'[11] can also be taken in another sense. Those who sell may be understood as flatterers who extol with false praises those who seem to do good deeds for the sake of human glory. Now when a man does some good for the sake of human praise, he does not do

---
7 Matt. 25.8.
8 Matt. 25.9.
9 *Ibid.*
10 Matt. 25.40.
11 Matt. 25.9.

any at all if no one praises him. From this it is understood that all who desire to receive the praises of men sell to human flattery what they seem to practice in God's work, and by accepting vain praise they lose eternal rewards. Now those virgins who had oil in their vessels place all of their good work within their conscience, because they do not do it for the sake of human praise but to obtain the divine mercy.

(4) Therefore, as we devoutly meditate, dearest brethren, on the fact that this parable pertains to the entire Church, those who are unable to preserve bodily virginity ought to observe purity of heart. Thus, if some cannot reach the crown of the martyrs or the virgins, they can at least merit to receive the forgiveness of all their sins. Moreover, virgins, who with God's help preserve their bodily purity, should strive with all their strength and labor by the grace of God to avoid talkativeness, to reject detraction or murmuring as the poison of the devil, to dread the disease of envy or pride as the sword of the ancient enemy, to maintain obedience with humility, never to despise the commands of a superior, to engage in reading and prayer. If they are not prevented by infirmity, they should rise for the vigils with all alacrity, and whether in church or at table or in any place whatever, they should strive to say with their lips whatever is in accord with obedience or humility. If they see anyone sad, they ought to console them, and if they recognize disobedience, they should not fail to rebuke it.

(5) In every walk of life we find good and bad people, and so in the Church of Christ which is now compared to a threshing floor where chaff as well as the wheat is found. What is worse, we even find there, not only lay people, but even clerics and monks and religious who are so careless and lukewarm that they do not produce the sweet honey of souls like spiritual bees, but like most cruel wasps they pierce the hearts of their brothers or sisters with the poisoned darts of their tongue. People like these are not helpers of Christ, but they are shown to be defenders of the devil. If perchance they see a

brother or sister haughtily standing up against a superior, they do not endeavor to calm him but by their evil words try, rather, to arouse him to still greater wrath, saying that this situation neither can nor should endure any longer. They even encourage others to answer their superiors with great bitterness or wrath, so that the superiors themselves regret having wanted to admonish or reprove them with paternal devotion. As we said above, in every profession there are not only helpers or ministers of the devil, but also vessels of Christ and defenders of justice. When the devil's assistants arouse men to disobedience or pride through their clever whispering, Christ's helpers strive to recall them to humility or meekness by their soothing encouragement and their holy, salutary advice. The former instill death, the latter life; the ones give poison, while the others supply an antidote; the former cause wounds, the latter obtain healing remedies; those bring perdition, these salvation; those inspire wrath, these gentleness; those foster pride, these teach humility; the former induce resentment, the latter urge patience; those arouse hatred, these charity. But no matter what the wicked do, the healing remedies of Christ are more powerful than the wounds of the devil.

(6) If those who are among the clergy or in a monastery exalt themselves and others to pride, like quivers which are full of the devil's arrows, they try to pierce the hearts of simple souls and to extinguish in them humility and meekness. But since through the goodness of God wheat is found in the midst of the chaff, holy souls are shown to be full of spiritual antidotes, like treasure chests of Christ. Whenever the wicked have inflicted wounds, they do not cease to heal them by applying heavenly remedies, saying to each sinner: Do not be proud, brother, because it is written: 'God resists the proud.'[12] Do not be angry, because we read: 'Anger lodges in the bosom of a fool';[13] and again: 'The wrath of man does not work the

---

12 James 4.6; 1 Peter 5.6.
13 Eccles. 7.10.

justice of God.'[14] If they perchance see disobedience, they say kindly and humbly: Do not be disobedient, brother, because it is written: 'Obedience is above sacrifice';[15] and the Apostle exclaims: 'Obey your superiors and be subject to them, for they keep watch as having to render an account of your souls.'[16] These souls are full of God if, when they see someone lukewarm or negligent, they try to arouse him to compunction by offering healing remedies out of the spiritual treasure chest, that is, out of a good heart. If they see someone uttering words of slander or murmuring, they tell him the words of the blessed Apostle: 'Neither murmur, as some of them murmured, and perished at the hands of the destroyer';[17] and do not slander, because it is written: 'He who speaks against his brother, speaks against the law';[18] and elsewhere: 'He who speaks against his brother, will be erased from the book of life.'[19] If they deter them from evil speech by this holy advice, they begin to encourage them to praise God. If they know someone who is talkative or quarrelsome, they apply the healing remedy of silence, saying what is written in the Old Testament: 'Listen, O Israel, and be silent';[20] and what was prophesied concerning our Lord and Savior: 'Like a sheep before the shearers, he was silent and opened not his mouth';[21] and again: 'Of every idle word men speak, they shall give account on the day of judgment.'[22] With these and similar remedies the vessels of Christ struggle and strive to restore to health whatever the vessels of the devil have endeavored to wound. Let every cleric or monk or religious examine his own conscience. If by speaking well he recognizes that he is Christ's helper and a defender of justice, let him rejoice and give

---
14 James 1.20.
15 Cf. 1 Sam. 15.22.
16 Heb. 13.17.
17 1 Cor. 10.10.
18 James 4.11.
19 Prov. 20.13. This is the Scriptural reference given in the text, but the Latin citation is completely different from the Vulgate version.
20 Cf. Deut. 27.9.
21 Cf. Isa. 53.7; Ps. 37.14.
22 Matt. 12.36.

thanks to God, and with His help let him persevere to the end, for not he who has begun, but he who 'Perseveres shall be saved.'²³ But if anyone feels that he is a helper or agent of the devil because of pride, disobedience, or envy, let him grieve over the past and be careful for the future. Through humility let him rebuild what the tyranny of pride had destroyed; let meekness soothe what anger had aroused; let the sweetness of charity put in order what malice or disobedience had disturbed; and as long as that gloomy soul which was wont to serve the devil remains in this mortal body, let him seek for a remedy against his time of need. Then he will be transferred from the left hand to the right, and together with the sheep of Christ may deserve to hear: 'Come, blessed, receive the kingdom prepared for you from the foundation of the world.'²⁴ Although this is true, brethren, still the good should not rejoice too much in their holy merits, nor should sinners be too much depressed with despair. However, the former should persevere with humility in their good deeds, and the latter should be quickly corrected of their evil. Then, when the day of judgment comes, a good life will be able to crown the just, and a reformed life can excuse the wicked: with the help of our Lord Jesus Christ, who lives and reigns as God with the Father and the Holy Spirit forever and ever. Amen.

Sermon 157

On the Gospel Passage Where It Says: 'Come, Blessed, Receive the Kingdom.'¹ On the Third Rogation Day

(1) When the Gospel text was read just now, dearest brethren, we heard the Lord say: 'Come, blessed, receive the king-

---
23 Matt. 10.22; 24.13.
24 Cf. Matt. 25.34.
---
1 Cf. Matt. 25.34.

dom prepared for you from the foundation of the world.'[2] In order that you may be able to hear this word and to escape from the evil hearing, endeavor with all your strength and by the grace of God to read this divine lesson frequently in your homes and to listen to it in church willingly and obediently. For just as desirable as is that word whereby it is said to the merciful: 'Come, blessed, receive the kingdom,' so dreadful and exceedingly terrible, on the other hand, is the word which the unfruitful and unmerciful are going to hear when it is said to them: 'Depart from me, accursed ones, into the everlasting fire.'[3] May God avert this from us, dearest brethren, and may He deign to free us from the evil hearing, so that what is written may be fulfilled in us: 'The just man shall be in everlasting remembrance. An evil report he shall not fear.'[4] This, indeed, will be the evil hearing which the wicked will endure: 'Depart from me, accursed ones, into the everlasting fire.' Irrevocable will be this sentence, which our most loving God is telling us much earlier for the very purpose of putting us on our guard with all our might. For if our God wanted to punish us, He would not admonish us so many centuries ahead of time. Since He shows us much earlier how we can avoid it, He punishes unwillingly; for if a man shouts to you: Look out! he does not want to strike you.

(2) Consider further what He is going to say to those who are on His right hand: 'Come, blessed, receive the kingdom prepared for you from the foundation of the world.' Notice, brethren, that the kingdom of heaven is predestined for us; hell, however, is not prepared for us but for the devil. Finally, those who are on the left hand are going to hear this: 'Depart from me, accursed ones, into the everlasting fire which was prepared'; He did not say 'for you,' but 'for the devil and his angels.'[5]

(3) I beseech you again, brethren, faithfully and carefully

---
2 *Ibid.*
3 Matt. 25.41.
4 Ps. 111.7.
5 Matt. 25.41.

listen to that sentence which the wicked are going to hear and to the one which the saints are destined to hear. 'Come, blessed,' it says, 'receive the kingdom.' Why? 'For I was hungry and you gave me to eat; I was thirsty and you gave me to drink,'[6] and so forth. But to sinners: 'Depart from me, accursed ones, into the everlasting fire. For I was hungry, and you did not give me to eat.'[7] Therefore, those who will be on the right hand do not receive the kingdom because they never sinned, but because they strove to wash away their sins through almsgiving. Moreover, those who will be on the left will not be cast into eternal fire because they were sinners, but because they refused to redeem their sins by almsgiving. Thus, generosity alone will give glory to the former and fruitlessness alone will condemn the latter. Just as it is impossible for any man to be able to live without sin, so through God's mercy it is possible for each one to ransom himself from sin by good works and especially by almsgiving. Then there will not be fulfilled in him what is written: 'Judgment is without mercy to those who have not shown mercy,'[8] but that other thought will rather refer to him: 'Blessed are the merciful, for they shall obtain mercy';[9] and still another: 'Lavishly, he gives to the poor; his generosity shall endure forever.'[10]

(4) Consider further, brethren, the reason why they will be cast into eternal fire. It is not going to be said: Because you committed murder, because you committed adultery, because you seized the property of another, but only this are they going to hear: 'For I was hungry, and you did not give me to eat.' I beseech you, brethren, do not think of this in a passing way, or believe that this was said only about the Jews or pagans or heretics. Believe most firmly that Christians and Catholics are going to hear it, if they will to persevere in evil deeds. Neither pagans nor heretics nor Jews are coming to judgment,

---

6 Matt. 25.35.
7 Matt. 25.41, 42.
8 James 2.13.
9 Matt. 5.7.
10 Ps. 111.9.

because it is written of them: 'He who does not believe is already judged.'[11] Now among those who will be sent to the left hand will not only be the laity, but also many bishops, and what is worse, wicked clerics, even avaricious or proud monks, as well as angry, haughty, or covetous religious and widows. If fruitful repentance does not come to their assistance, they are going to hear that dreadful, irrevocable sentence: 'Depart from me, accursed ones, into the everlasting fire.' If we are willing to listen to this sentence devoutly and with great trepidation, it will be able to recall us from every evil deed.

(5) Pay careful attention, then, to what truth has said: 'Depart from me, accursed ones, into the everlasting fire. For I was hungry, and you did not give me to eat.' If the man who has not given his own bread to one who is hungry is cast into the fire, where do you think he should be sent if he has taken what belongs to another? If one who has not clothed the naked is thrown into the fire, where should a man be sent if he strips another of his clothing? If the man who has not offered the hospitality of his home to guests is condemned with the devil, where do you suppose a man is to be sent if he takes away the home of another? If the man who has not visited those in prison is destined to perish, what will become of the man who perhaps unjustly threw a man into prison? As a result of this I beseech you, brethren, notice what expectation men who do evil have, when those who do no good are going to perish. Finally, in still another place, the Lord admonishes us in a terrifying manner when He says: 'Every tree that does not bear good fruit is cut down and thrown into the fire.'[12] He did not say every tree that bears evil fruit, but 'that does not bear good fruit.' From this we can clearly recognize what punishments the thorny tree will suffer on judgment day, when the one that does not bear fruit will be cut down and cast into the fire.

(6) Let no one deceive himself, dearest brethren, or sur-

---
11 John 3.18.
12 Matt. 7.19.

round himself with false hope: merely the dignity of the title Christian does not make a Christian. It is not profitable for a man to be called a Christian in name, if he does not show it in his actions, for it is written: 'Faith without works is useless.'[13] If a man believes but does not perform good works, Sacred Scripture exclaims to him: 'Thou believest that there is one God? Thou dost well. The devils also believe, and tremble.'[14] Therefore, those who believe but do not perform good works seem to have the faith of devils. Moreover, what the Lord says should be considered carefully: 'He who hears my commandments and keeps them, he it is who loves me';[15] and again: 'If anyone loves me, he keeps my commandments.'[16] If the one who keeps them loves, doubtless one who does not keep them does not love. Greatly to be feared is what the Lord again says: 'What does it avail you to call me, "Lord, Lord," and not to practice the things that I say?'[17] We ought to know, brethren, that it is useless to express our faith in words and to abandon the truth by our deeds. For just as it does not please us if our servants admit in words that they are our property and still refuse to fulfill their tasks, so it does not please God if a man pronounces himself a Christian in words only but neglects to fulfill the works which Christ commanded to be done. Finally, the blessed Apostle, when he spoke about rendering an account on judgment day, announced it thus: 'All of us must stand before the tribunal of Christ, so that each one may receive what he has won through the body, according to his works, whether good or evil.'[18] And the Lord said further in the Gospel: 'Then he will render to everyone according to his conduct.'[19] He did not say 'according to his faith,' but 'according to his conduct,' since, as I already mentioned above, the Apostle James exclaims: 'Faith without

---

13 James 2.20.
14 James 2.19.
15 Cf. John 14.21.
16 Cf. John 14.23.
17 Luke 6.46.
18 2 Cor. 5.10.
19 Matt. 16.27.

works is useless.' Therefore, if we want to avoid punishment and arrive at eternal bliss, brethren, we should not only believe in God but also love Him with our whole heart and, as far as we can with His help, endeavor to perform good deeds. When we have done what He commanded with the help of His grace, we may deserve to receive as His reward what He promised: through our Lord Jesus Christ, who together with the Father and the Holy Spirit lives and reigns as one God in the Trinity, for all ages and ages. Amen.

Sermon 158

On What is Said in the Gospel:
'Come, Blessed'; Also on Almsgiving

(1) When the Gospel was read, we heard that word which is at the same time both terrible and desirable, the sentence of our Lord which is equally dreadful and desirable. It is terrible because of what He says: 'Depart from me, accursed ones, into the everlasting fire';[1] it is desirable because of the words: 'Come, blessed, receive the kingdom.'[2] Who would not at the same time tremble and rejoice upon hearing these words: rejoice, because Christ deigns to promise a kingdom to Christians who are His servants; tremble, because He threatens sinners with eternal fire? I beseech you, brethren, listen to this lesson with an attentive heart and most alert senses. Since it is not difficult to prepare it, always hold it in your memory, and constantly think about its power. For if a man carefully heeds this lesson, even if he cannot read the rest of the Scriptures, this lesson alone can suffice for him to perform every good act and to avoid all evil.

(2) Therefore, listen, brethren, and see what it is that our

---
1 Matt. 25.41.
2 Cf. Matt. 25.34.

Lord promised that He will say to those who are going to be on His right hand. 'Come, blessed,' He says, 'receive the kingdom; for I was hungry and you gave me to eat; I was thirsty and you gave me to drink,'[3] and the other things which follow. But what is He going to say to those who are at His left? 'Depart from me, accursed ones, into the everlasting fire which was prepared for the devil and his angels. For I was hungry, and you did not give me to eat; I was thirsty and you gave me no drink.'[4] Therefore, pay attention, brethren, and notice that He did not say: 'Depart from me, accursed ones,' because you committed theft, because you bore false testimony, because you committed murder or adultery which is more grievous. This He did not say, but: 'For I was hungry, and you did not give me to eat; I was thirsty and you gave me no drink.' Moreover, He did not say: 'Depart from me' because you took away the property of another which is more unjust, but He says because you did not give of your substance to the poor; not because you did evil deeds, but because you refused to do good ones. Thus, too, mercy alone will free those who are going to be at the right hand, while avarice alone will condemn those on the left. What was said to those who will be on the right hand: 'Come, blessed, receive the kingdom,' they are not going to hear because they have not sinned. So also He is not going to say to those on the left: 'Depart from me, accursed ones,' because you have sinned, but because you were unwilling to redeem your sins by almsgiving. No man can live without sin, and yet with the Lord's help every man can redeem his sins by almsgiving.

(3) In that sentence of the Lord in which He said that He will cast into eternal fire the man who has not fed the hungry and clothed the naked, we can readily see, brethren, to what kind of torment or punishment men are to be condemned if they do evil, since those who do no good are cast into the fire. For if the man who has not given his bread to the poor is

---

3 Cf. Matt. 25.34, 35.
4 Matt. 25.41, 42.

condemned with the devil, where should be condemned the man who has taken what belongs to another? If the man who has not clothed the naked is cast into the fire, where do you think a man is to be thrown if he has stripped his neighbor? If the man who has not received a stranger into his home is condemned to hell, where do you think a man should be condemned if he takes away the home of another?

(4) For this reason, beloved brethren, let us devoutly meditate on these truths, and let us strive as much as we can to perform good works. According to our means let us give of our poverty to pilgrims and the poor, in order that we may redeem the sins which we have committed and prepare for ourselves eternal rewards as a result of these good works. Let us listen to the Lord when He says: 'Blessed are the merciful, for they shall obtain mercy.'[5] You have now heard the true sentence of our Lord, in which He promises us the kingdom of heaven if we practice almsgiving, feed the hungry, give drink to the thirsty, clothe the naked according to our means, and receive strangers. If we piously do all these things, we will come with assurance before the tribunal of the eternal judge, for then the just will be in eternal remembrance and will not fear the evil hearing. What is the evil hearing? That (may the Lord deign to avert it from us!) which those on the left are going to hear: 'Depart from me, accursed ones, into the everlasting fire.'[6]

(5) Therefore, hold fast to almsgiving or works of mercy, for: 'Alms deliver from death, and do not suffer their giver to go into darkness.'[7] Let each one stretch out his hand to the poor as much as he can in accord with his strength. If a man has gold, let him give gold; if he has silver, he should bestow silver; and if a man has no money, let him with a good intention extend a morsel to a stranger; if he does not have a whole loaf, he should break a piece off of what he has and

---
5 Matt. 5.7.
6 Matt. 25.41.
7 Cf. Tob. 4.11.

offer it. Such comfort and security the Lord through the prophet deigned to give to the poor that He did not say: 'Give all of your bread to the hungry,' but: 'share your bread with the hungry.'[8] Even if you do not have a whole loaf, share a little morsel.

(6) Now in order that you may know how acceptable to God is anything you give with a good intention, listen to the Lord in the Gospel speaking about that widow who offered two mites: 'This widow, who gave two mites, has put in more than all. For the rest were rich, and out of their abundance have given something; but she has put in all that she had,'[9] and for this reason she deserved to have the Lord praise her with His own lips. Therefore, let each one do what he can. Except for moderate food and simple clothing, whatever exceeds this should be given to the poor in a happy and cheerful spirit. Why happy and cheerful? Because he gives little and receives much; he extends a mite and prepares a kingdom; he has given a little money and receives eternal life; he gives temporal goods in exchange for eternal ones; he has stretched out fleeting possessions and receives those which will endure without end. Behold why we ought to give cheerfully and with a good intention. If a trustworthy man said to you: Give me one gold coin, and I will repay you one hundred solid gold coins, would you not gladly give him the one in order that you might receive the hundred? Now the God of heaven and earth says to you: 'He who has compassion on the poor lends to God';[10] moreover: 'As long as you did it for one of the least of these, you did it for me';[11] and in the Psalms: 'Well for the man who is gracious and lends.'[12] How much more, then, should you lend to God on earth, in order that you may receive a manifold return in eternal life? Then you will deserve to come before the tribunal of the eternal judge in the

---

8 Isa. 58.7.
9 Cf. Luke 21.3, 4.
10 Cf. Prov. 19.17.
11 Matt. 25.40.
12 Ps. 111.5.

sight of the angels, and can say with assurance and a clear conscience: Give, Lord, because I have given; have mercy because I have shown mercy. I did what you commanded; you pay what you promised. Again and again I admonish you, brethren, always keep in your memory this Gospel lesson, and labor with God's help and all your strength, so that you may be able to avoid the eternal fire and may happily arrive at the kingdom of heaven: with His assistance, to whom is honor and glory forever and ever. Amen.

* *Sermon 158A*

A Sermon of Admonition on the Last Judgment

(1) When the Gospel was read we heard that word which is at the same time both terrible and desirable, the sentence of our Lord which is equally dreadful and desirable. It is terrible because of what He says: 'Depart from me, accursed ones, into the everlasting fire';[1] . . .

Now as the holy prophet Daniel says: 'O king, take my advice; atone for your sins by good deeds,'[8] you will knock at the door of heaven in vain if you neglect it. Oh soul, which dwells within the frail walls of the flesh, watch, pray, knock, and seek: watch by begging, pray by seeking, knock by spending on the poor. If you watch and seek, the Lord says: 'Here I am,'[9] and 'If you pass through fire,' I am with you 'and the flames shall not consume you.'[10] If you ask through prayer,

---
1 Matt. 25.41. This sermon is a second version of the preceding one. According to Dom Morin, Sermon 158 is entirely the work of St. Caesarius, while Sermon 158A is partially abridged and in part interpolated from other sources. The latter begins the same as the preceding one as far as #5 . . . 'do not suffer their giver to go into darkness.'7 Footnotes 2-7, therefore, are those of Sermon 158.
8 Cf. Dan. 4.24.
9 Isa. 58.9.
10 Cf. Isa. 43.2.

you will find, and if you knock through giving to the poor, Christ opens the doors to you in order that you may enter and possess paradise. Now if you still think that anything will remain at the end of the world, consider your own end. Gradually all the existing good things are taken away, and the evils which were not present approach, for it is written: 'Naked I came forth from my mother's womb, and naked shall I go beneath the earth.'[11] Therefore, give alms. While you have the price in your hands give to yourself out of your possessions, because what you are holding easily slips away and is always strange to you. Pay attention to your price, look at your Lord, and consider what price He paid for you. He shed His blood for you; He loved you so tenderly that He redeemed you so dearly. Avoid the example of the rich man whose dogs fed on the wounds of Lazarus while the rich man did not even see him. Although they were alike in the flesh when they were born, riches made them different; and still they are the same in death. They exchanged places in the Lower World, for then the rich man said: 'Father Abraham, have pity on me.'[12] And Abraham said to him: 'Son, remember that thou in thy lifetime hast received good things, and Lazarus in like manner evil things; but here he is comforted whereas thou art tormented.'[13] Oh man, you hear the just provision of the sentence: the man who has not given to the poor has no refuge. You who became my brethren under the hand of God, listen to the word of the Lord: fulfill His desire, in order that you may receive the inheritance in the kingdom of your Father. Out of a slave you were made a friend, so reject what you were born, and pay attention to what you have been reborn. Cleverly make the exchange for yourself: in return for earthly possessions God offers you heaven. Then your Father and Lord and friend, with whom you have made a heavenly transaction, will say: 'Amen I say

---

11 Cf. Job 1.21.
12 Luke 16.24.
13 Luke 16.25.

to you, what you did for one of the least of these, you did for me.'¹⁴ What I have received I do not repay only a hundred times, but a thousand times a hundredfold. Moreover, as I promised through John, I will give eternal life to come, companionship for a thousand years, and a kingdom at the right hand of the Father. Therefore, I beseech you, brethren, let each one with a good intention extend as much as he can to the stranger. Listen to the Lord say concerning the widow in the Gospel . . . (as in the preceding Sermon 158, #6: 'This widow, who gave two mites' . . . do you pay what you promised.) Then you may deserve to hear: 'Come, blessed of my Father, take possession of the kingdom which was prepared for you from the foundation of the world':¹⁹ with the help of our Lord Jesus Christ, who lives and reigns forever and ever. Amen.

* *Sermon 159*

On What Is Written: 'If Anyone Wishes to Come After Me, Let Him Take Up His Cross.'¹

(1) It seems difficult, dearest brethren, and it is considered as harsh that the Lord commanded in the Gospel: 'If anyone wishes to come after me, let him deny himself.'² However, what He commands is not difficult, since He helps to effect what He commands. True, indeed, is what is said in the psalm: 'According to the words of your lips I have kept the ways of the law,'³ and also true is what He Himself said: 'For my yoke is easy, and my burden light.'⁴ Charity makes whatever

---
14 Cf. Matt. 25.40. Footnotes 15-18 correspond to 9-12 of the preceding sermon.
19 Matt. 25.34.

---
1 Cf. Mark 8.34.
2 *Ibid.*
3 Ps. 16.4.
4 Matt. 11.30.

is difficult in the precepts light. We know that this is true, for very often even earthly love, or wicked and wanton love, endures with patience things that are exceedingly difficult and burdensome in order to reach what it madly desires. If a man loves money he is called avaricious, if he loves honor he is called ambitious, and if he loves beautiful bodies he is called lustful. Consider how much those men who love perishable goods labor in sailing the sea, in accomplishing an earthly journey, or in enduring heat and cold. They do not even feel what they are suffering, and they strive all the more when they are kept from the effort. For if a man has taken a position in military service, when he has begun to acquire temporal gains through the intolerable sufferings of warfare and countless deaths, if the military service is taken away he is afflicted and becomes exceedingly sad, because the labor itself is withdrawn.

(2) I beseech you, brethren, if transitory possessions are sought in this fashion, how should eternal goods be sought? Therefore, dearly beloved, our whole attention should be directed to this, the choice of what we should love. There are, indeed, many lovers of the world, but through the goodness of God there do not also cease to be lovers of eternal life. For if there were only lovers of the world in this life, it would make us despair of eternal life. But wheat is also found among the chaff, and sometimes a rose is gathered among the thorns. Truly, there are many souls who not only patiently, but even willingly, accept many labors because of love for Christ. Why, then, do you wonder if a man who loves Christ and wishes to follow Him in loving Him denies himself for his own benefit? Just as a man is lost through loving himself, so he is found by denying himself. Love of self was the ruin of the first man, for if he had not loved himself in the wrong order and had preferred God to himself, he would have been willing to be subject to God. However, he was not, but turned aside to neglect God's will and to do his own. Truly, this is not to love; it is not to do one's own will, but to prefer the will of

God to perishable loves. Learn, then, to love yourself by not loving yourself.

(3) In order that you may know that it is a vice to love oneself carnally, the Apostle speaks thus: 'For men will be lovers of self.'[5] Does not one who loves himself stand in himself? When he has deserted God, he begins to love himself and he is driven away from himself to love things which are outside of him. This is so true that, when the Apostle said: 'For men will be lovers of self,' he immediately added: 'lovers of money.'[6] Now you see that he is outside of himself. You have begun to love something outside of yourself: stay within yourself, if you can. Why do you go outside? Did you not hear the thought of the wise man? 'The prudent man does not meet with evil.'[7] Behold, through money the rich man has become a lover of money. You have begun to love what is outside of yourself: you have gone outside of yourself. When a man's love goes away from him toward things that are outside of him, he begins to become vain along with the useless goods, and somehow to spend his substance like the prodigal son. He is emptied, he is poured forth, he becomes a beggar. However, we must not despair even of such men when they begin to repent. May God grant this to them: 'He came to himself.'[8] Now if he came to himself, he had gone outside of himself. Just as he remained in himself when he fell away, so he should not remain in himself when he returns; therefore, let him keep himself close to God. Let him deny himself so he will not fall again. What does to deny oneself mean? Let him not presume upon his own strength, let him realize that he is a man, and let him look to the prophetic word: 'Cursed is the man who trusts in human beings.'[9] Let him withdraw from himself in order that he may cling to God. If a man possesses any good, let him attribute it to the One from whom it came;

---
5 2 Tim. 3.2.
6 Cf. 2 Tim. 3.2.
7 Cf. Ecclus. 19.7.
8 Luke 15.17.
9 Cf. Jer. 17.5.

if he possesses any evil, let him blame himself, because he did it to himself. Let him deny himself, take up his cross, and follow Christ.

(4) Now where should Christ be followed, except whither He has gone? We know that He arose and ascended into heaven; that is where He must be followed. Evidently, we are not to despair because He Himself promised it, not because a man promised it. Heaven was far from us before our Head went to heaven. But why do we now despair of being there, if we are members of that Head? Then what? Since there is labor on earth along with many fears and pains, let us follow Christ where there is the highest happiness, the greatest peace, perpetual security. If a man desires to follow Christ, let him listen to the Apostle when he says: 'If anyone says that he abides in Christ, he ought himself to walk just as he walked.'[10] Do you wish to follow Christ? Be humble where He was humble; do not despise His humility if you wish to reach His height. Truly, the path became rough when man sinned, but it is smooth since Christ through His Resurrection trod upon it and made a royal road out of the exceedingly narrow path. Men run upon this way with two feet, that is, through humility and charity. Loftiness delights all men on it, but humility is the first step. Why do you stretch your foot beyond you? You want to fall, not to rise. Begin with the first step, that is, with humility, and you have risen.

(5) For this reason our Lord and Savior not only said: 'Let him deny himself,' but He added: 'take up his cross, and follow me.'[11] What does this mean, 'take up his cross'? Let him bear whatever is troublesome: thus let him follow Me. When he has begun to follow Me according to My morals and precepts, he will have many people who contradict him and stand in his way, many who not only deride but even persecute him. Moreover, this is true, not only of pagans who are outside of the Church, but also of those who seem to be in it

---

10 Cf. 1 John 2.6.
11 Mark 8.34.

corporally but are outside of it because of the perversity of their deeds. Although these men glory in merely the title of Christian, they continually persecute good Christians. Such men belong to the members of the Church in the same way that bad blood is in the body. Therefore, if you wish to follow Christ, do not delay in carrying His cross; tolerate sinners, but do not yield to them. Do not let the false happiness of the wicked corrupt you. You ought to despise all things for the sake of Christ, in order that you may deserve to arrive at His companionship. The world is loved, but let the One who made the world be preferred to it. The world is beautiful, but much fairer is the One by whom the world was made. The world is flattering, but more delightful is He by whom the world was created.

(6) Therefore, let us labor as much as we can, dearest brethren, so that love of the world may not steal over us, and so that we may not want to love a creature more than the Creator. God has given us earthly possessions in order that we may love Him with our whole heart and soul. But sometimes we provoke God's wrath against us when we love His gifts more than God Himself. You know very well that this same practice is observed among men, so that if someone gives a gift to his protege, if the latter begins to despise the man but to love the gift which he gave, not only does he no longer consider him as a friend, but he even despises and condemns him as an enemy. Now just as we love more those who seem to love us for ourselves rather than our gifts, so God is known to love those who prefer eternal life to earthly substance. Therefore, if we want to fulfill what our Lord said: 'If anyone wishes to come after me, let him take up his cross, and follow me,'[12] let us, with God's help, endeavor to fulfill what the Apostle says: 'Having food and clothing, with these let us be content.'[13] Otherwise, if we seek more earthly wealth than we should and want: 'To become rich,' we may fall

---
12 Cf. Mark 8.34.
13 Cf. 1 Tim. 6.8.

'into temptation and a snare and into many useless and harmful desires, which plunge men into destruction and damnation.'[14] From this temptation may the Lord deign to free us under His protection: who lives and reigns together with the Father and the Holy Spirit forever and ever. Amen.

Sermon 160

On What Is Written in the Gospel:
'The Good Man from the Good Treasure of
His Heart Brings Forth That Which Is Good.'[1]

(1) When the Gospel was read, dearest brethren, we heard that our Lord said to His disciples and to the multitudes: 'The good man from the good treasure of his heart brings forth that which is good; and the evil man from the evil treasure of his heart brings forth that which is evil. For out of the abundance of the heart the mouth speaks.'[2] If we notice carefully, brethren, Christ our Lord indicated two kinds or two locations of treasures: good treasure in the good heart, and evil treasure in an evil heart. For this reason, brethren, let us examine our own consciences. Let us consider the inner compartments of our soul and see whose treasure we have hidden there. Then, we will truly be able to know to whose domain both we and our treasure belong. If, with God's help, we always have good thoughts and perform honorable deeds, we not only keep Christ's treasure in our hearts, but we ourselves are the treasure of Christ. But if our soul is often occupied with unclean or wicked thoughts, there is no need to say to whom the treasure of our heart belongs. Each one will have the same kind of a master as the treasure he possesses. That Christ dwells in good

---
14 1 Tim. 6.9.
---
1 Luke 6.45.
2 *Ibid.*

men even the Apostle testifies: 'To have Christ dwelling through faith in the inner man';³ while we read in the Gospel concerning Judas that the devil inhabits the wicked: 'The devil having already put it into the heart of Judas to betray the Lord.'⁴

(2) Therefore, know well, brethren, that each man will be the possession of Christ or of the adversary, according to the way he wants to prepare himself with the help of God. Now since, as we already said: 'Out of the abundance of the heart the mouth speaks,'⁵ if you want to know what is kept in the heart of a man, notice what comes out of his mouth. If he speaks words that are holy, just, and pious, Christ who dwells in his heart Himself speaks in his mouth; but if you see obscene language, insults, curses, abuse, slander, or murmuring coming out of a man's mouth, you can clearly recognize who dwells within him. These two like guests instill themselves and somehow offer themselves at the door of your heart, your Lord and your adversary. The one shows you life, the other, death; one inspires light, the other, darkness; the one brings you hell, the other, heaven. Therefore, O man, with God's help you have it in your power to choose what you want. However, notice whom you are receiving and whom you reject; know for certain that whichever of the two you take in this world will inevitably receive you in the life to come. If you accept Christ, you are destined to reign with Him in heaven, but if (may God forbid it!) you choose the devil, you will be plunged with him into hell.

(3) For this reason guard both your hearts and your bodies with all watchfulness, brethren. It can happen that a devout soul repels the Holy Spirit from her if she is careless, while a sinful soul can drive away the devil if she loves God. Therefore, let not the soul which is holy be puffed up with pride or relax in any kind of assurance; neither let the sinner be over-

---

3 Eph. 3.16, 17.
4 Cf. John 13.2.
5 Luke 6.45.

whelmed with excessive despair. One who possesses God should courageously keep Him, and one who has lost Him should strive with all his might to recover Him. For Christ, dearest brethren, is invited to come down and dwell within us by our good works; the devil, on the contrary, is delighted with evil deeds, so that he may dominate the sinful soul. Now just as Christ quickly deserts us if He does not find good works in us, so the devil is speedily put to flight if he is not fed with evil deeds. Know for a fact, brethren, that no man can be empty: in each one of us either the king or a tyrant dwells. If Christ is driven from our heart by negligence, at once a place is provided for the adversary, but if the devil is driven out of our soul, Christ immediately enters. We ought to prepare a banquet in our heart of the same kind as the guest we wish to entertain.

(4) Under the inspiration of Christ, beloved brethren, let us hasten to store up in the cellar of our heart the wine of justice, the oil of mercy, the sweetness of charity, the lard of devotion, the spices of chastity, the burnt-offering of patience. With these and similar food Christ our Lord is delighted, and if He recognizes that they are in our hearts He doubtless will fulfill what He promised: 'Behold, I stand before the door and knock. If any man opens the door to me, I will come in to him and will sup with him, and he with me.'[6] Blessed is the soul, brethren, which strives to adorn and arrange his heart with good works in such a way that he deserves to receive God there as his guest. On the contrary, how unhappy is that soul, and even to be mourned with a whole fountain of tears, who is continually overwhelmed with evil deeds, is wounded with evil thoughts, and stained with foul or wanton spots, so that he merits to receive the devil at the banquet of his heart rather than Christ. Therefore, dearest brethren, if you wish to possess true joys, you ought to store up in your heart what you would like to find there continually. If you conceal bitterness in your heart, you long in vain to find

---
6 Apoc. 3.20.

sweetness there; if you hide darkness, you cannot possess the light. Finally, wicked men are wont to promise good things, but because they refuse to store them up first in the cellar of their heart, they cannot give what they promise. No one is able to give what he was unwilling to gather in the first place.

(5) Therefore, brethren, like good sons of the Church, strive to store up continually in your hearts the good works, which can please God, in order that what was promised by you with your lips may be fulfilled in deed. Then may happen in you what the Lord said before: 'The good man from the good treasure of his heart brings forth that which is good; for out of the abundance of the heart the mouth speaks.'[7] Refresh Christ in this world by your good deeds in order that He may refresh you in the world to come with His gifts. Reject the devil and receive Christ; despise death and choose life; cast forth darkness and accept the light. Receive Christ in this life which is full of labors in order that He may receive you into everlasting bliss. Give up transitory things, since you are destined to receive eternal goods. Then, when judgment day and the time for rendering an account comes, you may be able to hear with assurance that happy and desirable word: 'Come, blessed, receive the kingdom which was prepared for you from the foundation of the world; for I was hungry and you gave me to eat, naked and you covered me.'[8] Then, if repentance and abundant almsgiving do not come to their aid, the avaricious, dissolute, envious, and proud are going to hear: 'Depart from me, accursed ones, into the everlasting fire,'[9] while you will happily hear this if you are adorned with a holy life and good deeds: 'Come, blessed, receive the kingdom.' May the Lord bring us to this under His protection, who lives and reigns forever and ever. Amen.

---

7 Luke 6.45.
8 Cf. Matt. 25.34-36.
9 Matt. 25.41.

Sermon 160B

On What Is Written: 'The Good Man From the Good Treasure of His Heart Brings Forth That Which Is Good.'[1]

(1) When the Gospel was read, dearest brethren, we heard that our Lord said to the multitudes ... (this sermon continues like the preceding one as far as the end of #3).

(4) Therefore, beloved brethren, if a man under Christ's inspiration does not possess the wine of justice, the oil of mercy, the sweetness of charity, the lard of devotion, the spices of chastity, and the burnt-offering of patience, by the testimony of Christ he is found to be naked and an exile, a stranger to His domain. If a man first despises the gift of grace, he rejects the greater offering; he cannot reach the inheritance if he has been unwilling to conform to the covenant. Embrace the peace which Christ has sent, O Christian. Show that the will of the Lord is translated in you, and by worshiping God cling to your good inheritance. 'Blessed,' He says, 'are the peacemakers, for they shall be called children of God,'[6] and if you are not a peacemaker you cannot be a child of God. You will not be able to receive the promises if you are unwilling to be reconciled with your brother. It is not possible to have peace with Christ if a man wills to be in disagreement with a Christian. For how can you lay down your life for Christ if you refuse to preserve the peace which was assigned by Him? It is truly a sin of stubbornness to despise what is commanded, to refuse what is ordered, to turn away from what is a matter

---

1 Luke 6.45. Sermon 160A and 160B are additional versions of the preceding sermon. Sermon 160A is identical with 160 as far as #5; then, after a short paragraph on good works, there is a repetition of several paragraphs from Sermon 26, followed by a lengthy closing sentence. Since Dom Morin considers Sermon 160A of the non-Caesarian type and because of the brevity of its independent thought and expression, it has been omitted in the translation. Footnotes 2-5 correspond to those in Sermon 160.
6 Matt. 5.9.

of precept. Wars are never devised by peacemakers, nor peace treaties by the discordant. The Lord says: 'Love your enemies.'[7] If a man loves his enemy, he will be able to hate no one; if he prays to the Lord for his enemies, he envies no one; if he shows himself kind to the enemy, he will not be able to envy his brother. If we are commanded to love our enemies, whom of our brothers will we be able to hate? If we do not exchange insults, how do we presume to injure a brother? Kindness toward an enemy is the perfection of charity. It cannot be right to hate a brother if we are compelled to love a stranger. An enemy cannot exist for a brother, since we are commanded to honor an enemy. Does a man receive the peace of Christ if he burns with enraged lips and unbridled heart in perversity against a brother? Such a person contrives insults, plans deceit, seeks perversion; he attempts plots and pretends peace with his lips while he contrives wars in his heart. He envies the happiness of others, and with look askance follows a passing brother whose ears are open to slander; he willingly commits sin and rejects the good. He believes falsehood and refuses to accept the truth; the good fortune of another is punishment for him, the progress of his neighbors a torment, and the glory of a brother torture. He feeds upon envy and is nourished by slander; he rejoices in the misfortune of another, grieves over his success, and weeps at his advantages. If only the Lord would strike such a despiser of the law here with the scourge of His kindness and bestow upon him the discipline of reproof. Then, if he were corrected, he might learn the precepts of peace and, after his conversion from vice, give a good example to all the Christians who see him. Whoever is a solicitous and careful brother and is admonished by Christ, fulfills His peace in love for his brother. Keep the advice and fulfill the commands in order that when Christ is the judge you may hear: Receive what I promised, because you did what I commanded. With the help of Him who reigns forever and ever. Amen.

---
7 Matt. 5.44.

* Sermon 161

On What Is Written: 'A Certain Man Was Going Down from Jerusalem to Jericho.'[1]

(1) When the Gospel lesson was read, dearest brethren, we heard our Lord and Savior expound a parable concerning the sin of the first man. 'A certain man,' He said, 'was going down from Jerusalem to Jericho, and he fell in with robbers, who stripped him.'[2] That man who was going down from Jerusalem to Jericho was Adam. He went down from Jerusalem to Jericho: that is, he came from paradise into the world. Jerusalem is interpreted as a vision of peace, but Jericho typified this world. Now Jericho presents a figure of the world because it is interpreted as the moon. For just as the moon begins, increases, and wanes, so the human race is born, grows, becomes old, and dies. Therefore, Adam 'was going down from Jerusalem to Jericho, and he fell in with robbers.' If he did not come down he would not fall among robbers, for when he fell into sin from the height of virtue, then he came into the world from paradise. 'He fell in with robbers,' it says: that is, among the devil and his angels. 'Who stripped him,' that is, took away from him the glory of immortality. 'After beating him they went their way, leaving him half dead.'[3] The blows which were inflicted are understood as evil wishes, and according to the Apostle: 'Many useless and harmful desires.'[4] The fact that he said they left him half dead signifies this, that although he lived in the flesh he nevertheless was dead in soul, as the Apostle says: 'In Adam all die';[5] and elsewhere: 'Only the one who sins shall die.'[6] In those two men

---
1 Luke 10.30.
2 Ibid.
3 Ibid.
4 1 Tim. 6.9.
5 1 Cor. 15.22.
6 Ezech. 18.4, 20.

who passed by, that is, the priest and the Levite, we understand the Law and the Prophets. For the human race lay wounded by the devil, and neither the Law nor the prophets could free him; it was necessary for a Samaritan to come. Now a Samaritan is interpreted as a protector. Who, then, was that Samaritan, that is, the protector, except our Lord, of whom it is written: 'Indeed he neither slumbers nor sleeps, the guardian of Israel'?[7] Therefore, that Samaritan, 'as he journeyed,' that is, as He arranged the dispensation of the Incarnation, 'came upon him.'[8] What does it mean that He came upon him, except that He assumed human flesh? 'And he went up to him and bound up his wounds.'[9] What does it mean to bind up his wounds, except to give the grace which can resist sins? Moreover, by the fact that 'He poured on oil and wine,'[10] we understand mercy in the oil and justice in the wine; the anointing with chrism is surely in the oil, the consecration of the Eucharist in the wine. When he further said: 'He set him on his own beast,'[11] the Incarnation is understood as the beast. He put us on this beast when, as it is written: 'It was our guilt that he bore.'[12] Or the beast is certainly understood as the assistance of grace; for just as He carried back to His sheepfold on His own shoulders that lamb which had strayed, so He brought back this weak man to the inn. The inn to which he was carried is considered as the Church, and the innkeeper to whom he was entrusted is known to be the Apostle Paul. Because there are many changes in the Church of our day, like spiritual inns, through which men run to eternal bliss, for this reason the Apostle Paul like a steward of Christ encourages and admonishes us saying: 'So run as to obtain it [the prize].'[13] Now the fact that the Apostle Paul can be understood as the steward and glorious innkeeper

---

7 Ps. 120.4.
8 Luke 10.33.
9 Luke 10.34.
10 *Ibid.*
11 *Ibid.*
12 Cf. Isa. 53.4, 11.
13 1 Cor. 9.24.

of Christ, he himself indicates: 'There is my daily pressing anxiety,' he says, 'the care of all the churches.'[14] And because he was solicitous about the changes of Christ, he justly received the name of innkeeper. When it is said further: 'The next day he took out two denarii,'[15] the next day is understood as after the Resurrection; the first day is the Passion, the second the Resurrection. We can understand the two denarii as the Old and New Testament, or surely as the two precepts of love upon which 'Depend the whole Law and the Prophets,'[16] that is, 'Thou shalt love the Lord,'[17] and 'Thou shalt love thy neighbor.'[18]

(2) Now, in order that you may more easily know what is signified in this lesson as often as it is read to you, let us briefly repeat what we said. In the man who fell among the robbers, Adam is understood; in the robbers, the devil and his angels. When he was stripped, immortality was taken away from him. The blows which were inflicted upon him are known as evil desires, and he was left half dead because he was alive in body but dead in soul. The Law and the Prophets are seen in the priest and the Levite who passed by, while Christ is signified in the Samaritan, who is interpreted as a protector. The fact that mercy was moved at the sight of him when he was wounded, even though he neither asked nor cried out, shows that grace is bestowed without any preceding merits. In the oil and wine, we see mercy and justice. The beast upon which the man was placed is recognized as the Incarnation of our Lord and Savior; the inn to which he was brought is the Church, and the Apostle Paul is the innkeeper. The next day signifies after the Resurrection, and the two denarii are understood as the two testaments or the two precepts. As you spiritually eschew these facts like clean animals, brethren, provide for your holy souls food that is useful for eternal life.

---
14 2 Cor. 11.28.
15 Luke 10.35.
16 Matt. 22.40.
17 Matt. 22.37.
18 Matt. 22.39.

May He deign to grant this, to whom is honor and might forever and ever. Amen.

* *Sermon 162*

A Beautiful Homily of St. Augustine on the Fig Tree Which Did Not Bear Fruit for Three Years; Also That the Tears of a Penitent Are Like a Field in Which Dung Is Spread; and Still Further That If Dung Is Not Put in Its Proper Place It Does Not Make a House Clean, But When It Is Put in Its Right Place It Is Proven to Produce Much Fruit

(1) The condition of our misery and the mercy of God, brethren, are so arranged that the time for joy is preceded by a time of sadness. In other words, the time of sadness comes first, and the time for joy later; first, there is the time for labor, and then the time of rest; first is the time of calamity, and later the time of good fortune. If we first labor in the world by performing good deeds, then afterwards when the Lord repays, we may reach the kingdom, according to what the Apostle says: 'Through many tribulations we must enter the kingdom of God.'[1] This is the fact of our condition and the mercy of God. Our sins have produced for us the time of labor and calamity, but the time of joy, rest, and happiness does not come to us as a result of our own merits, but through the grace of the Savior. Although we deserved one thing, we hope for another; we merited evil, but we expect good things. This is effected through the mercy of Him who both created and recreated us, who made us and remade us.

(2) Now in the time of our misery, dearly beloved, and, as Scripture says: 'In my vain days,'[2] we ought to know where the source and place of our sadness should be. In the region of this world, no one will ever be able to find real rest and true

---
1 Acts 14.21.
2 Eccles. 7.16.

joy. In this land is fulfilled what the Lord said: 'Blessed are they who mourn,' but only in eternal life is to be fulfilled what He added: 'for they shall be comforted.'³ Since our life is known as a journey to eternal life, out of longing for eternal life, we must grieve on the way, in order that we may reach true joy in our heavenly country. Let each one of us be solicitous on the road, in order that we may be able to be secure in our true land. Then, there may be fulfilled in us what is written: 'Those that sow in tears shall reap rejoicing.'⁴ Perhaps someone may say: It is disgraceful to weep, it is hard to endure sadness. If whoever among you says this had eyes of the heart, you would know what great beauty arises from that ugliness. For sadness and tears for sins are just like dung in the fields. Now if you carefully pay attention to this, they seem to produce ugliness, but are shown to bring forth much fruit. Therefore, we ought to notice diligently that our tears are not shed over an earthly loss, but in longing for eternal life. Dung that is not put in its proper place makes a house unclean, but when it is spread in its right place it makes a field fertile. Look at the place of dung which was foreseen by the farmer. The Apostle Paul says: 'Who can gladden me, save the very one that is grieved by me?'⁵ And in another place: 'The sorrow and repentance that are according to God produce salvation that is never regretted.'⁶ If a man is sad according to God he is repentant, for he is sad because of his sins. A sorrow which arises from one's iniquity effects justice. For this reason, let what you are first displease you, in order that you may be able to be what you are not. 'The sorrow and repentance that are according to God produce salvation that is never regretted.' 'Repentance tends to salvation,' it says. What kind of salvation? 'That is never regretted.' What does it mean, that is never regretted? That which you can never regret. For this reason, I have said that there is good repentance and bad. It

---

3 Matt. 5.5.
4 Ps. 125.5.
5 2 Cor. 2.2.
6 Cf. 2 Cor. 7.10.

is good repentance when a man regrets having done evil; it is bad repentance when he regrets having done well. Behold, a man has done a good deed for his neighbor, he has freed him from a grave danger. After a while perhaps he suffers an injury from that man and says: I repent of having done the good deed. See there bad repentance. By doing well he had acquired eternal life, but by his bad repentance he not only lost what he had gained, but even offended God by his evil repentance. For this reason, the Apostle said: 'It produces salvation that is not regretted.' If a man repents of his sins, then he will always rejoice and will never be able to regret it. When we were first overwhelmed with many sins, we had a life of which we should have repented. Let us also have a repentance that cannot be regretted, since we cannot arrive at a life without regrets except through repentance for an evil life. Therefore, as we began to say above, dearest brethren, do you find dung in the substance of wheat that has been purified? Nevertheless, through dung we arrive at brightness, fruitfulness, fertility, splendor, and beauty. Ugliness was the path to beauty. Now just as grain is produced from the ugliness of dung, so the adornments of good works are generated by the tears of a penitent.

(3) In the Gospel our Lord said concerning a certain barren tree: 'Behold, for three years now I have come to this fig tree, and I find no fruit on it. I will cut it down, lest it still encumber my ground.'[7] Then the farmer pleaded with the man who was already threatening an axe and was almost striking it because of its barren roots, just as Moses interceded with God. Therefore, the farmer pleaded and said: 'Sir, let it alone this year too; I will dig around it and manure it. If it bears fruit, very well, but if not, then thou shalt come and cut it down.'[8] That tree is the human race. The Lord visited it at the time of the patriarchs, as if in the first year. He visited it at the time of the Law and the Prophets as though in the second

---
[7] Cf. Luke 13.7.
[8] Cf. Luke 13.8, 9.

year, and behold the third year shone in the Gospel. Because it was found without fruit both then and now, it should, as it were, have been cut down. But let the merciful intercede with mercy: since He wanted to show Himself merciful He supplied an intercessor with Himself. Sir, let it alone this year, too, He says, and dig around it. The ditch is a sign of humility. Let a basket of dung be applied, that is, the sorrow of a penitent. Lest perchance it bring forth fruit, it says, or rather because it does so. It will produce fruit in part, but in part it will not. What does this mean, it will produce fruit in part, but in part it will not? If there were all good men in the Catholic Church, it would bring forth good fruit entirely; and if there were all wicked men, it would bring forth all evil. But since both good and bad are found at the same time, for this reason, it will produce good fruit in part, but in part it will not. This is that one servant, that is, the one people, of whom the Lord says in the Gospel: 'His master will come, and will cut him asunder and make him share the lot of the unfaithful.'[9] Can one servant be cut asunder? This is not written about one servant but, as we said, concerning the one Christian people, one part of which is going to receive the kingdom, while the other is destined to suffer punishment. For there are good and bad established in the one unit and body of the Church, just as in the womb of Rebecca two children were joined together as a type of the Church.

(4) So in order that we may deserve to be found, not in the bad part, but in the good part, dearest brethren, just as we do not lack daily sins, so the daily remedies should never be lacking through repentance. For this reason, let us endeavor with all our strength to fulfill what the prophet advises us when he says: 'Come, let us bow down in worship before the Lord; let us kneel before the Lord who made us.'[10] Because there are many who weep but do not gather fruit, let us weep in such a way that we may deserve to gather the fruit of eternal life.

---

9 Luke 12.46.
10 Ps. 94.6.

Those who bewail the loss of temporal possessions derive no fruit for their souls, because, as I said above, the proper place for dung produces fruit, but the wrong area makes it unclean. I find someone sad in church: I see the dung and I look for the area. Tell me, my friend, why are you sad? I lost some money, he says. It is an unclean place and there is no fruit. Let him listen to the Apostle say: 'The sorrow that is according to the world produces death.'[11] Not only is there no fruit, but there is even great destruction. This is also true concerning other things which pertain to joys of the world, and they are not easily counted. I see another man sad, weeping, and groaning: I see much dung and again I look for the area. And when I saw him sad, weeping, and groaning, as I beheld him praying, a correct meaning occurred to me. And yet here, too, I look for the area. What if that man who is praying and groaning with much weeping entreats the death of his enemy? Even if he now weeps, begs, and prays, the place is unclean and there is no fruit. What we find in Sacred Scripture, dearest brethren, is even more: if he wills that his enemy should die, he falls upon the curse of Judas: 'May his plea be in vain.'[12] Again I looked back upon another soul groaning, weeping, and praying: I recognize the dung and ask the area. I turn my ears to the prayer and I hear him say: 'Once I said, O Lord, have pity on me; heal me, though I have sinned against you.'[13] He is groaning over his sin: I recognize the field and I expect fruit. Thanks be to God that the dung was put in a good place and produces grain.

(5) This is the time for fruitful sadness, dearest brethren. As we consider the condition of our frailty, the abundance of temptations, the creeping in of sins, the opposition of passions, the destructive force of unlawful desires which are always raging against good thoughts, let us ever grieve and groan. Then we may merit to rejoice without end at the

---
11 2 Cor. 7.10.
12 Ps. 108.7.
13 Ps. 40.5.

time of joy, repose, happiness, and eternal life which will come later. Then, too, will happily be fulfilled in us what we said above: 'Those that sow in tears shall reap rejoicing';[14] and also that other word: 'Although they go forth weeping, carrying the seed to be sown, they shall come back rejoicing, carrying their sheaves.'[15] To this joy may the Lord lead us under His protection: who lives and reigns forever and ever. Amen.

* Sermon 163

On the Prodigal Son and the One Who Always Remained with His Father

(1) In the Gospel passage which was just read, beloved brethren, we heard that a certain man had two sons, and one of them asked his father for his share of the property, and when he had received it, he wasted it with harlots. That man to whom the two sons belong is understood as God the Father. In his two sons are designated two people, the elder people, the Jews, and the younger Gentiles. The elder son, that is, the Jewish people, are said to have stayed with the father always because of the fact that they received the Law and adhered to the worship of one God. Although the Jews frequently worshiped other gods, still the elder son typified them because they kept the commands of the Old Testament. But the younger son, that is, the Gentiles, withdrew from the worship of God, served the demons, and together with harlots wasted the substance which they had received from their Father. Now what was that substance which was received from the Father, except wisdom, justice, fortitude, temperance, and other things like these? Therefore, the younger son wasted this excellent substance which he received from his father in the

---
14 Ps. 125.5.
15 Ps. 125.6.

company of harlots, that is, in various pleasures of different kinds. When it is said: 'He took his journey into a far country,'[1] this is to be believed, not concerning his change of place, but with regard to the wickedness of his life. For how did he take his journey into a far country, except by going from good to evil, from chastity to dissipation, from justice to iniquity? Although it says: 'Into a far country,' perhaps he was with his father in the same city or on a single farm. It is said, however, in the same way in which we speak of those who begin to be dishonest after an honorable life: That man has gone out of himself. He was patient, but has become irascible; he was chaste, but behold he has become dissipated. Then again, if such a man is finally converted to a good life we say: Thanks be to God, now that man has returned to himself. Thus, we must understand concerning that prodigal son that he withdrew from good works and every kind of an honest life. Finally, in order that you may be able to see this more clearly, remember what was said about him in the Gospel: 'But he came to himself.'[2] Behold from where he had gone: surely he had gone out of himself. 'When he came to himself, he said: "I will get up and go." '[3] Why did he say, I will get up? Because he had fallen down. Why did he say, I will go? Because he had departed. Moreover, when it was said: 'He joined one of the citizens of that country,'[4] it is understood that he had been subject to one of the chiefs of the devil. When he was sent from the farmhouse, the measure of that diabolical chief's power is recognized. When he fed the swine by the wickedness of his life, he refreshed the unclean spirits who are delighted with wicked and dissipated deeds. Our evil deeds are their food. For just as when we act well we feed Christ, so if we are wicked we provide food for the devil by killing our own soul. The husks which the swine were eating seem to signify the vanity of worldly literature. For husks

---
1 Luke 15.13.
2 Luke 15.17.
3 Luke 15.17, 18.
4 Luke 15.15.

seem to be, as it were, food; but they are light and useless. So also is the food in worldly writings, which by their dangerously sweet vanity have instilled deceitful fables into this world by wickedly uttering the continuous praises of the idols and even of the demons in different kinds of verse. Now what are the husks of swine, except the pages of secular books which sound but do not heal? For they are able to make a noise to no purpose; they cannot possess food that is useful for the soul. That the swine themselves, which ate the husks, are understood as unclean spirits, is clearly known from the Gospel. For when demons were to be driven out of men, they asked that they might deserve to enter swine.

(2) 'I will get up,' he says, 'and go to my father, and will say to him, I have sinned against heaven; make me as one of thy hired men.'[5] Now what hired men does God the Father have, except doctors of the Church or other clerics, who seem to preach doctrine and serve God, not for the sake of the kingdom of heaven, but for earthly gain? Of these the Apostle says: 'Speaking the word of God not sincerely.'[6] 'But while he was yet a long way off, his father saw him.'[7] What does it mean that he saw him, except that he had compassion on him? In the same way, we sometimes are wont to say concerning those to whom God has granted some good: God saw him. Finally, see what follows: 'He was moved with compassion.'[8] Now when he says: 'He fell upon his neck,'[9] he put his arm upon him. Christ is understood in the arm, as it is written: 'To whom has the arm of the Lord been revealed?'[10] God truly put His arm around the prodigal son when He clothed His Son in human flesh. Then He exclaimed and said to all: 'Take my yoke upon you.'[11] Whoever accepts the yoke of Christ is embraced as with the arm of a father and is known to be recon-

---
5 Luke 15.18, 19.
6 Cf. Phil. 1.17.
7 Luke 15.20.
8 Ibid.
9 Ibid.
10 Isa. 53.1.
11 Matt. 11.29.

ciled with God. And when the father said: 'Fetch the best robe,'¹² he gave him immortality, which Adam had lost by his sin. In the ring which was given, the Holy Spirit is understood, concerning whom the Apostle says: 'Having a pledge of the Spirit.'¹³ A ring is usually given to a spouse as a pledge. Now because that prodigal son, that is, the Gentiles, had sinned against God with different demons, they received the Holy Spirit as a pledge, in order that they might realize that they had returned to the lawful spouse. Of such the Apostle says: 'I betrothed you to one spouse, that I might present you a chaste virgin to Christ.'¹⁴ Moreover, when it is said: 'Bring out the fattened calf,'¹⁵ what does it mean to bring it, except preach the sufferings of Christ? Then, Christ is truly killed for each one when he believes that He has died for him. How is that calf fattened, unless as a result of the many sufferings, insults, and scourges which He patiently suffered for the human race as though for the prodigal son? Behold, the goodness of our Lord: in order that an adopted and prodigal son may be received, His own Son is killed. Listen to the Apostle Paul saying this: 'He who has not spared his own Son but has delivered him for us all.'¹⁶

(3) 'Now when his elder brother who was in the field came to the house, he heard music and dancing. And calling one of the servants he inquired what this meant.'¹⁷ That elder brother is understood as the Jewish people who were in the field because they served the Lord for the sake of earthly possessions. In the Old Testament especially, earthly happiness was promised to those who worship God. Then he came to the house and heard music. A harmonious voice is called music, for when all who serve God agree in charity, they fulfill what the Apostle says: 'I beseech you that you all say the same thing.'¹⁸

---
12 Luke 15.22.
13 Cf. Rom. 8.23.
14 2 Cor. 11.2.
15 Luke 15.23.
16 Rom. 8.32.
17 Cf. Luke 15.25, 26.
18 1 Cor. 1.10.

When Christians are like this they render music, that is, a harmonious sound which is pleasing to God, and there is fulfilled in them what is written: 'They were of one heart and one soul.'[19] He further said: 'He inquired of one of the servants,'[20] that is, he read one of the prophets. One of the servants is understood as Isaia or Jeremia or Daniel, for they all preached the coming of Christ and joy because of the reconciliation of the Gentiles. 'Then the servant answered and said: "Thy brother has come, and thy father has killed the fatted calf." But he was angered and would not go in.'[21] The fact that he was angry signifies the Jewish people who would be opposed to the salvation of the Gentiles: indeed, even to this day that zeal against the Church persists among them. The further fact that: 'His father came out and entreated him,'[22] may indicate that through the mercy of God, it is said that at the end of the world all the Jews are going to believe. According to what the Apostle Paul says: 'When the full number of the Gentiles shall enter, then all Israel will be saved.'[23] Now that elder son then said: 'Behold, these many years I have been serving thee, and have never transgressed one of thy commands; and yet thou hast never given me a kid that I might make merry with my friends.'[24] When he said: 'I have never transgressed one of thy commands,' it signifies that the Jews have seemed to worship one God, and when he complained: 'thou hast never given me a kid,' this is understood concerning Christ. For Christ, who is the Lamb of God, was judged as a kid by the Jews, that is, he was condemned as a sinner. Therefore, Christ is a lamb to us, but a kid to them, and those who have believed that Christ is not just, but a sinner, have not deserved to feast upon the slain kid and sacrificed lamb. When the father said to the elder son: 'Thou art always

---

19 Acts 4.32.
20 Cf. Luke 15.26.
21 Cf. Luke 15.27, 28.
22 *Ibid.*
23 Cf. Rom. 11.25, 26.
24 Luke 15.29.

with me, and all that is mine is thine,'²⁵ it signified that the worship of one God, the writings of the Old Testament and the prophets, which surely belong to God, have always been with the Jews. Surely, it is the Jews who faithfully believed in God, who were prefigured in that elder son.

(4) Now in order that you may be able to know these truths more fully, let us briefly repeat what we have said. In the father of the two sons, God the Father is understood, while in the two sons we find the two people of the Jews and the Gentiles. In the robe which the son received is accepted the immortality which Adam had lost; in the ring, the Holy Spirit; in the fattened calf, the sufferings of Christ; in the dancing with music, the united will of the Christian people, according to the words: 'They were of one heart and one soul.'²⁶ Through the goodness of God I know that the rest which follows will be in your memory and kept in your minds, and so it is not necessary to repeat it again. Let us thank God with our whole hearts because everything which was written prefigured the salvation of the Gentiles, and let us endeavor to engage in good works so continually that such great kindnesses of our God may not bring judgment to us, but may avail as a remedy for our soul before the tribunal of the eternal judge. May He Himself deign to grant this, who lives and reigns with the Father and the Holy Spirit world without end. Amen.

* Sermon 164

On the Rich Man and Lazarus

(1) When the Gospel was read just now, dearly beloved, we heard a parable about the rich man who was clothed in purple and fine linen and Lazarus who was full of ulcers. If we pay

---
25 Luke 15.31.
26 Acts 4.32.

attention only with the eyes of the body, we long for the adornments and delicacies of that rich man, while we shudder at the poverty and misery of Lazarus; but if we look with the eyes of the heart, we have to struggle with Lazarus for a short time in order that we may be able to avoid the eternal fire of that rich man. As a result of this, let your charity look and make a choice. I know indeed that many choose evil, so that they do not fear to offer the undesirable; but for the sake of those who accept it, I will not be silent. I propose to you those two men: the rich man who feasted daily and the other poor man who lay at his door full of ulcers, whose sores the dogs licked, and who longed to be satisfied with the crumbs falling from the table of the rich man. These two I propose, but I add further that the one was wicked, the other good; the one pernicious, the other blameless; the one pious, the other impious; the one intent upon God, and the other intent upon riches; the one mocking the word of truth, and the other awaiting the divine promise. Behold, I have proposed the two. I am afraid to say: Choose; for there are many present with bodily eyes but lacking the eyes of the heart. And still I say: Make your choice. Now let those who have ears to hear listen. And who does not have ears in his body? Few have them in the interior man. Make your choice. Finally, I speak to Christians and I address your faith. If you do not adorn the seat of shame, that is, your forehead, with the sign of the cross in vain, if you do not hear the prophets and the Gospel to no avail, choose. Why are you afraid to make a choice? You have heard the difference: choose, for in any case you have heard the end. Behold, the Lord follows, and the true teacher who deceives no one adds: 'It came to pass that the poor man died and was borne away by the angels into Abraham's bosom.'[1] Now make your choice. For when I mentioned: 'A certain rich man used to clothe himself in purple and fine linen, and feasted every day in splendid fashion,'[2] your passions were

---

1 Cf. Luke 16.22.
2 Luke 16.19.

tickled, and your weakness was flattered. It gave you pleasure to clothe yourself in purple and fine linen, and to feast every day in splendid fashion. When the final ends have been proposed, the man who possesses faith will choose rightly. He prefers to share in the labors of that poor man in order to reach his end, a goal without end, good without evil, true happiness, the strongest assurance. Does any wise man prefer to rejoice for a time like that rich man, and to be afflicted with his infinite torments, to thirst, and in hell to long for a drop of water along with the man who had refused a crumb? After his death his brothers, of whom he had said: 'I have five brothers,'[3] wasted his substance in the company of drunken men, and not as much as a drop of cold water could come to relieve him.

(2) Every man who does not notice this carefully judges that the rich man was fortunate. But if a man has eyes of the heart, he clearly understands that the rich man, because of the fact that he was proud and passionate, was miserable even though he enjoyed those adornments and delicacies. Lazarus, however, was blessed, even when he was licked by the dogs. Why? Because I am not looking at the body of the poor man, but his spirit. I do not shudder at his limbs which are full of sores, because I see the purity of his mind. The dogs licked his sores on the outside, but inside his conscience remained pure and undefiled. On the other hand, that proud man who was wicked and raving, who despised the poor man who lay before his door, is filthy and sluggish if you examine his soul. The soul of a wicked rich man is more corruptible than the flesh of the poor man; it possesses nothing healthy or whole. Now these are the facts if you watch with the eyes of the heart: the rich man possessed better what is worse, while the poor man kept better what is truly better. Do we perhaps hesitate because of the fact that man consists of body and soul? If I could question an ox and if he could answer, he would say that the soul is better than the body, for the guide is

---
[3] Luke 16.28.

better than the one who is led. It is the soul which has sensation in the body; there are bodily senses, but the soul uses them as its instruments. There are eyes, but if there is no inhabitant within, in vain will the windows lie open; there are ears, but I ask who hears through them; there is a tongue, but tell me who moves it; there are feet, but I ask who directs the step; there are hands, but tell me who directs their movements. If the one who dwells within withdraws, the house will lie empty. Now since no one doubts that the soul is better than the body, for this reason see where that rich man was happy, and see where the poor man was happy. The one was fortunate in his body which is the inferior part; the other one was blessed within in his soul which is the better part. It is as though the one was like an inhabitant who is sick in a marble house with a fluted ceiling; the other was like a lord who seems to dwell safely in a mean and empty home.

(3) Therefore, if we examine those two men interiorly, brethren, the expectation of the poor man was more fortunate than the possessions of the rich man. The abundance of earthly substance of the one was great, the hope of the other; the great wealth of the one in prosperity was a good thing in difficult times, but the hope of the other was great in the midst of adversity. However, that rich man laughed at those who said there was something afterwards. But he began to burn in hell and to beg, saying to Abraham: 'Father Abraham, let Lazarus dip his finger in water and cool my tongue, for I am tormented in this flame.'[4] A crumb, and a drop of water: the one begged a crumb from the feast of the rich man, while the other entreats a drop of water from the finger of the poor. But the poor man more easily obtains the crumb than that rich man receives the drop of water, for the reply is given to him: 'Son, remember that thou in thy lifetime hast received good things.'[5] Now these good things of yours belong to the foolish soul, not to the wise; they are to be considered great, or rather small.

---

4 Cf. Luke 16.24.
5 Luke 16.25.

'Thou in thy lifetime hast received good things.' If you followed your own will during your life, then what belongs to Lazarus justly does not belong to you. However, see, brethren, the judgment of our Lord Jesus Christ. 'There was a certain rich man.'⁶ He did not say what his name was: 'He used to clothe himself in purple and fine linen, and feasted every day in splendid fashion.'⁷ But what was the name of the poor man? Lazarus, and He mentioned his name. Do not wonder, for he was written in the book of life, while that other man was not to be named before God since he had already been named among men. However, he did not displease God because of the fact that he was rich or renowned, but because he was proud and merciless. Riches are not blamed by our Lord, for surely they are not given except by Him. Riches are not blamed, but men who are proud because of their riches are condemned.

(4) When we consider these truths, brethren, as far as our strength allows, let us think of the misery of the poor with kindly intent. Then, if we are freed from the evil hearing, we may happily hear that desirable word: 'Come, blessed of my Father, receive the kingdom which was prepared for you from the foundation of the world.'⁸ May He Himself deign to grant this, who lives and reigns together with the Father and the Holy Spirit forever and ever. Amen.

* Sermon 165

Likewise on the Rich Man and Lazarus

(1) 'There was a certain rich man who used to clothe himself in purple and fine linen, and who feasted every day in

---
6 Luke 16.19.
7 *Ibid.*
8 Cf. Matt. 25.34.

splendid fashion,'[1] and other words of the Gospel may be accepted allegorically in this way. That rich man typified the Jews who boasted about their own merits: 'Ignorant of the justice of God and wishing to establish their own.'[2] The purple and fine linen are the dignity of the kingdom, for thus it is written in the Gospel concerning the Jews: 'And the kingdom of God will be taken away from you and will be given to a people yielding justice.'[3] The feasting in splendid fashion is the empty display of the Law in which they gloried, wrongly using it for the pomp of pride rather than for the needs of salvation. Now the beggar who was named Lazarus, which is interpreted as help, signifies the Gentiles who are helped all the more, the less they presume upon the abundance of their wealth. Therefore, in the rich man, as was already said, the Jewish people are signified, and the Gentiles in Lazarus. The fact that the Gentiles or Lazarus longed for crumbs from the table of the rich man indicates the Gentiles who desired to receive knowledge of the spiritual law like heavenly delicacies. Moreover, the crumbs falling from the table are certain words of the Law which, by their boasting, they, as it were, threw on the ground when they spoke haughtily to the people. The sores with which Lazarus was filled signify the confession of sins which burst forth from inside like bad blood.

(2) We ought to know further, dearest brethren, that wounds are one thing and sores another. Wounds are inflicted from the outside, while sores break out from within. Now the sores signify the confession of sins for this reason, because when they erupt outside they show that there is already some evidence of health within. Therefore, when a man humbly confesses his sins, he seems full of sores on the outside, but he is known to be already healed within. But if, like that rich man, a person adorns his body and disdains to confess his sins, he is adorned outwardly but remains inwardly full of

---

1 Luke 16.19.
2 Cf. Rom. 10.3.
3 Cf. Matt. 21.43.

sores. Such was that rich man whose body was clothed in purple and fine linen, but whose soul was marked with the contagion of leprosy. For this reason in the sight of the angels, the soul of the rich man was as the body of the poor man looked to the eyes of men, while in his soul the poor man appeared like the rich man in his body. After death they exchanged places: after his sores Lazarus was adorned with the pearls of virtues and lifted up by the angels into the bosom of Abraham, while the rich man after his purple robes was struck with the leprosy of sin and plunged into the depths of hell. However, that rich man was not tortured in hell because of the fact that he was rich, but because he was proud and merciless. Furthermore, the dogs who licked the sores are understood as most wicked men who love their sins, for with a wide tongue they do not cease even to praise their evil deeds.

(3) The bosom of Abraham signifies the rest of the blessed to whom the kingdom of heaven belongs, and there they are received after this life. Burial in hell is the lowest depth of all punishments, which devours the proud and merciless after this life. The fact that he wanted to cool his tongue when he was completely enveloped in flames signifies what is written: 'Death and life are in the power of the tongue';[4] and that: 'With the mouth profession of faith is made unto salvation.'[5] For this reason, the tongue of that man endured greater burning because he not only refused to say that the poor should receive alms, but he even frequently injured him with exceedingly harsh words. In the tip of the finger is understood the grace of the Holy Spirit, as the Lord Himself said: 'If I by the finger of God,' that is, by the Holy Spirit, 'cast out devils.'[6] In the tip of the finger is indeed signified the least work of mercy whereby help is given to all men through the Holy Spirit. When it is further said to him: 'For thou in thy lifetime hast received good things,'[7] we understand the fact

---
4 Prov. 18.21.
5 Rom. 10.10.
6 Luke 11.20.
7 Luke 16.25.

that he loved the happiness of the world and wished to seek no other life nor to love anything except that life in which he was puffed up with pride. Moreover, it says that Lazarus received evil things because it is understood that he endured labors and pains, the trials and penalties of this mortal life. Truly, it is written: 'Not a child who has lived one day upon earth is free from sin,'[8] because surely we all die in Adam who became subject to death as a result of his transgression. Moreover, when it says: 'Between us and you a great gulf is fixed,'[9] so that, even if they wish it, the just cannot cross over into the places where the wicked are tortured, it means that after this life the wicked are to be received in the prison of hell in such a way that they may not leave it until they pay the last farthing. From this we understand that all the holy and just men can come to the aid of sinners by their prayers as long as the sinners themselves are still left in this life and ask for their help, but when the sinners have left this world overwhelmed with serious sins and without the remedy of repentance, even if they want it, the just cannot assist them at all.

(4) Now that rich man, that is, the Jewish people, says he has five brothers in his father's house. By these are meant all the Jews who were held under the Law which 'was given through Moses,'[10] for he wrote five books. But when Abraham says: If they wish to believe, 'They have Moses and the Prophets and do not hearken; they will not believe even if someone rises from the dead,'[11] this is meant to be understood concerning Christ, as if he would say: If they do not listen to Moses and the prophets, neither will they believe Christ Himself, who has risen from the dead. Therefore, as we meditate upon these truths, brethren, let us in a kindly spirit devise mercy for the poor as much as our strength allows, in order that we may deserve to be crowned by the Lord on the

---
8 Cf. Job 14.4.
9 Luke 16.26.
10 John 1.17.
11 Luke 16.29, 31.

day of judgment. May He Himself deign to grant this, who lives with the Father.

Sermon 166

Another Sermon, This Time on What Is Written in the Gospel: 'The Kingdom of God is Within You';[1] Also That We Should Decide with a Just Judgment Between the Body and the Soul; Further That We Can Never Possess Peace with God If We Murmur Against Him, and How We Possess Justice and Peace and Even Joy

(1) When the Gospel was read we heard the Lord say: 'The kingdom of God is within you.' Now He knew that not everyone would be able to understand what He said in the words: 'The kingdom of God is within you.' So for this reason, as if He were questioned by someone, He explained and added to it, saying: 'The kingdom of God does not consist in food and drink, but in justice and peace and joy.'[2] I exhort you, dearest brethren, let us examine our consciences to see whether we have the kingdom of God reserved within the treasury of our soul. If justice, peace, and joy are there we may rest with assurance, because we know that the kingdom of God is within us. But carefully notice what that justice, peace, and joy are.

(2) Justice is true and perfect when it does not do to others what it does not desire for itself. Now someone may say: Who can treat all men well? At least he can will to do good to all men, and when you have done this the Evangelist says to you: 'Glory to God in the highest, and on earth peace among men of good will.'[3] Someone may be able to say: I possess no wealth; but can anyone say: I cannot possess good will? For this reason, true is the justice which desires to have happen

---
[1] Luke 17.21.
[2] Rom. 14.17.
[3] Luke 2.14.

to all men what it chooses and wants for itself. That justice is true which loves not only friends, but even enemies out of love of God. Now if we wish to possess that true justice ourselves, brethren, we apply it well to others, for how can anyone bestow upon others what he is not known to possess in himself? But perhaps someone may ask how we ought to preserve justice in ourselves.

(3) Listen, brethren, justice appears to me what the word derives from it, because it is wont to reach a just decision between two opposing and contrary parts. Well, brethren, let us notice in ourselves, too, what the two contrary forces are: for 'The flesh lusts against the spirit, and the spirit against the flesh.'[4] Therefore, we have an interior and an exterior man, we have a body and a soul, that is, a mistress and a handmaid. Now if you want me to believe that you are able to decide justly the cause of another, I want to recognize it first in your own self. Be a just judge in your own case; give to the soul what is worthy, and reserve for the body what it needs. Grant to the mistress what is sufficient for it for eternity, and keep for the handmaid only enough to live upon in this world. If the mistress is brought down low, the handmaid is exalted; if little or nothing is stored up for the mistress in heaven and the whole is kept for the handmaid in the world, behold already we are known not to be just in our own case. How do we hear the case of another in the right order, when nothing is reserved for justice in our own case within us? This alone I know, brethren, that a man will never be able to judge the cause of another justly if he is unwilling to observe justice between his own soul and his body. For we have been made according to the image of God in both soul and mind, but we have been formed from the slime of the earth in body. Therefore, if a man loves his body more than his soul, he wants to bring down the image of God and to lift up the earth. If he is so unjust in himself, doubtless, he will not observe justice when he hears the case of another. For this reason,

---
4 Gal. 5.17.

a man who desires to observe justice should begin with himself and observe it first in himself, growing accustomed to being a just judge between his soul and his body. Let him keep simple and moderate food and clothing for his body in the world, and let him store up in heaven by almsgiving what is better for the soul. If he does otherwise and does not correct himself, willingly persevering in this, he is going to be judged in the future life in the same way in which he passes judgment in this one. Let these brief remarks suffice on the subject of true justice.

(4) You ought to know further what true peace is. It is not true peace when adulterers seem to be peaceable toward each other, or when robbers and drunkards, slanderous and proud men appear to be mutually agreeable. This should not be called peace, because it does not arise from the root of charity. If a man desires true peace, he should first strive to possess it with God. But someone may say: Who is there who would not want to have peace with God? Surely, anyone who does not live in such a way as God has commanded us to live. Who is there who does not have peace with God? One who is displeased by God. Again someone may say: Who is so mad as to be displeased by God? If I examine you, perhaps I will find that you are the very one to whom God is displeasing. Tell me, I beseech you, have you never murmured against an abundance of rain? Have you never been angry at the violence of the winds? Have you never complained about the dryness of droughts? Have you never murmured against the good fortune of wicked men? And, to speak even further, have you never blasphemed when rather abundant fruit was not gathered from the vines? Now if in all these matters you see and realize that you have never murmured against God, know that you possess true peace with God. In everything which happens to you exclaim what that most blessed man, Job, cried out with a safe conscience: 'The Lord gave, and the Lord has taken away; blessed be the name of the Lord!'[5] Now

---

[5] Job 1.21.

if you praise God when things go well for you, but murmur against Him when they go badly, you do not have peace with God and you cannot say with the psalmist: 'I will bless the Lord at all times.'⁶ Who is there who blesses the Lord at all times? The man whom good fortune does not corrupt or adversity frighten. This, then, is the first and real peace, to be at peace with God. When this has been accomplished, then we can also possess peace within ourselves. However, if a man is unwilling to have peace with God, he will not be able to possess peace with himself. Therefore, may our soul be at peace with God, so that our body may be subject to our soul; for if the higher faculty does not rule, the lower one afflicts and torments you. Let your soul bend its neck beneath the yoke of God, in order that your body may subject its neck to the yoke of the soul. Then there will be true and perfect peace, when we are at peace, not only with others, but also with ourselves. But just because we are still at battle and fight against the devil, let us not despair of victory. If we are at peace with God and are united to Him, how can it happen that we fear the devil? You have such a general with you, and are you afraid of the devil? You fight under such a king, and are you in doubt about victory? To be sure, the devil daily opposes you, but Christ is near: the one wishes to press you down, the other wills to lift you up; the one longs to kill you, and the other wishes to give you life. But be assured, brethren: Christ is better able to lift you up than the devil is able to overcome you. Therefore, if we observe justice and peace with all our heart, as we said above, then we will also be able to possess true joy.

(5) What is true joy, brethren, except the kingdom of heaven? And what is the kingdom of heaven, except Christ our Lord? The fact that Christ is true joy, we read in the Gospel, for thus the angels spoke to the shepherds: 'Behold, we bring you good news of great joy.'⁷ Listen, brethren, and see

---
6 Ps. 33.2.
7 Luke 2.10.

that there is no true joy except Christ our Lord. This the
angels also confirmed by their testimony, for when they had
said: 'Behold, we bring you good news of great joy which
shall be to all the people,' they immediately added: 'for today
a Savior has been born to you, who is Christ the Lord.'[8] I
know, brethren, that all men want to possess true joy. But a
man deceives himself if he is unwilling to cultivate his field
and still wants to rejoice in the harvest; he deceives himself
if he refuses to plant a tree but wishes to gather fruit. A man
does not possess true joy unless he keeps peace and justice.
Justice is like the first root, peace is the second, and joy the
third. Peace is born of justice, and joy is produced by peace.
Justice and peace seem to be like good works, but joy is understood
to be the fruit of good works. Therefore, we now labor
for a short time in observing justice and preserving peace, as
in good works, but afterwards we will rejoice without end as
the fruit of our good deeds. Listen to the Apostle say concerning
Christ: 'He himself is our peace, he it is who has
made both one.'[9] That Christ Himself is our joy, we already
said above. Moreover, in the Gospel when our Lord Jesus
Christ was speaking to His disciples, He exhorted them in this
way, saying: 'I will see you again, and your heart shall rejoice,
and your joy no one shall take from you.'[10] What does 'your
joy no one shall take from you' mean, except, no one shall take
me, your Lord, from you? Look at your own consciences, dearest
brethren. If justice abides there, that is, if you will and
desire and choose for all men the same as for yourself, and if
peace is within you, extending not only to friends but also
to enemies, then know that the kingdom of heaven, that is,
Christ the Lord, dwells in you. However, if when he examines
his conscience, a man does not find justice there, but avarice,
not peace but discord, not joy arising from hope in eternal
life but carnal joy springing from a love for dissipation, then

---

8 Luke 2.10, 11.
9 Eph. 2.14.
10 John 16.22.

he may know and understand that there reigns in him, not Christ the legitimate king, but a cruel tyrant. As long as we still live in this body, brethren, we can now, with God's help, correct and amend our lives. But if the last day finds us overwhelmed with many sins, there will be no time for amendment. For just as there will then be eternal joy for all the saints, so there will be endless punishment for sinners. This will be the lot of those who have refused to amend their lives by repentance. Then Christ is going to say to those on His left hand: 'Depart from me, accursed ones, into the everlasting fire';[11] and to those at His right: 'Come, blessed, receive the kingdom which was prepared for you from the foundation of the world.'[12] May our Lord lead you to this bliss under His protection: to whom is honor and might together with the Father and the Holy Spirit world without end. Amen.

* Sermon 167

From the Gospel According to John Where It Says That on the Third Day a Marriage Took Place at Cana of Galilee

(1) When the divine lesson was read just now, dearest brethren, we heard the Evangelist say: 'On the third day a marriage took place at Cana of Galilee.'[1] The third day is the mystery of the Trinity, while the miracles of the nuptials are the mysteries of heavenly joys. It was both a nuptial day and a feast for this reason, because the Church after the Redemption was joined to the spouse who was coming: to that spouse, I say, whom all the ages from the beginning of the world had promised. It is He who came down to earth to invite His beloved to marriage with His Highness, giving her for a

---
11 Matt. 25.41.
12 Cf. Matt. 25.34.

1 John 2.1.

present the token of His blood, and intending to give later the dowry of His kingdom. The six water-jars prefigure six ages, and they bespeak the cause of our salvation which occurs in the sixth age; for you may think that in a comparison with the reborn the idea of Baptism is expressed in them. There is the same liquid but not the same taste in the water which remained in the water-jars; what it was is another thing, and what it seems to have been has not perished. The measure remains in quantity, but grace is added in quality. Nothing is visibly added in increase, and the hidden addition fittingly takes place in an invisible manner. The measure is not increased, but improvement is acquired; the waters retain their fullness, but by a secret infusion they receive another power. In the same way through the water of Baptism, although a man seems to be the same outwardly, still he becomes different interiorly. He was born with sin, but is reborn without sin; he perished in the first instance, but progresses in the next. He is stripped of what is worse and renewed in what is better; his person is not touched, but his nature is changed. Nothing is seen to have been added, and still what is added is perceived through faith as with the taste and savor of the mind. When a man lays aside his past sinfulness, he is suddenly endowed with new dignity, with that cup of divine love of which it is said: 'And thy cup which inebriated me, how it overflows!'[2] Inebriated with that cup, I repeat, hearts taste the sweetness of heavenly things through the strength of spiritual wisdom. Then they may merit to hear: 'Taste and see how good the Lord is.'[3] Now he said: 'Taste,' because love of God can refresh the soul but cannot satisfy the desire, regardless of the amount of faith or longing with which it is sought. More and more, it arouses thirst when it is, as it were, tasted beforehand with the edge of the lips, and for this reason He says of Himself: 'He who eats of me will hunger still, he who drinks of me

---

2 Cf. Ps. 22.5.
3 Ps. 33.9.

will thirst for more.'⁴ Because of its sweetness, it arouses an appetite for itself, but it does not cause disgust from satiety. Just as men who are experienced in drinking wine are wont to thirst all the more when they have become drunk, so it is with the devout and chaste soul which is prudent and contrite, and which can, therefore, say with the psalmist: 'You have given us stupefying wine,'⁵ when it has begun to think about hope in a future life and to imbibe a thirst for heavenly goods. It knows how to be filled, but not how to be satisfied, so that the more it consumes according to its capacity, the more it lacks in its eagerness, and it can join with the prophet in that word of longing: 'My soul pines for your salvation';⁶ and again: 'My flesh and my heart waste away, O God of my heart';⁷ moreover: 'My soul yearns and pines for the courts of the Lord.'⁸

(2) On the other hand, when the soul that is careless and forgetful of God begins to be filled with the surfeit and intoxication of vices, and to be corrupted with the dregs of sins, a deadly and hostile pleasure draws after itself the enslaved senses. Now just as happens when the bodily skin is infected by moisture or itching and because of it, corruption makes it sore and scratching irritates it, so it is with the soul. Because of the pleasure of sins, guilt increases as the result of carelessness, the seduction is augmented by dissipation, and perdition delights all the more the one who is perishing. Pleasure that is finished does not satisfy, but through its exercise the desire for vices is inflamed more than it is ended. Although it can never be consumed, it destroys only its follower. Thus, indeed, the devil deceives hearts which have once been overcome by the most pleasing enticements; thus, he conceals the allurements of sin in the cunning of old tricks and manifold inventions. In the same way, malicious men are wont to act, as

---

4 Ecclus. 24.29.
5 Ps. 59.5.
6 Ps. 118.81.
7 Ps. 72.26.
8 Ps. 83.3.

also those who mix the deadly juices of herbs are wont to administer them to those who do not know it in a cup that is seasoned or sweetened with honey. This they do to appease the taste with a false pleasure. They conceal the strength of the bitterness with deceitful sweetness. The first smell of the cup is tempting, the taste of the poison is checked but suffocates. What rises to the lips is honey, but what goes down to the stomach is gall. So also the devil flatters men externally through the lust for carnal possessions and unlawful desires, but interiorly he plots against the soul. He kills the spirit while he pleases the affections, as the prophet said: 'For a time he sweetens the mouth, but in the end is found to be more bitter than gall.'[9] Sin gives pleasure now, but it will not be pleasant to burn afterwards.

(3) Now the soul advances in whatever habit operates in her. When through the exercise of fear of God and amendment of life, she begins to cross from the left hand to the right as from water to wine, in the cleansed state of a purified mind shrinking from the filthy contagions of sins, then she does not see the things which are before her eyes in the manner of a drunkard, but reaches out to the things which are promised in the future. For in proportion to the way you withdraw yourself from earthly concerns, to that extent you will arrive at heavenly things. The more you retreat from vices, the more you will approach virtues, for the rejection of sins means the acquisition of merits. And for this reason, the man who is temperate in the world and intoxicated with God is prepared for the desired heavenly joys as if for a wedding feast.

(4) From this banquet that sinner was cast into the darkness outside with his hands and feet bound, for it is said to him in the Gospel: 'Friend, how didst thou come in here without a wedding garment?'[10] That man who had lost his wedding garment, I believe, in losing the grace of Baptism had broken his water-jar and had lost the gift of the sacred font, pouring

---
9 Cf. Prov. 5.3, 4.
10 Matt. 22.12.

out the wine of the blessed redemption. To such men, it is further said that they should go: 'Into the everlasting fire which was prepared for the devil and his angels.'[11] Of them, I say, we read: 'It is a fearful thing to fall into the hands of the living God';[12] and of such the evangelist testifies: 'Every tree that is not bringing forth good fruit is to be cut down and thrown into the fire.'[13] Do you see that it is worthy of damnation, not only to have done evil, but even not to have accomplished good? We will be dissatisfied with ourselves too late in the presence of the eternal fire which will question our marrow and bones and even our thoughts. How much each one then will want to be punished for ever desiring the wife of another, for ever staining the clothing of his body and the silk cloth of Baptism, for ever neglecting the advice and admonitions of priests! For if it is a great danger not to rebuke the faults of another, how much more dangerous to have refused to correct one's own life, and not only to have failed to amend it, but even to have defended it and by defending it to have added still more?

(5) For this reason, the unquenchable fire there will have to burn whatever healing penance and a salutary conversion of life here has failed to cure. The burning pit of hell will be open, and to it there will be a descent but no means of return. Souls which have been stripped of the garment of faith and are mortally dead will be buried there forever, destined to be cast into the darkness outside where they will not be visited for all eternity. They will be unhappily shut out in exterior darkness, I repeat, or rather they will still more unhappily be enclosed in it. Concerning this pit the prophet relates: 'Let not the abyss swallow me up, nor the pit close its mouth over me.'[14] He said: 'Let not the pit close its mouth over me' for this reason, because when it admits the guilty, it will be closed above and opened below, extending to the depths. No breath-

---

11 Matt. 25.41.
12 Heb. 10.31.
13 Matt. 3.10.
14 Ps. 68.16.

ing space will be left, no breath of air will be available when the doors press down from above. Those who say farewell to the things of nature will be cast down there; since they have refused to know God, they will no longer be recognized by Him, and dying to life they will live for endless death. The happy souls who now use their wealth wisely, content with bodily necessities and generous with their possessions, pure in themselves, and not cruel toward others, free themselves from the fiery night of this infernal region. This punishment will detain those who will perish for all eternity, since they have lost the grace of Baptism and have not restored it through repentance. To them it is said: 'The chaff he will burn up with unquenchable fire.'[15]

(6) However, to souls which have committed deeds worthy of temporal punishments this word of God is directed, that they may not depart from there, 'Until they pay the last penny.'[16] They will pass through the stream of fire of which the prophetical word relates: 'And a stream of fire flowed out before him,'[17] through the river of flame and a terrible lake of boiling masses. The delay in passing through here will be as great as was the material sin; the reasonable discipline of flames will punish a man as much as his guilt demands, and wise punishment will range as long as foolish iniquity committed sin. In a certain passage the divine word compares the sinful soul to a brass pot when it says: 'Then I will set the pot empty on the coals till its metal glows red hot, till the impurities in it melt.'[18] There perjury, false testimonies, unjust judgments, wraths, vices, and unlawful desires which had stained a noble nature will melt away; there the pool or lead of different passions which had spoiled the divine image will be consumed: all the things which might have been removed from the soul here in a quick exchange through almsgiving and tears. Behold, in this way God must demand an account

---
15 Matt. 3.12.
16 Matt. 5.26.
17 Cf. Dan. 7.10.
18 Cf. Ezech. 24.11.

of man, since He gave His own self as man and by being pierced with nails cancelled the law of death.

(7) There the bodies of the just will travel as though through pleasant pools, untouched by the burning flames which do not even observe their true nature. In the midst of the burning fire which shrinks from them, they will receive evidence of their merits, for the bodies of these men, I repeat, will be unscathed, even honored by the punishments themselves, because they have not been burdened with sins. The flames with their cruel heat will have no power over them, since the fire of passions has not touched them; and the reasonable heat will not know how to inflict any injury on those to whom purity has given respect. In fact, it will rather prepare a path of harmlessness with its cooling air, and since it will find no place where it has to exercise judgment, it will spontaneously offer submission. Now perhaps someone will think within himself: How can it happen that human bodies do not burn in the midst of flames? Let us question the ancient examples which are famous in the Sacred Books: let us ask the glorious triumphs of the Hebrews. Thus, the faith and justice of the three children did not feel the fires of the Babylonians, but amazing coolness was found in the midst of the roaring furnace. The heat of the flames withdrew from the merits of their virtues and in a wonderful way covered those who were given over to it as guilty with fire like a mist; however, the ministers of the wicked king who were stationed afar off and stood around at a distance were destroyed. How much the merits of devotion and the privileges of sanctity obtain even in the present! Behold, the clouds of fire somehow blowing terribly and boiling up fifty cubits rage outside but spare them within: the wise fire is furious outside of the furnace, but serves those who are enclosed in it. It rages without consideration against the wicked, as much as savage cruelty attacks the saints. See how the fire like a witness knows how much reverence is due to chaste bodies. Imbued with respect it licks the food which is thrown to it, and wonders that it has no

power against bodies which have been consecrated by fear of God and chaste fasting; not only does it by a secret dispensation fail to violate its sacred trust, but it even protects it.

(8) Since these facts are true, beloved, let us realize that men will not be able to escape intolerable punishments and eternal flames unless they have first extinguished in themselves the fire of various carnal passions. For this reason, dearest brethren, let us be converted to a better life while the remedies are still in our power. Let us hurry while we still have the light, and let us not neglect the fleeting days of salvation. By dying to sins let us, with the Lord's help, extinguish death, and by the merits of our life here let us prepare for ourselves eternal life.

* *Sermon 168*

On the Words of the Gospel According to John: 'On the Third Day a Marriage Took Place,'[1] and So Forth

(1) As to the fact that when the Gospel was read just now, dearest brethren, you heard that on the third day a marriage took place and water was changed into wine, let us see what that marriage was. Our gain or re-instatement is shown in the nuptial vows and feast, just as in another place the return of the younger son was received with music and dancing. Now the six water-jars are the six ages of this world which prefigured the just and typified our Lord, and they take two or three measures each because they contain within them faith in the Trinity. But let us see what the divine word says; let us examine again the sacred words of the Gospel.

(2) He changed the water into wine at Cana of Galilee, and He concealed God who was hidden beneath the Man by the power of His works. 'And on the third day a marriage took

---

1 John 2.1.

place,' it says. What are those nuptials, except the joys of human salvation? Why on the third day? Either because it shows the mystery of the Trinity, or because He arose from the dead on the third day. Therefore, He came down to earth 'as a groom comes forth from his bridal chamber,'[2] and by accepting the Incarnation was to be joined to the Church which was composed of all nations. To this Church, which we surely are, He gave both a pledge and a dowry: He gave a pledge when He was promised to us according to the Law, and He gave a dowry when He was immolated for us. This can also be taken in another way: we may understand the pledge as present grace and the dowry as eternal life. Let us see what He does at Cana of Galilee, for as a result of it the wonderful miracles of the Lord now come to us.

(3) Placed there are: 'Water-jars, each holding two or three measures.'[3] The jars are filled, but suddenly the water is changed, just as men are destined to change afterwards. When they are changed for the better, as if they bespeak the force of Baptism, in the same way similarity to the sacrament of regeneration is expressed in them. When they are changed from one thing into another, the inferior creature being transformed into a more pleasing form, the mystery of the second birth is revealed. In the waters themselves nothing of their quality is diminished, and as long as they remain they do not become at all worse through this splendid alteration. Their own substance disappears, but another is acquired: a stronger taste is added to the weak elements, and a hidden power is infused into the smooth liquid; the nature of the waters is saturated, and so in a new way they confess the power of their Creator. Who can change these things, except the One who was also able to create them?

(4) Therefore: 'The wine having run short, the mother of Jesus said to him, "They have no wine." '[4] Let us now ask in

---

2 Ps. 18.6.
3 John 2.6.
4 John 2.3.

the first place what is the wine that is said to have failed, and what is that other wine which was miraculously provided and which the chief steward proclaims is better when he says: 'Every man at first sets forth the good wine, and when they have drunk freely, then that which is poorer. But thou hast kept the good wine until now.'[5] On many occasions we accept the wine as the divine precepts and the Sacred Scriptures which contain the purest life of heavenly wisdom. Through them the senses are kindled to fear God and the affections are inebriated, according to what is said concerning wisdom: 'She has spread her table, and mixed her wine in a bowl.'[6] If ever the power of the divine writings fills the inner being of man, he will be able to say with the prophet: 'You have given us to drink of the wine of compunction; your cup overflows!'[7] For this reason, when Christ was active at Cana of Galilee, the wine failed and wine was made: that is, the shadow was removed and truth presented itself. The Law withdrew and grace succeeded, carnal possessions were exchanged for spiritual ones, the old observance was transferred to the New Testament, as the blessed Apostle says: 'The former things have passed away; and behold, they are made new.'[8] Just as those water-jars which were filled with water lost nothing of what they were and still began to be what they were not, so the Law which is finished with the coming of Christ does not perish but progresses. For this reason, when the wine failed another wine was supplied: the Old Testament, indeed, was good, but without spiritual understanding it disappears with the letter; the New Testament through grace restores the odor of life.

(5) Since these facts are true, let us see who we can believe is the chief steward who is in charge of the house of the bridegroom. Who else should we think it is, except blessed Paul? After he had received the exceedingly sweet odor or taste of the mysteries of the New Testament following the letter of the

---
5 John 2.10.
6 Cf. Prov. 9.2.
7 Cf. Ps. 22.5.
8 2 Cor. 5.17.

Law, he was filled and saturated with the fragrance of their spiritual meaning, so that he exclaimed in admiration: 'Thou hast kept the good wine until now.'[9] Let us further see how he praises the wine itself: 'Eye has not seen nor ear heard,' he says, 'what things God has prepared for those who love him.'[10] Behold, the true and praiseworthy miracle which He works in us when He makes us good from the worst, humble from proud, chaste from shameful, friends of God from followers of the world. What greater miracles can He perform than when He deigns to promote a worm and rottenness to the stature of the angels, to put us away from earthly things to a position among the heavenly, and to take us to the grace of His own adoption?

(6) What, then, will we give to the Lord in return for all the things which He has granted to us? Or when will we be able to repay what we are not even able to think about? However, we should not despair because we have nothing with which to repay Him. So great is the goodness of our Lord that with Him the perfect will to act is considered as the completion of the deed, for if a man has done what he could he has fulfilled everything. What, then, will we give to the Lord, except humbly to say to him with prostrate body and contrite heart: 'O Lord, be merciful to me the sinner'?[11] He who does not despise a contrite and humbled heart loves a holocaust, and He does not ask of us what He knows we cannot accomplish. Therefore, men who are not able to give rather abundant alms should at least with a good intention dispense a little something according to their strength. Those who are unable to retain the glory of virginity should at least, with God's help, strive to observe chastity with their own wives. Let them love justice, possess charity, cultivate patience, avoid drunkenness as a pitfall of the devil, and love all men in a perfect spirit. They should pray for the good, that they may not withdraw

---

9 John 2.10.
10 Cf. 1 Cor. 2.9.
11 Luke 18.13.

from a holy life, and should intercede for the wicked in order that they may quickly be converted to a better life. Now these and similar actions, dearest brethren, are proven not to be excessively difficult or insupportable. Nothing will be impossible, provided only that there is a good will. For in order to prepare for eternal life, God does not make us travel to the east or the west on difficult journeys; He merely directs our attention to ourselves. What He has bestowed upon us through His grace, this He demands of us, for as He Himself said in the Gospel: 'The kingdom of God is within you.'[12] Therefore, may true charity and a good will abide in our hearts, so that the word of the Gospel may be fulfilled in us: 'Peace among men of good will.'[13] May He Himself deign to grant this, who lives and reigns forever and ever. Amen.

Sermon 169

On the Fact That Our Lord Changed Water Into Wine

(1) As we have occasionally indicated to your charity, dearest brethren, those six water-jars which the Gospel passage just mentioned and the water of which was changed into wine, prefigured the six ages of this world. As you usually hear, one age was completed from Adam to Noe, the second was from Noe to Abraham, as the Gospel mentions the third extended from Abraham to David, the fourth lasted from David to the transmigration to Babylon, the fifth extended from the transmigration to Babylon until John the Baptist, and the sixth age has been going on from John the Baptist and the coming of our Lord and Savior. This sequence of events is also clearly recognized in the course of human life: for the first step is like the first period of infancy, the second is boyhood, the third is

---
12 Luke 17.21.
13 Luke 2.14.

adolescence, the fourth young manhood, the fifth is middle age, and the sixth is that very old age which is also called decrepitude. Therefore, let it not seem strange to you when you hear that this world is covered in six ages, when you see the same thing fulfilled in the lives of men. In these six ages of the world, as in the six water-jars, prophecy was not wanting. For this reason those water-jars were filled with the mysteries of the Old Testament, but when Christ was not understood in them, not wine, but water was drunk from them.

(2) Now the first water-jar was fulfilled in the days of Adam, when: 'The Lord cast a deep sleep upon him: and he took one of his ribs and made it into a woman.'[1] What else did it then signify, except the Passion of our Lord and Savior? Adam sleeps and a rib is taken from his side to form Eve. When He bowed His head upon the cross, Christ slept and the Church was formed from His side. Now when He was pierced in the side: 'There came out blood and water';[2] the blood of Redemption, and the water of Baptism. Just as though, brethren, God in reality could not have made Eve from the same source from which He had created Adam. However, even then in that old Adam, from whose rib Eve was made, was signified the new Adam from whose side the Church was to be formed. Now because in that prophecy the Jewish people did not understand Christ, it tasted water and not wine.

(3) The second water-jar was fulfilled in Noe, in whose day the human race was saved through the mystery of the ark or the deluge. In the same way the whole world was rescued from eternal death through the mystery of the cross or of Baptism at the coming of our Lord and Savior.

(4) The third water-jar was fulfilled in Abraham, whom the Lord commanded to offer his own son as a holocaust in likeness to our Lord and Savior. For just as blessed Isaac then carried his own wood to the place of sacrifice, so Christ, the

---

1 Cf. Gen. 2.21, 22.
2 John 19.34.

true Isaac, bore the gibbet of His own cross to the site of His Passion.

(5) The fourth water-jar was fulfilled in David, who prefigured Christ our Lord in humility and meekness and in many tribulations. Among other things which our Lord deigned to say through him, He even exclaimed this: 'Rise, O Lord; judge the earth.'[3] To what God is it said, 'Rise,' except to one who has been asleep? 'Rise, O Lord,' he says, 'judge the earth.' You slept when you were judged by the earth; arise, to judge the earth, so that what the same Scriptures predicted may be fulfilled in you: 'For yours are all the nations.'[4]

(6) The fifth water-jar was fulfilled in the days of Daniel, who said that he saw: 'A stone hewn from a mountain without a hand being put to it,'[5] and that the stone grew until it filled the whole face of the earth. See, brethren, that the mountain from which the stone was cut did not fill the whole earth, while the stone which was cut out did fill it. That mountain signified the kingdom of the Jews, and from this mountain a stone was cut, that is, Christ was born. When it says, 'without a hand being put to it,' we understand this, without any effort of the bridegroom, for works are recognized by the hands. For this reason the mountain, that is, the kingdom of the Jews, did not fill the earth, because before Christ came 'in Juda' only was 'God renowned.'[6] But after Christ came, His grace filled the whole world to such an extent that: 'The sound' of the apostles 'resounds through all the earth, and their message to the ends of the world.'[7]

(7) The sixth water-jar was fulfilled through blessed John the Baptist, for when he saw the Jews coming to his Baptism he said to them: 'Brood of vipers! who has shown you how to flee from the wrath to come? Bring forth therefore fruits befitting repentance, for God is able out of these stones to raise

---
3 Ps. 81.8.
4 *Ibid.*
5 Dan. 2.34.
6 Ps. 75.2.
7 Ps. 18.5.

up children to Abraham.'⁸ What stones did he want to be recognized as those from which children of Abraham could be raised? What ones, to be sure, except all nations? And why were the nations stones? How could they not be stones, when they cared for stones? But someone may say: If some people care for stones, are they, therefore, stones? Listen to the Scriptures say: 'Their makers shall be like them, everyone that trusts in them.'⁹ For this reason those six ages of the world, like the six water-jars, were filled by the servants, that is, by the patriarchs and prophets. At His coming Christ did not throw away that water and add others, but He changed that same water into wine. Why is this? Because He did not come 'To destroy the Law, but to fulfill.'¹⁰ He did not reject the Old Testament and thus build the New; but what tasted like water in the letter of the Law He changed into wine and thus made it spiritually understood.

(8) Finally, before the coming of Christ, the Old Testament was water to this degree, that those who read it and did not recognize Christ were called foolish by Christ the Lord Himself. For after the Passion of our Lord, as two of His disciples were traveling, anxious to go to the small town by the name of Emmaus, our Lord and Savior joined them and said to them: 'What words are these that you are exchanging as you walk and are sad?'¹¹ And among other things they replied to him: 'Concerning Jesus of Nazareth, who was a prophet, mighty in work and word.'¹² O blessed disciples, the faith in you is so weak that you call the Lord of the prophets a prophet? Did you not hear the blessed Apostle Peter confess Him in that way? Do you not remember what Peter replied when the Lord questioned him? 'Thou art the Christ,' he said, 'the Son of the living God.'¹³ He confessed Him to be the Son of the living

---

8 Matt. 3.7-9.
9 Ps. 113B.8.
10 Matt. 5.17.
11 Luke 24.17.
12 Luke 24.19.
13 Matt. 16.16.

God, and do you believe He was a prophet? And yet this name may be applied to our Lord and Savior, according to what Moses said: 'The Lord your God will raise up a prophet whom you will hear as Me. If any man will not hear that prophet, he will be expelled from the people.'[14] Moreover, when those disciples said this they did not believe that Christ was the true God at all. Finally, see what they said: 'We were hoping that it was he who should redeem Israel.'[15] O disciples, you were hoping: do you now despair? The robber said on the cross: 'Lord, remember me when thou comest into thy kingdom';[16] and you say: 'but we were hoping.' Behold, you did not even believe that He would rise from the dead, and the robber already believed that He would reign. Therefore, since faith had grown so cold in the disciples that they spoke such words, the Lord replied and said: 'O foolish ones and slow of heart to believe!'[17] Why were they foolish? Because they were still drinking water; Christ had not yet spiritually changed the water into wine. And what did the Lord add after this? 'Thus is it not written, that thus the Christ should suffer, and should rise again from the dead on the third day; and that repentance and remission of sins should be preached in his name to all the nations? And beginning with Moses and with all the Prophets, he interpreted to them in all the Scriptures the things referring to himself.'[18] When He interpreted the Scriptures to them, then the water was changed into wine. Finally, when they drank the water, those who said concerning Christ: 'But we were hoping that it was he who should redeem Israel,'[19] were cold water. But after He changed the water to wine by interpreting the Scriptures for them, they no longer spoke unbelief as though they were cold or lukewarm, but glowing with the Holy Spirit they preached faith in God, saying: 'Was not our

---

14 Cf. Deut. 18.18, 19.
15 Luke 24.21.
16 Luke 23.42.
17 Luke 24.25.
18 Luke 24.26, 46, 47, 27.
19 Luke 24.21.

heart burning within us while he was speaking on the road and explaining to us the Scriptures?'[20] For now through the grace of Christ, who had interpreted the Scriptures for them, they had drunk spiritual wine. Therefore, their heart glowed with the love of Christ, because He had kindled within them that fire of which He Himself said: 'I have come to cast fire upon the earth, and what will I but that it be kindled?'[21] He had given them a taste of that new wine with which He deigned to spiritually fill the blessed apostles on Pentecost, and for this reason they said: 'Was not our heart burning within us because of Jesus?'[22]

(9) Now we ought not to consider carelessly, dearest brethren, what we read about those water-jars, because they held 'each two or three measures.'[23] He did not say: 'They each held two or three measures,' so that some might take two measures and others three; but he said of all that: 'They held each two or three measures.' Moreover, since this cannot be understood literally, let us see what we can believe spiritually in them. We already said above that the water which was in the water-jars can be taken as prophecy and the Old Testament; why, then, two or three measures? Doubtless, because of the mystery of the Trinity. But why two? Because of the two precepts of charity. In the Law and the Prophets, not only the mystery of the Trinity is recognized, but the two precepts of charity are also preached continually. Let us further see whether we can find the two or three measures in the Gospel. 'I and the Father are one,'[24] it says; behold you have two. Give the three also: 'Go,' it says, 'baptize all nations in the name of the Father, and of the Son, and of the Holy Spirit';[25] see, you have three.

(10) What Christ effected in the apostles, beloved brethren, He has also deigned to fulfill in us, that we who were luke-

---

20 Luke 24.32.
21 Luke 12.49.
22 Luke 24.32.
23 John 2.6.
24 John 10.30.
25 Cf. Matt. 28.19.

warm or cold with unbelief now glow with faith and merit to be in the service of God. Therefore, with His help, let us labor as much as we can, so that we may deserve to persevere to the end in our good works. Let us endeavor to exercise ourselves continually in the lessons of Sacred Scripture, so that we may be able to say with the prophet: 'You have given us stupefying wine';[26] and again: 'My cup overflows'![27] For just as our water was changed into wine through the love of God, so on the contrary we ought to fear that by loving the world and choosing its pleasures our wine may be changed again into water. Therefore, let us engage in good works as much as we can and beseech the mercy of God that He Himself may in His goodness preserve His works and His benefits in us: who lives and reigns together with the Father and the Holy Spirit forever and ever. Amen.

* *Sermon 170*

On the Samaritan Woman, and On Not Postponing Baptism

(1) In the Gospel lesson the holy evangelist has shown us most abundantly that our Lord Jesus Christ assumed the weakness of the human race. Indeed, when he said that the Lord came: 'To a town of Samaria called Sichar, near the field that Jacob gave to his son Joseph, and Jacob's well was there,' he added: 'wearied as he was from the journey, Jesus was sitting at the well.'[1] Our Lord Jesus Christ came to the field which holy Jacob had left to his son, Joseph. I do not think that this field was left to Joseph as much as to Christ, whom holy Joseph the patriarch prefigured, for truly the sun and moon adore Him, while all the stars bless Him. For this reason the Lord came to this field, in order that the Samaritans, who were

---
26 Ps. 59.5.
27 Ps. 22.5.

---
1 John 4.5, 6.

longing to claim for themselves the inheritance of the patriarch of Israel, might recognize their owner and be converted to Christ who became the legitimate heir of the patriarch.

(2) 'Wearied as he was from the journey,' it says, 'Jesus was sitting at the well.' Notice the difference in the mystery. When He was in the midst of the apostles He rejoiced in spirit; when He was situated on the mountain He not only consoled them, but even revealed to them His own glory; when He was located in Samaria, wearied as He was from the journey, He was sitting at the well. Could the power of God be exhausted? Certainly not. But he was wearied because He could not find the people faithful. Christ was wearied, then, because He recognized no virtue in His people. Today, too, our disobedience wearies Him, as does also our weakness. For we are weak when we do not pursue the things which are strong and enduring, but follow what is temporal and fleeting. It says indeed: 'He was sitting at the well,' but He was not resting, for He could not rest among the Samaritans. 'And it was about the sixth hour,'[2] it continues. On the sixth day God formed man out of the slime of the earth, and at the sixth hour He came to visit Samaria in order that the Samaritans might believe in Him and He Himself might begin to rest in them. Then, He might celebrate that true sabbath of rest, and for this reason the Lord 'was sitting at the well.'

(3) 'And there came a Samaritan woman to draw water.'[3] It is a great mystery. The woman came to the well and found a spring which she did not expect. 'The Lord said to her, "Give me to drink." '[4] The good Lord spontaneously offers Himself to her even though she did not ask it, in order to fulfill that prophecy: 'I appeared openly to those who sought me not, I was found by those who asked me not.'[5] He asks her, even though He intends to give her to drink; He sat at the well so that we might not look for water in a high place; but might

---
2 Ibid.
3 John 4.7.
4 Ibid.
5 Cf. Isa. 65.1.

draw draughts that are salutary for us from the fountain which surpasses all waters. What is this fountain, except our Lord Jesus Christ, to whom it is said: 'For with you is the fountain of life, and in your light we see light'?[6] It is a good fountain which cools us after the heat of this life, and with its flood tempers the aridity of our heart.

(4) Then He says to the woman: 'If thou didst know the gift of God, and who it is who says to thee, "Give me to drink," thou, perhaps, wouldst have asked of him, and he would have given thee living water.'[7] Not all men know the gift of God, because not all desire the living water, for if they did desire it they would never postpone the sacrament of Baptism. Therefore, they pass judgment on themselves and give testimony of their life, if they want to be baptized later in order that they may commit many sins and crimes. Do not delay, O man, the remedies of your salvation, because you do not know when your soul may be demanded of you. Finally, the Samaritan woman, who was ignorant of the mystery, said: 'Sir, thou hast no pail for drawing water, and the well is deep.'[8] Before the coming of the Lord, the well was also deep, and without a pail no one could draw water for himself. Our Lord, the living fountain, came to cleanse the hearts of all people, to quench their thirst, and to satisfy their souls. Moreover, He did not look for a pail to draw the water, but of His own accord poured Himself into the minds of each one. And He added: 'Everyone who drinks of this water will thirst again. He, however, who drinks of the water that I will give him shall never thirst; but it shall become in him a fountain of water, springing up unto life everlasting.'[9] Christ teaches one Baptism, for after entrance into the eternal fountain and the mystery of the heavenly draught He does not allow any one of us to thirst. Now since divine mercy has bestowed upon us so many benefits without any preceding merits on our part, for this reason

---
6 Ps. 35.10.
7 John 4.10.
8 Cf. John 4.11.
9 John 4.13, 14.

let us labor as much as we can and with His help, so that the favor of such great goodness may bring us progress and not judgment. May He Himself deign to grant this, to whom is honor and glory forever and ever. Amen.

Sermon 171

On the Pool of Siloe

(1) The passage of the holy Gospel which speaks about the pool of Siloe, beloved brethren, addresses us in particular, because we are freed from all the listlessness of sin through the grace of Baptism. Just as that paralytic whom the Lord cured was weak in all his members so that he could accomplish no good act, so before the coming of our Lord the entire human race was weakened interiorly in soul by the paralysis of sin. Before the coming of the Savior, the human race was so feeble that it could do nothing that was connected with faith and mercy or even justice. But just as that paralytic who was overwhelmed with weakness was lifted up at the word of the heavenly physician, so the entire human race which was sick interiorly in soul, almost even to the point of death, was recalled to its former state of health at the coming of our Lord and Savior. Now the couch on which that paralytic lay typified the human body, while the paralytic himself prefigured the soul. For just as that paralytic lay on the couch in a weakened condition, so also the soul of man reposed languid in his body. But what did our Lord, the physician and Savior, say to him? 'Rise,' He said, 'take up thy pallet and walk.'[1] What does this mean, take up thy pallet, except carry and govern your body? Conduct that which carried you: for when you were under the dominion of sin your flesh first carried you to evil, but now

---
1 John 5.8.

since grace is in control you conduct and direct your body to what is good. In the wrong and wicked order your flesh was first in control and the soul served, but now through the mercy of Christ the soul holds sway and the flesh is subject to it in servitude. 'Rise, take up thy pallet and go into thy house.'[2] When you were thrown out of your house, that is, out of the land of paradise at the intervention of sin, your flesh hurled you down into the world. But now through the gift of divine mercy take up your pallet and in every good work govern your little body, and return to your house, that is, return to eternal life on the path of justice. Before sin our house was eternal life, and from it we were thrown into the exile of this world. Therefore, when you hear it said to the paralytic: 'Take up thy pallet and go into thy house,' believe that it is said to you: govern your flesh in all chastity and return to paradise, as if to your own home and your original country.

(2) In the fact that many people lay in those five porticoes and only one was cured, the unity of the Catholic Church is prefigured. That pool typified Baptism. Unity descended and was cured; only one came down and was healed in the Church. What does it mean to come down, except humbly to believe in Christ crucified? For the human race which fell down from paradise through pride rises again by humbly descending in Baptism.

(3) Therefore, dearest brethren, preserve the sacrament of Baptism within you. Avoid drunkenness as a pit of hell; fear greatly pride, envy, and vanity as the sword of the devil. Do not speak ill of another, because it is written: 'He who speaks ill of his brother shall be rooted up.'[3] Do not slander, because we read: 'Nor the evil-tongued will possess the kingdom of God.'[4] Do not bear false witness, for it is written: 'The false

---

[2] Cf. John 5.8.
[3] Cf. Prov. 20.13. Dom Morin notes that this quotation is cited in this way rather frequently by Caesarius, Jerome, and others, although it shows little similarity to the original version.
[4] 1 Cor. 6.10.

witness will not go unpunished.'[5] Do not lie to one another, because of what we read: 'A lying mouth slays the soul.'[6] Do not retain hatred for each other, because it is written: 'Everyone who hates his brother is a murderer.'[7] Do not commit theft, and do not practice deceit in any kind of business. Go to church rather frequently, respecting and loving your priests. Pay tithes even out of your poverty, and give alms according to your ability. By telling you these truths I absolve myself in the sight of God and His angels. Moreover, if you willingly listen to the things which we have said and, with God's help, strive to fulfill them faithfully, you will both give me joy and prepare for yourselves a kingdom: with the help of our Lord Jesus Christ, who lives and reigns forever and ever. Amen.

Sermon 172

On the Man Born Blind

(1) When the Gospel was read just now, dearest brethren, we heard that Jesus gave sight to the man who was blind from birth. Why do you wonder? Jesus is the Savior. If Jesus is the Savior, He did something in keeping with His name, for by His kindness He restored what He had given to a lesser degree in the womb. Now when He made his eyes less powerful, surely He did not make a mistake, but He deferred it for the miracle. Do you perhaps say to me: How do you know this? We have heard it from Him, for when the disciples questioned Jesus Christ, saying: 'Lord, who has sinned, this man or his parents, that he should be born blind?'[1] He replied to them: 'Neither has this man sinned, nor his parents, but the works of God

---
5 Prov. 19.9.
6 Wisd. 1.11.
7 1 John 3.15.

---
1 John 9.2.

were to be shown in him.'² Behold, why Christ delayed when He made the eyes less powerful in the womb. Do not think, brethren, that the parents of that blind man had no sin, and that the blind man himself, when he was born, did not contract original sin; because of the fact of original sin even very little children are baptized. However, that blindness was not due to the sin of his parents nor due to the sin of the blind man, but in order that the glory of God might be made manifest in him. For when we are born we all contract original sin, and still we are not born physically blind. That blind man, brethren, was prepared as a salve for the human race: he was bodily restored to light, in order that by considering his miracle we might be enlightened in heart.

(2) Now although the blind man was illuminated, he still erred. Perhaps you may say: In what did he err? First of all, because he thought Christ was a prophet. Then we heard his reply, which without any doubt is false, for he said: 'We know that God does not hear sinners.'³ If God does not hear sinners, what hope do we have, or why do we pray? Do not be afraid, brethren. That man who said that God does not hear sinners was still blind in heart and he lied; he was, indeed, bodily enlightened, but he was still blind in spirit. If God does not hear sinners, where is that publican who went up into the temple with the Pharisee? While that Pharisee was boastfully publishing his own merits, the publican stood afar off and kept his eyes fixed on the ground, striking his breast and confessing his sins. And he departed from the temple justified, rather than that Pharisee. Surely, God hears sinners, brethren. However, the man who said that had not yet washed the face of his heart in Siloe. The mystery had gone ahead in his eyes, but the benefits of grace had not yet affected his heart; he had, indeed, received bodily sight, but had not yet recovered the eyes of his heart. When, then, did the blind man recover the eyes of his heart? When he was sent out by the Jews. He found the Lord,

---
2 John 9.3.
3 John 9.31.

who admitted him to Himself. 'He found him,' surely because he looked for Him; and He said to him: 'Dost thou believe in the Son of God?' And the blind man replied: 'Who is he, Lord, that I may believe in him?' And Jesus said to him: 'I am he who speaks with thee.'[4] The blind man did not hesitate; he immediately washed the face of his heart, and he saw. To recover bodily sight he washed his face in Siloe; in order to see with the eyes of his heart he believed in Christ the Lord. That pool of Siloe typified our Lord and Savior, because Siloe is interpreted as one who has been sent. Who is the one who has been sent, except Christ, who said: 'I was not sent except to the lost sheep of the house of Israel';[5] and again: 'I do the will of my father who sent me'?[6] For this reason Christ was that pool of Siloe. That blind man listened, and adored, and believed; he washed his face, and with his bodily eyes saw Christ the Lord.

(3) Now in order to effect cures our Lord only spoke and did nothing with His hands. As a result of this there was open calumny among the Jews, because they falsely accused Him when He spoke, just as though the Jews themselves did not speak on the sabbath. We might say that, not only on the sabbath, but on no day did the unhappy Jews speak, since they withdrew from praises of the true God. In reality how can they speak, when they have denied the word of God and there is fulfilled in them what Christ had predicted concerning them: 'Let dumbness strike their lying lips that speak insolence against the just in pride and scorn'?[7] This was especially prophesied concerning Christ and the Jews. Therefore, Christ 'Spat on the ground and made clay with the spittle.'[8] In the ground we understand the Law, and grace is designated in the spittle. What does the Law effect without grace, O unhappy Jews? What does the ground do without the spittle of Christ?

---

4 Cf. John 9.35-37.
5 Matt. 15.24.
6 Cf. John 4.34.
7 Cf. Ps. 30.19.
8 John 9.6.

What does the Law do without grace, except make men still more guilty? Why? Because the Law knows how to obey, but not how to help; the Law can point out sin, but it cannot take sin away from man. [Therefore, let the spittle of Christ go down to the ground and gather together the earth. Let He who made the earth remake it, and He who created it reform and recreate it. Likewise, in the spittle is understood the word of God, His real human body on earth. For this reason let the spittle of Christ come down, in order that the earth may be gathered up: let the grace of Christ come, in order that the Law may be fulfilled.] 'He made clay with the spittle.' What is spittle mixed with clay, except the Incarnate Word? That blind man presented an image of the whole human race, and, therefore, the spittle was mixed with clay and the blind man was made to see: the Word became incarnate and the world was illumined.

(4) Now, beloved brethren, since we in Christ have recovered the eyes of the heart which we had lost in Adam, let us give abundant thanks to Him who deigned to enlighten us to behold Him, without any preceding merits on our part. Let us endeavor, with as much strength as we can and with His help, to open our eyes to the good and close them to evil, according to what the prophet begs of the Lord when he says: 'Turn away my eyes from seeing what is vain.'[9] Who lives and reigns forever and ever. Amen.

* *Sermon 173*

The Bishop, Augustine, on What Is Written:
'He Who Loves His Life, Loses It.'[1]

(1) When the divine lesson was read just now, brethren, we

---
9 Ps. 118.37.

---
1 John 12.25.

heard the Lord say: 'He who loves his life, loses it.' What the Apostle says seems, as it were, to be contrary to this thought: 'No one ever hated his own flesh.'[2] Therefore, if there is no one who hates his own flesh, how much more so is it that there is no one who hates his own soul? Surely, the soul is much preferred to the body, since it is the inhabitant, while the body is the dwelling. Moreover, the soul is in domination, while the body serves; the soul is the superior and the body the subject. Therefore, if no one ever hates his body, who is there who hates his soul? For this reason the present Gospel passage has proposed a not small question to us when we heard: 'He who loves his life, loses it.' It is dangerous to love one's life, lest it perish. But if it is dangerous for you to love your life for the reason that it might perish, therefore, you ought not to love it, because you do not want it to perish. Moreover, if you do not want it to perish, you love it. What is this? If I love, I perish; therefore, let me not love, so I will not perish. But because I am afraid to perish, for this reason I do not love, and still, since I am afraid of perishing, I love. The Lord also says elsewhere: 'What does it profit a man, if he gain the whole world, but suffer the loss of his own soul?'[3] Behold, the soul is to be loved in such a way that it is preferred to the gain of the whole world. And still the man who loves his own soul should notice that if he loves it, he will lose it. Do you not want it to perish? Do not love it. But if you do not want it to perish, you cannot fail to love it.

(2) There are people who love their own soul wrongly. The word of God wants to correct them to this end, not that they may hate their soul, but that they may love it rightly. By loving it wickedly they destroy it and it becomes, as it were, a great confusion and contradiction. Nevertheless, it is true that if you love it wickedly you destroy it, but if you hate it rightly you preserve it. So there is a wicked love of your soul and a correct hate of it. Love is perverted by hatred, while hatred is

---

2 Eph. 5.29.
3 Matt. 16.26.

corrected by love. What is a perverse love for the soul? When you love your soul in sin. Listen to the fact that love which arises from hatred is wicked love: 'But he who loves iniquity hates his own soul.'[4] See what a correct hatred is which comes from love, when the Lord continues there and says: 'But he who hates his life in this world, will find it unto life everlasting.'[5] Surely, you love very much what you wish to find in eternal life. For of what advantage is what you love in time? Either you will be taken away from it, or it will be removed from you. When you are withdrawn the lover himself perishes, and when that is taken away, what you loved perishes. Therefore, love should not be placed there, where either the lover or what is loved perishes. But what is to be loved? What can remain with us in eternity. If you want to keep your soul safe forever, hate it in time. For this reason a right hatred comes from love, and perverse love proceeds from hate.

(3) What, then, is the measure in loving life? Do you think that the martyrs did not love their life? Surely, you see how, when a man's life is endangered in this present world, his friends hurry on his behalf. They run to the church and entreat the bishop to intercede if he has influence; they ask him to hurry and run. Why? Because of life. Moreover, they all tremble, and believing that haste is necessary, they forego all other matters. All haste is praised, and every delay is blamed. Why? For the sake of life. What does it mean, for the sake of life? So a man will not die. Did not the martyrs know how to love their life? And still this is for the sake of life, lest a man die. The death of man is a calamity. If you run a hundred miles for this life, how many miles should you run for the sake of eternal life? If you hasten to acquire a profit for a few days, and those uncertain—for if a man is freed from death today, he does not know whether he will die tomorrow—if you hurry so much for the profit of a few days, because very few are the days even to old age, how should we hasten for

---
4 Cf. Ps. 10.6.
5 Cf. John 12.25.

the sake of eternal life? And still in this matter men are listless: with difficulty will you find a man who will even move a foot slowly for the sake of eternal life. Therefore, a perverse love of life abounds, but very few possess a correct love. For just as there is no one who does not love his soul, so there is no one who does not love his body. Thus, it happens that what the Apostle said is true: 'No one ever hated his own flesh,'[6] and the soul is not loved. Therefore, brethren, let us learn how to love our souls. Every pleasure of the world is transitory. There is salutary love and harmful love, for love may be hindered by love. Let harmful love withdraw, and salutary love take its place. Because men do not want it to depart, for this reason the other cannot enter them. They are full, so they cannot take any more; they should pour it out, in order that they may be able to receive. They are, indeed, full of the love of carnal pleasures, they are filled with love for the present life, they are full of love for silver and gold, possessions of this world. Now when men are full they are like vases. Do you want honey to go in where you have not yet removed the vinegar? Pour out what you have, in order that you may be able to receive what you do not possess. First, there must be a renunciation of this world, and then conversion to God. When a man renounces himself he empties himself, and when he is converted he is filled. Moreover, this should take place, not only in the body, but also in the heart.

(4) Perhaps you may ask, brethren, how this love grows: for it has its beginning, its increase, and its perfection. Now we ought to know who has begun, so that we may encourage him to growth; also who has not begun, so we may advise him how to begin; finally, who has begun and increased, so that we may urge him to perfection. Let your charity first notice this: all loves and affections in man first come from himself, and then to another object which they love. If you love gold you love yourself first and then the gold, because if you are dead there will be no one to possess the gold. Therefore, the

---
6 Eph. 5.29.

love of every man begins with himself and cannot arise except from himself. Moreover, no one is advised to love himself, for this not only is in the nature of man, but also exists in the beasts. For you see, brethren, how not only the huge animals and large beasts, like oxen and camels or elephants, but even flies and the smallest worms do not want to die and love themselves. All creatures flee from death. Therefore, they love themselves and want to preserve themselves: some by speed, others by disguise, by resisting or attacking. All animals fight for their life, do not wish to die, and want to protect themselves. For this reason they love themselves. Another also begins to be loved. What is that other? Whatever you love; this is either the same as yourself, below you, or above you. If what you love is beneath you, love it to comfort it, to take care of it, to use it, but not to adhere to it. For example, you love gold. Do not become attached to the gold, for how much better are you than the gold? Gold, indeed, is a shining piece of earth, while you have been made to the image of God in order that you may be illumined by the Lord. Although gold is a creature of God, still God did not make it according to His own image, but you He did; therefore, He put the gold beneath you. This kind of love should be despised. Those things are to be acquired for their usefulness, but we should not cling to them with the bond of love as if with glue. Do not make for yourself members over which, when they have begun to be cut away, you will grieve and be afflicted. What then? Rise from that love with which you love things that are lower than you, and begin to love your equals, that is, things that are what you are. But what need is there of many words? If you will, you can understand briefly.

(5) The Lord Himself has told us in the Gospel and clearly showed us in what order we may have true love and charity. For He spoke thus: 'Thou shalt love the Lord thy God with thy whole heart, and with thy whole soul, and with thy whole strength; and thy neighbor as thyself.'[7] Therefore, first love

---
7 Luke 10.27.

God and then yourself; after these love your neighbor as yourself. First learn how to love yourself, and then love your neighbor as yourself; for if you do not know how to love yourself, how will you be able to love your neighbor in truth? Now some men think that they love themselves in the lawful order when they seize the property of another, get drunk, are slaves of lust, and acquire unjust profits through different kinds of deceit. Such men should listen to the Scriptures say: 'He who loves iniquity hates his own soul.'[8] If by loving iniquity, then, you not only do not love yourself but even hate, how will you be able to love either God or your neighbor? Therefore, if you wish to observe the order of true charity, exercise justice, love mercy, and avoid dissipation; according to the Lord's precept begin to love, not only your friends, but even your enemies. When you faithfully strive to observe this with all your heart, you will be able to ascend by those virtues as if by steps, and then you will merit to love God with your whole soul and with all your strength. After you come to that happy state of perfection, you will consider all the pleasures of this world as dung, and with the prophet you will be able to say: 'But for me, to be near God is my good.'[9]

* *Sermon 174*

On the Blessing of Peace, From the Gospel of John

(1) Here is a word of our Lord: 'My peace I give to you, my peace I leave with you.'[1] As we are about to speak of peace, let us first see what the holy rewards of peace are. Peace, indeed, is serenity of mind, tranquillity of soul, simplicity of

---

8 Cf. Ps. 10.6.
9 Ps. 72.28.

---

1 John 14.27.

heart, the bond of love, the fellowship of charity. This it is which removes hatred, settles wars, restrains wrath, tramples upon pride, loves the humble, pacifies the discordant, makes enemies agree. For it is pleasing to everyone. It does not seek what belongs to another or consider anything as its own. It teaches men to love, because it does not know how to get angry, or to extol itself, or become inflated with pride. It is meek and humble to all men, possessing rest and tranquillity within itself. When the peace of Christ is exercised by a Christian, it is brought to perfection by Christ. If a man loves it he will be an heir of God, while anyone who despises it rebels against Christ. When our Lord Jesus Christ was returning to the Father, He left His peace to his followers as their inherited good, teaching them and saying: 'My peace I give to you, my peace I leave with you.' Anyone who has received this peace should keep it, and one who has destroyed it should look for it, while anyone who has lost it should seek it. For if a man is not found with it, he will be disinherited by the Father and deprived of his inheritance.

(2) Either tomorrow, or certainly on Sunday, you will without any physical weariness more fittingly hear the things which follow concerning the good man who brings forth good things out of the treasure of his heart: with the help of our Lord Jesus Christ, to whom is honor and glory forever and ever. Amen.

* *Sermon 175*

On the Gospel Lesson Where the Lord Appeared to His Disciples When the Doors were Closed; Also Against Heretics Who Baptize a Second Time

(1) Some men are wont to ask, concerning the Gospel text which was read to us, dearest brethren, how our Lord and

Savior could appear to His disciples when the doors were closed. Some are so stirred by this fact that they almost run into danger by summoning the judgments of their own reasoning against the divine miracles. For thus they argue: If there was a body, there was also flesh, and if flesh, bones, too. Now if what hung on the cross arose from the grave, how could it enter through closed doors? If it was not possible, they say, it was not done; and if it could, how could it? If you understand the manner, it is not a miracle; and if it does not seem to be a miracle, you approach denial that He arose from the grave. Look at the miracles of your Lord from the very beginning, and give me individual reasons for them. No man came near and a virgin conceived: give me a reasonable explanation how the virgin conceived without a man. Reason fails there where there is the edifice of faith. Behold, you have one miracle in the conception of the Lord; listen to it also in the birth. A virgin gave birth, yet remained a virgin. Even then, before He arose, the Lord was born through closed doors, for He produced the members of an infant through the undefiled virginal womb, just as He later brought the members of a young man in through closed doors.

(2) You ask me and say: If He entered through closed doors, where is the bulk of His body? And I reply: If He walked upon the sea, where was the weight of His body? But the Lord did that as the Lord. Did He, then, because He arose, cease to be the Lord? What about the fact that He also made Peter walk upon the sea? What divinity could do in the one, faith fulfilled in the other. Christ was able to do it, and Peter could because Christ willed it. Therefore, when you begin to examine the reasonableness of miracles by your human senses, fear that you may lose your faith. Do you not know that nothing is impossible for God? So when anyone tells you: If He entered through closed doors there was no body, answer him on the contrary: Nay, if He was touched there was a body, and if He ate there was a body. The one thing He did by a miracle, the other by nature. Is not the daily course of nature itself to be

admired? Everything is full of miracles, but they have become of trifling value because of their frequency. Give me a reasonable explanation—I will ask something about the usual and the ordinary—give a reasonable explanation as to why the seed of such a large fig tree is so small that it can scarcely be seen, while the lowly gourd produces such a large seed. If you consider, and look with your mind and not your eyes, in that very small grain of the seed of the fig tree, in that littleness and narrow space the root lies hidden and the strength is imbedded. The future leaves are already begun, and the fruit which is going to appear on the tree has already been sent ahead in the seed. It is not necessary to examine many things. No one gives a reasonable explanation for everyday matters, and do you ask me for an explanation of miracles? Therefore, read the Gospel and believe the facts which are miraculous. What God creates is still more, and we do not wonder that He exceeds all of His works. There was nothing and there now exists a world.

(3) But, you say, the bulk of a body could not enter through doors which were closed. How great was that bulk, I ask you? Surely as much as there is in men. As much as there is in a camel? Definitely not that much. Read the Gospel and listen to the Lord Himself: 'A camel more easily enters through the eye of a needle, than a rich man enters the kingdom of God.'[1] When they heard this the disciples despaired of salvation for the rich. But what did He reply to the disciples when they were sad? 'Things that are impossible with men are very easy for God.'[2] God can transfer a camel through the eye of a needle, and He can also bring a rich man into the kingdom of heaven. Why do you falsely accuse me because of the closed doors? Closed doors have some kind of a crack, and compare the crack of doors to the eye of a needle. Compare the bulk of human flesh to the huge size of camels, and do not falsely accuse the miracle of divine power.

---
1 Cf. Luke 18.25.
2 Cf. Luke 18.27.

(4) You, brethren, who were sons of darkness and have merited to become sons of light, rejoice because, as the Evangelist says: 'It has pleased your Father to give you the kingdom.'³ In the Gospel pages, as if by a marriage contract, our mother was united to her heavenly spouse. She knows no other man, she does not know any adulterer, she hates the husband of another. At a single birth she filled her womb with her young: she knew how to bear a child once, but does not know how to beget another. Moreover, unhappy is the heretic who draws the children already born through the womb of another. He does not give life, but kills, according to that Gospel text: 'Can a man enter a second time into his mother's womb and be born again?'⁴ O impious presumption of heretics! Restrain your hands from that wicked crime, if you want to recall to the womb a son that is already born. Although you want to destroy the man by sacrilege, you are doing violence to the spiritual nature; you are attacking the common rights of birth and the law of all life. If carnal generation cannot be sought a second time, how can spiritual birth be repeated? The Apostle says: 'One God, one faith, one Baptism.'⁵

(5) Since we have merited to be freed from the power of the devil through the grace of Christ and without any preceding merits of our own, dearest brethren, let us endeavor as much as we can with His help always to engage in good works. Let us further fear what is written: 'Behold, thou art cured; sin no more, lest something worse befall thee';⁶ and what the Apostle Peter proclaims in terrible words: 'If after escaping the defilements of the world they are again entangled therein and overcome, their latter state has become worse for them than the former.'⁷ The Apostle Paul also attests this: 'If a man again touches a corpse after he has bathed, what did he gain

---

3 Luke 12.32.
4 Cf. John 3.4.
5 Eph. 4.5.
6 John 5.14.
7 2 Peter 2.20.

by the purification?'⁸ As great as what we have received is, we ought to preserve it with even greater care and solicitation. It is a serious matter for a pagan to refuse the grace of God, but it is no less grave for a Christian to accept it and then to lose it. For not only the dignity of the title Christian makes a man a Christian. It is not at all profitable for you to be called it in name if you do not show it in deed. Thus, the Lord Himself also said in the Gospel: 'Why do you call me, "Lord, Lord," and not practise the things that I say?'⁹ For this reason let us strive to live so chastely, justly, and piously that when we come before the tribunal of the eternal judge, we may not be punished with the wicked and sinners, but may deserve to arrive at eternal rewards together with the just and those who fear God: with the help of our Lord, to whom is honor and might forever and ever. Amen.

Sermon 176

A Homily Taken From a Work of the Bishop,
St. Augustine, on the Vision of Blessed Peter, the Apostle,
and Cornelius, the Centurion

(1) When the text from the Acts of the Apostles was read just now, we heard that blessed 'Peter went to the upper room about the sixth hour; but he got very hungry, and wanted something to eat. But while the disciples were getting it ready, he fell into an ecstasy, and saw a large vessel like a great sheet, weighed down at the four corners and let down from heaven; and in it were all the four-footed beasts and creeping things of the earth. And a voice from heaven sounded, "Peter, kill and eat." But he said, "Lord, thou knowest that never did I eat anything common or unclean." And there came a voice a

---
8 Ecclus. 34.25. Caesarius credits St. Paul with this quotation, but, as Dom Morin notes, these actually are words from Ecclesiasticus.
9 Luke 6.46.

second time, "What God has cleansed, do not thou call common." This happened three times, and the vessel was taken up into heaven.'[1] Now what these things signify we are willing to reveal briefly to the ears of your charity, if you bid us do so. All the animals which the Jews are forbidden to eat are signs of things and, as it is said: 'Shadows of things to come.'[2] For it is written to them that they should eat animals which chew their cud and with a cloven hoof, while those which lack one or both of these qualities they should not eat. In these animals are signified certain men who do not belong to the company of the saints, for the cloven hoof refers to a good life, while chewing the cud is related to wisdom. Why does a cloven hoof refer to a good life? Because it slips only with difficulty, and falling is a sign of the sinner. Moreover, how is chewing the cud related to the wisdom of doctrine? Because Scripture said: 'Precious treasure rests in the mouth of the wise, but the fool consumes it.'[3] Therefore, when a man listens and then becomes forgetful through carelessness, he, as it were, destroys what he heard, so that he no longer tastes it in his mouth, burying the lesson itself in oblivion. But if a man meditates on the Law of the Lord both day and night, he, as it were, chews his cud, delighting in the taste of the word, as in the palate of the heart. For this reason what was commanded to the Jews signifies that men do not belong to the Church, that is, to the body of Christ and the pleasant company of the saints if they are careless listeners or lead a wicked life or are rebuked for both vices. Thus, the other things which were given to the Jews as commands in this way are shadowy expressions of things to come. After our Lord Jesus Christ, the light of the world, came, they were read only for understanding, and not in order that they might be observed. Therefore, permission was given to Christians, not to act in accord with this vain custom, but to eat what they will with moderation, benediction, and

---

[1] Cf. Acts 10.9-15.
[2] Col. 2.17.
[3] Cf. Prov. 21.20.

thanksgiving. Perhaps for this reason it was also said to Peter: 'Kill and eat,'[4] so that he might no longer keep the observance of the Jews, although there was not commanded to him, as it were, excess in eating and disgraceful gluttony. But in order that you may understand that this was shown in figure, there were creeping things in that vessel. Now could the creeping things eat anything? What, then, does this explanation mean?

(2) That vessel signifies the Church, and the four corners by which it was let down indicate the four corners of the earth throughout which the Catholic Church is extended and spread everywhere. Therefore, anyone who wishes to go to one corner and to be cut off from the whole by heresy, does not belong to the mystery of the four corners. But if he has no part in the vision of Peter, neither will he have a part in the keys which were given to Peter. That vessel was let down by the four corners because of the fact that God says His saints are to be gathered together at the end of the world from the four winds. For this reason the faith of the Gospel is now spread on those four hinges. Those animals are further the nations: for all the nations which were unclean before the coming of Christ because of errors and superstitions and wickedness, have been made clean when their sins were forgiven at His coming. Why, then, after the remission of their sins, are they not received into the body of Christ which is the Church of God, and which Peter personified? In many places Peter appears personifying the Church. If Peter prefigured the Church, and the Church is the body of Christ, He is to receive as for His food the cleansed nations whose sins have been forgiven.

(3) After this Cornelius, a Gentile, sent for him, as did also the Gentiles who were with him. The alms of this man had been accepted and had cleansed him in a certain measure, and there now remained for him to be united to the Church, that is, the body of the Lord, like clean food. Now Peter trembled at giving the Gospel to the Gentiles, because those who believed in circumcision forbade the apostles to hand over the

---

4 Acts 10.13.

Christian faith to those who were not circumcised. They said that people should not approach to share in the Gospel unless they had received circumcision, which had been handed down to their fathers. Therefore, that vessel removed doubt from Peter, and so after that vision he was advised by the Holy Spirit to go down and proceed with those who had come from Cornelius, and he went. Cornelius and the men with him were considered like those animals which were pointed out in the vessel, for God had already cleansed them when He accepted their alms. Therefore, they were to be killed and eaten, that is, their past life in which they had not known Christ was to be killed, and they were to cross over into His body, as if into the new body of the company of the Church. For when Peter himself came to them, he briefly recalled what had been pointed out to him in that vision. And he said: 'You know it is not permissible for a Jew to associate with foreigners or to visit them; but God has shown me that I should not call any man common or unclean.'[5] Surely, God showed the same truth when that other word resounded: 'What God has cleansed, do not thou call unclean.'[6]

(4) Perhaps it may also be asked why there was a sheet which contained those animals. Surely, this was not without reason. Now we know that a moth, which destroys other garments, does not eat a sheet. For this reason anyone who wants to reach the mystery of the Catholic Church should exclude from his heart the corruption of evil desires. He should be confirmed in the faith so imperishably that he is not pervaded with evil thoughts as with moths, if he wants to reach the mystery of that sheet which prefigures the Church. Why was it let down from heaven three times, except because all the nations which belong to the four parts of the earth where the Church is spread are baptized in the name of the Trinity? The Church was signified in the four corners which fastened the vessel, for they renew all who believe in the name of the

---
5 Acts 10.28.
6 Cf. Acts 10.15.

Father, and of the Son, and of the Holy Spirit, in order that they may reach the company and communion of the saints. For this reason the four corners, the four parts of the world, and the triple lowering show the mystery of the Trinity. This fact also indicates the number of the twelve apostles, with three each delegated to the four, four times three equals twelve. And since the twelve apostles were destined to preach the mystery of the Trinity in the four corners of the world, for this reason the four corners were let down from heaven three times.

(5) As we mentioned above, blessed Peter typified the Catholic Church. The fact that he went up to the roof signifies that the Church was to ascend on high spiritually, away from earthly desires, and to lift up the heart in accord with what the Apostle said: 'But our citizenship is in heaven.'[7] The fact that Peter hungered further signified that the Church would hunger for the salvation of the Gentiles. The sheet which was let down from heaven also indicated the Church, and the animals which were in the sheet presented an image of all nations. Moreover, the four corners by which that vessel was lowered seem to have signified the four corners of the world in which the Gospel of Christ is preached. The fact that the vessel was let down from heaven three times showed the mystery of the Trinity and the sacrament of Baptism. And when it was said to Peter: 'Kill and eat,'[8] this indicated that the Catholic Church was destined to kill first and then eat all who believe in Christ. In other words, their unbelief would be slain in order that faith might be instilled. For no one can believe in Christ unless what he was first dies, according to what the Apostle says: 'For you have died and your life is hidden with Christ in God.'[9] Just as those who are surrounded by heretics are devoured by death while they are still alive, so those who come to Christ die to their past, in order that they may live

---
[7] Phil. 3.20.
[8] Acts 10.13.
[9] Col. 3.3.

for the things to come. They perish to the devil and are gained for Christ; they die to death and happily are planted in life. Let us beg with continual prayers that the divine goodness may deign to fulfill and confirm this in us: with the help of our Lord Jesus Christ, who together with the Father and the Holy Spirit lives and reigns forever and ever. Amen.

* *Sermon 177*

St. Augustine on Original Sin

(1) Where or how original sin is contracted, dearest brethren, how we continually suffer disturbances because of it, and how, with God's help, we can overcome the evil desires which are planted in us, the blessed Apostle clearly shows us, when Christ speaks through him: 'I see another law in my members, warring against the law of my mind and making me prisoner to the law of sin that is in my members.'[1] This law was born at the time when the former law was transgressed; it was born, I repeat, when the former law was despised. What is the former law? The one which man received in paradise. Were they not naked, and still not ashamed? Why were they naked and still not ashamed, except because not yet was there a law in their members resisting the law of their mind? Man committed a deed worthy of punishment, and then he found within himself a movement of shame. They ate contrary to the prohibition, and their eyes were opened. Were their eyes at first closed in paradise, so that they wandered about blind? Far from it: for how could Adam have imposed names on the birds and the beasts, when all the animals were brought to him? On whom did he confer names if he did not see them? Then it was said: 'The woman saw the tree, because it was pleasing to the eyes

---

1 Rom. 7.23.

to behold.'² Therefore, they had their eyes open; they were naked, but they were not ashamed. Their eyes were opened to something which they had never feared. They were opened to look, but not to see; because they felt shame, they were careful to cover themselves. 'They sewed fig leaves together,' it says, 'and made themselves aprons.'³ They covered themselves where they felt shame. Behold the source of original sin, because no one is born without it. Notice that the Lord, who was conceived by a virgin, did not want to be conceived in the same way. He dispelled it, since He came without it. Therefore, the two are distinct: the one leads to death, the other to life; the first man led to death, the second one leads to life. Why does the one lead to death? Because he is only man. And why does the other lead to life? Because He is both God and man.

(2) Now the Apostle does not accomplish what he wants. Therefore, since you know the source of original sin, carefully notice what it tries to accomplish in us by continuous assault. Behold, as he himself says, the Apostle wills not to sin, and still he sins; therefore, he does what he does not will. Did that evil inclination drag the Apostle, when he was subject to it, to wickedness, to fornication? Far from it. Do not let such thoughts enter your heart. He struggled against them and was not overcome. But because he did not want to possess that against which he was struggling, he spoke as follows: 'It is not what I wish that I do,'⁴ and still I do not consent to the wickedness. For he would not say in another place: 'Do not fulfill the lusts of the flesh,'⁵ if he were fulfilling them. He has put his own battle before your eyes, in order that you may not be afraid of your own. For if the blessed Apostle had not said this, perhaps you would despair when you saw the evil inclination to which you did not consent nevertheless aroused. If I belonged to God, I would not be tempted in this way. See the Apostle struggling, and do not despair in your own case.

---

2 Cf. Gen. 3.6.
3 Cf. Gen. 3.7.
4 Rom. 7.15.
5 Cf. Gal. 5.16.

'I see another law in my members,' he says, 'warring against the law of my mind.'⁶ Now because I do not want it to overcome me—for it is my flesh, I am myself, it is a part of me—'It is not what I wish that I do, but what I hate, that I do,'⁷ that I desire. Then what good do I accomplish? The fact that I do not consent to the evil inclination. I do good, even though I accomplish no good, because I do not consent to evil inclinations at all. Then, again, how does my enemy do evil and still accomplish no evil? He does evil because he arouses a wicked desire; but he accomplishes no evil because he does not attract me to it.

(3) The entire life of the saints is engaged in this war, for there happens in them what is written: 'The flesh lusts against the spirit, and the spirit against the flesh.'⁸ They, indeed, fight, but they are not overcome. What shall I say about wicked, carnal, and dissipated souls who do not struggle, but are carried along in subjection? [And still they are not carried along,] because they follow willingly, and of their own accord devote themselves to wicked deeds. With such souls the devil does not condescend to fight at all, because they never or only with difficulty oppose his counsels. But with the saints he has daily struggles, because it is written of him: 'His repast is sumptuous.'⁹ This, I repeat, is the life of the saints, and in this war man is always in danger until he dies. But what are the saints going to say at the end, that is, in the triumph of victory? 'O death, where is thy struggle?'¹⁰ This will be the word of the triumphant. 'O death, where is thy sting? The sting of death is sin,'¹¹ and death arises from remorse over it. Sin is like a scorpion: it stings us and we are dead. But when is it that we may say: 'O death, where is thy victory?'¹² This is not promised to us in this life, but at the resurrection. Then

---
6 Rom. 7.23.
7 Rom. 7.15.
8 Gal. 5.17.
9 Cf. Hab. 1.16.
10 Cf. 1 Cor. 15.55.
11 Cf. 1 Cor. 15.55, 56.
12 1 Cor. 15.55.

it will be granted to the saints neither to wish to sin nor to be able to do so at all.

(4) For this reason, dearest brethren, along with the blessed Apostle we are exercised in this war. Finally, when the Apostle was laboring in this battle he also said: 'I see another law in my members, warring against the law of my mind and making me prisoner to the law of sin that is in my members.'[13] This is an unseemly law, namely, evil desires, wounds, disease, and weakness. When the Apostle was struggling in the midst of these, he exclaimed: 'Unhappy man that I am! Who will deliver me from the body of this death?'[14] And as he was groaning help came to him. How did it come to his aid? 'The grace of God through Jesus Christ our Lord.'[15] The grace of God through Jesus Christ our Lord will free you from the body of this death; it will deliver you from the law of death. However, as was already said, this is going to take place at the resurrection, when you will possess a body in which no evil inclination remains. 'When this mortal body puts on immortality,'[16] then this corruptible body will put on incorruption. Then it will be said to death: 'Where is thy struggle?' and there will be none. And likewise it will be said: 'O death, where is thy sting?' and it will be found nowhere. In the meantime, while we are still in the midst of this battle which we have to wage, let us heed the blessed Apostle. 'I myself with my mind serve the law of God,' by not consenting to evil, 'but with my flesh the law of sin'[17] by evil desires. With my mind I serve the law of God and with my flesh the law of sin: I am delighted with this and am inclined to it; indeed, I am inclined to it, but I am not overcome. It tickles, it plots, it pushes me on and tries to drag me. 'Unhappy man that I am! Who will deliver me from the body of this death?' I am unwilling to be victorious always, but sometimes I want to arrive

---

13 Rom. 7.23.
14 Rom. 7.24.
15 Rom. 7.25.
16 1 Cor. 15.54.
17 Rom. 7.25.

at peace. But since this peace is impossible in this world, cling to that measure and resist faithfully. Serve the law of God with your mind, and the law of sin with your flesh. Let it be from necessity that you have evil inclinations, but not because you consent. Sometimes, this evil inclination steals over even the saints and good Christians in such a way that it effects in them when they are asleep what it cannot do when they are awake. How many times they are defiled by temptations unwillingly and against their volition. Now I ask you, brethren, if that temptation which creeps up on people when they are asleep or unwilling cannot be without sin, how do men judge themselves if they either commit adultery or enjoy their own wives without moderation? When a man knows his wife except with the desire for children, he should not doubt that he has committed sin, for thus speaks the Apostle: 'Every one learn how to possess his vessel in honor and holiness, not in the passion of lust like the Gentiles who have no hope.'[18]

(5) These words are not my own, dearest brethren, but those of the blessed Apostle. He says that those who use their wives without moderation are like the Gentiles who have no hope. Since all animals observe their own time, so that we see no kind of animals mixed after conception, doubtless men who are made according to the image of God ought to observe this even more fully. We are ashamed to stay here a long time, but let us not be ashamed to pray to God afterwards. Since the weakness of our flesh compels us to exceed the limits of the sin which we commit through dissipation, it should be redeemed by continuous prayer and more abundant almsgiving. By granting full pardon to all of our enemies we may especially say, and say in all truth: 'Forgive us our debts, as we also forgive our debtors.'[19] If we are willing to fulfill this in humility and charity, we will appear in the sight of the eternal judge free from not only small sins, but even from serious offenses. May He deign to grant this, to whom is honor and

---

18 1 Thess. 4.4, 5, 12.
19 Matt. 6.12.

might together with the Father and the Holy Spirit forever and ever. Amen.

* *Sermon 178*

A Homily on a Thought of Peter. Also on Judgment Day, and on What the Apostle Says: 'Laying Aside the Works of Darkness, Put on the Armor of Light.'[1]

(1) We have frequently heard the blessed Apostle Paul, dearest brethren, as he admonishes us in a salutary way and says: 'Laying aside the works of darkness, put on the armor of light.' What does it mean to lay aside the works of darkness, except to renounce the devil, his pomps and his angels? And what does it mean: 'Put on the armor of light,' except believe in God the Father almighty? However, let us first examine who or what the devil is, dearly beloved, and what his pomps are which we renounce when we lay aside the works of darkness. Then, at last, we may talk to your charity as much as He allows about God the Father almighty, who is the true light.

(2) What is the devil? An angel separated from God through pride, who 'has not stood in the truth.'[2] He is the author of lying, and since he was deceived by himself, he is anxious to deceive another. The adversary of the human race, he is the inventor of death, the originator of pride, the root of wickedness, the chief of sins, the leader of all vices, and the persuader of sinful desires. When he saw the first Adam, who surely is the father of all of us, made from the slime of the earth according to the image of God, adorned with virtue and clothed with immortality, he was hostile and envious. He was struck with the poison of interior malice when he saw that earthly man had received what he himself had lost through pride when he was still an angel. Filled with insatiable longing for our

1 Cf. Rom. 13.12.
2 John 8.44.

deaths, he ruined our first parents, at the same time stripping them of those gifts and great blessings. For when he had taken from man such a great benefit, dearly beloved, including faith, modesty, continency, charity, and immortality, he left him naked and in disgrace. Laughing at the filthy rags of vices which he had occasioned, he subjected him to his dominion and bound all his offspring to himself by the same tie. Adam, indeed, took the disgraceful rags. When he was stripped of modesty by the devil, he was clothed with immodesty; when he lost temperance, he became intemperate. When charity was destroyed, he became wicked; and when he was deprived of immortality, he was delivered over to death. See what he lost and what he acquired.

(3) Now since 'We have become orphans,'[3] brethren, let us renounce this harmful inheritance before the avenging judge comes. If anyone has neglected to renounce the inheritance which includes the rags of the devil, which surely are his pomps and his angels, then when judgment day comes, as the Gospel says: 'The debtor will be delivered to the judge, and the judge will shut the debtor up in prison. Amen I say to thee, saith the Lord, he will not come out from it until he has paid the last penny.'[4] Each one should watch and look out, lest, if he does not completely renounce them, after his confession of faith the devil may still recognize within him the rags of his vices. Then he will begin to be held in guilt, although Christ wanted to free him by His grace. Men who are unwilling to be corrected after receiving this grace should not wickedly deceive themselves and return again to their evil pleasures. The day of judgment is awaited, and there will be the most just judge who admits no one because he is powerful, and whose palace no one spoils with gold and silver. All the souls will stand near: 'So that each one may receive according to what he has won through the body, whether good or evil.'[5]

---

3 Lam. 5.3.
4 Cf. Matt. 5.25, 26.
5 Cf. 2 Cor. 5.10.

The devil, our adversary, will also be on hand, and the words of our confession will be read. And if anyone is found to have departed from this life as his debtor, then that adversary will rejoice.

(4) Consider this, brethren. If anyone recognizes many sins in himself, let him quickly have recourse to the healing remedies of repentance. As long as that shadowy soul is still retained in this little body, he should seek a remedy for himself in his day of need. With God's help, he should hasten to labor as much as he can to lay aside the filthy rags of vice and to put on the stole of good works. Then, when he has merited to enter that heavenly nuptial feast on the day of judgment, it will not be said to him: 'How didst thou come in here without a wedding garment?'[6] Then it will further be said to the servants, when he is silent: 'Bind his hands and feet and cast him forth into the darkness outside, where there will be the weeping and the gnashing of teeth.'[7] There eyes will weep if they were occupied with vain pleasures, and teeth will gnash if they rejoiced in a gluttonous appetite. Let us pray, beloved brethren, that we may be freed from this evil hearing and may merit to hear that desirable word: 'Come, blessed of my Father,'[8] and the rest. May He Himself deign to grant this.

Sermon 179

An Admonition on the Gospel Text Where it Says: 'If a Man's Work Abides He Will Receive Reward; If His Work Burns He Will Lose His Reward.'[1]

(1) In the Gospel text which was read to us a little while

---
6 Matt. 22.12.
7 Matt. 22.13.
8 Matt. 25.34.

1 Cor. 3.15.

ago, dearest brethren, we heard the Apostle say: 'Other foundation no one can lay, but that which has been laid, which is Christ Jesus. But if anyone builds upon this foundation, gold, silver, precious stones, wood, hay, straw—the work of each will be made manifest, for the day of the Lord will declare it, since the day is to be revealed in fire. The fire will assay the quality of everyone's work: if his work abides which he has built thereon, he will receive reward; if his work burns he will lose his reward, but himself will be saved, yet so as through fire.'[2] There are many people who understand this text incorrectly, deceiving themselves with a false assurance. They believe that if they build serious sins upon the foundation of Christ, those very offenses can be purified by transitory flames and they themselves can later reach eternal life. This kind of understanding must be corrected, dearest brethren, because men deceive themselves when they flatter themselves in this way. For in that passing fire, of which the Apostle said: 'He himself will be saved, yet so as through fire,' not serious, but slight sins are purged. What is worse, not only greater sins, but even small ones, if they are very many, ruin a man. For this reason, even though not all sins are to be mentioned, at least some of them should be, whether more or less serious, lest anyone foolishly try to excuse himself by saying that he does not know which are lesser sins and which are serious offenses.

(2) Although the Apostle has mentioned more serious sins, nevertheless we briefly say what they are, lest we seem to prompt despair. Sacrilege, murder, adultery, false testimony, theft, robbery, pride, envy, avarice, and, if it is continued for a long time, anger, drunkenness if continuous, and slander are included in their number. If anyone knows that some of these sins have dominion over him, unless he does penance in a worthy manner and for a long time, if he enjoys it, and further gives abundant alms and refrains from those same sins, he cannot be purged by that passing fire

---

[2] 1 Cor. 3.11-15.

of which the Apostle spoke. Instead, eternal flames will torture him without any remedy.

(3) Although what the slight offenses are is known to all of you, still it is necessary to name at least a few of them, since it would take too long to mention them all. As often as anyone takes more than he needs in food or drink, he knows that this amounts to slight sins. As often as a man speaks more than he should or is silent more than is proper; as often as he provokes a poor man who is begging rudely; as often as he wills to eat when others are fasting, even though he is in bodily health, and rises too late for church because he had surrendered to sleep; as often as he knows his wife without the desire for children; as often as he looks tardily for those who are placed in prison, and even more rarely visits the sick; if he has neglected to recall the discordant to harmony; if he has irritated his neighbor or his wife or his child or a servant more than he should; if he has flattered himself more than is right; if he has willingly flattered a superior either of his own accord or out of necessity; if he has prepared exceedingly luxurious or sumptuous feasts for himself while the poor were hungry; if he has occupied himself, either in church or outside of it, with idle stories for which an account must be rendered on the day of judgment; if when we carelessly take an oath we swear falsely, when we could not have done this because of any necessity, and curse with all facility and temerity, although it is written: 'Nor the evil-tongued will possess the kingdom of God';[3] when we rashly suspect something which usually is not proven to be as we thought, without any doubt we commit sin. There is no doubt that these actions and similar ones belong to the slight offenses which, as I already said, can scarcely be counted. From these sins, not only all the Christian people, but even all the saints sometimes cannot be free, and they never will be. Although we do not believe that the soul is killed by these sins, still they make it ugly by filling it with some kind of blisters and, as it were, a

---
[3] 1 Cor. 6.10.

horrible scab. For this reason they allow the soul to come to the embraces of that heavenly spouse only with difficulty or with great confusion, for it is written concerning Him: 'He prepared for Himself the Church not having spot or wrinkle.'[4]

(4) Therefore, they may continuously be redeemed by constant prayer, frequent fasting, more abundant almsgiving, and the forgiveness of those who sin against us. Otherwise, perhaps when they are collected and form a great heap, they may bury us. Whatever remains of these sins and is not redeemed by us will have to be purged in that fire of which the Apostle said: 'It is to be revealed in fire, and if his work burns he will lose his reward.'[5] As long as we live in this world, we ourselves exhaust ourselves in penance, or at least with the will and permission of God, we are afflicted with many tribulations because of those sins. If we are further grateful to God, we are set free. This happens as often as a husband or wife or child dies, or if our substance, which we love more than is necessary, is taken away—although we should love Christ more than that same possession, and if need be, should prefer to lose our substance rather than to deny Christ. Still, as I already said, because we love it more than we should, we cannot lose it either in life or in death without great sorrow. And still, if like good children, we give thanks to God who like a kind father permits it to be taken away, and admit with true humility that we suffer less than we deserve, in this way the sins themselves are purged in this world. Moreover, that fire of purgatory will find nothing in the future life, or at least very little, to burn away. But if we neither give thanks to God in tribulations nor redeem our own sins by good works, we will have to stay in that fire of purgatory as long as those above-mentioned slight sins are consumed like wood and hay and straw.

(5) Perhaps someone may say: It makes no difference to me how long I will have to stay, as long as I pass on to eternal

---

[4] Cf. Eph. 5.27.
[5] 1 Cor. 3.13, 15.

life. Let no one say this, dearest brethren, because that fire of purgatory will be more difficult than any punishment in this world can be seen or imagined or felt. Since it is written concerning the day of judgment: 'One day will be as a thousand years, and a thousand years as one day,'[6] how does anyone know whether he is going to pass through that fire days or months or perhaps even years? Moreover, if a man is unwilling to put even one finger into the fire, why should he not fear that it might then be necessary to be tortured both in soul and body for a considerable time? For this reason, let each one labor with all his strength to avoid serious sins, and to redeem his slight offenses by good works in such a way that either very little or nothing of them may be seen to remain for that fire to consume. If those who commit serious sins refuse to correct them during life by the healing remedy of repentance, they will not be able to come to that fire of which the Apostle says: 'But he himself will be saved, yet so as through fire.'[7] As was already said, they are going to hear instead that hard and irrevocable sentence: 'Depart from me, accursed ones, into the everlasting fire.'[8] Therefore, those who desire to be freed from that eternal punishment and from the fire of purgatory should not commit serious sins. If they have already committed them, they should perform fruitful penance, not ceasing to redeem by good works also those small and even daily offenses.

(6) I now wish to explain more fully to you by what works slight offenses may be redeemed. As often as we visit the sick, look into prison, recall the discordant to harmony, fast on the days appointed by the Church, wash the feet of guests, attend vigils rather frequently, give alms to the poor who pass before our door, and forgive our enemies as often as they ask it, by these and similar works slight offenses are redeemed every day.

---

6 2 Peter 3.8.
7 1 Cor. 3.15.
8 Matt. 25.41.

(7) This alone, however, does not suffice for serious sins. Tears and crying and groaning must be added, as also continuous fasting which is extended over a long time, and the gift of even more abundant alms than we are able to bestow. Of our own accord withdrawing from communion with the Church, and continuing for a long time in grief and sadness, we should also perform public penance, because it is just for a man to redeem himself by the building up of many things, since he ruined himself by the destructive power of many things. Finally, what I suggest is not impossible or even difficult. Let us mourn for our soul when it is dead in the same way in which we bewail the dead body of another. If a wife or child or husband has died, men dash themselves upon the ground, tearing their hair and striking their breasts, continuing for some time in their mourning and fasting and tears. I beseech you, brethren, let us exhibit for our soul what those men show for the body of another. And notice, brethren, how wrong it is to ask for what is impossible, and not to seek the possible. We bewail a body, which we cannot revive, and we do not mourn for a dead soul which we can recall to its former condition. What is still worse on our part, we bewail the dead body which we love, but the dead soul which we do not love we neither mourn nor lament. For this reason, let us exchange places and begin to love the Lord more than the servant, that is, the Creator of the body more than the body. Let us love the mistress more than the handmaid, that is, the soul which was made according to the image of God, more than the body which was formed from the slime of the earth. Then, on the last day when our body has begun to rot and to be devoured by worms in the grave, our soul may be lifted up to the bosom of Abraham by the hands of angels, and after our body has been restored in the resurrection, we may deserve to hear on judgment day: 'Well done, good servant; enter into the joy of thy master.'[9]

(8) Now in order that the things which we said above may

---
9 Matt. 25.21.

be able to be fixed more firmly in your hearts, and the lesson of the Apostle may be understood more fully, I want to review them briefly for your charity. All the saints who faithfully serve God, striving to take time for reading and prayer and to persevere in good works, do not build serious sins or slight offenses, that is, wood, hay, and straw upon the foundation of Christ, but rather good works, that is, gold, silver, and precious stones. Such souls will pass without any violence through that fire of which the Apostle said: 'It is to be revealed in fire.'[10] However, souls which are ready to commit slight offenses, even though they do not commit serious sins, if they are careless in redeeming them, they are not going to come to eternal life because of the fact that they believed in Christ and did not commit serious sins. Through the justice and mercy of God, as was already said, they must first be purified by the bitterest tribulations in this world, or through the goodness of God, they may free themselves by abundant almsgiving and kind forgiveness of enemies. Otherwise, they will have to be tortured for a long time by that fire of which the Apostle spoke, in order that they may reach eternal life without spot or wrinkle. Souls which have committed either murder or sacrilege or adultery or other sins like these, as was already said, if they have not been helped by worthy repentance, will not deserve to reach life by passing through the fire of purgatory, but they will be thrown to death in the eternal fire.

(9) Therefore, as often as you hear in the Gospel text: 'If anyone builds upon the foundation of Christ gold, silver, precious stones,'[11] accept it with reference to the saints and perfect Christians, who, like purified gold, will merit to reach eternal rewards. However, those who build upon it wood, hay, and straw understand, as was often said, as good Christians who, nevertheless, are careless in purging themselves of slight offenses. If divine justice has not purged such sins through many tribulations, and no one has redeemed them by an

---
10 1 Cor. 3.13.
11 Cf. 1 Cor. 3.12.

abundance of alms, not without great grief will there be fulfilled in them what the Apostle said: 'If his work burns he will lose his reward; he himself will be saved, yet so as through fire.'[12] Let no one deceive himself, as was already said above, in thinking that this can happen in the case of serious sins, too, if they have remained uncured. For this reason, let us labor as much as we can with God's help, as I have often said, so that we may be able to avoid serious sins, and so that we may redeem the slight offenses without which we cannot live, by continually loving our enemies and an abundance of alms: with the help of our Lord Jesus Christ, who together with the Father and the Holy Spirit lives and reigns forever and ever. Amen.

* *Sermon 180*

On What Is Written: 'Put Away Lying.'[1]

(1) When the divine lesson was read just now, dearest brethren, we heard the Apostle say: 'Put away lying and speak truth each one with his neighbor.'[2] Let no one think that truth is to be spoken with a Christian, and lying with a pagan. Speak the truth with your neighbor. Every man is your neighbor: anyone who was born of Adam and Eve with you is your neighbor. We are all neighbors in the condition of our earthly birth, but otherwise we are brothers in that hope of a blessed inheritance. You ought to think that every man is your neighbor, even before he is a Christian. For you do not know what kind of a man he will be in the presence of God; you do not know how God has foreknown him. Sometime the man whom you are mocking because he worships idols will be converted and worship God, perhaps more piously than you

---
12 1 Cor. 3.15.

1 Eph. 4.25.
2 *Ibid.*

who laughed at him a little before. Our neighbors lie hidden in those men who do not belong to the Church, and they also are concealed from us in the Church. For many who seem to be Christians are to be excluded from the Church because of their wicked life and their perseverance in evil. Similarly, those who seem to be outside are going to believe and persevere in a good life in such a way that they will be united to the Church forever. Therefore, the former should not become proud or the latter despair, for we cannot know what the future will be. Let us consider every man a neighbor, not only because of the condition of human mortality whereby we come to earth by the same destiny, but also in the hope of that inheritance. For we do not know what is going to happen to a man who now is either a Jew or a heretic or a pagan. Perhaps, as was said, through the mercy of the Lord he will be converted to God in such a way that he will deserve to hold the first place among the saints.

(2) 'Put away lying and speak truth each one with his neighbor, because we are members of one another. "Be angry and do not sin." '[3] Therefore, if you are angry at your servant because he has done wrong, be angry at yourself, so you yourself will not sin. 'Do not let the sun go down upon your anger.'[4] Truly, this is understood in terms of time, brethren. For if anger steals over a Christian because of his human condition and the weakness of the mortality which we bear, it should not be kept a long time and become a daily occurrence. Cast it out of your heart, before this visible light of life dies, so that invisible light may not desert you. This is understood better in another way, that Christ is our sun of justice and of truth. He is not the sun which is adored by pagans and Manichaeans and is even seen by sinners, but that other one by whose truth the human soul is illuminated, and in which the angels rejoice. Moreover, if the weakened eyes of the heart of men tremble beneath its rays, they still are purged through

---
3 Eph. 4.25, 26.
4 Eph. 4.26.

His commands, so that they may contemplate it. When the sun itself has begun to dwell in a man through faith, let it not behold in you anger which is arising, so that the sun will set on your wrath, that is, Christ may desert your mind, for God does not want to dwell along with your anger. For He seems, as it were, to die at your hands when you are killed by it, for when anger is of long standing, it becomes hatred; when it has become hatred, you are already a murderer. As the Apostle John says: 'Everyone who hates his brother is a murderer.'5 Likewise, he says again: 'He who hates his brother is in the darkness.'6 It is no wonder that he remains in darkness when the sun is killed by him.

(3) Perhaps what you also heard in the Gospel pertains to this: 'The boat on the lake was in peril, and Jesus fell asleep.'7 In this life we are sailing, as it were, on a kind of lake, and there is a wind, and storms are not lacking. Our boats are almost completely filled with the daily trials of this world. How does this happen, except because Christ is asleep? If He were not asleep in you, you would not suffer those trials, but you would possess interior peace if Jesus were keeping watch with you. Now why is it that Jesus is said to be asleep within you, unless because your faith which arises in Jesus, is sound asleep in your heart? What are you to do, in order that you may be set free? Arouse Jesus, and say: 'Master, we are perishing.'8 He will awake, that is, your faith will return to you, and with His help you will consider within your soul that the earthly possessions which are given to the wicked will not continue with them. Either they will desert them while they are still alive, or will be abandoned by them when they die. But what is promised to you will remain forever, while what is granted to them for a time will quickly be removed: it will blossom like the flower of grass. For: 'All mankind is grass, the grass withers and the flower wilts, but

---

5 1 John 3.15.
6 1 John 2.11.
7 Cf. Luke 8.23.
8 Cf. Luke 8.24.

the word of our Lord stands forever.'⁹ Therefore, turn your back to what is transitory, and your face to that which endures. Since Christ is keeping watch, if that storm does not sink or completely fill your ship, soon your faith will command the winds and the waves and thus it will pass through the danger. Also pertinent to this matter, brethren, is everything that the Apostle said about stripping off the old man: 'Be angry and do not sin: do not let the sun go down upon your anger: do not give place to the devil.'¹⁰ Since the old man gave place, let not the new one do so. 'He who was wont to steal, let him steal no longer.'¹¹ The old man stole, so let not the new one do so. He is a man, one man, he was Adam; but he was the old man, and has become the new.

(4) We have often said, we often repeat, and as long as we live we ought to say that the Church of our time has both chaff and grain. Let no one seek to remove all the chaff, except at the time of winnowing. Let no one leave the threshing floor before it is time, lest perchance while he is unwilling to bear sinners, he may be found to have been gathered by the birds near the threshing floor before he enters the barn. Now notice, brethren, how we are saying these things. When the grain has begun to be threshed along with the chaff, it no longer touches itself and, as it were, does not know itself, because the chaff comes in between. Moreover, if anyone watches the threshing floor a rather long time, he thinks there is only the chaff. Unless he looks more carefully and stretches out his hand, separating it with the air from his mouth, that is, with a purging breath, he succeeds in separating the grain only with difficulty. Sometimes the ears of grain themselves are, as it were, separated from each other, so that they do not touch each other. This comparison refers to the man who thinks he is the only good man as soon as he has made some progress. This thought even tempted so great a

---
9 Isa. 40.6-8.
10 Eph. 4.26, 27.
11 Eph. 4.28.

man as Elias, brethren. Thus, the Book of Kings relates: 'They have slain thy prophets, they have thrown down thy altars, and I alone am left: and they seek my life. But the divine response came to him: I have left me seven thousand men who have not bent the knee before Baal.'[12] He did not say: You have two or three others like yourself. Do not think you are the only one, he says. There are seven thousand others, and do you think you are the only one? However, let your holiness heed with me what I had begun to say, and may the mercy of God dwell in your hearts. Listen briefly. Whoever is still wicked should not think that no one is good, and the man who is good should not think he is the only one. Remember this, behold, I repeat it. Notice what I am saying: whoever is wicked should question his own conscience, renounce the evil in himself, and not think that no one is good; and whoever is good should not think that he is the only good man. Moreover, the good man should not be afraid to mix with sinners, for the time will come when they will be separated; the time will come for the wicked to be separated from the good. Meanwhile, as was already said, those who are good should bear with the wicked, and those who are wicked should imitate the good. Good men should not be lifted up in pride, nor should sinners be broken by dangerous despair. For now the chaff can be converted into wheat, and the wheat can be changed into chaff. If those who are good lead a careless life, they may offend God, while if those who are wicked quickly amend their lives, they may merit the mercy of God. As long as we are in the body this exchange can take place, but when we have departed from this life no good man will be able to be evil, nor can one who is wicked arrive at goodness any longer.

(5) As we meditate upon these truths in a salutary manner, dearest brethren, let us labor as much as we can on behalf of the salvation of our soul. Let us not be deaf or with hardened hearts when the Lord mercifully invites and encourages us,

---

12 Cf. 3 Kings 19.10, 15, 18.

saying: 'Delay not your conversion to the Lord, put it not off from day to day';¹³ and again: 'Seek the Lord while he may be found.'¹⁴ For He is found if He is sought. But if a man does not seek Him while there is time to find Him, he will not be able to find Him forever. Therefore, with the help of God, let us endeavor to live in such a way that the precepts and commands of our Lord may avail as a remedy for us because we have followed them, rather than as a judgment because of our transgression. May He Himself deign to grant this, who together with the Father and the Holy Spirit lives and reigns forever and ever. Amen.

* Sermon 181

On the Lesson of the Apostle Where It Says: 'Making the Most of Your Time, Because the Days are Evil';¹ and Also: 'You Give Coins to Buy Bread for Yourself; Forgive a Wicked Man Something, in Order That You May Buy Rest for Yourself.'²

(1) When the lesson was read you heard the Apostle telling us, or rather we all heard him say: 'See to it that you walk with care: not as unwise but as wise, making the most of your time, because the days are evil.'³ Two things make days evil, brethren, wickedness and misery. Days are called evil because of the wickedness and the misery of men. However, those days, as far as refers to the space of hours, have been arranged, take their turns, and tell the times. 'The sun rises and the sun goes down';⁴ again it rises and goes down, times come and

---
13 Ecclus. 5.8.
14 Isa. 55.6.
---
1 Eph. 5.16.
2 No reference is cited for this quotation.
3 Eph. 5.15, 16.
4 Eccles. 1.5.

they pass away. To whom are times troublesome, if men are not troublesome to themselves? Therefore, as I said, two things make days evil, the misery of men and their wickedness. Now although the misery of men is common, their wickedness ought not to be common.

(2) From the time of Adam's sin, we have all been born wretched, and misery is common to us all. But in opposition to the birth which made us all wretched, God provided a rebirth by which He might free us from misery. Birth sends us into misery; rebirth marks us for blessedness. Now just because I said that regeneration frees us from misery, we are not immediately blessed as soon as we are reborn. If we were then at once blessed, and enjoyed good days as soon as we were regenerated, the Apostle would not say to us what he speaks to those who are already reborn and devout: 'Making the most of your time, because the days are evil.' Even the regenerated suffer evil days until the penalty of mortality is ended and the grace of the highest happiness takes its place. If it does not profit us for the future life that we worship God, why do we adore Him? In order that we may possess happiness here? How many who do not worship God possess that? In order that we may grow old here, and become decrepit? How many blasphemers of God grow old? Is God, then, to be worshiped in order that His worshipers may have children and not be sterile? God also gives children to lions and wild asses and serpents. Therefore, He is not to be sought because of any great and true good which is granted to Jews and pagans and heretics, and even to wild beasts. Moreover, even the wicked possess gold and silver, honors, children, and much property. One who is a true Christian ought not look for all those passing things, but he should devote the whole weight of his attention and prayer in search of eternal bliss. Whenever God grants those temporal goods, thanks should be given to Him, and when He takes them away He should be similarly thanked. He may give those things whenever He wishes, and He may take them away when He wills; the only important

thing is that He may not take Himself away from us.

(3) Therefore, let no one say in his heart, brethren, when you hear that lesson of the blessed Apostle: 'Making the most of your time, because the days are evil'; let no one say in his heart: Our parents had good days, but we have evil days. Why did our parents have those? Were they not Christians? Was this lesson not read in the times of the apostles? When it was read so many years ago, did they not groan at it, and did they know what it said? From the time when Adam fell and was thrown out of paradise, there never were any days except evil ones. Let us ask the children who are born why they begin life with crying, since they can also laugh. A person is born, and he immediately cries; I do not know how many days later he laughs. When he wept at his birth he was a prophet of his own calamity, for tears are the witness of misery. He does not yet speak, and already he predicts that he is going to be in labor and in fear. If he lives well and is just, certainly he will always be afraid when placed in the midst of temptations. For why is it that he is just? Behold, he is just. What does the Apostle say? 'All who want to live piously in Christ will suffer persecution.'[5] Behold why days are evil: the just cannot live here without persecution.

(4) But you say to me: How do those who live piously suffer persecution, when there is peace, when the Church does not suffer from hostile kings, when all laws are to promote it? Those who live among the wicked suffer persecution. Why? Because all sinners persecute the good, not with the sword and stones, but by their life and morals. Was anyone persecuting holy Lot among the Sodomites? No one was troublesome to him, and yet he was living among the wicked, the impure, the unchaste, the proud, and the blasphemous. He suffered persecution, not by being beaten, but by living among the wicked. For whenever anyone who is just and good sees other men living an evil life, a slave to dissipation, not observing justice, pursuing pride, and despising charity; when those who

---
5 2 Tim. 3.12.

are good see such men they grieve, are afflicted, and become sad. With the Apostle they grieve over those 'who sinned and have not repented.'⁶ If anyone who hears me does not yet live piously in Christ, begin now to lead a devout life in Him. On whose behalf do I speak? The Apostle Paul lived at a time when the new faith was still being sown in the world and it was necessary to endure many adversaries, because it was said of Christ: 'A sign that shall be contradicted.'⁷ Does he recall only the persecutions which he suffered at the hands of the Jews and the Gentiles? Not only those, for he tells as follows: 'From the Jews five times I received forty lashes less one; I was stoned,'⁸ and the other things which we recognize when we read them. Those also were persecutions, without which no just man can live in this world: 'Conflicts without, and anxieties within.'⁹ Finally, when he recalls his dangers he says: 'In perils in the sea, in perils from floods, in perils in the wilderness, in perils from robbers, in perils from false brethren.'¹⁰ Other perils men can suffer quietly, but perils from false brethren they do not know how to suffer quietly, even until the end of the world.

(5) For this reason let us make the most of time, since the days are evil. Perhaps you expect to learn from me what it means to make the most of time, and how we have to do this. I am going to say what few heed, few bear, few approach, and few practice. However, I will say it, for the few who are going to listen to me live among the wicked, and their days are evil. To make the most of your time means this: whenever anyone starts a quarrel with you, lose something, in order that you may be free for God and not for strife. Lose something: out of what you lose you will have the price of time. Surely, whenever you appear in public because of your wants, when you pay money and buy bread for yourself, or wine, or oil, or wood,

---
6 2 Cor. 12.21.
7 Luke 2.34.
8 2 Cor. 11.24, 25.
9 2 Cor. 7.5.
10 Cf. 2 Cor. 11.26.

or clothing, or any household goods, or whatever you need, you give and you receive. You lose something and gain something; this is what it means to buy. For if you lost nothing and possessed what you did not have, either you found it or you accepted it as a gift or you acquired it by inheritance. But whenever you lose something in order that you may have something, then you buy. What you have is the object bought, and what you lose is the price. Therefore, just as you lose money in order to buy bread for yourself, so lose money in order to buy repose for yourself. Behold, this is what it means to make the most of your time.

(6) Listen to that ancient proverb which is both useful and necessary: 'Trouble comes to your door and asks for a coin; give it two, and it will depart.'[11] Trouble is the wicked man who wants to spoil you through slander: trouble is the sinner, the slanderer, the traitor. Such a man is like a bad blister on the body. When a man suffers a blister, he wants it to quickly form a callous, and he is anxious for that bad blister without any delay to remove a small particle from the body, and to go away with it so the poison of it will not take hold of the whole body and even seek his life. In the same way, when an unjust and wicked man who is unwilling to be free, except for strife, starts some slander against you, think that he is a bad blister and agree to lose some small part of your substance. For if you are too busy quarreling, you will not be able to have a heart at peace and free for God. Does not that above-mentioned proverb seem to have sprung from the Gospel? Did not the Lord tell further how to make the most of time when He said: 'If anyone would go to law with thee and take thy tunic, let him take they cloak as well'?[12] He wants to go to law and to take your tunic: he has to call you away from your God to quarrel. You will not have a quiet heart, nor will you possess a tranquil soul. Your thoughts will be driven away when you are aroused against that adversary of yours. Behold, you have

---
11 The author or source of this proverb is not indicated.
12 Matt. 5.40.

lost time. How much better is it to lose money and to make the most of your time? Certainly, what was said has been pleasing to everyone. We come to your business, and there I find you.

(7) In your cases and in your business, my brethren, when matters to be decided come to us, if I tell a Christian that he should lose something of his own in order to make the most of his time, with how much greater anxiety and confidence should I tell him to repay what belongs to another? For I hear both Christians. The cunning man who wants to plead a case for another and to take money from him as a compensation, rejoices at these words. The Apostle said: 'Making the most of your time, because the days are evil.' I slander a Christian: whether he wills it or not, he gives me something in order to make the most of time, because he listened to the Apostle. Watch out, lest perchance when you think yourself shrewd you find that you are quarrelsome, preferring to spend in order that it may conquer you, rather than to lose something in order that it may free you. However, if I am going to say to him: Lose something quietly, make the most of the time, you hear the Apostle say: 'Because the days are evil.' Now if I say to the man who is good and just: Lose something, in order that you may be at peace, am I not going to say to you: Malicious and lost soul, child of the devil, you have no case, and you are plotting to take away the goods of another; you have no case and are full of slander? You, too, are a Christian. Do I want to acquire him and lose you? If I say to him: Give that man something, in order that he may go away from the slander, where will you be, who have money as a result of calumny? That man who made the most of time in order to avoid slander endures evil days here. You who feed upon slander also have evil days here, and after these days you will suffer even worse ones on the day of judgment. But perhaps you laugh because you pay attention to the money. Laugh, laugh and scorn: Let me pay, for the one who exacts an account will come. But we believe that in God's mercy the

good Lord Himself will deign to inspire all men, not only the saints and Christians who fear God, but also those who trouble both themselves and others with many quarrels. Then, when all contention and jealousy have been removed, they will strive for peace and charity in such a way that they will not merit to incur the wrath of God because of discord, but rather to arrive at eternal rewards because of love and peace: with the help of our Lord Jesus Christ, to whom is honor and might together with the Father and the Holy Spirit forever and ever. Amen.

Sermon 182

An Admonition of St. Augustine on the Love of Charity and Hatred of Carnal Desires; That the Kingdom of Heaven Can Be Bought, Not Only With Two Mites, But Even with Good Will; Also on the Tribulation of Grapes and Olives

(1) In order to recommend to us the sweetness of true and perfect charity, dearest brethren, the blessed Apostle Paul explained to us the bitterness of carnal desires. Like a very skilled spiritual physician, he shows what we ought to avoid and what we should seek. Since 'Covetousness is the root of all evils,'[1] and charity is the root of all good things, both cannot exist together at the same time. Unless the one is torn out by the roots, the other cannot be planted. A man attempts to cut off the branches to no purpose, if he does not strive to tear out the root. For thus the Apostle speaks about the same truth: 'Covetousness is the root of all evils, and some in their eagerness to get rich have strayed from the faith and have involved themselves in many troubles. But thou, O man of God, flee these things.'[2] Let us, therefore, heed the advice of the one in whose person Christ our Lord spoke, and strive

---
1 1 Tim. 6.10.
2 1 Tim. 6.10, 11.

as much as we can to flee from the bitterness of avarice, if we want to arrive at the sweetness of charity.

(2) Whenever we talk about contempt for riches, some rich man replies to me: I have learned not to hope in the uncertainty of riches, I do not want to be rich, lest I fall into temptation; but since I am rich already, what am I to do with the possessions which I now happen to have? The Apostle continues: 'Let them give readily, sharing with others.'³ What does it mean to share with others? To share your possessions with the man who does not have any. Therefore, if you begin to share with others, you will not be that plunderer and robber who broods over the wants of the poor as over the property of another. If you have shared your goods with those who do not have possessions, you give even more, because you have become a dispenser to the poor. As much care as you exert so that the poor will have food without fear you dispense mercy, and for this reason God confers honor upon you and, as it were, says to you: First, take from your common goods what is necessary for the needs of your household, and give to Christ what is left. Be prepared to hear: 'Come, blessed of my Father, receive the kingdom which was prepared for you from the foundation of the world; for I was hungry and you gave me to eat.'⁴ Perhaps you used to despise a certain poor or needy person. Do not despise Christ who is seated in heaven but is in want upon earth, for He will come with recompense, either eternal life or eternal fire. For this reason you can even be rich with some hope when you think over this truth. But if you still wish to become rich and not only refuse to spend on the poor what is superfluous for your own needs, but even desire to increase your property, perhaps you also have some hope of robbery. Unless perchance you say this: God knows that I do not want to increase my estate by robbery. How do you expect to increase it? By purchase. Do you think that you are innocent because you want to increase it by buying? You

---
3 Cf. 1 Tim. 6.18.
4 Cf. Matt. 25.34, 35.

are not wicked because of robbery, but because of your intention. If someone says to you: Sell your possessions, you tremble and are afraid, thinking it a curse. So now when you wish to buy, do you not desire the same thing, that other people should sell their possessions? For how can you buy if someone else has not been forced to sell?

(3) Notice further, brethren, how much a man labors when he is anxious to beautify his clothes, and how the man who is willing to clothe the naked is without any effort. For if a man has possessions, he brings them forward and gives them; if he has none, a good will suffices for him in the sight of God. Behold, he does not labor if he has them. But if he does not, he is poor in his treasury but rich in conscience, provided that he has what is most necessary. He is poor in his house, but rich in soul. Suppose that you perchance possess nothing, but have a good will. Listen to the angels exclaiming at the birth of the Lord: 'Glory to God in the highest, and on earth peace among men of good will.'[5] Upon what a small price the kingdom of heaven depends! At how cheap a price such a great possession is offered! It is offered on earth, in order that you may possess it in heaven; what is offered in time you may possess in eternity. You cannot say: I do not have the means to buy it, because so great is that possession that I cannot find a suitable price. Is not as much as you may have enough? Even this is superfluous. How much was possible for Zachaeus? Half of his wealth, for he was a rich man. 'I give one-half of my possessions to the poor,'[6] he said. But because he bought first, do you perhaps find nothing to buy? He bought the kingdom of heaven. He bought it, and still what you buy is kept intact for you. Do not be afraid that a joint owner will make it difficult for you. What charity possesses is wide enough for all. A certain widow bought the kingdom of heaven for two mites; she put two coins into the treasury of the Church. 'Amen I say to you, no one has put more into the house of

---
5 Luke 2.14.
6 Luke 19.8.

God than this widow; for they have put in out of their abundance, but she has put in all that she had.'⁷ Since the Lord gave her food, she now had two coins over and above to live on for one day. Therefore, she put them into the house of God and bought for herself the kingdom of heaven. Look, since you feared that it was too costly and that you were not capable, see that it is possible for two mites. If the price which Zachaeus gave frightened you, be consoled by the price which this widow gave. I add more, dearest brethren, but even the very small amount is sufficient. A cup of cold water is more trifling, and good will alone is very little, but listen to the angels exclaim: 'Peace on earth among men of good will.'⁸ Perhaps we did not say well that good will is very little? Nay, it is more costly than all things, and the man who has good will has everything. If Zachaeus had not possessed good will, he would have given nothing even in the half of his possessions. For good will is also called charity. And what does the Apostle say? 'If I distribute all my goods to the poor, yet do not have charity, it profits me nothing.'⁹ Therefore, the man who possesses good will has everything. This alone can be sufficient if there are no other things, but if it alone is lacking, whatever a man possesses profits nothing. If it is present, it alone suffices, but everything else avails nothing if charity alone is lacking. If you had in your house treasures with which you might feel secure, you would rejoice and exult; you possess good will in your heart, and are you sad? You could fear a thief in your treasury, but whom do you fear in your heart? Do not allow an enemy in your heart; if you possess good will, you fear nothing.

(4) Perhaps someone may think about this and say: If I begin to give my wealth to the poor and refuse to punish my opponents out of love of God, striving to be meek and humble, it will immediately be necessary for me to endure the persecu-

---

7 Cf. Mark 12.43, 44; Luke 21.3, 4.
8 Luke 2.14.
9 Cf. 1 Cor. 13.3.

tions of wicked men. If you are afraid of these things, have you not read: 'Through many tribulations we must enter the kingdom of God'?[10] Did you not hear the Scriptures say: 'My son, when you come to serve the Lord, prepare yourself for trials'?[11] It is true that when you begin to seek God in truth you will have to endure the wickedness of proud and sinful men, because Christ is not worshiped by them in the same way in which He is daily preached to them. Whatever they desire and ask of God they want to spend on their own dissipation and entertainment, at the theater, in trifles, in fornication, and in drunkenness. In this sort of thing they want to spend that in which they long to abound, and then they think that God is good when He gives them the means of corrupting themselves.

(5) But someone may say: Behold, times are difficult, and they will become still more difficult. The Church makes more progress in these more difficult days, and those who have their hearts above also make progress. However, those who do not keep their heart above have it disturbed on earth, and they tell their heart to exchange places so that it may be above, singing within themselves: 'To you, I lift up my soul, O Lord.'[12] To say that the times are more severe is the same as for someone to say that the times of the olive are more severe when the fruit is gathered from it, because it is thrown into the press. When it hung on the tree the times seemed to be happy, and they do not notice that it was full of oil. A harder time comes, as it were, when the time for the press comes, and greater pressures come. Through the sins and crimes of the proud, through the avarice and dissipation of sinners, greater pressures are brought to bear on the human race. For all sinners and lovers of the world are like presses. Just as the grape and the olive are squeezed in presses so that wine and oil may be stored away in the cellar, so through the wicked-

---

10 Acts 14.21.
11 Ecclus. 2.1.
12 Ps. 24.1.

ness of sinful men those who are good and just are physically exhausted by many tribulations. Thus their souls, like the oil and the wine, will merit to be stored in eternal bliss. Therefore, do not despair of the justice and mercy of God as often as you see yourself wearied by unjust men. Remember that those who persecute you are considered like mills and presses in the sight of God. Like the real olive and grape, you are compelled to bear the pressure of wicked men for a short time, but afterwards they will suffer endless disgrace, while by a happy exchange you will cross over into the kingdom. Then, when you are freed from all evils you will be able to say with the prophet: 'We went through fire and water, but you have led us out to refreshment.'[13] But in order that you may deserve to reach this bliss, pray for those who persecute you. God is powerful, so that He can convert them to a good life, and those who now seem like chaff may change from tares to wheat, from oil to the olive. Moreover, those who now persecute others by their wickedness, afterwards will themselves suffer persecution for the sake of justice. Those who now cruelly wish to seize the possessions of another should begin to pay the poor in mercy. If the divine goodness in accord with its usual practice accomplishes this through your prayers, when the Lord repays, you will receive a twofold reward in eternal bliss, not only because of your own salvation, but also as the result of the salvation of others. May He Himself deign to grant this, who together with the Father and the Holy Spirit lives and reigns forever and ever. Amen.

---

[13] Ps. 65.12.

Sermon 183

A Homily of St. Augustine on the Peril of a Priest; Also on That Rich Man Whose Land Brought Forth Abundant Fruit, and on That Other One Who Was Clothed In Purple and Fine Linen

(1) If you notice carefully, dearest brethren, you realize that all priests of the Lord, not only bishops, but even the clergy and ministers of the churches, are in great danger. The Holy Spirit even bears witness to this truth when He says: 'Cry out full-throated and unsparingly, lift up your voice like a trumpet blast; tell my people their wickedness';[1] and again: 'If you do not speak out to dissuade the wicked man from his wicked conduct, I will hold you responsible for his death.'[2] The Apostle also says about them: 'Obey your superiors and be subject to them, for they keep watch as having to render an account of your souls.'[3] If each one will scarcely be able to render an account of his own soul on the day of judgment, dearest brethren, what will be the situation of priests, of whom the souls of all will be required? Therefore, when you consider our danger, pray for us, so that we may endeavor continually to provide spiritual food for the flock entrusted to us, and may thus merit to render a good account of them. For this reason consider what it is, dearest brethren, that I wish to suggest to your charity. With your prayers may I deserve to have Him help me, although He now frightens me.

(2) Among other precepts of his the blessed Apostle also says this, that a bishop should be strong in rebuking objectors with sound doctrine. It is a great work, but a heavy burden. However: 'My God, in whom I trust,' with you helping us by your prayers for us, 'will rescue us from the snare of the fowler,

---
1 Isa. 58.1.
2 Cf. Ezech. 3.18.
3 Heb. 13.17.

from the destroying pestilence.'⁴ There is no reason which makes the dispenser of God slothful in rebuking objectors more than fear of a harsh word. For as long as we fear the calumny, ridicule, and reproaches of proud men and fear to be burdened by them with respect to earthly possessions, when we are afraid of losing temporal goods, we preach eternal ones less than we should. As long as we dread to lose something worldly through the wickedness of such men, we neglect to take care of the wounds of their sins with spiritual remedies. For this reason it is to be feared that we will be compelled to render a difficult account on the day of judgment, both for ourselves and for those to whom we fail to speak because of our love for earthly possessions.

(3) Let us further see what it means to rebuke those who speak against us. Those who speak against us are not to be understood in only one way, for very few people contradict us in speech, but very many do so by a wicked life. When does a Christian dare to tell me that it is a good thing to seize the goods of another, and when does he not dare to say that it is good to defend his possessions closely? What about that rich man whose 'land prospered'?⁵ When he found that he had no place to store his crops, he rejoiced greatly because he had thought of the idea of destroying the old store-houses and building new and larger ones in order that he might fill them. When he further said to his soul: 'Thou hast many good things laid up for a long time; rejoice, live in luxury, glut yourself,'⁶ was that rich man seeking the goods of another? He was arranging to gather his own crops, and was thinking of where to put them, not planning violence for anyone. He was not making plans about the land of his neighbor, to confuse the boundaries, to plunder the poor, or to deceive the simple soul; he only thought about where he would store his own crops. Listen to what a man will hear if he holds his own

---
4 Cf. Ps. 90.2, 3.
5 Cf. Luke 12.16. This is an older version than that of the Vulgate.
6 Cf. Luke 12.19.

possessions very closely, and understand from this what those who seize the goods of another may expect. For this reason, although he thought he had discovered a very wise plan in tearing down the old and rather limited store-houses and building new ones which would be larger, God spoke to him as he was gathering his crops and storing them away, not coveting or seizing the goods of another. 'Thou fool,' He said—where you appeared wise to yourself, there you were foolish—'Thou fool, this night is thy soul demanded of thee; and the things that thou hast provided, whose will they be?'[7] If you have kept them they will not stay yours; if you have spent them, they will remain yours. Why do you store up what you are destined to leave? Let those things rather go ahead where you are going to follow. See, that foolish man who stored away goods unreasonably is rebuked. If the man who stores up his own possessions is foolish, you find a name for the man who seizes what belongs to another. If the one who stores up his own goods is filthy, one who seizes the property of another is filled with ulcers. However, he is not like that man full of sores who lay at the door of the rich man and the dogs licked his sores. That man was full of sores in his body, but the robber is so in heart.

(4) Perhaps someone may answer and say: It was not a very great punishment for that man to whom God said: 'Thou fool.' God does not say 'Thou fool' in the same way that man says it. Such a word of God to anyone is a judgment. Is God going to give the kingdom of heaven to foolish men? This is shown by those five foolish virgins who are read to have been locked outside the door. And what remains for those to whom He is not going to give the kingdom of heaven, except the punishment of hell? We ought to consider this more carefully in order that we may see it more clearly. Now that rich man, before whose door lay that very poor man who was full of sores, was not called a man who seizes the good of another. 'There was a certain rich man,' it says, 'who used to clothe

---
7 Cf. Luke 12.20.

himself in purple and fine linen, and who feasted every day in splendid fashion.'[8] There was a rich man, it says. It did not say a liar or an oppressor of the poor, one who seizes stolen goods or hands them over or receives them, the robber of orphans or the persecutor of widows. None of these, but: 'There was a certain rich man.' Why is this important? He was a rich man, but he was rich for his own benefit. To whom did he offer anything? Perhaps he would withdraw and the Lord would be silent about him and admit his person if he concealed his offenses? For we are told: 'Judge not personally.'[9] Therefore, if you want to hear the offense of that rich man, do not seek any farther than you hear from Truth itself. 'There was a rich man, he used to clothe himself in purple and fine linen, and he feasted every day in splendid fashion.'[10] What, then, was his offense, except the man lying at his door full of sores who was not helped by him? This is openly said about him, that he was merciless; not that he seized the goods of another, but that he refused to give of his own possessions. If that poor man lying at his door received sufficient bread from the rich man, would it be said of him that: 'He longed to be filled with the crumbs that fell from the rich man's table'?[11] Only because of his uncharitableness in despising the poor man who lay at his door and refusing to feed him fittingly and worthily: 'He died and was buried; and lifting up his eyes, being in torments in hell, he saw the poor man in Abraham's bosom.'[12] Why should I dwell upon more details? He longed for a drop, although he had not given a crumb. By a just sentence he did not receive it, since through cruel avarice he had not given. If this is the punishment of the avaricious, what is the punishment of robbers?

(5) Now one who seizes the goods of another says to me: I am not like that rich man. I give a feast for the poor, I send

---
8 Luke 16.19.
9 Cf. John 7.24.
10 Cf. Luke 16.19.
11 Luke 16.21.
12 Cf. Luke 16.22, 23.

food to those who are locked in prison, I clothe the naked, and I receive strangers. Do you think you are giving? Do not take away, and you have given. The one to whom you have given rejoices, but the one from whom you have taken laments. Which of those two is God going to hear? You say to the one to whom you gave: Give thanks, because you have received. But on the other hand another says to you: I groan, for you took away from me. You took away almost everything, and you gave very little to the other man. Even if you had given to the poor all that you took from the other, God does not love such deeds. He tells you: You fool, I commanded you to give, but not at the expense of another. If you have, give out of your possessions; and if you have nothing to give of your own, you will do better to give to no one rather than to rob another. When Christ the Lord sits in judgment and separates those on the right and those on the left, He is going to say to those who do good: 'Come, blessed of my Father, receive the kingdom.'[13] However, to the unfruitful, who have performed no good works to the poor: 'Go into the everlasting fire.'[14] Then what is He going to say to the good? 'I was hungry and you gave me to eat,'[15] and so forth. And they will answer Him: 'Lord, when did we see thee hungry?'[16] And He will reply: 'When you did it for one of the least of my brethren, you did it for me.'[17] Therefore, understand, foolish man, when you want to give alms as the result of robbery. If, when you feed a Christian, you feed Christ, when you rob a Christian you also rob Christ. Listen to what He is going to say to those on His left: 'Go into the everlasting fire.' Why? 'For I was hungry, and you did not give me to eat; I was naked, and you did not clothe me. Go.' Where? 'Into the everlasting fire.' Go at once. Why? 'For I was naked, and you did not clothe me.'[18] There-

---
13 Matt. 25.34.
14 Matt. 25.41.
15 Matt. 25.35.
16 Matt. 25.37.
17 Cf. Matt. 25.40.
18 Cf. Matt. 25.41-43.

fore, if the man to whom Christ is going to say: 'I was naked, and you did not clothe me,' will go into eternal fire, what place in the everlasting fire will be held by one to whom it will be said: I was clothed, and you stripped me?

(6) Perhaps at this point you will try to escape this word, so that Christ may not say to you, I was clothed and you stripped me. You may think that you can change your habit and instead of stripping a Christian who is clothed, strip a heretic or a Jew. Here, too, Christ will answer you, or rather He now replies to you through His servant, the least of His ministers. Thus He responds: Forbear this loss to me, for when you who are a Christian rob a Jew, you prevent him from becoming a Christian. However, perhaps you also will still reply: I am not inflicting punishment because of any hatred, but I am rather bestowing discipline because of love. I am robbing a Jew for the purpose of making him a Christian as the result of this harsh and salutary discipline. I would like to hear and believe that what you took from the Jewish man you gave to a Christian.

(7) Perhaps someone may also think within himself and say: There are many Christians who are rich, avaricious, and passionate; I am guilty of no sin if I take from them and give to the poor. For if I give alms I will be able to have a reward out of that money with which they do no good. Even in this matter each one should spare his soul. Thoughts of this kind are suggested by the cunning of the devil, for even if he gives away everything that he took, he adds to his sins, rather than lessens them.

(8) We have spoken against the one vice of robbery, whereby human property is destroyed everywhere; we have spoken and no one contradicts us. Who dares to contradict truth in speech when it is most evident? Therefore, we do not do what the Apostle advises, for we do not rebuke those who contradict. We address the obedient, instruct those who esteem us, and do not rebuke those who contradict. However, they do not contradict with their tongue, but with their life. I advise, and

he plunders; I teach, and he plunders; I command, and he plunders; I rebuke, and he plunders. How does he fail to contradict? Now I will say what I think is enough about this topic. Therefore, restrain yourselves, brethren, restrain yourselves, my sons, restrain yourselves from the habit of plundering. And you who groan under the hand of robbers, restrain yourselves from the desire to plunder. If another man is powerful and plunders, you groan under the hand of robbers. Because you cannot plunder, for this reason you do not do it. Have the ability to do so, and then I will praise your passion if it is restrained.

(9) Therefore, dearest brethren, if you listen devoutly and carefully in keeping with your custom, you will be able to avoid the wickedness of avarice and evil desires, and in return for your works of mercy will happily arrive at eternal rewards: with the help of our Lord.

Sermon 184

On the Martyrs, on Phylacteries, and on a Passage From the Eleventh Chapter of the Apostle's Letter to the Hebrews

(1) In the Gospel text we heard that the servants and friends of God 'of whom the world was not worthy'[1] suffered indignities and glorious calamities by the power of faith, as the divine word says: 'Others had experience of mockery and stripes, yes, even of chains and prisons. They were stoned, they were sawed asunder, they were put to death by the sword.'[2] Therefore, we read that some were tortured in prisons, while others, as the persecution acquired strength, were overcome by the whirling of a cruel storm and were struck with hard showers of rocks. Still others had their holy heads removed by the

---
1 Heb. 11.38.
2 Heb. 11.36, 37.

hostile sword of the wicked, but in the kingdom of the eternal Head they are exalted. 'They were stoned, and they were sawed asunder,' it says. With a new sword, the dreadful murderer drew a slow path through their heart, and the numerous bites of the teeth of wild beasts hurried through their triumphant entrails. Thus, the strange newness of the punishments produced a multitude of merits through their perservering faith.

(2) But perhaps someone may think within himself and say: Why is it that good and holy men are handed over into the hands of the wicked? You ask why this is? Because: 'Man's life on earth is a trial.'[3] In a worldly contest, those who sweat are tried in order that they may be proved, and they are proved in order that they may receive a reward. For this reason the devil also with the Lord's permission sometimes holds the saints in his power when he asks it. The purpose of this is not that he may harm them in the virtue of their soul, but in order that he may disturb them in the weakness of their body. If they do not surrender at all, but through fear of the Lord faithfully resist, the temptation to wickedness is an occasion of glory. The Lord Himself was handed over into the hands of sinners, and thus the wicked judge spoke to Him at the time of the Passion: 'Dost thou not know that I have power to kill thee, and to release thee?'[4] And the Lord said to him: 'Thou wouldst have no power, were it not given thee from above.'[5] Therefore, in order to instruct and strengthen us, He bore and overcame the troublesome misfortunes of this world. Thus, we should understand that we cannot avoid the evils of this life, but with God's help we can overcome them. For this reason the faithful of Christ have some portion with the holy martyrs, if out of fear of God they patiently and courageously bear the things which this world imposes. That is why the divine word tells us: 'If you are partakers of the sufferings, you will also be of the comforts.'[6]

---
3 Cf. Job 7.1.
4 Cf. John 19.10.
5 Cf. John 19.11.
6 Cf. 2 Cor. 1.7.

(3) Perhaps you may say: There is no persecutor of religion, and the persecutor of piety does not threaten; without an enemy how could I have a part with the martyrs? This is not true, dearest brethren. Only exercise your faith; for although a public tempter is absent, the hidden tempter is not lacking. Let us briefly offer some thoughts, if you will, about the hidden and wickedly flattering temptations of the enemy, and about his plots. For example, does someone rouse you to theft, to false testimony, or to some other unjust gains? Through his mouth the voice of the ancient serpent whispers. Does an ugly seducer trap you into committing shameful lust by dishonorable advice and flattering allurements, even urging you on to the depths of dissipation? Secret plots are laid out for you by the enemy.

(4) It usually happens, brethren, that a persecutor on the side of the devil comes to a sick man and says: If you had summoned that magician, you would already be cured. If you had been willing to hang those superstitious signs on you, you would already have recovered your health. If you consent to this persecutor, you have sacrificed to the devil; if you despise him, you have acquired the glory of martyrdom. Perhaps another man comes and says: Send to that soothsayer, transmit your cincture or fillet to him so he can measure it and look at it. Then he himself will tell you what to do, or whether you can escape. Still another says: That man knows very well how to fumigate; and everyone for whom he has done this immediately felt better, and every attack left his house. In as many people as consented, he has defiled the sacrament of Baptism. The devil is wont, in this way, to deceive careless and lukewarm Christians, so that if anyone has committed theft, that most cruel persecutor incites one of his friends. Then he says to him: Come secretly to a place, and I will arouse for you a person who can tell you who it is who stole your silver or your money. But if you want to know this, do not sign yourself when you come to that place. Behold to what evils lukewarm Christians are led. While they want to recover temporal

health, they do not tremble to commit such wicked crimes. If a man consents to such advisers of the devil, he should not doubt that by rejecting Christ he has made an agreement with the devil. Even women are wont to persuade each other that if their children are sick they should have recourse to some kind of incantation which is not proper to the Catholic faith. This is deception on the part of the devil.

(5) How much more proper and salutary it would be to hasten to church and receive the Body and Blood of Christ, devoutly to anoint both themselves and their children with blessed oil, and in accord with what the Apostle James says, to receive, not only bodily health, but also the forgiveness of sins. For thus the Holy Spirit has promised through him: 'If any one among you is sick, let him bring in the presbyters of the Church, and let them pray over him, anointing him with oil in the name of the Lord; and the prayer of faith will save the sick man, and if he be in sins, they shall be forgiven him.'[7] But perhaps someone will say: Why is it that our bishop admonishes us so frequently on this subject? For this reason, brethren. Although we admonish you so often, still we know that through the words of many men these wicked deeds are committed by some people. Therefore, I beseech you, brethren. Let those who have not yet committed this never do so, and if anyone has done so, he should hasten to do suitable penance as soon as he can.

(6) For our part, brethren, whenever we wish to celebrate the festivals of the saints and the martyrs, let us, with God's help, strive to prepare ourselves as much as we can and to adorn our hearts with good works. Therefore, as each one examines his conscience, if he knows that he is in truth chaste, pious, humble, and merciful, let him rejoice and give thanks to God. With all his strength and with the help of God, let him endeavor, not only to preserve, but even to increase the divine gifts within him. But if he sees that he is careless or inclined to drunkenness, irascible, envious, and proud, or per-

---
[7] James 5.14, 15.

haps stained with the filth of dissipation, he should quickly have recourse to the healing remedies of repentance. Before that gloomy soul leaves his most unhappy body, let him acquire for himself a remedy against his day of need. Let him give such abundant alms and so frequently engage in vigils, fasting, and prayer with crying and groaning, that before his soul, as I already said, is snatched from his poor little body which is guilty of sin, he may provide for himself the remedies of a contrite and humbled heart which will be profitable for all eternity, since: 'A heart contrite and humbled, O God, you will not spurn.'[8] It is fitting that no sinner should ever despair beneath the hand of the almighty physician. So great is the multitude of His mercy, that He in truth not only grants the forgiveness of sins to those who have amended their lives, but He even allows them to arrive at eternal rewards.

(7) For this reason we should neither despair nor hope in the wrong way. A man despairs if he thinks that God will not forgive the many sins with which he is overwhelmed, even if he does penance. Moreover, he hopes wickedly when he believes that even if he wills to remain in sin until the end of his life, he can still merit the mercy of God. Truly, our God, who knows how to repay merits, also knows how to punish sins. The same one who said: 'If you return and groan, you shall be saved,'[9] also said: 'Delay not your conversion to the Lord, put it not off from day to day.'[10] Fear, O man, the justice of Him whose mercy you are seeking. The longer He waits for you to amend your life, the more severely He will punish you if you refuse to correct yourself quickly. God, indeed, dispenses mercy in this world, but He exercises justice in the world to come. Here He offers the money of His admonition and patience, but there He is going to demand interest, for then will be fulfilled what is written: 'Then he will render to everyone according to his conduct.'[11] He did not say, accord-

---
8 Cf. Ps. 50.19.
9 Cf. Isa. 30.15.
10 Ecclus. 5.8.
11 Matt. 16.27.

ing to mercy, but 'according to his conduct.' This the Apostle Paul also confirms when he says: 'All of us will stand before the tribunal of Christ, so that each one may receive what he has won through the body, according to his works, whether good or evil.'[12] With the Lord's help, then, brethren, let us live in such a way that whatever He gave us when He was judged He may find intact when He comes to judge. Then the festivals and relics of the holy martyrs will not avail to judgment for us, but progress. Moreover, let us as far as we can endeavor to live in such a way that we may be able to obtain in heaven the companionship of those whose feasts we will celebrate in the world: with the help of our Lord Jesus Christ, who lives and reigns forever and ever. Amen.

* *Sermon 185*

On Harmony Between Brothers

(1) In many places of Sacred Scripture the Holy Spirit advises us to speak to you about harmony between brothers, and for this reason anyone who has a quarrel against another should end it, lest he be finished. Do not despise these words, my brethren. For this life is constantly in danger in the midst of so many and such great temptations, and it prays that it may not be overwhelmed. Mortal and fleeting as it is, no just man can live in it without some kind of sins, but there is one remedy by which we may live, and our God and teacher taught us to say it in prayer: 'Forgive us our debts, as we also forgive our debtors.'[1] We have made a pact and agreement with God, writing the condition of our debt being forgiven in a pledge. We ask with full confidence to be forgiven then only, if we

---

12 2 Cor. 5.10.

1 Matt. 6.12.

also forgive. But if we do not forgive, with what kind of a conscience do we trust that our sins will be forgiven for us? Man should not deceive himself, for God deceives no one. It is human to get angry, although we wish that we would not do this. It is human to get angry, but it is not right for the small twig which arose through your anger to be watered by different kinds of suspicion and to reach the beam of hatred. For anger is one thing, hatred is another. A father, indeed, often becomes angry at his son, but he does not hate his son; he is angry in order to correct him. If he becomes angry for the purpose of correction, he is angry through love. For this reason it is said: 'Thou dost see the speck in thy brother's eye, and yet dost not consider the beam in thy own eye.'[2] You blame anger in another, and keep hatred within yourself. In comparison with hatred, anger is a mote. However, if you encourage a mote, it will be a beam, but if you tear it out and throw it away, it will be nothing.

(2) If you noticed, when the epistle of blessed John was read, you should have been frightened. For he says: 'The darkness has passed away and the true light is now shining';[3] then he continued and added: 'He who says that he is in the light, and hates his brother, is in the darkness still.'[4] Perhaps a man thinks that such darkness is like that which men suffer when they are locked in prison. If only it were like that! And even so no one wants to be in such a situation. However, in this darkness of prison even the innocent can be enclosed, for in such darkness the martyrs were locked. Darkness was spread all around, but light was burning in their hearts. Their eyes did not see in the darkness of prison, but love for a brother was able to see God. Do you want to know what kind of darkness it is concerning which it is said: 'He who hates his brother, is in the darkness still'? In another place he said: 'Everyone who hates his brother is a murderer.'[5] The man who hates his

---
2 Matt. 7.3.
3 1 John 2.8.
4 1 John 2.9.
5 1 John 3.15.

brother walks about, departs, enters, goes forward, is burdened with no chains, and is locked in no prison; and still he is bound because of sin. Do not think that he can be without a prison, for his prison is his heart. When you hear: 'He who hates his brother, is in the darkness still,'[6] lest perhaps you may despise the darkness, he adds to it and says: 'Everyone who hates his brother is a murderer.' You hate your brother, and you walk about with assurance. You do not want to live in harmony, and you do not know why God has given you this space of time: behold, you now are a murderer and you still live. If you had God angry you would quickly be carried off along with your hatred for your brother. God spares you, so do you also spare yourself; live in harmony with your brother.

(3) Perhaps you wish it, but he does not? This is enough for you, and you have a reason to grieve over him; you have absolved yourself. Say with assurance, if you are willing to live in harmony but he is not: 'Forgive us our debts, as we also forgive our debtors.'[7] Perhaps you have sinned against him; you want to live in harmony with him, and you want to say to him: Brother, forgive me for the sin I committed against you. He is unwilling to forgive, he does not want to forgive you your debt; what you owe him he refuses to forgive. Let him notice when he has to pray, if he has refused to forgive you for the offense which you perhaps committed against him. Let him notice when he comes to the prayer, and see what he is going to do. He says: 'Our Father, who art in heaven.'[8] Let him say it, and let him continue: 'Hallowed be thy name.'[9] Still continue: 'Thy Kingdom come.'[10] Proceed: 'Thy will be done on earth, as it is in heaven.'[11] Go still farther: 'Give us this day our daily bread.'[12] You have said it, and now what

---

6 1 John 2.9.
7 Matt. 6.12.
8 Matt. 6.9.
9 *Ibid.*
10 Matt. 6.10.
11 *Ibid.*
12 Matt. 6.11.

follows? Watch out, lest perhaps you might want to cross over now and say something else. There is no way for you to pass, and you will be held there. Therefore, say it, and tell the truth, or, if you have no sin so that you should say: 'Forgive us our debts,' do not say it. But where is that other statement which the same Apostle made: 'If we say that we have no sin, we deceive ourselves, and the truth is not in us'?[13] But if a consciousness of weakness stings us, because iniquity abounds everywhere in this world, then say: 'Forgive us our debts.' But also notice what follows, for you refused to forgive your brother an offense, and you are going to say: 'As we also forgive our debtors.' Or do you not intend to say it? If you are not going to say it, you will receive nothing. Therefore, say it, but tell the truth. How are you going to speak the truth, when you have refused to free your brother from his offense?

(4) I have admonished him, and now I comfort you, whoever you are who have said to your brother: Forgive me the offense which I committed against you. If you said it from your heart, with true humility and unfeigned charity, said it as God sees in your heart, but he has refused to forgive you, do not be worried. You are both servants, and you have one Lord. You owe a fellow-servant, and he has refused to forgive you; address the Lord of both of you. Let the servant exact of you what the Lord has forgiven you, if he can.

(5) Something else I must say. I have admonished the man who is unwilling to forgive his brother. When he asks to be forgiven, he should do what he is praying, or else he will not receive what he desires. I have also admonished the man who seeks pardon from his brother for an offense and does not obtain it. He may be confident that he will receive from his Lord what he has not obtained from his brother. There is still another warning that I have to give. Your brother has offended you, and he is unwilling to say to you: Forgive me for having offended you. This kind of grass abounds. If only God would uproot it from His field, that is, from your hearts.

---
13 1 John 1.8.

For there are many who know that they have offended their brothers, but they are unwilling to say: Forgive me. They did not blush to commit the offense, but they are ashamed to ask for pardon; they did not blush over the iniquity, but they are ashamed of the humiliation. Do I, then, admonish you first? If any of you are out of harmony with your brothers, return to yourself, and examine yourself. Render a just judgment of yourself within your hearts, and you will find that you should not have done what you did, or should not have said what you did. Ask for pardon, brethren, from your brothers; do what the Apostle says: 'Forgiving one another, as also God in Christ has generously forgiven you, so do you also.'[14] Do it, and do not blush. Do not remain guilty before the eyes of God, and do not be ashamed to ask for pardon. Behold, I am speaking to everyone, men and women, the clergy and the laity, and I am even speaking to myself. Let us all listen, and let us all fear, if we have offended our brothers. We have still received the days of grace of life; we are not yet condemned. As long as we live let us do what the Father, who will be our judge, commands. Let us ask pardon from our brothers whom we have perhaps offended or injured in some way by sinning against them.

(6) There are some lowly persons according to worldly rank who are lifted up with pride if you ask them for pardon. This is what I mean: sometimes a man who is a lord offends his servant. Now the one is the master, and the other is the servant—however, they are both servants of still another, because they were both redeemed by the blood of Christ. Now it may seem hard that I should order this, but I do command that if perchance the master offends his servant by judging him unfairly or striking him unjustly, and if that man should say: Forgive me, grant me pardon—not that he should not do it, but let not the other begin to grow proud. Then what? He should repent before the eyes of God, and punish his heart in the sight of God. Moreover, if he is unable to say to his

---

14 Cf. Eph. 4.32.

servant: Give me pardon, because he should not, let him address him kindly; for a kind word is a plea for forgiveness.

(7) For my part, my brethren, when I suggest these truths to you I absolve my conscience in the sight of God. Before the tribunal of Christ, no one of you will be able to say that he was not admonished, that he was not invited to the things which are good and warned against the things which are evil. In accord with the precept of my Lord I offer this money at the table of your heart, but when He comes He is going to exact the interest. For among other sins, we commit none more serious than when we keep enmities in our heart. We should know that because of our hatred and enmities at such times we do not merit to receive the rain of grace. Therefore, those who know that they hold in their heart hatred against some of their brothers should hasten to be reconciled with them at once, lest this evil be seen to overflow in their soul if the whole area is forced to sustain it. For this reason let us forgive our brothers, and let us confidently hold our Lord to the bond of His promise, since He said: 'Give, and it shall be given to you; forgive, and you shall be forgiven.'[15] May He Himself deign to grant this.

Sermon 186

An Exhortation to the People on the Words of Blessed John the Evangelist: 'Everyone Who Believes That Jesus Is the Christ Is Born of God.'[1]

(1) In his epistle blessed John the Evangelist, dearest brethren, has not only given us consolation, but he has also inspired solicitude and fear. There is comfort, indeed, if we are willing to fulfill the things which he preaches about charity;

---

15 Luke 6.38, 37.

1 1 John 5.1.

but there ought to be intolerable fear if we neglect to fulfill them. For thus he says: 'Everyone who believes that Jesus is the Christ is born of God.' Who is there who does not believe that Jesus is the Christ? Whoever does not live in the way which Christ commanded. For many say: I believe; and they think that faith alone without good works is sufficient. People who are of this sort should heed the blessed Apostle James when he says: 'Faith without works is useless.'[2] They should also listen to Paul: 'Faith, which works through love.'[3] Everyone who believes that Jesus is the Christ is born of God. But what does it mean to believe? 'And everyone who loves him who begot, loves also the one begotten of him.'[4] He immediately joined love to faith, because without love faith is useless. According to charity, faith belongs to Christians, but without love it belongs to the demons. Moreover, those who do not believe are worse than the demons, and even slower. If someone refuses to believe in Christ, he still does not imitate the demons. Now a man believes in Christ, but he does not do what Christ commands: he has a confession of faith in the fear of hell, but not in the love of justice.

(2) Moreover, we ought to know, dearest brethren, that there are two cities in this world, namely, Babylon and Jerusalem. Babylon is interpreted as confusion, and Jerusalem as the vision of peace. These two cities have their own people and their own citizens. Do not attach yourself to the Babylonians if you desire to reach the eternal country. When you see a man possess charity and seeking eternal joy, you have found a citizen, a fellow-citizen of the angels, a pilgrim sighing on the way. Join him, for he is your companion; run along with him. Do not love anything outside of the will of God. You labor in loving avarice, and what you love is loved with effort, for the world is loved through labor; God is loved without effort. Avarice is going to command labors, perils, bruises, and trib-

---

2 James 2.20.
3 Gal. 5.6.
4 1 John 5.1.

ulations, and you are going to obey. To what end? In order that you may have the means of filling your treasury, you may lose your security. Perhaps you were more secure before you possessed it than when you have begun to have it. Behold what avarice commanded. You have filled your house, and robbers are feared; you have acquired gold, and you have lost your sleep. See how you have done for yourself what avarice commanded. What does God command? Love Me. You love gold, are going to seek it, and perhaps you will not even find it; whenever anyone seeks Me, I am with him. You love honor, and perhaps you will not attain it; you love Me, and immediately you find Me. How many men love gold, and they do not immediately possess it? But who has ever loved God and not found Him merciful? Behold, God says to you: You want to win a patron, or a powerful friend, and for this reason you go through another inferior. Love Me, for one does not go to Me through another; love itself makes Me present to you. What is sweeter than this love, brethren? If perchance anyone doubts that the love of God possesses in itself a great sweetness, he should listen to the psalmist when he says: 'Taste and see how good the Lord is.'[5]

(3) We who are pilgrims and strangers in this world, dearest brethren, ought to understand that we are still on the way, and not yet in our true country. Truly, life is this road. When man is born he begins the road, when he dies he is known to have finished it. For this reason men are wise if they show anxiety about the salvation of their soul and do not love the road. By running along the road, they long for their true country. But lovers of dissipation, who love present things more than future ones for the sake of fleeting pleasures, love the road, and as long as they wish to rejoice on the road they do not merit to reach the eternal country. Therefore, is fulfilled in them what is written: 'The burdens of the world have made them miserable.'[6] Now since no man should love the

---
[5] Ps. 33.9.
[6] As has already been noted, the source of this quotation is unknown.

earthly road, but should hasten as much as he can to arrive quickly at his place of destination, why do we not blush when we love the road of this life in the wrong order and with perverse love, so that we do not desire to reach our true country? For love of the present life is wont to press our necks down under a harsh yoke, and to impose chains and fetters on the feet of souls. In order that we may deserve to be freed from these bonds, let us exclaim with the prophet: 'Let us break their fetters and cast their bonds from us';[7] and further: 'You have loosed my bonds, to you will I offer sacrifice of thanksgiving.'[8] Therefore, let us not love the road, but let us listen to the Apostle saying: 'So run, as to obtain it';[9] and again: 'I have finished the course';[10] and still again: 'I, however, so run as not without a purpose.'[11] Now when the Apostle said these things, he did not want it to be understood as concerning bodily feet, but rather the affections of souls. Since there are two feet of the soul on which men run to eternal bliss, with God's help, let us use effort to keep them sound. What are these two feet on which we run to that heavenly Jerusalem, except the two precepts of charity, that is: 'Thou shalt love the Lord,' and 'Thou shalt love thy neighbor'?[12] If you love God and do not love your neighbor, you have one foot; you will remain on the road and will not be able to reach your true country. Again, if you love your neighbor but do not love God, you will be lame and not able to run at all.

(4) For this reason I beseech you again and again, brethren. As long as we live, let us believe that we are still on the road. By devoting ourselves to good works, let us hasten to run to that eternal life of bliss. Now as the Apostle says: 'While we are in the body we are exiled from the Lord,'[13] and in another place the prophet says: 'I am but a wayfarer before you, a

---
7 Ps. 2.3.
8 Ps. 115.16, 17.
9 1 Cor. 9.24.
10 2 Tim. 4.7.
11 1 Cor. 9.26.
12 Luke 10.27.
13 2 Cor. 5.6.

pilgrim on earth.'[14] For this reason let us, on the road of this life, that is, in the laborious life of this world, keep for ourselves as much out of the result of our labor as will be enough for reasonable food and clothing for us as we pursue our journey. Whatever God has given us more than this, let us through alms to the poor direct there 'Where neither rust consumes, nor thieves break in and steal.'[15] For the things that we keep in this world through avarice we will leave either during our lifetime or when we die. Therefore, let each one redeem himself with his own possessions while they still belong to him. If a man rejoices that he is in a sound condition and knows that he is without any serious sins, he should provide adornments for himself by giving alms. If, when he examines his conscience, he feels that he is weak and liable to punishment because of many sins, through his acts of mercy to the poor, let him acquire a remedy for himself in his day of need. For if, perchance, he appears at that heavenly banquet and in that sublime abode of the marriage-chamber, wrapped in the filthy rags of his vices, he will merit to hear: 'Friend, how didst thou come in here without a wedding garment?'[16] and when he is speechless, it may be said: 'Bind his hands and feet and cast him forth into the darkness outside where there will be the weeping, and the gnashing of teeth.'[17] May we deserve to be freed from this evil hearing, and rather be the just in everlasting remembrance who hear that desirable word: 'Well done, good and faithful servant; I will set thee over many things; enter into the joy of thy master.'[18] Let almsgiving begin to send ahead for us into eternal bliss everything of our substance that avarice had been wont to keep or dissipation had devoured in worse fashion. Then, when our soul has been freed from this body as from a prison, we may merit to be lifted up to the bosom of Abraham by the hands of the angels;

---
14 Cf. Ps. 38.13.
15 Matt. 6.20.
16 Matt. 22.12.
17 Cf. Matt. 22.13.
18 Matt. 25.21.

and when the company of the saints has been assembled, we may deserve to hear that sweet word: 'Come, blessed of my Father, receive the kingdom which was prepared for you from the foundation of the world.'[19] To this happiness may the Lord lead us under His protection: who lives and reigns together with the Father and the Holy Spirit forever and ever. Amen.

---

19 Cf. Matt. 25.34.

The indices to this and the previous volume (Vol. 31 of this Series) will be combined with the indices of the third volume of this work which will be published at a later date.

THE FATHERS
OF THE CHURCH

(A series of approximately 100 volumes when completed)

Volume 1: THE APOSTOLIC FATHERS (1947)
    The Letter of St. Clement of Rome to the Corinthians
    The So-called Second Letter of St. Clement
    The Letter of St. Polycarp to the Philippians
    The Martyrdom of St. Polycarp
    The Didache or Teaching of the Twelve Apostles
        translated by F. Glimm
    The Letters of St. Ignatius of Antioch
    Letter to Diognetus
        translated by G. Walsh
    The Shepherd of Hermas
    The Fragments of Papias (first printing only)
        translated by J. Marique
                            OCLC 367814

Volume 2: SAINT AUGUSTINE (1947)
    Christian Instruction
        translated by J. Gavigan
    Admonition and Grace
        translated by John Courtney Murray
    The Christian Combat
        translated by R. Russell
    Faith, Hope and Charity *(Enchiridion)*
        translated by B. Peebles
                            OCLC 728405

Volume 3: THE WRITINGS OF SALVIAN THE PRESBYTER (1947)
    The Governance of God
    Letters
    The Four Books of Timothy to the Church
        translated by J. O'Sullivan
                            OCLC 806839

Volume 4: SAINT AUGUSTINE (1947)
    The Immortality of the Soul

        translated by L. Schopp
   The Magnitude of the Soul
        translated by J. McMahon
   On Music
        translated by R. Taliaferro
   The Advantage of Believing
        translated by L. Meagher
   On Faith in Things Unseen
        translated by R. Deferrari, M–F. McDonald

                                                      OCLC 856032

Volume 5:   SAINT AUGUSTINE   (1948)
   The Happy Life
        translated by L. Schopp
   Answer to Skeptics *(Contra Academicos)*
        translated by D. Kavanagh
   Divine Providence and the Problem of Evil
        translated by R. Russell
   The Soliloquies
        translated by T. Gilligan

                                                        OCLC 728405

Volume 6:   WRITINGS OF SAINT JUSTIN MARTYR   (1948)
   The First Apology
   The Second Apology
   The Dialogue with Trypho
   Exhortation to the Greeks
   Discourse to the Greeks
   The Monarchy or Rule of God
        translated by T. Falls

                                                        OCLC 807077

Volume 7:   NICETA OF REMESIANA   (1949)
   Writings of Niceta of Remesiana
        translated by G. Walsh
   Prosper of Aquitaine: Grace and Free Will
        translated by J. O'Donnell
   Writings of Sulpicius Severus
        translated by B. Peebles
   Vincent of Lerins: The Commonitories
        translated by R. Morris

                                                        OCLC 807068

Volume 8:   SAINT AUGUSTINE   (1950)

    The City of God (books 1–7)
     translated by D. Zema, G. Walsh
                 OCLC 807084

Volume 9: SAINT BASIL ASCETICAL WORKS (1950)
    translated by M. Wagner
                  OCLC 856020

Volume 10: TERTULLIAN APOLOGETICAL WORKS (1950)
    Tertullian Apology
     translated by E–J. Daly
    On the Soul
     translated by E. Quain
    The Testimony of the Soul
    To Scapula
     translated by R. Arbesmann
    Minucius Felix: Octavius
     translated by R. Arbesmann
                 OCLC 1037264

Volume 11:   SAINT AUGUSTINE   (1957)
    Commentary on the Lord's Sermon on the Mount
    Selected Sermons (17)
     translated by D. Kavanagh
                 OCLC 2210742

Volume 12:   SAINT AUGUSTINE   (1951)
    Letters (1–82)
     translated by W. Parsons
                 OCLC 807061

Volume 13:   SAINT BASIL   (1951)
    Letters (1–185)
     translated by A–C. Way
                 OCLC 2276183

Volume 14:   SAINT AUGUSTINE   (1952)
    The City of God (books 8–16)
     translated by G. Walsh, G. Monahan
                 OCLC 807084

Volume 15: EARLY CHRISTIAN BIOGRAPHIES (1952)
    Life of St. Ambrose by Paulinus
     translated by J. Lacy
    Life of St. Augustine by Bishop Possidius

Life of St. Cyprian by Pontius
translated by M. M. Mueller, R. Deferrari
Life of St. Epiphanius by Ennodius
translated by G. Cook
Life of St. Paul the First Hermit
Life of St. Hilarion by St. Jerome
Life of Malchus by St. Jerome
translated by L. Ewald
Life of St. Anthony by St. Athanasius
translated by E. Keenan
A Sermon on the Life of St. Honoratus by St. Hilary
translated by R. Deferrari

OCLC 806775

Volume 16: SAINT AUGUSTINE (1952)
The Christian Life
Lying
The Work of Monks
The Usefulness of Fasting
translated by S. Muldowney
Against Lying
translated by H. Jaffe
Continence
translated by M–F. McDonald
Patience
translated by L. Meagher
The Excellence of Widowhood
translated by C. Eagan
The Eight Questions of Dulcitius
translated by M. Deferrari

OCLC 806731

Volume 17: SAINT PETER CHRYSOLOGUS (1953)
Selected Sermons
Letter to Eutyches
SAINT VALERIAN
Homilies
Letter to the Monks
translated by G. Ganss

OCLC 806783

Volume 18: SAINT AUGUSTINE (1953)

Letters (83–130)
translated by W. Parsons
                                                 OCLC 807061

Volume 19:   EUSEBIUS PAMPHILI   (1953)
Ecclesiastical History (books 1–5)
translated by R. Deferrari
                                                 OCLC 708651

Volume 20:   SAINT AUGUSTINE   (1953)
Letters (131–164)
translated by W. Parsons
                                                 OCLC 807061

Volume 21:   SAINT AUGUSTINE   (1953)
Confessions
translated by V. Bourke
                                                 OCLC 2210845

Volume 22:   FUNERAL ORATIONS   (1953)
Saint Gregory Nazianzen: Four Funeral Orations
translated by L. McCauley
Saint Ambrose: On the Death of His Brother Satyrus I & II
translated by J. Sullivan, M. McGuire
Saint Ambrose: Consolation on the Death of Emperor Valentinian
Funeral Oration on the Death of Emperor Theodosius
translated by R. Deferrari
                                                 OCLC 806797

Volume 23:   CLEMENT OF ALEXANDRIA   (1954)
Christ the Educator
translated by S. Wood
                                                 OCLC 2200024

Volume 24:   SAINT AUGUSTINE   (1954)
The City of God (books 17-22)
translated by G. Walsh, D. Honan
                                                 OCLC 807084

Volume 25:   SAINT HILARY OF POITIERS   (1954)
The Trinity
translated by S. McKenna
                                                 OCLC 806781

Volume 26:   SAINT AMBROSE   (1954)

Letters (1–91)
translated by M. Beyenka

OCLC 806836

Volume 27: SAINT AUGUSTINE (1955)
The Divination of Demons
translated by R. Brown
Faith and Works
The Creed
In Answer to the Jews
translated by L. Ewald
Adulterous Marriages
translated by C. Huegelmeyer
The Care to be Taken for the Dead
translated by J. Lacy
Holy Virginity
translated by J. McQuade
Faith and the Creed
translated by R. Russell
The Good of Marriage
translated by C. Wilcox

OCLC 855069

Volume 28: SAINT BASIL (1955)
Letters (186–368)
translated by A–C. Way

OCLC 2276183

Volume 29: EUSEBIUS PAMPHILI (1955)
Ecclesiastical History
translated by R. Deferrari

OCLC 708651

Volume 30: SAINT AUGUSTINE (1955)
Letters (165–203)
translated by W. Parsons

OCLC 807061

Volume 31: SAINT CAESARIUS OF ARLES I (1956)
Sermons (1–8)
translated by M–M. Mueller

OCLC 806828

Volume 32: SAINT AUGUSTINE (1956)

Letters (204–270)
    translated by W. Parsons
                                              OCLC 807061

Volume 33:   SAINT JOHN CHRYSOSTOM   (1957)
  Commentary on St. John The Apostle and Evangelist
  Homilies (1–47)
    translated by T. Goggin
                                              OCLC 2210926

Volume 34:   SAINT LEO THE GREAT   (1957)
  Letters
    translated by E. Hunt
                                              OCLC 825765

Volume 35:   SAINT AUGUSTINE   (1957)
  Against Julian
    translated by M. Schumacher
                                              OCLC 3255620

Volume 36:   SAINT CYPRIAN   (1958)
  To Donatus
  The Lapsed
  The Unity of the Church
  The Lord's Prayer
  To Demetrian
  Mortality
  Works and Almsgiving
  Jealousy and Envy
  Exhortation to Martyrdom to Fortunatus
  That Idols Are Not Gods
    translated by R. Deferrari
  The Dress of Virgins
    translated by A. Keenan
  The Good of Patience
    translated by G. Conway
                                              OCLC 3894637

Volume 37:   SAINT JOHN OF DAMASCUS   (1958)
  The Fount of Knowledge
  On Heresies
  The Orthodox Faith (4 books)
    translated by F. Chase, Jr.
                                              OCLC 810002

Volume 38: SAINT AUGUSTINE (1959)
Sermons on the Liturgical Seasons
translated by S. Muldowney

OCLC 810000

Volume 39: SAINT GREGORY THE GREAT (1959)
Dialogues
translated by O. Zimmermann

OCLC 3713482

Volume 40: TERTULLIAN (1959)
To the Martyrs
Spectacles
translated by R. Arbesmann
The Apparel of Women
The Chaplet
Flight in Time of Persecution
translated by E. Quain
Prayer
Patience
translated by E. Daly

OCLC 810006;804160

Volume 41: SAINT JOHN CHRYSOSTOM (1960)
Commentary on St. John the Apostle and Evangelist
Homilies 48–88
translated by T. Goggin

OCLC 2210926

Volume 42: SAINT AMBROSE (1961)
Hexameron
Paradise
Cain and Abel
translated by J. Savage

OCLC 806739

Volume 43: THE POEMS OF PRUDENTIUS (1962)
The Book of Hymns for Every Day
The Book of the Martyrs' Crowns
translated by C. Eagan

OCLC 806750

Volume 44: SAINT AMBROSE (1963)
The Mysteries
The Holy Spirit

The Sacrament of the Incarnation of Our Lord
The Sacraments
translated by R. Deferrari

OCLC 2316634

Volume 45:   SAINT AUGUSTINE   (1963)
The Trinity
translated by S. McKenna

OCLC 784847

Volume 46:   SAINT BASIL   (1963)
Exegetic Homilies
translated by A–C. Way

OCLC 806743

Volume 47:   SAINT CAESARIUS OF ARLES II   (1963)
Sermons (81–186)
translated by M. M. Mueller

OCLC 2494636

Volume 48:   THE HOMILIES OF SAINT JEROME   (1964)
Homilies 1–59
translated by L. Ewald

OCLC 412009

Volume 49:   LACTANTIUS   (1964)
The Divine Institutes
translated by M–F. McDonald

OCLC 711211

Volume 50:   PAULUS OROSIUS   (1964)
The Seven Books of History Against the Pagans
translated by R. Deferrari

OCLC 711212

Volume 51:   SAINT CYPRIAN   (1964)
Letters (1–81)
translated by R. Donna

OCLC 806738

Volume 52:   THE POEMS OF PRUDENTIUS   (1965)
The Divinity of Christ
The Origin of Sin
The Spiritual Combat
Against Symmachus (two books)
Scenes from Sacred History Or Twofold Nourishment
translated by C. Eagan

		OCLC 806750
Volume 53:	SAINT JEROME	(1965)

On the Perpetual Virginity of the Blessed Mary
Against Helvidius
The Apology Against the Books of Rufinus
The Dialogue Against the Pelagians
  translated by J. Hritzu

OCLC 806757

Volume 54:   LACTANTIUS   (1965)

The Workmanship of God
The Wrath of God
The Deaths of the Persecutors
The Phoenix
Appendix
  translated by M–F. McDonald

OCLC 806760

Volume 55:   EUGIPPIUS   (1965)

The Life of Saint Severin
  translated by L. Bieler, L. Krestan

OCLC 806735

Volume 56:   SAINT AUGUSTINE   (1966)

The Catholic and Manichaean Ways of Life
The Way of Life of the Catholic Church
The Way of Life of the Manichaeans
  translated by D. Gallagher, I. Gallagher

OCLC 295838

Volume 57:   THE HOMILIES OF SAINT JEROME   (1966)

Homilies 60–96
  translated by L. Ewald

OCLC 412009

Volume 58:   SAINT GREGORY OF NYSSA   (1967)

On Virginity
On What It Means to Call Oneself a Christian
On Perfection
On the Christian Mode of Life
The Life of Saint Macrina
On the Soul and the Resurrection
  translated by V. Callahan

OCLC 806734

Volume 59:   SAINT AUGUSTINE   (1968)
    The Teacher
    The Free Choice of the Will
    Grace and Free Will
        translated by R. Russell
                                           OCLC 712674

Volume 60:   SAINT AUGUSTINE   (1968)
    The Retractations
        translated by I. Bogan
                                           OCLC 712676

Volume 61: THE WORKS OF SAINT CYRIL OF JERUSALEM I (1969)
    Procatechesis
        translated by A. Stephenson
    Lenten Lectures 1–12 (Catecheses)
        translated by L. McCauley
                                           OCLC 21885

Volume 62:   IBERIAN FATHERS I   (1969)
    Writings of Martin of Braga
        Sayings of the Egyptian Fathers
        Driving Away Vanity
        Exhortation to Humility
        Anger
        Reforming the Rustics
        Rules For An Honest Life
        Triple Immersion
        Easter
    Paschasius of Dumium
        Questions and Answers of the Greek Fathers
    Writings of Leander of Seville
        The Training of Nuns and the Contempt of the World
        Sermon on the Triumph of the Church for the Conversion of the Goths
        translated by C. Barlow
                                           OCLC 718095

Volume 63:   IBERIAN FATHERS II   (1969)
    Braulio of Saragossa
        Letters of Braulio
        Life of St. Emilian
        List of the Books of Isidore of Seville
    Writings of Fructuosus of Braga

Rule for the Monastery of Compludo
General Rule for Monasteries
Pact
Monastic Agreement
translated by C. Barlow

OCLC 718095

Volume 64:   THE WORKS OF SAINT CYRIL   (1970)
OF JERUSALEM II
Lenten Lectures (Catcheses) 13–18
translated by L. McCauley
The Mystagogical Lectures
Sermon on the Paralytic
Letter to Constantius
translated by A. Stephenson

OCLC 21885

Volume 65   SAINT AMBROSE   (1972)
Seven Exegetical Works
   Isaac or the Soul
   Death as a Good
   Jacob and the Happy Life
   Joseph
   The Patriarchs
   Flight from the World
   The Prayer of Job and David
translated by M. McHugh

OCLC 314148

Volume 66:   SAINT CAESARIUS OF ARLES III   (1973)
Sermons 187–238
translated by M. M. Mueller

OCLC 1035149; 2494636

Volume 67:   NOVATIAN   (1974)
The Trinity
The Spectacles
Jewish Foods
In Praise of Purity
Letters
translated by R. DeSimone

OCLC 662181

Volume 68:   SAINT JOHN CHRYSOSTOM   (1978)
            Discourses Against Judaizing Christians
                translated by P. Harkins
                                              OCLC 3003009

Volume 69:   MARIUS VICTORINUS   (1981)
            Theological Treatises on the Trinity
                Letter of Candidus the Arian to Marius Victorinus
                Rhetor On the Divine Begotting
                Letter of Marius Victorinus Rhetor of the City of
                Rome to Candidus the Arian
                Letter of Candidus the Arian to the Most Illustrious
                Marius Victorinus
                Against Arius Book I A
                Against Arius Book I B
                Against Arius Book II
                Against Arius Book III
                Against Arius Book IV
                On the Necessity of Accepting the Term *Homoousios*
                Hymns on the Trinity
                translated by M. T. Clark
                                              OCLC 5029056

Volume 59:   SAINT AUGUSTINE   (1968)
    The Teacher
    The Free Choice of the Will
    Grace and Free Will
        translated by R. Russell
                                        OCLC 712674

Volume 60:   SAINT AUGUSTINE   (1968)
    The Retractations
        translated by I. Bogan
                                        OCLC 712676

Volume 61: THE WORKS OF SAINT CYRIL OF JERUSALEM I (1969)
    Procatechesis
        translated by A. Stephenson
    Lenten Lectures 1–12 (Catecheses)
        translated by L. McCauley
                                        OCLC 21885

Volume 62:   IBERIAN FATHERS I   (1969)
    Writings of Martin of Braga
        Sayings of the Egyptian Fathers
        Driving Away Vanity
        Exhortation to Humility
        Anger
        Reforming the Rustics
        Rules For An Honest Life
        Triple Immersion
        Easter
    Paschasius of Dumium
        Questions and Answers of the Greek Fathers
    Writings of Leander of Seville
        The Training of Nuns and the Contempt of the World
        Sermon on the Triumph of the Church for the Conversion of the Goths
        translated by C. Barlow
                                        OCLC 718095

Volume 63:   IBERIAN FATHERS II   (1969)
    Braulio of Saragossa
        Letters of Braulio
        Life of St. Emilian
        List of the Books of Isidore of Seville
    Writings of Fructuosus of Braga

Rule for the Monastery of Compludo
General Rule for Monasteries
Pact
Monastic Agreement
translated by C. Barlow

OCLC 718095

Volume 64: THE WORKS OF SAINT CYRIL (1970)
OF JERUSALEM II
Lenten Lectures (Catcheses) 13–18
translated by L. McCauley
The Mystagogical Lectures
Sermon on the Paralytic
Letter to Constantius
translated by A. Stephenson

OCLC 21885

Volume 65 SAINT AMBROSE (1972)
Seven Exegetical Works
Isaac or the Soul
Death as a Good
Jacob and the Happy Life
Joseph
The Patriarchs
Flight from the World
The Prayer of Job and David
translated by M. McHugh

OCLC 314148

Volume 66: SAINT CAESARIUS OF ARLES III (1973)
Sermons 187–238
translated by M. M. Mueller

OCLC 1035149; 2494636

Volume 67: NOVATIAN (1974)
The Trinity
The Spectacles
Jewish Foods
In Praise of Purity
Letters
translated by R. DeSimone

OCLC 662181

Volume 68:   SAINT JOHN CHRYSOSTOM   (1978)
Discourses Against Judaizing Christians
translated by P. Harkins

OCLC 3003009

Volume 69:   MARIUS VICTORINUS   (1981)
Theological Treatises on the Trinity
Letter of Candidus the Arian to Marius Victorinus Rhetor On the Divine Begetting
Letter of Marius Victorinus Rhetor of the City of Rome to Candidus the Arian
Letter of Candidus the Arian to the Most Illustrious Marius Victorinus
Against Arius Book I A
Against Arius Book I B
Against Arius Book II
Against Arius Book III
Against Arius Book IV
On the Necessity of Accepting the Term *Homoousios*
Hymns on the Trinity
translated by M. T. Clark

OCLC 5029056

www.ingramcontent.com/pod-product-compliance
Lightning Source LLC
Chambersburg PA
CBHW032021290426
44110CB00012B/621